LOVE

WASHINGTON

GUIDE

I

LOVE

WASHINGTON

GUIDE

THIRD EDITION

Marilyn J. Appleberg

Illustrations by Albert Pfeiffer

COLLIER BOOKS
Macmillan Publishing Company
New York

Maxwell Macmillan Canada • Toronto
Maxwell Macmillan International • New York • Oxford • Singapore • Sydney

Acknowledgments

The following people helped to make the task of revising this book a labor of love:

To Maria Hyman, Sara and Bob Haft, Katerine Yelloz, Veneta Acson, and Howard Streicher, thank you for the warm welcome, the hospitality, and the knowledge you so generously shared. To Thomas Murphy at the Washington, DC, Convention and Visitors Association, your knowledge and accessibility were invaluable.

To Jane Herman, Theresa A. Czajkowska, and Sharon L. Gonzalez, for bringing order out of chaos, thank you.

A big THANK YOU as well to Sharlonlee Johnson at the Washington Metropolitan Area Transit Authority, Wendy Lim at the Smithsonian Institution, and Stephanie Sferra of Tourmobile ® Sightseeing. And thanks to Michael Sussman for sharing his knowledge.

Last, but always first in my book, Albert Pfeiffer, for his continuing friendship and creativity.

MAP CREDITS

Taxicab Zone Map, page 4, courtesy of the DC Public Service Commission. Smithsonian Mall Map, page 85, courtesy of the Smithsonian Institution.

Map Section: Washington DC Street Maps, © Copyright Rand McNally & Company, R. L. 87-S-4. Washington Metro System Map reproduced by permission of the Office of Public Affairs, Washington Metropolitan Area Transit Authority. Tourmobile Map, courtesy of Tourmobile® Sightseeing.

Collier Books
Macmillan Publishing Company
866 Third Avenue
New York, NY 10022

Maxwell Macmillan Canada, Inc.
1200 Eglinton Avenue East
Suite 200
Don Mills, Ontario M3C 3N1

Macmillan Publishing Company is part of the Maxwell Communication Group of Companies.

Library of Congress Cataloging-in-Publication Data

Appleberg, Marilyn J.
  I love Washington guide / Marilyn J. Appleberg; illustrations by Albert Pfeiffer.—3rd ed.
  p. cm.
  Includes index.
  ISBN 0-02-097292-X
  1. Washington (D.C.)—Description—1981–   —Guidebooks
  I. Title.
  F192.3.A69 1992
  917.5304′4—dc20   91-38400

Macmillan books are available at special discounts for bulk purchases for sales promotions, premiums, fund-raising, or educational use. For details, contact:

Special Sales Director
Macmillan Publishing Company
866 Third Avenue
New York, NY 10022

10 9 8 7 6 5 4 3 2 1

Extreme care has been taken to see that all information in this book is accurate and up to date, but the Publisher cannot be held responsible for any errors that may appear.

Printed in the United States of America

CONTENTS

Contents

INTRODUCTION

The White House

Washington! A planned city, carved out of swampland along the Potomac to house a dream. Like the new nation it was to serve, Washington was conceived on a grand scale. But broad boulevards, *rond points*, and monumental statues didn't stop British diplomats assigned here from drawing hardship pay because of the weather.

Myths about Washington abound, but annually 19 million people spend their vacation time in America's capital city—and that's a fact. They come to see their government in action at the Capitol, visit the awe-inspiring monuments to America's great leaders—Washington, Lincoln, and Jefferson—and to see money being printed. They come to see a profusion of pink and white blossoms, two giant pandas, the president's house, and the profoundly moving Vietnam Memorial. And that's just the beginning, because no visit to Washington would be complete without a trip to the "nation's attic," the Smithsonian Institution. The National Air and Space Museum at the Smithsonian has been the top tourist attraction on the Mall since it opened in 1976; go and you'll see why.

The Old Downtown has been revitalized, and Metro brings you right to its heart. Make time to visit the recycled Old Post Office Building, The Shops at National Place, and glamorous Union Station, now a destination in and of itself.

Washington is no longer thought of as a cultural backwater, thanks in great part to the Kennedy Center for the Performing Arts, where ballet, theater, opera, and the National Symphony, directed by Mstislav Rostropovich, thrive. (Don't just tour it, attend it! Call (800) 444-1324 and find out what will be there when you are.) Don't forget, too, the beautifully restored National Theater, the Folger Productions, and the glorious Wolf Trap Farm Park. The East Wing of the National Gallery and the Hirshhorn Museum have become national showpieces, and the burgeoning local art scene in a fascinating setting nearby merits a visit. Dine in some of Washington's unique ethnic restaurants—including Ethiopian and Afghan—and at least one of the many cafeterias. In fine weather, outdoor cafes abound. You'll no doubt also visit Georgetown and, across the Potomac,

Alexandria, Virginia—two historic ports rich in tradition and charm. This guide covers their delights as well.

John F. Kennedy once quipped that Washington had Northern charm and Southern efficiency; geography aside, you'll find Washington a special place to visit or to live. And as an extra bonus, no other American city offers so much cultural and artistic diversity that is absolutely FREE!

HOW TO USE THIS BOOK

General categories are listed in the table of contents; for more specific information on what is included in the book, use the index.

To save space, abbreviations have been used for days of the week and for months.

Small shops in busy shopping areas usually conform to the policies of their larger neighbors; the hours of the department stores are listed, as the only major change occurs during the Christmas shopping season, when they are all open every evening. Others conform to the eccentricities of their area of town; if they are unusual they are listed. If unsure, call ahead.

Where a shop or restaurant accepts credit cards, the following key is used:

AE	American Express
CB	Carte Blanche
DC	Diners' Club
MC	MasterCard
V	Visa

I
LOVE
WASHINGTON
GUIDE

BASIC
INFORMATION

HELPFUL HINTS

Washington, DC, was a planned city, laid out on a grid. It is therefore relatively easy to navigate, once you know the following: The U.S. Capitol is the geographic center of the city. There, at the intersection of East Capitol, South Capitol, and North Capitol streets and the Mall (in lieu of West Capitol), the city is divided into quadrants: Northeast (NE), Northwest (NW), Southeast (SE), Southwest (SW). (More than likely, you'll be spending the bulk of your time in NW and SW.)

Streets are either numbered—they run north to south—or lettered—they run east to west. On lettered streets, the first two digits of the address indicate the nearest cross street, so 1739 N Street is near 17th Street. On numbered streets, the digits of the address correspond to the alphabet, so 516 10th Street is near E Street. (NOTE: There is no J Street, making K the tenth letter.) Avenues bear state names and cut through the grid pattern diagonally. Where they intersect, circles are created and sometimes confusion you may lose the avenue or street you were on. The pattern in each quadrant is generally repetitive, with the coordinates (NW, NE, SE, SW) pinpointing your location. Note: There is no B or J Street. B is Independence and Constitution avenues (on either side of the Mall); J doesn't exist ostensibly because Pierre L'Enfant, the city's planner, didn't like Chief Justice John Jay, but more likely because in those days I and J were used interchangeably.

When in doubt, consult the easy-to-read street map in the map section of this guide.

WEATHER

Though much in the nation's capital is predictable, the weather is not necessarily so. The average mean temperature in summer is 76°F (24°C); in winter 37°F (3°C). But winter's heavy snowfalls and summer's high humidity are not reflected in those numbers, and each in its way can make getting around in the city difficult.

Spring (56°F, 12°C), short but sweet, enhanced by the arrival of the cherry blossoms, and fall (59°F, 15°C), with its colorful appearance, are ideal times to visit.

Layering of clothing is best for any season, except perhaps summer when you will want to wear as little and as light as possible. But even then, a sweater will be needed in those places where the air-conditioning is set at frigid. Comfortable shoes are a must, as well as an umbrella, in any season.

GETTING AROUND

Washington's Metro subway system is modern, clean, carpeted, quiet, and efficient. It covers 103 miles of the Washington Metropolitan Area; where and when it is in operation, it makes getting around a breeze. (NOTE: There are no Metro stops in Georgetown.)

The Metrobus system, which operates on the city's main arteries and in parts of Maryland and northern Virginia, is at best complex.

Taxis are easily hailed and can be surprisingly inexpensive because of the unique zone system on which the fare is based. Also, it is possible to find out in advance how much your trip will cost. Most touring will be done in Zone 1.

Using your car in the city may eat up precious touring time, especially if you get caught in rush hour when things get confusing as well as slow. (Some arteries change direction in the afternoon to facilitate the traffic flow out of town.) Best advice regarding your car: Park it while touring the downtown areas.

Last, but in some ways best, there is walking. Still the only real way to see a city, especially one as pleasing to the eye as Washington.

CAVEAT

The reality of life in today's urban areas dictates the use of common sense while visiting and touring. Wandering into deserted areas of a city with which you are unfamiliar can be foolhardy. When going out at night, know your destination, how you are getting there, and, perhaps more important, how you are getting back. But do not allow unreasonable fears to keep you from enjoying your stay in Washington to the fullest.

INFORMATION CENTERS

These are the main information sources for tourists about places, events, or travel.
Washington, DC, Convention & Visitors Association
1212 New York Avenue, NW (20005). (202) 789-7000. Helpful information available by mail or phone *only* in the form of brochures on hotels, sightseeing, restaurants, and special events. *OPEN Mon-Fri 9am-5pm.* Other times, dial 737-8866 for a recorded announcement of current events in DC. For in-person tourist information, visit the Washington Visitor Information Center (*see* below).
Washington Visitor Information Center
1455 Pennsylvania Avenue, NW (20004). 789-7038. Located in the Willard Collection of Shops, one block from the White House. This is a one-stop resource center for free brochures, maps, and information on where to stay, dine, and the latest on special events. Staffed by knowledgeable personnel from the Washington, DC, Convention & Visitors Association, as well as by trained volunteers from the International Visitors

Information Service. *OPEN Mon-Sat 9am-5pm; Apr-Oct, Sun as well.*

The International Visitors Information Service (IVIS)

733 15th Street, NW, Suite 300; 783-6540. And *Dulles Airport, International Arrivals Building. Their emphasis is on foreign visitors, with complete information on DC sightseeing, entertainment, and hotels. Brochures and maps. Telephone language bank for foreign visitors, 783-6540, staffed by volunteers till 11pm; 24-hour emergency answering service. Multilingual escorts are available, but only for government-sponsored visitors who don't speak English. They also feature a "Home Hospitality" program, for government-sponsored visitors, which enables the foreign visitor to spend an evening in the home of an American family. Three days' notice is needed for IVIS to make the arrangements. Nonprofit organization, but donations are accepted. *OPEN Mon-Fri 9am-5pm. *OPEN 7 days noon-7pm.*

Information Kiosks

In the Mall and monument area. Operated by the National Park Service. Park Rangers provide information and copies of their monthly calendar *Kiosk. OPEN June 1-Sept 1, 7 days 8:30am-5pm.*

Ramsay House Visitors Center

221 King Street, Alexandria, Va. (703) 838-4200. A restored 18th-century town house is headquarters for the Alexandria Tourist Council. Available: hotel and restaurant guides, annual event information, and walking tour maps. Also, a short film on local history. Some maps and sightseeing information on DC. (*See also* HISTORIC & NEW WASHINGTON, Historic Buildings & Areas.) *OPEN 7 days 9am-5pm.*

BUS & SUBWAY INFORMATION

For information and directions to anywhere in the city by Metrorail or Metrobus, call 637-7000 (TDD 638- 3780), 7 days 6am-11:30pm.

Buses

Fare within Washington: $1 at all times. Handicapped persons and senior citizens ride for 30¢ at all times (50¢ in Maryland and Virginia; 55¢ when crossing the DC line), with a Metro authorization card. Children under age 5 accompanied by an adult ride free. Transfers are free. Exact fare is required; *the driver cannot make change.* Tickets or tokens may be purchased at Metrobus Ticket Outlets; for locations, call 637-1328. Metrobuses run on varying schedules; for exact times, call 637-7000.

Fare to Maryland: $1.65 during nonrush hours; $1.65-$1.90 during rush hours.

Fare to Virginia: $1.35-1.80 during nonrush hours; based on a zone system during rush hours, $1.90-$2.85.

Subways (Metro)

Fare $1 during nonrush hours. During rush hours —Monday to Friday from 5:30 to 9:30am and from 3 to 7pm—fare is calculated according to distance traveled. Senior citizens and handicapped ride for half fare all the time. Up to two children under age 5 ride free when accompanied by an adult. Free transfer to Metrobus (but not vice versa) is available. Farecards are needed to enter and exit the Metro system. Insert bills and/or coins in the farecard vending machines they all accept change (no pennies) and $1 and $5 bills; some take $10 and $20 bills, *but* change is returned in coins. Then select the farecard value you want, press the white button, and you will get your farecard and change if you have any coming. If your farecard has an unused value at the end of your ride, it will be returned to you upon exiting and may be used at any time. No refunds are given.

Family/Tourist passes, providing unlimited travel for up to four people (there are four passes, so travel may be on an individual basis), are available for the Metrorail or Metrobus for $8. Valid for a specific Saturday, Sunday, or federal holiday (excluding July 4). Available at Metro sales offices and selected hotels. For details, call 637-7000 (daily, from 6am to 11:30pm).

Bike-on-Rail program permits riders 18 and older to take their bicycles on the last car of any Metro train after 7pm Monday through Friday and all day Saturday, Sunday, and holidays (except July 4). For information or to obtain the required permit, call 962-1116. Ages 12 to 17, call 962-1327.

Metro stations are indicated by tall, brown-colored pylons, with a large white letter "M" at the top. Each station has a color-coded map to help you calculate fare and destinations. Attendants are also present in information booths to assist you. A Metro map is included in the map section of this guide.

HOURS OF OPERATION: Mon-Fri 5:30am-midnight; Sat 8am-midnight; Sun 10am-midnight.

TAXIS

Taxis are readily available downtown except during rush hours. Fares are calculated on a zone system—$2.60 for the initial zone. NOTE: There are additional charges for baggage, evening rush hours (4 to 6:30pm weekdays), and telephone dispatch. During rush hours, taxis are permitted to pick up additional passengers. The standard tip is 10-15 percent of the fare. For problems or complaints call the DC Taxicab Commission at 767-8370.

The following have taxis available 24 hours a day, 7 days a week.

Capitol Cab: 546-2400
Diamond Cab: 387-6200
Yellow Cab: 544-1212

TAXICAB ZONE MAP

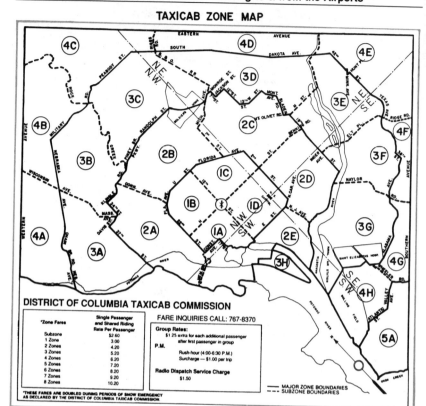

DISTRICT OF COLUMBIA TAXICAB COMMISSION

FARE INQUIRIES CALL: 767-8370

*Zone Fares	Single Passenger and Shared Riding Rate Per Passenger
Subzone	$2.60
1 Zone	3.00
2 Zones	4.20
3 Zones	5.20
4 Zones	6.20
5 Zones	7.20
6 Zones	8.20
7 Zones	9.20
8 Zones	10.20

Group Rates:
$1.25 extra for each additional passenger after first passenger in group

P.M.
Rush-hour (4:00-6:30 P.M.)
Surcharge — $1.00 per trip

Radio Dispatch Service Charge
$1.50

—— MAJOR ZONE BOUNDARIES
- - - SUBZONE BOUNDARIES

*THESE FARES ARE DOUBLED DURING PERIODS OF SNOW EMERGENCY AS DECLARED BY THE DISTRICT OF COLUMBIA TAXICAB COMMISSION.

Suburban cabs utilize meters. They can take you to the suburbs from DC and vice versa, but they cannot transport you within the city.

Also try the area north of the White House and the Mall.

PARKING

Street parking is completely prohibited in the downtown area of the city during rush hours, Monday to Friday from 7 to 9:30am and from 3:30 to 6:30pm. On Georgetown's main thoroughfares, parking is nixed on Friday and Saturday nights. If you are lucky enough to find a spot, note the regulations to avoid being ticketed or towed away.

Commercial parking in Washington is limited and relatively expensive. If you do park in a garage, make note of its closing time to avoid having your car locked in for the evening—or weekend. On the Mall, the only visitor parking for a fee is available at the National Air & Space Museum at 7th Street and Independence Avenue, SW.

GETTING TO & FROM THE AIRPORTS

Train (Metro)

Take the Metro Blue or Yellow Line. It's inexpensive, air-conditioned, and takes approximately 40 minutes to or from Washington National Airport. *HOURS OF OPERATION: Mon-Fri 5:30am-midnight; Sat 8am-midnight; Sun 10am-midnight.* For information, call 637-7000 daily from 6am to 11:30pm.

Bus

The Washington Flyer Buses
(703) 685-1400. *To National Airport*: From the Sheraton, Shoreham, Washington Hilton, Capital Hilton, Mayflower, and J. W. Marriott hotels start-

ing at 6:10am till 9:10pm. *From National Airport*: To the above hotels starting at 5:30am till 10:30pm. Buses leave every half hour. The cost is $5 one way; round trip $8.

To Washington Dulles Airport: From the Washington Hilton starting at 6am till 11pm (they also stop at the Capital Hilton and the Mayflower). *From Washington Dulles Airport*: Starting at 5:05am till 10:05pm, buses leave every half hour. The trip takes one hour and costs $11 one way; $19 round trip.

Taxi

DC taxis do not run on meters. The fare is based on a zone system within DC and on mileage when you are outside DC. It's possible to find out your fare to the airport in advance, just call 331-1671. Tipping is up to the individual. If you have a problem or complaint, note the driver's and cab's numbers, located on the righthand visor, and call the DC Taxicab Commission, 767-8319. For fare inquiries outside of the DC area, call 331-1671.

TELEPHONE SERVICES

Emergency calls: 911
Area Codes
Note: Unless otherwise noted, the area code is 202.
Washington: 202
Virginia: 703
Maryland: 301
Telephone Information
Directory Assistance (Information): 411
Operator Assistance: 0
Out-of-Town: 1 + area code + 555-1212
International Calls
Many countries can now be dialed direct. 011 + country code + city code + the number. Dial 0 (operator) for information concerning the code number of a particular country. Otherwise, have the operator assist in placing the call.
Capitol Switchboard
To locate the office of your senator or congressman, call 224-3121.
Recorded Services
Daily Tourist Information: 737-8866
Dial-a-Museum: 357-2020
Dial-a-Park: 619-7275
Dial-a-Phenomenon: 357-2000
Dial-a-Sermonette: 338-1240
Dial-a-Story: 638-5717
National Archives: 501-5000
Passport Office Information: 647-0518

Postal Answer Line: 526-3920
Prayer: 347-4341
Time: 844-2525
Weather: 936-1212
Public Library Services
Washington, DC, Public Library
For any information you might need about the library, call 727-1111.
Telephone Reference Information Service
Dial 727-1126. They will try to answer any ready reference question you might have. *Mon-Thurs 9am-9pm; Fri & Sat 9am-5:30pm.*

POSTAL SERVICES

Post Offices
Main Post Office, Brentwood Station, 900 Brentwood Road, NE. *OPEN Mon-Fri 8am-8pm; Sat 10am-6pm; Sun noon-6pm.*
The Postal Answer Line, 526-3920, is a recorded selection service line for information on all services. Call for location of post office nearest you. Local post offices are *OPEN Mon-Sat 8am-5pm.*
Stamps
Available at all post offices, *OPEN Mon-Sat 8am-5pm*, and at self-service stations located in many post office lobbies. Otherwise, stamps may be obtained from vending machines in most pharmacies, though at a premium.
Express Letters
Dial 636-1401. Guaranteed 24-hour delivery of any mail brought to one of the specially designated post offices before 5pm; to major cities only. Call for location of the post office nearest you that features the service.
Zip Codes
For zip code information, call 682-9595.

DC PUBLICATIONS

For current happenings in DC at any given time, these are the best sources, available at any newsstand.
City Paper
Every Thursday. Lively free weekly available at shops and cafes.
Washingtonian
Slick, informative monthly magazine.
The Washington Post
The famed daily DC newspaper. The Friday Weekend section is very helpful.
The Washington Times
Daily in the am; good Weekend section on Friday.

HOTELS

The Willard InterContinental

Washington is, and has been for the last several years, experiencing an unprecedented hotel building boom; most are in the ultra-luxurious or pampered business executive class. The good news for families are the older buildings that have been converted from apartment residences to all-suites accommodations offering more space and an opportunity to save on eating out. There are close to 50,000 hotel rooms in the city, but Washington, in addition to being a popular tourist destination, is also, since the opening of the convention center, a popular business destination. So be forewarned: Book early, especially during peak travel times

NOTE: In DC, there is an 11 percent tax added to your hotel bill as well as a $1.50-per-day surcharge.

WEEKEND PACKAGES & RATES

From the deluxe class to the mid-level chains, almost all of the hotels offer some sort of reduced rate on the weekend when the business traveler has left for home. Some of these have extra amenities, others are only well-reduced rates; I have included the toll-free 800 number for hotels listed in this section. Call and ask what is available in this category; availability may vary with the season. Fall and spring are the busiest times in DC. Most of the hotels have some sort of corporate, family, senior citizen, or active-duty military personnel rate. Inquire.

CHOOSING A HOTEL

The Washington, DC, Convention & Visitors Association has a brochure of DC-area accommodations entitled "A Guide to Lodgings in the Nation's Capital." Write to them at 1212 New York Avenue, NW, Washington, DC 20005. **The Hotel Association of Washington, DC** also offers a free brochure, with special emphasis on reduced seasonal rates. Write to them at 1201 New York Avenue, NW, Suite 601, Washington, DC 20005, or call (202) 289-3141. A "Weekends" brochure is also offered by the **Committee to Promote Washington**; write to them at P.O. Box 27489, Washington, DC 20038-7489, or call (202) 724-4091 or (800) 422-8644.

RESERVATIONS SERVICES

Capitol Reservations
1730 Rhode Island Avenue, NW, 20036. (202) 452-1270; (800) 847-4832. This highly regarded knowledgeably staffed agency exists to help the visitor to DC find good, decently priced hotel rooms. They do the looking and the booking. They represent over 70 hotels and there is absolutely no cost to you (the hotel pays the commission). They are up on all the discounts and seasonal rates and often are able to offer exclusives on deeply discounted rates; they are highly reliable. Service available *Mon-Fri 9am-6pm; Sat 9am-1pm*.

Washington DC Accommodations
1720 20th Street, NW, 20009. (202) 289-2220; (800) 554-2220. Expert personal service to help visitors find the best rates available, be it economy or deluxe accommodations. The service is completely free to the traveler and reservations are confirmed immediately. Service available *Mon-Fri 9am-5pm*.

DELUXE

More than just expensive, these are the crème.

Carlton Hotel
923 16th Street, NW, 20006. (202) 638-2626; (800) 325-3535. Fax (202) 638-4231. The grande dame at K Street; a remodeled jewel built in 1926, now a Sheraton property, has undergone a $22 million restoration. Refined ambience; distinguished address two blocks north of the White House. Magnificent block-long lobby; tastefully decorated rooms boast every amenity. Health club on premises; pool privileges at the Sheraton Washington (they'll shuttle you there). Concierge; 24-hour room service; butler service on every floor. No- smoking floor. Children under age 17 in parents' room free. No pets. Deluxe restaurant and paneled lounge. Meeting rooms. 197 rooms; 13 suites. Weekend packages.

The Four Seasons Hotel
2800 Pennsylvania Avenue, NW, 20007. (202) 342-0444; (800) 332-3442. Fax (202) 944-2076. Outstanding hotel on the fringe of Georgetown overlooking the C&O Canal. European ambience and impeccable service. Furnished with period antiques, many of the elegant, silk-walled guest rooms boast views of Rock Creek Park. Multilingual staff, concierge, 24-hour room and valet service, state-of-the art fitness facilities including an indoor swimming pool. Children under age 18 in parents' room free. No-smoking rooms available. Afternoon tea or cocktails in the Garden Terrace Lounge; and brunch at Aux Beaux Champs (*see* RESTAURANTS, French). Underground garage; complimentary use of limousine. Small pets accepted. Deluxe meeting facilities. 197 rooms, including 30 suites. Weekend packages.

The Grand Hotel
2350 M Street, NW, 20037. (202) 429-0100; (800) 848-0016. Fax (202) 429-9759. In the West End, just three blocks east of Georgetown, a luxurious newcomer designed to pamper the so-phisticated international traveler. Behind the elegant Beaux Arts facade are lovely public spaces and beautifully appointed rooms decorated in soothing colors; marble bathrooms with telephones and TV speaker; some rooms have kitchenettes, some suites have whirlpools and fireplaces. Plush terry robes for guest use, nightly turndown; 24-hour room service. Executive business center, health club, and heated swimming pool overlooking the secluded courtyard. The Promenade Lounge for afternoon tea. Small pets permitted. 265 rooms and suites. Weekend packages.

The Hay-Adams Hotel
One Lafayette Square, NW, 20006. (202) 638-6600; (800) 424-5054. Fax (202) 638-2716 or -3803. Washington's classic personal hotel, restored to its former elegance. Built in 1927 as a private guest house, inspired by an Italian palazzo, on the site of the former houses of statesman John Hay and historian Henry Adams, it offers a prestigious location overlooking Lafayette Square directly across from the White House (rooms with a view for a premium). Dignified European ambience, personal service. Fresh flowers in the traditionally decorated high-ceilinged rooms; complimentary use of terry robes; nightly turndown service; 24-hour butler and concierge service; complimentary limousine service. International clientele; multilingual staff. One child under age 10 in parents' room free. Pets allowed. The oak-paneled John Hay Room for classic French cuisine; the Tea Room for afternoon tea. Meeting room available. 145 rooms; 18 suites. Weekend and summer rates.

Henley Park Hotel
926 Massachusetts Avenue, NW, 20001. (202) 638-5200; (800) 222-8474. Fax (202) 289-8576. A special spot downtown within sight of the Capitol, two blocks from the Convention Center, and close to Union Station; a rejuvenated 1918 Tudor-style former apartment house. Rooms have Queen Anne furnishings and English prints, mini-bars, free in-room movies on HBO; nightly

Hay-Adams Hotel

turndown service and shoe shine. Concierge; 24-hour room service. Off the intimate lobby, the Wilkes Room for breakfast and afternoon tea as well as a clubby lounge. Also on premises the respected Coeur de Lion restaurant (see RESTAURANTS, French). Guest privileges at a nearby health club. Children under age 14 in parents' room free. Parking for a fee. 96 rooms.

Jefferson Hotel
1200 16th Street, NW, 20036. (202) 347-2200; (800) 368-5966. Fax (202) 331-7982. Fine, intimate, sedate, 69-year-old personal-service hotel four blocks from the White House, now expanding into an adjacent town house. Favored by much of official Washington (indeed, temporary home to then vice president George Bush before he moved to official residence). One- or two-bedroom suites with parlors. Rooms are spacious and airy with English period furnishings; some kitchen suites available. Pets accepted. Valet parking. Restaurant and bar; afternoon tea. Hand laundry; 24-hour concierge and butler service; nightly turndown. Banquet room. 100 rooms, including 32 suites. Weekend package.

The Madison Hotel
15th & M Streets, NW, 20005. 862-1600; (800) 424-8577. Fax (202) 785-1255. One of Washington's finest and most elegant classic old hotels; popular with foreign diplomats and heads of state (even Gorby and Raisa once slept here). Contemporary exterior with federal-period furnishings and exquisite oriental art objects. Superior service; multilingual staff; 24-hour concierge and room service. Refrigerator in room; nightly turndown with sweet dreams Godiva mint at bedside. Children, pets, and parking for a fee. 374 rooms. Weekend packages.

The Mayflower Hotel
1127 Connecticut Avenue, NW, 20036. 347-3000; (800) 468-3571. Fax (202) 466-9082. This longtime (since 1925), traditional yet elegant hotel with its classic block-long skylit lobby was recently and expensively refurbished. Often called the "hotel of presidents," it was officially opened for President Calvin Coolidge's inaugural ball and its magnificent ornate Grand Ballroom has been the scene of every one since then. Conveniently located on fashionable Connecticut Avenue, four blocks from the White House. Draws businesspeople, conventioneers, and tourists. J. Edgar Hoover dined here daily for 20 years. Both JFK and LBJ stayed here, and so did Truman, after his presidency. Amenities include complimentary coffee and morning newspaper. Children under age 18 in parents' room free. Pets allowed. Parking. Concierge; 24-hour room service. No-smoking rooms. Nicholas restaurant (see RESTAURANTS, American). Convention facilities. 724 rooms. Weekend rates.

The Morrison-Clark Inn
1015 L Street, NW, 20001. (202) 898-1200; (800) 332-7898. Fax (202) 289-8576. This historic property (actually, twin townhouses built in 1865) at Massachusetts Avenue was once the Soldiers, Sailors, Marines and Airmen's Club. Elegant and inviting public spaces and guest rooms; furnished with period antiques and reproductions, it's an extremely civilized choice close to the Convention Center. Concierge service; in-room movies. Well-regarded restaurant on premises (see RESTAURANTS, American: Morrison-Clark Inn). 54 rooms. Weekend rates.

The Ritz Carlton
2100 Massachusetts Avenue, NW, 20018. 293-2100; (800) 241-3333. Fax (202) 293-0641. Outstanding choice on Embassy Row near Dupont Circle. Built in 1924, lovingly restored to become, in 1979, the elegant small hotel in Washington. Eight-story addition added 100 rooms in 1985. Beautiful, individually decorated rooms and suites (by Sister Parish of Kennedy White House redecorating fame) have two-line phones, marble baths, honor bars, and the use of plush terry robes. Emphasis on personal service in the European tradition: multilingual staff; 24-hour valet, concierge, and room service. No-smoking rooms available. Children under age 12 in parents' room free. The famed Jockey Club restaurant; the cozy Fairfax Bar (see RESTAURANTS, Continental, and NIGHTLIFE, Piano Bars). Small meeting rooms. 230 rooms. Weekend packages.

Watergate Hotel
2650 Virginia Avenue, NW, 20037. 965-2300; (800) 424-2736. (No fax.) Adjacent to Kennedy Center overlooking the Potomac River, a stroll away from Georgetown. Part of a commercial/apartment/hotel complex it's a stylish choice. Large luxury accommodations, predominantly suites, with balconies, most with Potomac-filled views; some with kitchens. Excellent service. Health club with whirlpool, steam bath, and sauna; indoor swimming pool. Children under age 12 in parents' room free. Pets allowed. Also within the complex, the fine Jean Louis Restaurant (see RESTAURANTS, French) and the prestigious Les Champs shopping arcade. Meeting rooms and convention center. 237 rooms and suites. Weekend packages.

Willard InterContinental
1401 Pennsylvania Avenue, NW, 20004. (202) 628-9100, (800) 327-0200. Fax (202) 637-7326. A beautifully restored Beaux Arts masterpiece, the Willard has regained its position as a jewel of Pennsylvania Avenue only a two-block stroll away from the White House and in the restored Old Downtown. (President Lincoln and his family were guests at the original Willard for nine days —at $2.75 per person per day when an assassination attempt was rumored.) Today, the opulent lobby (where the term *lobbyist* was coined), the fabled Peacock Alley, and the oak-paneled Willard Room (see RESTAURANTS, American) are all once more flourishing. Modern amenities in the charmingly decorated rooms include in-room movies, stocked honor bar; 24-hour room service, nightly turndown service, terry robes for guest use, and the morning papers delivered to the door. Children under age 15 in parents' room

free. Pets accepted. Fifteen meeting rooms and ballrooms; 394 rooms, 65 luxury suites. Weekend packages. (*See also* HISTORIC & NEW WASHINGTON, Historic Buildings & Areas.)

EXPENSIVE

ANA Hotel Washington, DC
2401 M Street, NW, 20037. (202) 429-2400; (800) 228-3000. Fax (202) 457-5010. A ten-story $80 million hotel built in 1985 (as the Westin Hotel) in the West End between Georgetown and the business district. Elegant accommodations; valet service; state-of-the art fitness center with swimming pool. Appealing formal courtyard garden. Two restaurants; 24-hour room service. Children under age 18 in parents' room free. Pets accepted. Executive Club floor; deluxe meeting facilities include video teleconferencing. 415 rooms. Weekend package.

The Canterbury Hotel
1733 N Street, NW, 20036. (202) 393-3000; (800) 424-2950. Fax (202) 785-9581. Near Dupont Circle, this small inviting European-style, all-suites hotel is on one of DC's quietest, prettiest residential blocks. Classic 18th-century English decor including some four-posters; gracious service. Complimentary continental breakfast served in Chaucer's, their very fine restaurant (*see* RESTAURANTS, Continental), also complimentary evening cocktail, nightly turndown, and free morning paper. Valet parking. Up to two children under age 12 in parents' room free. No-smoking rooms. Historic note: FDR lived at this address when he was assistant secretary of the navy. 99 junior suites. Weekend package.

The Capitol Hill Hotel
200 C Street, SE, 20003. 543-6000; (800) 424-9165. Fax (202) 547-2608. A small, all-suites hotel in a converted apartment building close to the Capitol. Comfortable, spacious accommodations; Queen Anne-style furnishings; fully equipped kitchens. Personal service; amenities include complimentary continental breakfast, the morning paper, nightly turndown; concierge. Executive membership for extra-special comfort. Children under age 12 in parents' room free. Small conference room. 152 suites. Good-value weekend package.

The Capitol Hilton
1001 16th Street, NW, 20036. (202) 393-1000; (800) 445-8667. Fax (202) 393-7992. A large, modern, highly commercial, very active Hilton at K Street near the White House indeed, near everything. The extra- large rooms have color TV with free in-room movies; some have refrigerators, some have balconies. Children in parents' room free. Pets allowed. Buses leave from here to all three airports. The Towers: a new, elite environment on the top four floors with private elevator and lounge, concierge service and health club access. Twigs, great spot to see Capitol types at breakfast; a newly redecorated

Trader Vic's, among others (*see* RESTAURANTS, Breakfast/Brunch *and* Polynesian). Well-used convention facilities; business center with everything from secretaries to personal computers available. 549 rooms, including 32 suites. Weekend packages.

Dupont Plaza Hotel
1500 New Hampshire Avenue, NW, 20036. 483-6000; (800) 421-6662. Fax (202) 328-3265. Located right on Dupont Circle, half a mile from the White House. Each attractive room has color TV, refrigerator, wet bar; suites overlook Dupont Circle Park. Children under age 14 in parents' room free. Parking for a fee. No-smoking rooms. Restaurant; lounge; room service. Convention facilities. 314 rooms. Weekend packages.

Embassy Row Hotel
2015 Massachusetts Avenue, NW, 20036. (202) 265-1600; (800) 424-2400. (No fax.) Just north of Dupont Circle in the heart of DC's prestigious Embassy Row. Gracious European ambience; international clientele. Nightly turndown service; in-room movies. Multilingual staff. Outdoor rooftop swimming pool and sun deck in season. Children under age 12 in parents' room free. Pets allowed. Parking charge. Restaurant and lounge on premises. Four meeting rooms. 196 rooms and suites. Weekend package.

Grand Hyatt Hotel
1000 H Street, NW, 20001. (202) 582-1234; (800) 228-9000. Fax (202) 637-4781. A 12-story atrium and a 7,000-square-foot lagoon distinguish this downtown Hyatt, just across from the Convention Center, with direct access to Metro Center station. Two-story health club with swimming pool, exercise rooms, sauna, aerobics, and juice bar. Free HBO, CNN; mini-bars; 24-hour room service. The Regency Club for enhanced amenities at a premium. Three restaurants, two lounges. Children under age 17 in parents' room free. 907 rooms including 60 suites.

Guest Quarters New Hampshire
801 New Hampshire Avenue, NW, 20037. (202) 785-2000; (800) 424-2900. Fax (202) 785-9485. In Foggy Bottom at H Street near the Kennedy Center. Quiet, all-suites luxury hotel; all accommodations have fully equipped kitchens. Rooftop swimming pool with a view. Continental breakfast Saturday and Sunday; room service; personalized valet service available. Small pets accommodated for a fee. Good for business travelers and families. 101 suites. Weekend rates.

Guest Quarters Pennsylvania Avenue
2500 Pennsylvania Avenue, NW, 20037. (202) 333-8060; (800) 424-2900. Fax (202) 338-3818. One block from historic Georgetown, three blocks from the Metro. Small, all-suites luxury hotel. One- and two-bedroom accommodations available. Cheerful contemporary decor. All have bedroom, living room, and dining areas; fully-equipped kitchens; color TV. Garden; health club and pool privileges nearby. Children and parking extra. Accommodations for small pets, too. Helpful concierge; room service; con-

tinental breakfast available. Well recommended by businessmen. Group rates available. 123 suites. Weekend rates.

Hyatt Regency Washington on Capitol Hill
400 New Jersey Avenue, NW, 20001. (202) 737-1234; (800) 233-1234. Fax (202) 737-5773. On Capitol Hill, two blocks from Union Station, a large, dazzlingly modern Hyatt popular with businesspeople. The Hyatt signature atrium lobby this one five stories with restaurants and glass-capsule elevators. On-premises health club; glass-roofed swimming pool; 24-hour room service. Children under age 18 in parents' room free. No pets except Seeing Eye dogs. Three restaurants, three lounges including the Capitol View Club (see RESTAURANTS, Rooms with a View; see also NIGHTLIFE, Piano Bars: Capitol View Lounge). Regency Club floor for extra pampering for a premium. Convention facilities 842 rooms. Good-value weekend rates.

J.W. Marriott
1331 Pennsylvania Avenue, NW, 20004. (202) 393-2000; (800) 627-7468. Fax (202) 626-6965. The Marriott flagship hotel, part of the successful restoration of Pennsylvania Avenue and the Old Downtown. The imposing lobby leads right into the lively SHOPS at National Place and National Press Building and the National Theater. Traditional rooms have extra-large beds, TV with HBO, and great views. The convention-size hotel has several restaurants; free limousine service to National Airport; health club with indoor swimming pool and exercise room with Universal equipment, hydrotherapy, sun deck. Children under age 18 in parents' room free. Concierge Level on floors 14 and 15 for extra-special care and a private lounge with a view for breakfast and cocktails. 773 rooms. Weekend rates.

Latham
3000 M Street, NW, 20007. 726-5000; (800) 368-5922. Fax (202) 337-4250. On M Street in historic Georgetown (formerly the Georgetown Marbury Hotel). Georgian exterior with attractively decorated rooms. Attention to comfort and service. Concierge; complimentary morning paper. Outdoor swimming pool; boutiques located in the building; three restaurants, lounge with entertainment. Valet parking. Banquet and conference facility; executive boardroom. 164 rooms. Weekend packages.

Loew's L'Enfant Plaza
480 L'Enfant Plaza East, SW, 20024. (202) 484-1000; (800) 243-1166. Fax (202) 863-4497. Ultra-modern, well-located (near Smithsonian and Hirshhorn museums, walk to the monuments) luxury hotel (recently refurbished) on floors 11 to 15 of a cosmopolitan complex. Luxuriously appointed rooms, all with remote-control TV, in-room movies, VCR, refrigerator, minibar; some with balconies and great views. Year-round rooftop-atrium swimming pool and state-of-the-art health club. Amenities abound: nightly turndown with sweet dreams mint; ice delivered daily; second TV in bathroom. Children under age 18 in parents' room free. Pets allowed. Two

restaurants and two bars. Club 480 for special amenities. Underground shopping promenade; Metro station. 372 rooms and suites. Weekend packages.

New Hampshire Suites
1121 New Hampshire, NW, 20037. (202) 457-0565; (800) 762-3777. Fax (202) 331-9421. Renovated hotel in the newly fashionable West End. Warm surroundings, courteous service. Choice of three sizes of contemporary suites: junior, standard, and master. All cable TV, kitchenettes with microwaves and coffee makers. Nightly turndown; complimentary breakfast daily. Multilingual concierge service. No-smoking rooms available. Business services available; executive boardroom. 75 units. Weekend packages.

Omni Shoreham Hotel
2500 Calvert Street, NW, 20008. (202) 234-0700; (800) 843-6664. Fax (202) 234-0700. Upper Northwest, on 11 acres of park and woodland, very resortlike yet only 10 minutes from downtown. Very large plush convention-size hotel overlooking bucolic Rock Creek Park. It has benefited greatly from Omni's renovations and management. Amenities include health club, sauna, tennis courts, Olympic-size outdoor swimming pool. The Art Deco-motif Marquee lounge for big band sounds, the Garden Court for a sumptuous champagne brunch on Sunday. Children under age 14 in parents' room free. Good-value family packages. 715 rooms including 55 suites. Weekend rates.

One Washington Circle Hotel
One Washington Circle, NW, 20037. 872-1680; (800) 424-9671. Fax (202) 887-4989. Well-regarded, luxurious, all-suite hotel between Georgetown and the White House. Traditional or contemporary decor; residential feel. Most suites have balconies, all have fully-equipped pantry kitchens and TV. Swimming pool and sun deck. Complimentary morning papers, free grocery delivery; nightly turndown service. Children under age 12 in parents' room free. Parking facilities. Room service. The very good West End Cafe (see RESTAURANTS, American). Conference room. 152 suites. Great weekend packages.

Park Hyatt Washington, DC
1201 24th Street, NW, 20037. (202) 789-1234; (800) 922-7275. Fax (202) 457-8823. Yet another pricey European-style luxury-class hotel in the West End, three blocks from Georgetown. This newest addition boasts elegant accommodations; personal service, 24-hour room service, valet parking; indoor swimming pool, health club, Jacuzzi, and sauna; lobby lounge for high tea. Children under age 18 in parents' room free. 224 rooms, including 130 bedroom suites. Weekend package.

Phoenix Park Hotel
520 North Capitol Street, NW, 20001. (202) 638-6900; (800) 824-5419. Fax (202) 393-3236. Just four blocks from the Capitol and one block from the renewed Union Station, this is one of DC's most charming small hotels. Named for a Dublin

park, warm Irish hospitality and personal service are the draw. Elegant period- style furnishings; TV with complimentary HBO; valet and room service till 1am; concierge; nightly turndown. Suites have brick walls and fireplaces. Children under age 16 in parents' room free. The masculine Powerscourt Restaurant, popular with congressional types (*see* RESTAURANTS, Continental), and the Dubliner, the city's best Irish pub, with entertainment every night (*see* NIGHTLIFE, Ethnic). Meeting facilities available. 84 rooms, including 15 suites. Weekend rates.

Pullman Highland
1914 Connecticut Avenue, NW, 20009. (202) 797-2000; (800) 424-2464. Fax (202) 462-0944. A $6 million renovation of the historic Highland Hotel by the France-based Pullman International Hotels. Situated on a hill overlooking the city, near embassies and fashionable Connecticut Avenue shops, four blocks north of the Dupont Circle Metro station. All rooms have color TV; refrigerator or mini-bar; fax access line. Concierge; multilingual staff. Children under age 14 in parents' room free. No pets. Valet parking. Restaurant; lounge. Business center; two small meeting rooms. 143 rooms. Weekend package.

Ramada Renaissance Techworld Hotel
999 9th Street, NW, 20001. (202) 898-9000; (800) 228-9898. (No fax.) This upscale Ramada, part of Techworld Plaza, a commercial mixed-use complex, is a giant newcomer to downtown. The Renaissance Club Tower provides extra pampering for a premium. Fitness center with 50-foot swimming pool; two restaurants and a bar/lounge. 720 rooms, 80 suites. Weekend rates.

River Inn
924 25th Street, NW, 20037. (202) 337-7600; (800) 424-2741. (No fax.) In residential Foggy Bottom, close to the Kennedy Center, a small hotel overlooking the Potomac. A guest-house feel in the all-suites accommodations with living, dining, and fully-equipped kitchen areas. Personal-service oriented, charming. Multilingual staff. Children under age 14 in parents' room free. Parking. On premises the trendy Foggy Bottom Cafe (*see* RESTAURANTS, American). 127 suites. Weekend rates.

Sheraton Washington Hotel
2660 Woodley Road, NW, 20028. (202) 328-2000; (800) 325-3535. Fax (202) 234-0015. Upper Northwest Connecticut Avenue, 2 miles from the White House but near the National Zoo and Rock Creek Park. DC's largest convention-oriented hotel on 12 acres of real estate. In summer, two outdoor swimming pools and sun deck; in winter, ice skating. Concierge services; multilingual staff; special corporate services available. Free in-room movies. Children under age 12 in parents' room free. Pets allowed. Five restaurants, some with entertainment; health club; post office; beauty salon and barber shop on premises. Full convention facilities. Shuttle bus to downtown. 1,505 rooms, 257 of which are specially equipped for handicapped guests. Good-value weekend rates.

Washington Hilton Hotel & Towers
1919 Connecticut Avenue, NW, 20009. (202) 483-3000; (800) 445-8667. Fax (202) 265-8221. Huge convention and family-oriented hotel. Comfortable rooms with color TV; first-run in-room movies; refrigerators. Family rates available. Children in parents' room free. Baby-sitters can be arranged. Pets allowed. Business services include stenographer, interpreters. Resort-like atmosphere with Olympic-size outdoor swimming pool, wading pool, poolside service, outdoor tennis courts, health spa, and jogging course. Restaurant, coffee shop, lounges. Some facilities and accommodations for handicapped. 1,154 rooms. Weekend package.

Washington Marriott Hotel
1221 22nd Street, NW, 20037. 872-1500; (800) 3   445. Fax (202) 872-1424. Midtown location near Georgetown. Business execs predominate at this attractive modern Marriott with a winning staff. Indoor swimming pool, fitness center, whirlpool, sauna. In-room movies available. Complimentary morning paper, juice, and coffee. No charge for a third person in the room. Pets accepted. Two bars; Atrium Restaurant. Meeting rooms available. 418 rooms. Weekend and holiday rates.

Washington Plaza Hotel
10 Thomas Circle, Massachusetts Avenue at Vermont, NW, 20005. (202) 842-1300; (800) 424-1140. Fax (202) 842-1300, ext 7082. Attractive, tastefully decorated, moderately expensive accommodations, five blocks from the White House and the Convention Center. Some rooms have balconies, all have in-room movies. Beautifully landscaped grounds with outdoor swimming pool in season; health club on premises. Popular restaurant and lounge; 24-hour room service. Children under age 18 in parents' room free. Newly designed banquet and group facilities. 340 rooms and suites. Very good value weekend rates.

Washington Vista—Hilton International
1400 M Street, NW, 20005. (202) 429-1700; (800) 847-8232. Fax (202) 785-0786. Five blocks from the White House and the Convention Center, a $50 million glass-and-concrete structure with a striking glass-canopied central atrium lobby and a 130-foot-high glass window facing M Street. Executive Floors on 11 and 12 for personal service; also an executive fitness center. Rooms have in-room movies and HBO. The American Harvest and Veranda restaurants, a wine bar, and the Lobby Court for afternoon tea accompanied by a string quartet; 24-hour room service. Underground garage; meeting facilities. 399 rooms. Weekend packages.

Wyndam Bristol Hotel
2430 Pennsylvania Avenue, NW, 20037. (202) 955-6400; (800) 822-4200. Fax (202) 775-8489. A wonderful small hotel located between the White House and Georgetown, four blocks from the Foggy Bottom Metro station. Spacious rooms

in classic English decor complete with four-poster beds, mini-bars, coffee makers, hair dryers; some are equipped with kitchenettes. Concierge; valet parking. Children under age 17 in parents' room free. No pets. On premises, the Bristol Grill Restaurant. 240 rooms. Weekend rates.

MODERATE

Bellevue Hotel
15 E Street, NW, 20001. (202) 638-0900; (800) 327-6667. (No fax.) Small, well-priced refurbished older hotel located on Capitol Hill, a stroll away from the Capitol, Union Station, and the Smithsonian. Old-world feel; great location for sightseeing. Family plan; special rates for groups and government personnel. No pets. Free parking. On premises, the Tiber Creek Pub; lounge with entertainment. 140 rooms and junior suites. Weekend rates.

Best Western Skyline Hotel
10 I Street, SW, 20024. (202) 488-7500; (800) 458-7500. Fax (202) 488-0790. A motel five blocks from the Capitol in the Southwest Redevelopment Area. Most rooms have nice views. Olympic-size, open-air swimming pool and sun deck in season. Grayline Sightseeing pickup point. Special family rates; kids under age 18 in parents' room free. Pets allowed. Free underground parking. Restaurant, lounge, and coffee shop. Meeting rooms available. 203 rooms. Weekend and group rates.

The Carlyle Suites
1731 New Hampshire Avenue, NW, 20009. (202) 234-3200. (No fax.) A newly renovated, moderately priced all-suites hotel with Art Deco styling, near lively Dupont Circle, three blocks to Metro. Units are spacious with fully-equipped kitchens, dining/sitting areas; color TV. Children under age 18 in parents' room free. No- smoking accommodations available. Restaurant, lounge. Meeting facilities. Limited free parking. Government and group rates. 176 suites. Weekend packages.

Channel Inn
650 Water Street, SW, 20024. (202) 554-2400; (800) 368-5668. Fax (202) 863-1164. A good choice newly renovated motel on the Washington Channel. All rooms have balconies overlooking the water. Outdoor swimming pool, boat docks. Children under age 18 in parents' room free. No pets. Restaurant, lounge with entertainment, coffee shop; room service. Meeting rooms. 170 suites.

Days Inn Downtown Convention Center
1201 K Street, NW, 20005. (202) 842-1020; (800) 562-3350. (No fax.) (Formerly Best Western Midtown Motor Inn) Within walking distance of the White House. In-room movies; outdoor swimming pool. Children under age 18 in parents' room free. Pets allowed. Free garage parking. No-smoking rooms available. Restaurant, lounge. 220 rooms.

Days Inn New York Avenue
2700 New York Avenue, NE, 20002. 832-5890; (800) 325-2525. (No fax.) About 2 miles from downtown, opposite the National Arboretum, near RFK Stadium. Swimming pool. Children under age 19 in parents' room free. Pets allowed. Restaurant; room service. Meeting rooms. 194 rooms. Weekend package.

Embassy Square Suites
2000 N Street, NW, 20036. (202) 659-9000; (800) 424-2999. Fax (202) 429-9546. Near Dupont Circle, ten-story full-service apartment hotel boasts a helpful staff and a pleasant garden courtyard with outdoor swimming pool. All of the nicely decorated suites have kitchens and balconies; best are those facing the park. Complimentary continental breakfast. Children under age 18 in parents' room free. No pets. No-smoking rooms. Parking for a fee. Dining room, bar, and lounge on premises. Small meeting room. 250 suites. Good- value weekend rates.

Georgetown Dutch Inn
1075 Thomas Jefferson Street, NW, 20007. (202) 337-0900; (800) 421-6662. Fax (202) 333-6526. Pleasant, small hotel just off historic Georgetown's bustling M Street close to the C&O Canal. Comfortable suites, all have separate bedroom and fully-equipped kitchen facilities. Complimentary continental breakfast. Children under age 13 in parents' room free. Small pets allowed. Free parking. 47 suites. Weekend package.

Hampshire Hotel
1310 New Hampshire Avenue, NW, 20036. 296-7600; (800) 368-5691. Fax (202) 293-2476. Former apartment building one block from the Dupont Circle Metro station. A short walk to Georgetown. Spacious junior suites with completely equipped kitchens (a few exceptions). Children under age 12 in parents' room free. No pets. Lafitte Restaurant features Creole cooking (see RESTAURANTS, American). Business-type clientele. 82 suites. Weekend and holiday rates.

Harrington Hotel
11th & E Streets, NW, 20004. (202) 628-8140; (800) 424-8532. Fax (202) 347-3924. Located between the White House and the Capitol. At the low end of moderate priced, a good, older hotel; central but still transitional location for downtown shopping and touring. Full of budget-minded groups, young and old. Good for families; special flat rates available; for students, too. Small pets allowed. Terrific cafeteria on premises. 275 rooms. Weekend rates.

Holiday Inn Capitol
550 C Street, SW, 20024. (202) 479-4000; (800) 465-4329. Fax (202) 479-4353. Six blocks from the Capitol and one block from the National Air & Space Museum. Outdoor swimming pool; in-room movies. Children under age 18 in parents' room free. Pets allowed. Free parking. Restaurant, lounge; room service. Meeting facilities. 529 rooms. Weekend package.

Holiday Inn Central
1501 Rhode Island Avenue, NW, 20005. (202) 483-2000; (800) 465-4329. Fax (202) 797-1078.

At Scott Circle, seven blocks from the White House; short walk to the Metro. Swimming pool; game room. Children under age 18 in parents' room free. Sightseeing tours depart daily. Free parking. Restaurant, lounge. Meeting rooms. 213 rooms. Weekend and holiday rates.

Holiday Inn Downtown Governor's House
1615 Rhode Island Avenue, NW, 20036. (202) 296-2100; (800) 821-4367. Fax (202) 331-0227. Convenient location close to the business district. In-room movies; outdoor swimming pool in summer. Complimentary use of YMCA health club. Children under age 18 in parents' room free. Daily sightseeing tours depart from hotel. Valet parking. Herb's Restaurant with pleasant garden patio dining (*see* RESTAURANTS, American). Meeting rooms. 152 rooms. Weekend and holiday rates.

Holiday Inn Georgetown
2101 Wisconsin Avenue, NW, 20007. (202) 338-4600; (800) 465-4329. Fax (202) 333-6113. Upper Wisconsin near Georgetown University and the National Cathedral. Outdoor swimming pool; in-room movies. Children under age 18 in parents' room free. Pets allowed. Sightseeing tours arranged. Restaurant, lounge, coffee shop; room service. Laundry service. Meeting rooms available. 296 rooms. Weekend packages.

Holiday Inn Thomas Circle
1155 14th Street, NW, 20005. (202) 737-1200; (800) 465-4329. Fax (202) 783-5733. Conveniently located at Massachusetts Avenue, five blocks from the White House, near the Metro. Newly renovated high-rise with comfortable rooms. Outdoor rooftop swimming pool in season. Children under age 18 in parents' room free. Pets allowed. Free valet parking. Restaurant, lounge. Convention/meeting facilities. 208 rooms. Weekend rates.

Hotel Anthony
1823 L Street, NW, 20036. (202) 223-4320; (800) 424-2970. Fax (202) 223-8546. Recently renovated modern hotel close to business, shopping, and nightlife area; one block to Farragut North Metro station. Each large studio has complete kitchen facilities or wet bar, color TV with first-run movies. Pleasant service. Children under age 16 in parents' room free. No pets. Parking facilities. Samantha's Restaurant (*see* NIGHTLIFE, Dance Bars & Clubs). 99 suites. Great weekend rates.

Hotel Lombardy
2019 I Street, NW, 20006. (202) 828-2600; (800) 424-5486. Fax (202) 872-0503. At Pennsylvania Avenue, one block from George Washington University. Near financial and business district; favored by businessmen. Comfortable accommodations, all with mini-bars, many with kitchenettes. Children under age 12 in parents' room free. Cafe Lombardy on premises. Conference room available. 126 rooms and suites. Weekend package.

Hotel Washington
515 15th Street, NW, 20004. (202) 638-5900; (800) 424-9540. Fax (202) 638-4275. Opposite the Treasury, one block from the White House. Large nine-story historic DC hotel at Pennsylvania Avenue. In continuous use since opening in 1918, recently refurbished to keep up with its tony renewed neighbor, the Willard. Guests in residence have included Vice President John Garner and Speaker of the House John McCormack. A winter season amenity: complimentary afternoon tea in the lobby. Newly added health club on premises. Children under age 14 in parents' room free. Small pets allowed. Parking facilities. The Two Continents in the Sky Restaurant and the popular Rooftop Terrace, which has one of the town's most breathtaking views (*see* RESTAURANTS, Rooms with a View). Meeting rooms available. 370 rooms. Weekend and holiday rates.

The Howard Inn
2225 Georgia Avenue, NW, 20001. (202) 462-5400; (800) 368-5729. Fax (202) 667-0973. At Howard University campus, hotel with African motif and view of DC skyline. Executive suites. Jacuzzi, heated indoor swimming pool, health spa. Children under age 14 in parents' room free. No pets. Parking facilities. Restaurant, two lounges with entertainment; room service. Meeting and banquet facilities. 147 rooms. Weekend and holiday rates.

Howard Johnson Motor Lodge
2601 Virginia Avenue, NW, 20037. (202) 965-2700; (800) 654-2000. Fax (202) 965-2700, ext. 7910. Across from Watergate Complex, two blocks from Kennedy Center; DC's only Ho Jo. Some rooms have balconies overlooking the Potomac and there's a rooftop swimming pool and a sun deck with a view. All rooms have color TV, radio, and refrigerator. Children in parents' room free. Small dogs allowed. Free garage parking. Lounge, 24-hour restaurant. 192 rooms.

Normandy Inn
2118 Wyoming Avenue, NW, 20008. (202) 483-1350; (800) 424-3729. Fax (202) 387-8241. Small, quiet, European-style hotel located approximately four blocks north of Dupont Circle in Kalorama, an area of embassies and old apartment buildings. Pleasant accommodations, all with queen-size beds; some have refrigerators. Amenities include in-room movies and wine and cheese receptions in the tearoom. Room service for breakfast only. Children under age 12 in parents' room free. Parking facilities. 76 rooms. Good-value weekend package.

Omni Georgetown Hotel
2121 P Street, NW, 20037. (202) 293-3100; (800) 843-6664. Fax (202) 857-0134. Actually in Dupont Circle, quite close to Rock Creek Park. Traditional apartment hotel with all-suites accommodations. Outdoor swimming pool in season; sauna and exercise room. Children under age 16 in parents' room free. Parking for a fee. Restaurant on premises; room service. No-smoking rooms and small meeting rooms available. 120 suites. Good-value weekend rates.

Quality Hotel Capitol Hill
415 New Jersey Avenue, NW, 20001. (202) 638-

1616; (800) 228-5151. Fax (202) 638-0707. On Capitol Hill, good family choice two blocks from Union Station and the Capitol. Moderately priced; newly decorated rooms. TV with free HBO; rooftop swimming pool in season. Children under age 18 in parents' room free. Pets allowed. Free indoor parking. Restaurant in children's menu, lounge. Convention/banquet facilities. Nine meeting rooms. 340 rooms. Good-value weekend package.

Quality Hotel Central
1900 Connecticut Avenue, NW, 20009. (202) 332-9300; (800) 842-4211. Fax (202) 328-7039. Relatively small low-frills hotel in embassy area north of business district, near George Washington University. No- smoking floor. Outdoor swimming pool in season. Children under age 18 in parents' room free. Pets allowed. Complimentary garage parking. Cappucino's Restaurant, lounge. 150 rooms. Weekend packages.

Quality Hotel Downtown
1315 16th Street, NW, 20036. (202) 232-8000; (800) 368-5689. Fax (202) 667-9827. Good location in embassy area. All rooms are spacious, with kitchen facilities; TV with free HBO. Children under age 18 in parents' room free. No pets. Parking facilities. Restaurant, lounge; room service. Meeting rooms available. 135 rooms. Weekend rates.

Radisson Park Terrace
1515 Rhode Island Avenue, NW, 20005. (202) 232-7000; (800) 424-2461. Fax (202) 332-7152. (Formerly Best Western Executive House Hotel.) Eight-story hotel downtown at Scott Circle, five blocks from the White House. Large, individually decorated rooms, some with kitchenettes; free HBO. Outdoor rooftop swimming pool and landscaped sun deck; poolside service. Children under age 12 in parents' room free. Free garage. Restaurant. Meeting rooms. 180 rooms and 40 suites. Weekend rates.

Ramada Inn Central
1430 Rhode Island Avenue, NW, 20005. (202) 462-7777; (800) 368-5690. Fax (202) 332-3519. Six blocks from the White House. Some rooms with kitchen facilities; free HBO. Outdoor rooftop swimming pool and sun deck in season; access to nearby health club. Children under age 18 in parents' room free. Family rates available. No pets. Limited parking facilities. Restaurant, lounge; room service. Seven meeting rooms; 18 boardrooms; banquet room. 186 suites. Good-value weekend package.

Savoy Suites
2505 Wisconsin Avenue, NW, 20007. (202) 337-9400; (800) 944-5377. Fax (202) 337-3644. (Formerly the Wellington.) Small Art Nouveau "revival" hotel in Upper Georgetown. Large rooms, some with fully-equipped kitchenettes and Jacuzzis; in-room movies. Small outdoor swimming pool. Children under age 18 in parents' room free. Pets allowed. Free parking. No-smoking rooms. Restaurant. Meeting facilities. 150 rooms. Very good value weekend rates.

State Plaza Hotel
2117 E Street, NW, 20037. (202) 861-8200; (800) 424-2859. Fax (202) 296-6481. Downtown location, across from the State Department, five blocks from Foggy Bottom Metro station. Accommodations in this all-suites hotel vary from a large bedroom with sitting area and separate kitchen to a deluxe suite with separate living room, dining room, kitchen, and bedroom. Children under age 16 in parents' suite free. Restaurant on premises with outdoor dining in season. Three meeting rooms and banquet facilities. 218 suites. Excellent-value weekend rates.

The Tabard Inn
1739 N Street, NW, 20036. (202) 785-1277. Fax (202) 785-6173. On one of DC's loveliest residential streets (just off Connecticut Avenue), a small hotel housed in three combined Victorian-era town houses where, in 1863, Edward Everett Hale wrote *Man Without a Country.* Charming, bordering on eccentric. No elevator; large rooms with old-fashioned iron beds; fireplaces; no TV. Not all rooms have private baths but room #62 has a skylight and sun deck, and #24 has a piano! Wonderful cozy fireplace lounge for a drink, informal bar and restaurant (*see* RESTAURANTS, Continental). Complimentary continental breakfast, on nice days taken in lovely outdoor garden patio. A find. Book well in advance. 45 rooms.

BUDGET

Remember there are bargains to be had within the Moderate category for weekend stays and in nonpeak seasons; make sure you investigate those. See also Hostels & Y's *and* Bed & Breakfast.

Best Western Regency Congress Inn
600 New York Avenue, NE, 20002. (202) 546-9200. Fax (202) 546-6348. Modest motel with outdoor swimming pool and sauna. Pets allowed. Free parking. Restaurant on premises. Tour groups predominate. 49 rooms.

Connecticut Avenue Days Inn
4400 Connecticut Avenue, NW, 20008. (202) 244-5600; (800) 325-2525. (No fax.) Approximately 1½ miles north of the zoo, close to Chevy Chase, Maryland. Complimentary continental breakfast; free HBO and parking. Children under age 18 in parents' room free. Pets allowed. Parking fee. 155 rooms.

Connecticut-Woodley Guest House
2647 Woodley Road, NW, 20008. (202) 667-0218. (No fax.) Very small, homey hotel in a turn-of-the-century building opposite the Sheraton Washington Hotel. Close to the National Zoo and 1½ miles from the White House, near the Woodley Park Zoo Metro station. Half of the rooms have private baths, the rest share. TV in the lounge only. No pets. Free parking. Family rates available. 14 rooms.

Econo-Lodge
1600 New York Avenue, NE, 20002. (202) 832-3200; (800) 344-7687. Fax (202) 832-1791. (Formerly Quality Inn North East.) Located near the Capitol and the Smithsonian, one block from the Metro. Sightseeing tours pickup point. Indoor heated swimming pool. Color TV. Children under age 18 in parents' room free. No pets. Free parking. Lounge; room service. 158 rooms.

Master Hosts Inn
1917 Bladensburg Road, NE, 20002. (202) 832-8600; (800) 251-1962. Fax (202) 529-7546. Adjacent to the National Arboretum, close to RFK Stadium and the Franciscan Monastery. Most pleasant are the rooms overlooking the enclosed courtyard with outdoor swimming pool and sun chairs. Children under age 12 in parents' room free. Small pets allowed. Free parking. Chinese-American restaurant with outdoor tables in season, lounge; room service. Sightseeing tours depart from here daily. Meeting room. 150 rooms.

University Inn
2134 G Street, NW. (202) 342-8020; (800) 842-1012. (No fax.) Renovated hotel, close to the Lincoln Memorial, on the George Washington University campus. Private and shared bath accommodations. Extended-stay rates available. 123 rooms.

BED & BREAKFAST

This is one way to avoid the impersonal aspect of some hotels and meet some city natives.

Adams Inn
1744 Lanier Place, NW, 20009. (202) 745-3600. Homey accommodations with private and shared baths. Charmingly cozy dining room with fireplace; complimentary continental breakfast. Carriage house apartment with fully-equipped kitchen also available. No pets. Smoking not permitted on premises. Two-night minimum. 26 rooms.

Bed & Breakfast League/Sweet Dreams & Toast
P.O. Box 9490, Washington, DC 20016. (202) 363-7767. Represents over 60 properties in DC, Maryland, and Virginia offering a variety of accommodations. Wide price range; all hosts are screened. Two-night minimum.

Bed 'n' Breakfast Ltd. of Washington, DC
P.O. Box 12011, Washington, DC 20005. (202) 328-3510. They make reservations for a network of 80 private homes in DC, and the nearby Maryland and Virginia suburbs, offering rooms and continental breakfast. Accommodations range from austere to lavish. Rigid inspection assures quality lodgings. Rates are based on location of host homes, number of guests, shared or private bath. Unhosted apartments are also available. Payment must be made in advance. Write or call for their guest application; be specific about requirements. AE, MC, V. (Money orders preferred; there is a surcharge for credit card transactions.)

Kalorama Guest Houses
At Kalorama Park: 1854 Mintwood Place, NW, 20009; (202) 667-6369. At Woodley Park: 2700 Cathedral Avenue, NW, 20008; (202) 328-0860. Borrowing a European tradition, bed and breakfast in a charming Victorian town house (there are actually six) and the former Rock Creek Park motel. Rooms have brass beds and a cozy, individual, old-fashioned charm. Complimentary continental breakfast in the parlor, where a warming fire greets you in winter. Shared and private baths available; two-room suites for three to six people; no phones in the rooms. Prepayment required. 50 rooms. Weekly rates available.

VIRGINIA HOTELS

Best Western Olde Colony Inn
625 First Street at North Washington, Alexandria, Va 22314. (703) 548-6300; (800) 528-1234. Fax (703) 548-8032. Near Crystal City, eight blocks from Old Town. Some rooms with kitchenettes. Indoor/outdoor swimming pool in season. Children under age 12 in parents' room free. Small pets allowed. Free parking. 332 rooms. Weekend rates.

Guest Quarters
100 South Reynolds Street, Alexandria, Va 22304. (703) 370-9600; (800) 424-2900. Fax (703) 370-0467. All-suite hotel with all the comforts of home and full hotel services, for long- or short-term stays. All suites have fully-equipped kitchens; color TV; air-conditioning. There are also three penthouses. Swimming pool. Children under age 16 in parents' room free. Small pets allowed, for a fee. Free parking. Book well in advance, not all suites are transient. Restaurant with lounge; room service. Two meeting rooms. 225 suites. Weekend packages.

Holiday Inn Crowne Plaza *DOUBLETREE*
300 Army-Navy Drive, Arlington, Va 22202. (703) 892-4100; (800) 848-7000. Fax (703) 521-0286. (Formerly Quality Inn Pentagon City.) Two blocks to Metro, one block from the Pentagon City mall. Cable TV and free HBO. Full fitness center with racquetball, rooftop indoor swimming pool, sauna. Free airport shuttle. Children under age 18 in parents' room free. No pets. Free indoor parking. Penthouse restaurant, The Sky Dome revolving cocktail lounge offering views of DC (*see* NIGHTLIFE, Dance Bars & Clubs), lounge, coffee shop. Convention facilities. 635 rooms and suites. Weekend rates.

Holiday Inn Dulles International Airport
1000 Sully Road (Box 17244), Sterling, Va 22170. (703) 471-7411; (800) 465-4329. Fax (703) 471-7411, ext 515. Convenient to airport; free airport shuttle. Indoor swimming pool; fitness equipment and game room. Children under age 18 in parents' room free. Pets allowed. Free parking. Restaurant, lounge. Convention facilities. 397 rooms. Weekend package.

Holiday Inn National Airport
1489 Jefferson Davis Highway, Arlington, Va 22204. (703) 521-1600; (800) 465-4329. Fax (703) 920-1236. Near Crystal City complex. Free shuttle to airport. Color TV; air-conditioning. Outdoor swimming pool. Children under age 13 in parents' room free. Small (under 20 pounds) pets allowed kennels available. Restaurant, lounge; room service. Ballroom; five meeting rooms. 279 rooms. Weekend package.

Holiday Inn Old Town
480 King Street, Alexandria, Va 22314. (703) 549-6080; (800) 465-4329. Fax (703) 549-7777. Brick-walled colonial hotel right on the main street in historic Old Town. Large heated indoor pool; access to nearby health club. Children under age 18 in parents' room free. Pets accepted. Complimentary shuttle service to National Airport. Restaurant, cafe. Meeting rooms. 227 rooms. Weekend package.

Howard Johnson's National Airport
2650 Jefferson Davis Highway, Arlington, Va 22202. (703) 684-7200; (800) 654-2000. Fax (703) 684-3217. Five minutes from downtown, half a mile from airport rooms are soundproof. Outdoor rooftop swimming pool, lake swimming. Children under age 18 in parents' room free. No pets. Courtesy car to airport. Free parking. Two restaurants, lounge. Conference facilities. 276 rooms. Weekend package.

Hyatt Arlington at Key Bridge
1325 Wilson Boulevard, Arlington, Va 22209. (703) 525-1234; (800) 228-9000. Fax (703) 875-3393. Across the Key Bridge from Georgetown, close to the Metro. Amenities include in-room movies. Children under age 18 in parents' room free. Baby-sitting service. No-smoking rooms on advance request. Small pets accepted. Free parking on weekends. Restaurant, two lounges; room service. 302 rooms. Weekend rates; honeymoon package.

Hyatt Regency Crystal City
Washington National Airport, Arlington, Va 22202. (703) 418-1234; (800) 228-9000. Fax (703) 418-1233. National Airport's largest hotel. A five-story atrium, glass elevators, and the comfort and convenience for which Hyatt hotels are known the bustle, too. Health club facilities include outdoor pool, Jacuzzi, and exercise room. The Regency Club for special amenities. Two restaurants. Complimentary transport to and from the airport. Large meeting facility and banquet room. 685 rooms and suites. Weekend package

Marriott Crystal City
1999 Jefferson Davis Highway, Arlington, Va 22202. (703) 521-5500; (800) 228-9290. Fax (703) 685-0191. Three minutes from National Airport in Crystal City complex (Metro station). Large and luxurious. Indoor swimming pool; sauna and whirlpool. Children under age 18 in parents' room free. Two restaurants, lounge; room service. Free transportation to airports. Convention facilities. 340 rooms. Weekend package.

Marriott Dulles International Airport
P.O. Box 17450, Dulles International Airport, Washington, DC 20041. (703) 471-9500; (800) 228-9290. Fax (703) 661-8714. Adjacent to Washington-Dulles Airport; 45 minutes to downtown DC. Busy, convention-oriented. Color TV with first-run in-room movies. Indoor and outdoor swimming pools; poolside service. Exercise room, whirlpool, steam, and sauna. Tennis, volleyball, softball, and basketball. Putting green, 18-hole golf privileges nearby. Picnic facilities. Children under age 18 in parents' room free. Free parking. Complimentary 24-hour transportation to and from the airport. Two restaurants. Convention facilities. 370 rooms. Weekend package.

Marriott Key Bridge
1401 Lee Highway, Arlington, Va 22209. (703) 524-6400; (800) 228-9290. Fax (703) 522-7480. Overlooking the Potomac; within shouting distance of Georgetown. In-room movies available. Indoor/outdoor swimming pool with poolside service. Health club (under age 16 not permitted), exercise room, sauna, whirlpool. Game room. Observation deck. Children under age 18 in parents' room free. Family rates available. Some rooms equipped for handicapped guests. Two restaurants and lounge with panoramic views. Convention facilities. 560 rooms. Weekend package.

Morrison House
116 South Alfred Street, Alexandria, Va 22314. (703) 838-8000; (800) 367-0800. Fax (703) 684-6283. A small, elegant colonial-style choice in Old Town. Multilingual concierge desk, 24-hour valet and room service. Afternoon tea served daily from 3 to 5pm in the parlor. Restaurant on premises. Baby-sitting and secretarial services available. 45 rooms, including 3 suites. Special weekend packages.

Quality Inn Arlington
1190-1200 North Courthouse Road, Arlington, Va 22201. (703) 524-4000; (800) 228-5151. Fax (703) 524-1046. One mile from downtown DC; courtesy shuttle to Metro. Color TV; air-conditioning. Outdoor swimming pool; game room. Children under age 16 in parents' room free. Corporate and government rates. Free parking. Restaurant and lounge. Efficiency units available. Convention facilities. 400 rooms. Weekend package.

Quality Inn Iwo Jima
1501 Arlington Boulevard, Arlington, Va 22209. (703) 524-5000; (800) 228-5151. Fax (703) 522-5484. Located close to Arlington Cemetery and the Iwo Jima Memorial; three blocks from the Roslyn Metro station. Outdoor swimming pool. Children under age 16 in parents' room free. No pets allowed. Restaurant. Laundry service. 141 rooms.

Ramada Hotel Old Town
901 North Fairfax Street, Alexandria, Va 22314. (703) 683-6000; (800) 272-6232. Fax (703) 683-7597. Three miles (5 minutes) from National Airport. Outdoor rooftop swimming pool. Tennis

and golf nearby. On weekends, children under age 18 in parents' room free; during the week the cost is $10. Pets allowed. Free indoor parking; courtesy limousine to airport. Restaurant, lounge. Convention facilities. 258 rooms. Weekend package.

Ritz-Carlton Pentagon City

1250 South Hayes Street, Arlington Va 22202. (703) 415-5000; (800) 241-3333. Fax (703) 415-5061. Luxury personal service newcomer to the area with 18th- and 19th-century antiques in the elegant public spaces. Indoor swimming pool, health and fitness facility. Ritz Carlton Club on the top two floors for extra pampering. No-smoking rooms available. 345 rooms, including 41 suites. Weekend packages.

Sheraton National

Columbia Pike & Washington Boulevard, Arlington, Va 22204. (703) 521-1900; (800) 468-9090. Fax (703) 521-2122. All national shrines and monuments within 2 miles. Color TV; some rooms have balconies and refrigerators. Soundproof. Indoor swimming pool; health club with gym and sauna. Free transportation to and from airport; free transportation to nearest Metro station. Children under age 17 in parents' room free. Free valet parking. Restaurant, lounge; room service. Ballroom, banquet facilities; ten meeting rooms. 416 rooms. Weekend packages.

Stouffer Concourse Hotel

2399 Jefferson Davis Highway, Arlington, Va 22202. (703) 418-6800; (800) 468-3571. Fax (703) 418-3763. Modern 14-story hotel located in Crystal City complex, 5 minutes from DC. In-room movies available; indoor swimming pool, sauna, and game room. Complimentary shuttle to and from National Airport. Sightseeing tours. Children under age 18 in parents' room free. Two restaurants and lounge; room service. Early wake-up with complimentary coffee or tea and the morning paper. Approximately 15 rooms equipped for handicapped guests. Convention and meeting facilities. 384 rooms. Weekend package.

Towers Hotel

420 North Van Dorn Street, Alexandria, Va 22304. (703) 370-1000; (800) 368-3339. Fax (703) 751-1467. Adjacent to Landmark Shopping Center. Homey apartments—studios, one- and two-bedroom suites with fully-equipped kitchens; color TV with free HBO. Outdoor swimming pool, exercise room, playground area. Maid service; laundry facilities. Children under age 12 in parents' room free. No pets. Comfortable inexpensive family choice 8 miles outside DC. Free parking. Snack shop. Conference room. 187 apartments.

MARYLAND HOTELS

Best Western Maryland Inn & Fun Dome

8601 Baltimore Boulevard, College Park, Md 20740. (301) 474-2800; (800) 528-1234. Fax (301) 474-0714. Pleasant accommodations; good family choice. "Fun Dome" includes enclosed pool, sauna, Jacuzzi, putting green, shuffleboard, exercise room, and more. Complimentary doughnuts and coffee in the morning. Restaurant. Free parking. Meeting rooms available. 120 rooms.

Colonial Manor Motel

11410 Rockville Pike, Rockville, Md 20852. (301) 881-5200; (800) 752-3800. Fax (301) 231-7668. Across the street from the White Flint Shopping Mall; half an hour from DC. Mainly business and military clientele. Some rooms have kitchen facilities; in-room movies. Outdoor swimming pool. Laundry room; baby-sitting service. Children under age 12 in parents' room free. Pets permitted in some rooms. Free parking. Restaurant, lounge. Meeting room. 169 rooms.

Holiday Inn of Silver Spring

8777 Georgia Avenue, Silver Spring, Md 20910. (301) 589-0800; (800) 465-4329. Fax (301) 587-4791. One block from Capitol Beltway, close to the Metro station. Outdoor swimming pool, sauna, and exercise room. Children under age 12 in parents' room free. Baby-sitters available. Rooms equipped for handicapped guests. Restaurant, lounge, coffee shop. Shopping mall; seven meeting rooms. 226 rooms.

Hyatt Regency Bethesda

1 Bethesda Metro Center, Bethesda, Md 20814. (301) 657-1234; (800) 233-1234. Fax (301) 657-6453. Large Hyatt with indoor swimming pool with lap lane and whirlpool; health club with exercise equipment and sauna. Regency Club floor offers extra amenities at a premium. No-smoking rooms available. Children under age 18 stay free in parents' room. 345 rooms, including 41 suites. Weekend packages.

Marriott Bethesda

5151 Pooks Hill Road, Bethesda, Md 20014. (301) 897-9400; (800) 228-9290. Fax (301) 897-0192. Twenty minutes from downtown DC at intersection of 495 and I-270. Indoor/outdoor swimming pool, health club, sauna, outdoor day/night tennis, game room, golf privileges nearby, jogging area. Children under age 18 in parents' room free. Facilities for handicapped guests. Pets allowed. Two restaurants, lounge; room service. Free parking. Convention facilities. 407 rooms. Weekend packages.

Quality Hotel Silver Spring

8727 Colesville Road, Silver Spring, Md 20910. (301) 589-5200; (800) 228-5151. Fax (301) 588-1841. Recently remodeled well-priced hotel close to Metro station. Indoor swimming pool, sauna, and exercise room. Laundry and valet service. Sightseeing tours arranged. Children under age 17 in parents' room free. Free parking. Two restaurants, lounge, coffee shop; room service. Convention and meeting facilities. 256 rooms. Weekend packages.

Ramada Inn Bethesda

8400 Wisconsin Avenue, Bethesda, Md 20814. (301) 654-1000; (800) 272-6232. Fax (301) 654-0751. Ten miles from the center of DC; near

White Flint Shopping Mall. All rooms have cable TV, some have kitchenettes. Outdoor swimming pool, access to health club facilities. Children under age 18 in parents' room free. Baby-sitting service available. Free parking. Restaurant, lounge with dancing. Meeting rooms available. 160 rooms. Weekend rates.

Sheraton Hotel/Exhibition Center

8500 Annapolis Road at I-95, New Carrollton, Md 20784. (301) 459-6700; (800) 325-3535. Fax (301) 459-8192. In suburban Maryland, 20 miles from downtown DC, 18 miles from Annapolis. Near Metro station. In-room movies; some rooms have kitchen facilities. Outdoor pool; poolside cabanas and suites available. Restaurant with lounge; room service. Children under age 17 in parents' room free. Ramps available for handicapped guests. Free parking. Convention and meeting facilities for up to 1,000 people. 237 rooms. Weekend packages.

HOSTELS & Y'S

Alexandria YMCA

420 East Monroe Avenue, Alexandria, Va 22301. (703) 549-0850. The only YMCA in the metropolitan area with housing facilities. Close to public transportation (6 miles from DC), near Old Town. Co-ed facility all rooms with air-conditioning, private bath, and shower. No kitchen facilities.

Swimming pool, weight room. Plenty of parking. No reservations. 44 rooms.

International Guest House

1441 Kennedy Street, NW, 20011. (202) 726-5808. Near 16th Street. Maximum stay for American visitors is one week, international guests two weeks, at this no-frills nonprofit guest house (run by Mennonite church). International students predominate. Co-ed; 11pm curfew. Communal lounge with TV. Small kitchen facilities, but they give you breakfast and tea and cookies at night. Air-conditioned. Half price for children under age 10; under age 5 free. No pets. 7 rooms.

International Student House

1825 R Street, NW, 20009. (202) 387-6445; (202) 232-4007. A short stroll from Dupont Circle. International and American students are welcome for a one-month minimum stay. Accommodations are shared; you must supply your own bed and bath linens; no maid service. Breakfast and dinner are included with lodging. Pleasant public rooms for dining and afternoon tea. 90 beds. No credit cards.

Washington International Youth Hostel

1009 11th Street, NW, 20001. (202) 737-2333. Rock-bottom rates for clean and secure dormitory-style (same sex) accommodations, 4 to 14 in a room. Community self-service kitchen facilities available. Maximum stay is three nights. 250 beds. No credit cards.

SIGHTSEEING

The Capitol

VIEWPOINTS

Washington, DC, was planned as a horizontal city, and in 1901 Congress established building height restrictions in an effort to prevent any commercial structures from dwarfing the city's federal monuments or from interfering with original planner Pierre L'enfant's broad vistas. This regulation, the bane of modern architects designing for the city, is probably the single most important reason why Dc abounds with viewpoints, many of which are awe-inspiring. Listed are a few of the best.

Arlington House, The Robert E. Lee Memorial (Custis-Lee Mansion)
Arlington National Cemetery, Arlington, Va. (703) 557-0613. The house is located on a bluff, and one of the best views of Washington is available from here. Fittingly, Pierre L'Enfant, who planned the capital city, is laid to rest just in front of the mansion. Below is the grave of President John F. Kennedy. (*See also* HISTORIC & NEW WASHINGTON, Historic Buildings & Areas.) Accessible via Tourmobile. *Metro: Arlington Cemetery.*

Francis Scott Key Bridge
In Georgetown, at M Street, NW. Walk across the Potomac to Virginia and you will be rewarded with a lovely view.

Grant Memorial
The East Mall at 1st Street. The view of the Capitol and the surrounding terraces is impressive. (*See also* HISTORIC & NEW WASHINGTON, Statues & Monuments.) *Metro: Capitol South, Union Station.*

Jefferson Memorial
Tidal Basin, West Potomac Park. Stand on the steps and look across the Tidal Basin for a most unforgettable sight—especially in the evening. The downtown Washington skyline, the Washington Monument, and the White House—all illuminated splendors. *OPEN Always.* (*See also* HISTORIC & NEW WASHINGTON, Historic Buildings & Areas.) *Metro: Arlington Cemetery.*

Kennedy Center for the Performing Arts
2700 F Street, NW. 523-5691. Individuals may go to the Center's Roof Terrace on their own. It's

a good vantage point overlooking the Potomac River. *OPEN 7 days 10am-midnight.* (*See also* HISTORIC & NEW WASHINGTON, Modern Architecture.) *Metro: Foggy Bottom.*

Lady Bird Johnson Park
On an island in the Potomac, access is only via a footbridge from a parking lot on the Virginia shore. Views of the Potomac and the Washington skyline from the eastern end of the island. (*See also* PARKS & GARDENS, Parks.)

Lincoln Memorial
West Potomac Park, west end. From the rear of the monument across the Potomac to Arlington National Cemetery. In the pm you can glimpse the Eternal Flame that glows at the grave of JFK; beyond it, on the hill, is Arlington House. *OPEN Always.* (*See also* HISTORIC & NEW WASHINGTON, Historic Buildings & Areas.) *Metro: Foggy Bottom, Arlington Cemetery.*

Old Post Office Clock Tower
1100 Pennsylvania Avenue, NW. 523-5691. Board a glass elevator and ride to the ninth floor of this 1899 treasure of a building and view the vast interior courtyard of the Pavilion. A second elevator takes you to the top of the 315-foot clock tower, the third highest structure in the city, from which you get a sweeping view of the Capitol and Pennsylvania Avenue and a close-up view of the clockworks and the bells of the carillon. A National Park Service Ranger is on hand to answer questions. *OPEN Apr 5-Labor Day, 7 days 8am-11pm; balance of the year 10am-6pm (last tour 5:45pm). CLOSED every Thurs 6-9pm for bell ringing practice. FREE.* (*See also* HISTORIC & NEW WASHINGTON, Historic Buildings & Areas: Old Post Office Building.) *Metro: Federal Triangle.*

George Washington Masonic National Memorial
King Street & Callahan Drive, Alexandria, Va. (703) 683-2007. From the tower, a panoramic view of metropolitan Washington. (*See also* SIGHTSEEING On Your Own.)

George Washington Memorial Parkway
Traveling south on the parkway from Cabin John Bridge you are treated to a lovely view of the Potomac and the city.

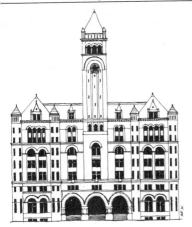

Old Post Office Clock Tower

Washington National Cathedral
Wisconsin & Massachusetts Avenues, NW. 537-6200. Pilgrim's Observation Gallery at the west end of the church, on the seventh floor, below the twin towers of St. Peter and St. Paul, offers a splendid panoramic view of Washington and the surrounding environs, as well as a close-up view of the gothic gargoyles and grotesques carved into the exterior stonework. (*See also* HISTORIC & NEW WASHINGTON, Churches & Synagogues.) Observation Gallery *OPEN Mon-Sat 10am-4pm; Sun noon-3:15pm.* FREE.

Washington Monument
The Mall, Constitution Avenue at 15th Street. 426-6841. The tallest structure in the city. Windows in the cap of the 555-and-a-bit-foot obelisk provide a magnificent view of the city, especially in the evening. (*See also* HISTORIC & NEW WASHINGTON, Historic Buildings & Areas.) *OPEN 7 days Apr 1-Labor Day 8am-midnight; balance of the year 9am-5pm. CLOSED Christmas Day.* FREE. *Metro: Federal Triangle, Smithsonian.*

Restaurants with a View

The following restaurants provide a vista with your meal. For details on each, see RESTAURANTS, Rooms with a View.

Capitol View Club
Hyatt Regency Washington, 400 New Jersey Avenue, NW, 11th floor.

Roof Terrace Restaurant
Kennedy Center, 2700 F Street, NW.

Rooftop Terrace, Hotel Washington
15th Street & Pennsylvania Avenue, NW. *See also* RESTAURANTS, Rooms with a View: Two Continents in the Sky.

Top o' the Town
Prospect House, 14th & North Oak Streets, Arlington, Va.

The View
Marriott Key Bridge, 1401 Lee Highway, Rosslyn, Va.

WASHINGTON TOURS

Old Town Trolley Tours
3150 V Street, NE. 269-3020. A fully-narrated 1-hour-and-45-minute tour of the city in an authentic (albeit not on tracks) all-weather trolley in distinctive orange and green. It's a great way to do your touring. You may stay on board or get off at any stop and reboard a later one. Catch the trolley at Union Station, the Hyatt Regency Washington on Capitol Hill, the Pavilion at the Old Post Office, the Grand Hyatt Hotel, the J.W. Marriott Hotel/SHOPS at National Place, the Capital Hilton Hotel, the Washington Hilton Hotel, the Omni Shoreham/Sheraton Washington, Georgetown Park, Lincoln Memorial, the Holiday Inn Capitol (near the Air & Space Museum), and at Neptune Fountain at the Capitol/Library of Congress. *Operates 7 days every 30 minutes, 9am-4pm.* Adults $14; children under age 12, $5. (Money-back guarantee if you are not pleased with the service.)

Tourmobile Sightseeing
1000 Ohio Drive, SW. 554-7950. A great way to see the major attractions on the Federal Mall, Arlington, and Mount Vernon. The largest sightseeing operation in DC and the only one allowed by the government to stop at all points of interest on the Federal Mall. Each tour is completely narrated, and you can get off at any stop and reboard at any time (the tour passes each stop every 30 minutes). There are five tours: Complete Tour of Washington and Arlington Cemetery (stops at 18 historic sites); Arlington Cemetery Tour; Mount Vernon Tour; tour of the home of abolitionist Frederick C. Douglass (March 1 to Labor Day only); and the Combination Tour of Washington, Arlington Cemetery, and Mount Vernon. Note: The minimum riding time for the Complete Tour is 1½ hours; for Arlington, 30 minutes; for Mount Vernon, 1½ hours; for Douglass's home, 30 minutes. Be forewarned: During peak season you may spend several hours just waiting to board and reboard—they can only take on passengers as others get off. Best for traveling around the Mall museums and monuments. Tickets, which range in price from $2.75 to $25, may be purchased at the blue-and-white Tourmobile ticket booth or from the driver. Cost is lower for children ages 3 to 11. *Mar 1-Labor Day 9am-6:30pm (tickets purchased after 4pm are good for the next day); balance of the year 9:30am-4:30pm (tickets purchased after 2pm are good for the next day).* Group rates available. See map section for routes.

By Coach

All About Town
519 6th Street, NW. 393-3696. Guided coach

tours of DC with accompanying lecture. Free pickup at downtown hotels.

American Sightseeing Road Tours
5400 Tuxedo Road, Tuxedo, Md (at the District line). (301) 386-8300. Nine tours of Washington and the surrounding area, concentrating on the major sights. Morning and afternoon tours. Air-conditioned buses. Free pickup. Tours last 3 to 8 hours. (Cannot accommodate foreign languages.) Set fee.

The Blue Line
2001 New York Avenue, NE. 529-7755. A variety of tours in and out of DC, such as the Federal City by night, all-day combination, interior government buildings. Also special tours and charters to suit businesses, organizations, and conventions.

Gray Line-Gold Line
Union Station, 50 Massachusetts Avenue, NW. 289-1995. A choice of 11 different guided tours, lasting from 4 hours to two days. All over DC and out-of-town historic areas. Eight local and three out-of-town tours, including Gettysburg, Williamsburg, and Charlottesville. (*See also* Day Trips, Escorted.) Free pickup and delivery for most hotels. Group rates; lower for children, under age 4 free.

Specialized Tours

The Capital Informer
3240 Prospect St, NW, 20007. 965-7420. This very professional operation offers customized tour programs for individuals and conventions, specializing in unique and VIP programs. Via coach, limousine, or the executive van. Call or write in advance of your visit.

The Guide Service of Washington, Inc.
733 15th Street, NW, Suite 1040. 628-2842. Custom tours for those interested in the historical and architectural aspects of DC. Licensed tour guides. Many different foreign languages are accommodated. Geared toward out-of-town groups but good for individuals, too. Charge is by half or full day. Phone is answered 24 hours a day.

National Fine Arts Associates
4801 Massachusetts Avenue, NW, Suite 400. 966-3800. Custom-designed, in-depth tour programs for groups—focus on art, architecture, and history—lasting either one day or one week. Walking and coach tours. Guides are experts on topic at hand. Many "behind-the-scenes" tours; wide range of conference services as well. Will arrange luncheons, dinners, and receptions. Call for additional information on the Washington, Maryland, and Virginia areas.

Scandal Tours of Washington
783-7212. The comedy group Gross National Product runs these tours of DC, which give a more than slightly jaundiced view of the capital city and those who inhabit it. During the 90-minute coach tour learn the high- and lowlights of scandals, from the first inhabitant of the White House to the current resident. Leaves from the Washington Hilton Hotel, 1919 Connecticut Avenue, NW, *year-round every Sat at 1pm.* Advanced reservation required. MC, V.

Special Interest Tours
P.O. Box 33033, Washington, DC, 20033. (202) 467-4402. Knowledgeable Washingtonian Maxine Atwater offers very personally constructed tours of the city with a unique point of view. Her most popular tour is Glittering Scenes, a nighttime view of DC with an emphasis on the city's social history (extra-special when done with limo, champagne, and chocolates); also popular, the Secret Gardens Tour. Coach tours for 40 plus, or more personal limousine or walking tours may be arranged.

Washington, Incorporated
1990 M Street, NW. 828-7000. Half- or full-day tours of museums, art galleries, historic homes, monuments, embassies. You choose what you want to see and for how long. For individuals or groups. Reserve at least 24 hours in advance.

Walking Tours

See also Specialized Tours, *as well as* ANNUAL EVENTS, April, May, September, *and* October *for scheduled garden, home, and walking tours.*

A good book for do-it-yourself walking tours is Washington on Foot *(Smithsonian). In addition, try bookstores in the particular area you wish to tour for specialized guides—chances are one will be available.*

Alexandria Guided Walking Tours
Ramsay House Visitors Center, 221 King Street, Alexandria, Va. (703) 838-4200. Guided walking tours through Old Town Alexandria. The leisurely tour covers six city blocks and lasts 1¼ hours. *End of Mar-end of Nov, Mon-Sat at 11am (June-Aug, Sat at 8:30am as well); Sun at 2pm.* Weather permitting. Admission. Also available, Lantern Light Ghost Tours *every Sat 8pm;* call for information, (703) 548-0010.

Doorways to Olde Virginia
P.O. Box 20485, Alexandria, Va 22320. (703) 548-0100. Walking tours of Old Town. Covers an eight-block area and takes approximately 1½ hours. Focuses on the historical and architectural aspects of the Market Square area. Well-informed tour guides. For groups of 12 or more. Charge per person doesn't include admission fees.

Steve Hoglund
387-8907. This knowledgeable local historian will arrange a group tour from his repertoire of 20 walks of Washington's upper-northwest neighborhoods, including Embassy Row, Dupont Circle, Adams-Morgan, and Kalorama, as well as Foggy Bottom, Federal Triangle, and The Great Avenues. *24-hour answering service.*

Smithsonian Resident Associate Program
1100 Jefferson Drive, SW, 20560. 357-3030. Walking tours of Washington neighborhoods and major historic and cultural institutions. The 2-hour tours are conducted by extremely knowledgeable guides. Open to members and non-

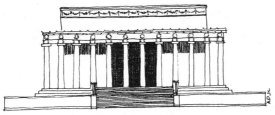

Lincoln Memorial

members, but the only real way to know what is scheduled is to get the monthly newsletter sent to members. Write or call for details. *Tours year-round, Sat & Sun.* Fee lower for members.

Tour de Force

P.O. Box 2782, Washington, DC, 20013. (703) 525-2948. Tailored walking tours with a fresh, unconventional point of view. Individually escorted by Jeanne Fogle, a fourth-generation Washingtonian and local historian. Neighborhood walks, specially focused art, history, or architecture tours; unusual sights and a highlights tour. All available for individuals or groups; pre-arrangement is a must. Also, step-on guide service for tour groups. Write or call for details.

ON YOUR OWN

See also HISTORIC & NEW WASHINGTON *for historic homes and sites open to the public;* ANNUAL EVENTS *for special happenings in the city; and* MUSEUMS & GALLERIES *for some of the city's top attractions.*

NOTE:*There are special VIP tours of the Capitol, the FBI, the Kennedy Center for the Performing Arts, and the White House. For arrangements, write as far in advance of your visit as possible to your senator: c/o of the U.S. Senate, Washington, DC 20510, or your congressperson: c/o U.S. House of Representatives, Washington, DC 20515.*

Bureau of Engraving and Printing

14th & C Streets, SW. 566-2000. Designs, engraves, and prints paper currency (no coins) and Treasury notes, bonds, and certificates; postage stamps; food coupons; permits; and award certificates. The face value of its annual production? $300 billion! Constantly replenishing the supply of dollar bills, which have a life of only 18 months. Visitors gallery allows observance of currency-producing operation, where high-speed presses turn out 8,000 sheets of bills an hour. Tickets for a 25-minute self-guided tour are issued on first-come basis. A souvenir shop sells shredded money. *OPEN Mon-Fri 9am-2pm. CLOSED Sat, Sun & holidays.* FREE. *Metro: Smithsonian.*

C&O Canal Barge Ride

Foundry Mall, at the foot of Thomas Jefferson Street, NW (south of M Street), in Georgetown, where the C&O begins. 472-4376. Mid-April to mid-October, Wednesday to Sunday, three to four times a day in summer (less in spring and fall), you can take a cooling, colorful ride on *The Georgetown,* a 15-ton reproduction of a 19th-century coal-hauling barge—pulled by two government-issued mules, Katie Lynn and Kit—up the Chesapeake and Ohio Canal, which had a short heyday in the 1860s. The 90-minute journey to Great Falls, Maryland—and into the past—is run by the National Park Service. On the journey, a five-member crew in suspendered trousers and calico dresses and bonnets sings, tells tales, and demonstrates crafts to illustrate life along the C&O back then. At the falls you may board the *Canal Clipper* and ride through the rugged woods at the gorge of the river. Fare for adults, $4; for seniors, $3, for children, $2.50. (*See also* HISTORIC & NEW WASHINGTON, Historic Buildings & Areas, *and* ANNUAL EVENTS, April.)

The Capitol

Capitol Hill, east end of the Mall. 224-3121. Approach the Capitol by the East Front steps (where every inauguration since Andrew Jackson has taken place—until Ronald Reagan's). It is the preeminent symbol of American democracy. On the right is the Senate, on the left the House of Representatives. An American flag flying above either wing tells you whether that body is in session (never in August). Night sessions are indicated by a lantern light atop the Capitol dome. Go to the Rotunda; from there, take the 35-minute guided tour, which leaves *every 15 minutes, 9am to 3:45pm, 7 days a week.* You'll see Statuary Hall (aka the Whispering Chamber because of the acoustics), the Crypt, the original Supreme Court Chamber, and the great Rotunda—96 feet in diameter, 180 feet high—where President Kennedy lay in state. To visit the galleries in either the House or Senate chambers you'll need a pass from your senator or congressperson; write ahead or visit their office for a same-day pass. No reservations required. (*See also* the Capitol Subway *and* HISTORIC & NEW WASHINGTON, Historic Buildings & Areas.) *Metro: Capitol South, Union Station.*

The Capitol Subway

Between the Richard B. Russell Senate Office Building & the Everett M. Dirksen Senate Office

Building. If you wander the Capitol on your own, don't miss this fun ride in a fast, quiet, open-car subway—and you just may be in some very impressive company. *In operation Mon-Fri 9am-4:30pm; Sat & Sun 9am-noon (till 9:30pm if night sessions are scheduled).* FREE.

The FBI
J. Edgar Hoover Building, Pennsylvania Avenue at 10th Street, NW. 324-3447. In this fortresslike building (the Bureau's home since 1975) you may tour the FBI crime labs, see video replays of bank robberies, visit the practice firing range, and gaze at photos of the current Ten Most Wanted Fugitives. The popular, free, guided tour lasts one hour and is given approximately every 15 minutes. *OPEN Mon-Fri 8:45am-4:15pm. CLOSED Sat, Sun & holidays.* Group tours must be booked in advance with your congressperson. (*See also* HISTORIC & NEW WASHINGTON, Modern Architecture: J. Edgar Hoover FBI Building.) FREE. *Metro: Federal Triangle.*

Kennedy Center for the Performing Arts
2700 F Street, NW. 416-8341. Guided tours of the building by volunteers, including the theaters and "places even the employees don't know about" peppered with history and trivia. The 45-minute tours, *7 days, 10am-1pm,* leave every 15 minutes or less from Motor Lobby A. Reserve in advance for groups. Congressional tours are conducted Monday to Saturday at 9:30pm; reserve in advance with the office of your congressperson. Also, scripts available in French, Spanish, German, Italian, Portuguese, Japanese, and Hebrew. (*See also* HISTORIC & NEW WASHINGTON, Modern Architecture.) FREE. *Metro: Foggy Bottom.*

The Metro
This attraction is spacious, serene, and safe (its corridors are watched by TV surveillance cameras). Begun in 1980, it now reaches 103 miles from DC to the major population centers in Virginia and Maryland. It is one of the most efficient, smoothest, and cleanest subways in the country —its walls are cleaned every other day, keeping them graffiti-free; its carpets (yes, carpets) are vacuumed and seats scrubbed every other day as well. If you have ever been on the subway in New York, you owe your senses a ride on this one. *See* BASIC INFORMATION for fare details; see the Metro map in the map section for desti-

nations. NOTE: There are no Metro stations in Georgetown (residents demurred); the closest is Foggy Bottom.

The National Archives
Constitution Avenue & 8th Street, NW. 501-5000. In this building are kept the originals of America's most cherished documents, the "Charters of Freedom": the Declaration of Independence, the Constitution, and the Bill of Rights. But since 1980 the "hot" attraction has been the continuous playing of the Nixon "Watergate" tapes, now housed in Alexandria,* where tourists may get an earphoneful of more current history in the making. Reserve in advance for group tours, 523-3184. Exhibition Hall *OPEN Apr 1-Labor Day, 7 days 10am-9pm; early Sept (day after Labor Day)-Mar 31, 7 days 10am-5:30pm. CLOSED Christmas Day.* Central Research & Microfilm Research Rooms *OPEN Mon-Fri 9am-10pm; Sat 9am-5:15pm. CLOSED federal holidays.* *Note: The Nixon tapes are kept at 845 South Pickett Street in Alexandria. There is a shuttle service six times a day between the Washington and Alexandria locations. Twelve and a half hours of tapes are played on a seven-day cycle, Monday to Friday from 9:15am till 4:30pm. You must register 15 minutes in advance at 9am. Call (703) 756-6498 for specific information on the tapes and which is being played that day. (*See also* HISTORIC & NEW WASHINGTON, Historic Buildings & Areas.) FREE. *Metro: Federal Triangle.*

The Pavilion at the Old Post Office
1100 Pennsylvania Avenue, NW. 289-4224. One of the newest attractions along Pennsylvania Avenue is actually one of the oldest. The Old Post Office Building (*see* HISTORIC & NEW WASHINGTON, Historic Buildings & Areas) was saved from the wrecker's ball for all our delight in a true spirit of cooperation between government and the private sector. Reopened in 1983, the Pavilion draws visitors to its 35 specialty shops, seven restaurants, and a Main Street and Embassy Row of fast but tasty food. Every day at noon there is free live entertainment on the Pavilion stage. It's lively, tempting, colorful, and fun. Don't miss the ride in the glass elevator to the clock tower and a wonderful view of DC. (*See also* Viewpoints.) Shops *OPEN Apr-Dec, Mon-Sat 10am-8pm, Sun noon-6pm; Jan-Mar, 7 days*

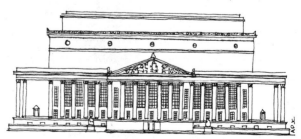

The National Archives

0am-6pm. Food *OPEN Mon-Sat 10am-9:30pm, Sun noon-8pm; in winter till 8pm. FREE. Metro: Federal Triangle.*

The Pentagon

Arlington, Va. (703) 695-1776. With 3.7 million square feet of floor space it's the world's largest office building (completed in 1943); 22,000 people work here. Headquarters for the Defense Department, the central command post for the army, navy, and air force. Walking tours take about 55 minutes (after all there are 17 miles of corridors) plus a 12-minute movie about the Pentagon, *Nov-Apr, Mon-Fri at 9:30, 10, 11 & 11:30am, noon, 12:30, 1, 2, 2:30 & 3:30pm; May-Oct, Mon-Fri 9:30am-3:30pm, every 30 minutes.* Tour includes the Commander-in-Chief Corridor, displaying etchings of presidents and memorabilia; the Executive Corridor, concentrating on important persons in the military; Time-Life Corridor, featuring artwork from WW II; and the Hall of Heroes, with its portraits of recipients of the Medal of Honor. Reserve for groups of 15 or more and for handicapped persons. The tour window is at the entrance to the Metro station. *OPEN Mon-Fri 9:30am-3:30pm. CLOSED Sat, Sun & holidays. FREE. Metro: Pentagon.*

State Department

200 C Street, NW. 632-3241. Created in 1789, the State Department is the oldest of the 13 cabinet departments. There are exhibits in the lobby depicting the agency's history, but this normally low-profile wing of the government boasts a lovely and valuable (estimated at $60 million) collection of art objects and furnishings (1740-1825)—mainly gifts to our government—which grace the 8th-floor Diplomatic Reception Rooms. Best: the John Quincy Adams State Drawing Room and the view from this vantage point. Also here are Thomas Jefferson's china and Francis Scott Key's Chippendale chairs. Accessible by reservation only. Write four to six weeks in advance to the State Department Tour Office, 2201 C Street, NW, Room 1493 FMSS/GS, Washington, DC 20520. Tours *Mon-Fri 9:30am, 10:30am & 2:45pm. CLOSED Sat, Sun & holidays. FREE.* Note: No strollers permitted; not recommended for children under age 12.

Union Station

50 Massachusetts Avenue, NE. 371-9441. The magnificent Beaux Arts beauty of a railroad station has not only been revitalized as a grand gateway for those arriving in the nation's capital by train, it has been positively metamorphosed into a dynamic shopping, dining, and entertainment complex—now very much a destination in and of itself, for both visitors and residents. (*See also* HISTORIC & NEW WASHINGTON, Historic Buildings & Areas.) Shops *OPEN 24 hours.* Shops *OPEN Mon-Sat 10am-9pm; Sun noon-6pm.* Cafes open even earlier to serve commuters, and the more upscale restaurants serve well into the evening for late-night dining and nightcaps following a movie at one of the nine theaters. A must-see!

United States Naval Observatory

34th Street & Massachusetts Avenue, NW, 20392. 653-1543. Developed in 1830, the observatory is the oldest scientific institution in the navy and is the standard time-setter for this country—using special telescopes and 30 atomic clocks. Fascinating nighttime tours are available *every Mon eve 8pm (except federal holidays).* Write or call for exact schedule. You get a chance to view celestial bodies (moon, planets, double stars) through the 26- and 12-inch refracting telescopes and astronomers on hand will answer your questions. Tickets available on a first-come basis to the first 100 individuals. Dress for outdoor weather conditions. Tours last 2 hours. Groups of 15 to 35 must reserve two to three months in advance; call 653-1541. The observatory library contains approximately 75,000 volumes, many of which date back to the 15th century. Of interest: To the left as you enter the gates is the official residence of the vice president of the United States (I know you wondered where he lived). FREE.

The Vietnam Veterans Memorial

Constitution Gardens, Constitution Avenue between 17th and 21st Streets, NW. 634-1568. Between the Lincoln and Washington memorials. One of the most evocative places in the nation's capital is a privately funded memorial, the design of which, when it was first shown, seemed destined to become as controversial as the war it was to commemorate. But from its unveiling on Veteran's Day 1982, the stark and somber polished black granite memorial, its 140 panels etched with a seemingly endless list (58,183 in all) of the American dead of the Vietnam War, has almost mystically become a vehicle for healing. A powerful cathartic for the still grieving, the still angry. Visitors come by the millions (over 10,000 a day) to see, to weep, and to give in to the overwhelming urge to touch the names on the wall. Some do pencil rubbings, others leave mementos that are now being catalogued by the Park Service, which since 1984 has had jurisdiction over the monument. A realistic bronze statue (a compromise for those who thought the wall too abstract) stands with a flagpole near the entrance. There is a directory (the names on the wall are in chronological order of death) and from 8am to midnight there is *always* someone there to talk to. Flashlights are provided in the pm. *OPEN 7 days, 24 hours a day.* (*See also* HISTORIC & NEW WASHINGTON, Statues & Monuments.) Accessible via Tourmobile.

Voice of America

330 Independence Avenue, SW, 2nd floor. 619-3919. The international radio broadcasting service of the United States. Each week it broadcasts 901¼ hours of news, editorials, lectures, and commentaries in 45 languages to an audience of over 80 million people. For the many who formerly lived behind the Iron Curtain, this was their only window on the west. The 45-minute tours are given *Mon-Fri at 8:40, 9:40 & 10:40am & 1:40 & 2:40pm. CLOSED Sat, Sun & holidays.*

Reserve in advance. FREE. *Metro: Federal Center.*

George Washington Masonic National Memorial

King Street & Callahan Drive, Alexandria, Va. (703) 683-2007. On Shooters Hill above the Potomac, an imposing classical building honoring fellow Mason George Washington. It is a repository of relics in the possession of the Alexandria-Washington Lodge #22, whose first master was Washington while he was president; also exhibits devoted to freemasonry. Fine views from the tower. Fully-guided 90-minute tours, every 70 minutes, excluding lunchtime. Last tour at 3:35pm. *OPEN 7 days 9am-5pm. CLOSED Thanksgiving, Christmas, New Year's Day.* FREE. *Metro: King Street.*

The Washington Post

1150 15th Street, NW. 334-7969. In business since 1877, but it gained international fame as the paper for which investigative reporters Woodward and Bernstein, who broke and reported the Watergate story, worked. Tour the newsroom, the pressroom, and other areas of this busy daily. Reserve in advance. Guided tours *every hour on the hour Mon & Thurs only, 10am-2pm.* (Children under age 12 not permitted on tour.) FREE. *Metro: McPherson Square, Farragut North.*

White House Tour

1600 Pennsylvania Avenue, NW. 456-7041 (recording); 456-2200. The tour of the presidential house includes the East Wing—the Jacqueline Kennedy Garden, the State Room, East Room, Green Room, Red Room, Dining Room, the lower level, and the Foyer. *Tour hours are year-round, Tues-Sat 10am-noon; tickets are distributed on the Ellipse at 8am.* The tickets give a specific time to be at the East Gate, on East Executive Avenue, for your tour. There is a live band on the Ellipse to entertain you while you wait, sponsored by the National Park Service. *Congressional tours are available Tues-Sat 8am-9am, by writing to your representative, and are limited to 1,200 a day.* The tour usually lasts half an hour. Note: No photographs may be taken inside the White House. (*See also* HISTORIC & NEW WASHINGTON, Historic Buildings & Areas.) FREE. *Metro: McPherson Square.*

RIVER TRIPS

The Dandy

Zero Prince Street, Alexandria, Va. (703) 683-6076 for reservations; (703) 683-6090 for information. *The Dandy,* a climate-controlled restaurant-cruise ship, sails year-round. There are public luncheon and dinner cruises plus special morning, luncheon, and midafternoon cruises for private and semiprivate parties. Fee includes cruise and meal; beverages, taxes, and gratuities are extra. Reservations are required. Luncheon cruises *Mon-Sun: board 11:30am-*

12:15pm; departs 12:30pm, docks 3pm. Cruise and three-course lunch. On Sunday, in addition to the meal, there is entertainment. Dinner cruises *Sun-Thurs: board 6:30-7:15pm; departs at 7:30pm, returns at 10:30pm (Fri and Sat docks at 11pm).* Cruise and five-course meal.

Spirit of Washington

Pier 4, 6th & Water Streets, SW. 554-8000. Popular newcomer to Washington waters (already in Boston and New York). Boats have carpeted climate-controlled dining rooms and fully-stocked bars. Features dancing to live bands and a "Salute to Broadway" revue with performing waiters and waitresses. All cruises board half an hour before departure. Reservations required. There is an Afternoon Lunch Cruise, noon to 2pm; an Evening Dinner Cruise, 7 to 10pm; a Sunday Brunch Cruise, 1 to 3pm, and a Moonlight Party Cruise, boarding at 10:30pm, cruising till 1:30am. Ask about their Mount Vernon Cruise.

DAY TRIPS

Escorted

Gray Line Tours

Union Station. 289-1995. An all-day trip to Harpers Ferry and the Gettysburg battlefield; the tour takes approximately 12½ hours. Harpers Ferry, near the Blue Ridge Mountains, known best as the site of John Brown's Raid in 1859, then on across the Mason-Dixon Line to Gettysburg, Pennsylvania. Go to the top of the National Tower, 300 feet above the battlefield. Also Cemetery Ridge, site of Lincoln's Gettysburg Address and Eisenhower's farm. Group charters only, may be scheduled any day, any time of the year. The Gray Line offers many other tours, lasting up to 10½ hours. Call for details.

On Your Own

Annapolis, Maryland

Chamber of Commerce, 152 Main Street. (301) 268-7676. Only 30 miles from DC. The capital of Maryland and for a short time the nation's capital (from November 1783 to the summer of 1784). Charm and history abound. Some of the sights include the U.S. Naval Academy (Visitors Information Center, Ricketts Hall, [301] 263-6933), established in 1845 on 300 acres with over 200 buildings, including the Chapel containing John Paul Jones's sarcophagus; the Chase-Lloyd House (CLOSED Sunday and Monday), where Francis Scott Key was married—built by Samuel Chase, a signer of the Declaration of Independence; Hammond Harwood House (CLOSED Monday), a five-part mansion built in 1774; Paca House (CLOSED Monday), with 18th-century formal gardens, built in 1765 for William Paca, signer of the Declaration of Independence and governor of Maryland. Also the Maryland State

House. For ghost-chasers there is Brice House, built in 1776 by William Buckland, where there have been reports of ghostly happenings.

You can take a 40-minute narrated cruise of Historic Annapolis Harbor aboard the *Harbor Queen*. Sails *Memorial Day-Labor Day, 7 days, every hour on the hour, 11am-4pm; Apr-Memorial Day & Labor Day-Sept 30, weekends only, 11am-4pm, every hour on the hour.* Ninety-minute cruises of Annapolis Harbor and the Severn River sail *Memorial Day-Labor Day, Wed-Sun 1:30pm & 3:30pm.* Also an all-day cruise to St. Michael's, *Memorial Day-Labor Day, Wed-Sun 10am-5:30pm.* Call 261-2719 in DC for more information.

In addition, there are many shops and restaurants, especially in the harbor vicinity. The Annapolis Arts Festival in June; the Maryland Seafood Festival in September; and Sailboat and Powerboat Shows in October.

Antietam National Battlefield Site

Visitors Center: one mile from Sharpsburg, Md, off Route 65. (301) 432-5124. The battle that was fought here, 65 miles from DC, on September 17, 1862—over an area of 12 square miles—was the bloodiest of the Civil War. It was the first of two attempts by Confederate Army general Robert E. Lee to carry the war into the north. There were 41,000 men fighting for the south, 87,000 for the north, and at the end of that single day the Confederates had lost 10,700 men, the Union 12,410. At the National Cemetery here, 4,776 Union Army soldiers are buried, including 1,836 unknown. Start at the Visitors Center Museum, where a slide presentation and a 26-minute film provide an orientation. The Observation Tower allows you to view the battlefield from 75 feet up. Tape tours are available. There is also a picnic area, nature trails, and areas for hiking and biking. The Visitors Center *OPEN 7 days 8:30am-5pm.* The cemetery *OPEN 7 days sunrise-sundown.*

Ash Lawn

I-64, Charlottesville, Va. (804) 293-9539. Home of President James Monroe. Built in 1799, this 550-acre estate is still a working plantation. To see: boxwood gardens complete with peacocks, demonstrations of spinning and weaving; inviting picnic areas. Site of the Summer Festival in June, July, and August and the Colonial Crafts Fair in July. *OPEN Mar-Oct, 7 days 9am-6pm; Nov-Feb, 7 days 10am-5pm. CLOSED Thanksgiving, Christmas & New Year's Day.* Admission.

Busch Gardens—The Old Country

Williamsburg, Va. (703) 529-1389; (804) 253-3350. At 3 hours, 150 miles from DC, it's a bit of a trip. On 360 acres, replicas of 17th- and 18th-century German, Italian, French, and English villages. There are shows, restaurants, and rides. Shops with imported merchandise and an animal habitat filled with native North American animals. Next to the Anheuser-Busch brewery—they have free tours and free beer tasting; there are also celebrity concerts. *OPEN June-Aug, Sun-Fri 10am-10pm, Sat 10am-midnight; Apr-*

May & Sept-end Oct, Fri-Tues only 10am-7pm. Admission; lower for senior citizens in September and October.

Catoctin Mountain Park

Route 77 West, just off U.S. 15 North, Md. (301) 663-9330. It's 65 miles north of DC and best known as the site of Camp David, the presidential retreat. Over 5,000 acres of park with opportunities for hiking, camping, and picnicking. There are fireplaces and tables; rest rooms. Nearby is Cunningham Falls State Park, with Big Hunting Creek cascading down a 40-foot gorge; boating and fishing; Cat Rock; Bob Hill; and Isobel Rock all provide incredible views. No trailers over 22 feet, please. Both parks are *OPEN 7 days sunrise to sundown.*

Colonial Williamsburg, Virginia

Take I-95, I-64 & Va 168 SW. Follow the signs to the Visitors Center, (804) 229-1000. Three hours from DC. The capital of the British Crown Colony of Virginia from 1699 to 1780. On 173 acres, a unique opportunity to view 18th-century colonial life. The restoration funded by John D. Rockefeller in the 1920s includes 83 buildings; a few hundred smaller structures have been reconstructed. Colonial life proceeds as it did in the 18th century, with traditional crafts workshops, costumed townspeople, horse-drawn carriages on tranquil tree-lined streets. Historic sights include the Governor's Palace and the College of William and Mary. Shops and restaurants. Great for history buffs and antiquers.

Fredericksburg, Virginia

Visitors Center: 706 Caroline Street. (703) 373-1776. Take Route 1 South. One hour from DC. Nearly three centuries old and rich in Revolutionary and Civil War history. It's the place where George Washington grew up—the famous cherry tree chopping and coin toss across the Rappahannock River occurred here. Visit the Mary Washington house, Saint James House, Rising Sun Tavern, Hugh Mercer Apothecary Shop, the Cultural Center (Old City Hall), James Monroe Law Office-Museum and Memorial Library, Belmont, Kenmore, and the Chimneys, now a restaurant. Tour tickets are available at the Visitors Center, allowing you admission to seven historic attractions at a discount. Otherwise, there are individual admissions at each site. Guided walking tours are also available, call in advance.

Harpers Ferry National Historical Park

Visitors Center, Old Stagecoach Inn. (304) 535-6223. Via I-270 & U.S. 340. Located in West Virginia, 65 miles from DC. The force of Harpers Ferry was established in 1747, but it is best remembered as the site of John Brown's Raid in 1859, one of the sparks that helped ignite the Civil War. One of two original federal arsenals, it has been restored to its 1860 appearance, many pre-Civil War buildings remain standing. There are free guided walking tours of the city from June to September—or a map is available at the Visitors Center for a self-guided tour—that take you to historic houses such as Master Armorers House, now a gun-making museum. Jefferson

Rock is named for our third president, who reportedly said the view from here was "worth a voyage across the Atlantic." Hikers follow the Appalachian Trail for 3 miles; it ends at the ruins of an old stone fort. There are unsurpassed views along the way of the Shenandoah and Potomac valleys.

Luray Caverns

Luray, Va. (703) 743-6551. Only 90 minutes from DC are over 64 acres of caverns. Discovered in 1878, the largest is 300 feet long, 500 feet wide, and 140 feet high. Take the one-hour guided tour of these natural, very colorful formations. The "stalacpipe" organ, the only one of its kind —from a master console, stalactites and stalagmites are played. *OPEN Mar-June, 7 days 9am-6pm; June 15-Labor Day, 7 days 9am-7pm; Labor Day-Nov 14, 7 days 9am-6pm; Nov 15-Mar 14, Mon-Fri 9am-4pm, Sat & Sun 9am-5pm.* Admission charge, lower for senior citizens and children ages 7 to 13; under age 7 free. Group rates available for 25 or more.

Manassas National Battlefield Park

Near the intersection of I-66 & Va 234. (703) 754-7107. Just 26 miles southwest of DC is the site of the two battles of Bull Run. There are 3,031 acres of battlefield with two nature trails covering 20 miles. To see: cannon from the Civil War; a statue of Stonewall Jackson, who received wounds here; and on Henry Hill, Mrs. Judith Henry, the first civilian casualty of the Civil War, is buried. Picnic areas with tables. *OPEN 7 days, sunrise to sundown.*

Monticello

Charlottesville, Va. (804) 295-8181. The 5,000 acre estate that was home and then burial place of Thomas Jefferson, America's third president. The classic design, construction, and remodeling were started by Jefferson in 1768 and continued for 40 years. Above the entrance door is the clock Jefferson had Peter Sprunk of Philadelphia build to his specifications. It tells not only the time but also the day of the week by weights that descend past markers on the wall, each indicating a day of the week (holes had to be cut in the floor because of a misjudgment of the fall of weights). There are 13 skylights for natural lighting. There are original furnishings in the house and the gardens have been restored to their original state. *OPEN 7 days 8am-5pm; Nov 1-Feb 28, closes at 4:30pm.* Admission.

Shenandoah National Park

Via I-66, Va 55 & U.S. 340 or via I-66 & U.S. 211. (703) 999-2266. At two hours, 80 miles southwest of the District, this is the closest national park to DC. Two Visitors Centers are located near the entrance to the park. The Skyline Drive, the road that winds through the park, is simply spectacular. Four campgrounds, 700 campsites, cottages, lodges, 94 miles of Appalachian Trail, and 200 miles of park trails. Fishing, riding, and tables and grills for picnicking. Park *OPEN always except during inclement weather.* Visitors Center *OPEN 7 days 9am-5pm.* Admission for children age 16 and over.

ANNUAL EVENTS

CALENDAR

These are some of the special events that occur annually in Washington, DC. They are like icing on a cake.

January

Unless it is an election year, Congress convenes on the first Monday in January. If it's an election year, the inauguration takes place on January 20, with the president taking the oath of office on the west front of the Capitol, followed by an extravagant parade down Pennsylvania Avenue from the Capitol past the White House. Then, incumbent and freshman senators and representatives go to work "on the Hill."

Washington Antiques Show
Omni Shoreham Hotel, 2500 Calvert Street, NW. First full week in January; hours vary. A very popular annual antiques show that benefits a number of charities. Hundreds of local and national dealers. In addition to browsing and buying there are lectures, appraisals, and exhibits on loan from museums in the area. Check ahead, not all days are open to the general public. For information, call 234-0700. Admission.

Lee Birthday Celebrations
Arlington House, Arlington National Cemetery. One Sunday in mid-January. An open house featuring 19th- century music, period foods, and exhibitions of restoration work. For information, call (703) 557-0613. Also, the fourth Sunday in January from 3 to 5pm at the **Boyhood Home of Robert E. Lee**, 607 Oronoco Street, and at the **Lee-Fendall House**, 614 Oronoco Street, Alexandria, Va. Joint celebrations in Old Town of the birthdays of "Light Horse" Harry Lee and son Robert E. Candlelight tours of the homes, refreshments, and period music. For information, call (703) 838-4200 or -8454. Admission.

Martin Luther King, Jr, Birthday Observance
At the Lincoln Memorial on the third Monday in January. Wreath-laying ceremony and a presentation of Dr. King's memorable "I Have a Dream . . ." speech. Guest speakers, local choirs, and a military honor guard gather to salute the life of the slain civil rights leader. For details, call 619-7222. FREE.

Ice Skating
National Sculpture Garden Rink, 9th & Constitution Avenue, NW, and **Pershing Park Rink**, 14th Street & Pennsylvania Avenue, NW. Outdoor ice skating throughout the winter in unique city settings. For information, call 737-6938 and 371-7222, respectively. Admission to each. FREE skating on the **Reflecting Pool** and on the **C&O Canal**, when conditions permit; check with the National Park Service, 619-7222.

U.S. Army Band Concerts
Fort Myer, Bruckner Hall, Arlington, Va. January through April, every Tuesday and Thursday at 8pm. Concerts featuring soloists and ensembles of the Army Band. For details, call (703) 696-3399.

February

U.S. Army Band Concerts
See January.

Black History Month
The entire month of February. In recognition of the contributions of African Americans to American life—special performances, readings, weekend craft workshops for kids, and exhibitions at the National Museums of American Art, American History, and African Art and at the Anacostia Neighborhood Museum. For information, call 357-2700. Also at the Martin Luther King, Jr., Memorial Library, call 727-0321. FREE.

Chinese New Year's Festival
Late January to mid-February, depending on the lunar calendar. Chinatown, H Street NW between 5th and 8th Streets. The traditional lunar celebration ushering in the Chinese New Year with firecrackers and dragon dancers through the streets of Chinatown. Many of the restaurants offer festive fixed-price holiday banquets. For information, call 724-4091. FREE.

Biennial Art Exhibition
Corcoran Gallery of Art, New York Avenue & 17th Street, NW. 638-3211, ext 301. Late winter/early spring, odd-numbered years, for six weeks. Exhibition of contemporary American paintings. Contribution suggested. (*See also* MUSEUMS & GALLERIES, Museums.)

Abraham Lincoln's Birthday Celebration
Lincoln Memorial, West Potomac Park at 23rd Street, NW. 426-6700. February 12 at noon for one hour. A traditional ceremony honoring the 16th president on his birthday, includes the laying of the presidential wreath, speeches by dignitaries, the Presentation of the Colors, and a reading of the Gettysburg Address. For information, call 619-7222. FREE.

Ice Capades
Capitol Centre, Landover, Md. (301) 350-3400. Mid-February. The annual spectacle on ice performed by the nation's best skaters. Tickets may be purchased in advance.

Washington's Birthday Celebration
Washington Monument, February 22 at 11:30am. Traditional wreath-laying ceremony honoring the nation's founding father. (If February 22 falls on a Saturday, the ceremony is held the following Monday.) Sponsored by the National Park Service and the Washington National Monument Society. For information, call 619-7222.

George Washington Birthday Celebrations in Old Town, Alexandria
Celebrations in Alexandria for native son George Washington are determined by the federal holiday, which usually falls on the third Monday in February. For exact information, call (703) 838-4200.

George Washington Birthnight Banquet & Ball
Gadsby's Tavern Museum, 134 North Royal Street. The Saturday of Washington's Birthday weekend. The traditional birthday ball started during Washington's lifetime—with him

in attendance—at this very same tavern! The banquet is at an Old Town restaurant from 7 to 9pm, the ball is at Gadsby's Tavern from 9pm to midnight Black tie, military, or colonial dress. Admission.

Revolutionary War Encampment

Fort Ward Park, 4301 West Braddock Road, Alexandria, Va. Sunday afternoon before the federal holiday commemorating Washington's birthday. Reenactment of a day in the life of a Revolutionary War camp from 11am to 2pm; skirmishes at 2pm. FREE.

George Washington Birthday Parade

Start: Wilkes & South St. Asaph's Streets. Reviewing stand on North Royal Street in front of Gadsby's Tavern Museum. Held on the federal holiday at 1pm. The nation's largest parade celebrating George Washington's birthday. Fife and drum corps, bagpipes, floats, military bands, and more wind their way through Old Town. FREE

March

The coming of spring is heralded in Washington with colorful profusions of wild flowers as well as formal displays in the Botanic Garden Conservatory. (See also PARKS & GARDENS, Gardens: Dumbarton Oaks Garden.)

All seem to anticipate the Cherry Blossom Festival, which, depending upon the weather, arrives at the end of March or the beginning of April.

U.S. Army Band Concerts

See January.

American Classic Antiques Show

The DC Armory, 2001 East Capitol Street. Early March for three days. An important antiques show with more than 185 dealers from 20 states, Canada, and Europe. For information, call (301) 738-1966 or, during the show, (301) 547-9215. Admission.

Annual Bach Marathon

Chevy Chase Presbyterian Church, 1 Chevy Chase Circle, NW. March 16 from 1 to 6pm. In honor of Johann Sebastian Bach's birthday, 16 organists play on the church's massive pipe organ. Box lunches and refreshments are available. For information, call 363-2202.

St. Patrick's Day Parade

On Constitution Avenue from 7th to 17th Streets, NW. The Sunday before March 17 from 1 to 3:30pm. Floats, military bands, Irish groups, dancers, bagpipes, and much wearin' of the green. For additional information, call 426-2200.

St. Patrick's Day

Arlington National Cemetery, Arlington, Va. On March 17 at about 12:30pm. The Ancient Order of Hibernians starts the ceremonies by placing a wreath on the grave of John F. Kennedy. Then on to the grave of George Washington Parke Custis, a supporter of Irish independence in the 19th century, for a shamrock-planting ceremony. Bagpipes are played; a member of the Irish embassy usually attends. There is period music and

food till 4pm at the Arlington House open house immediately following the ceremonies. For information, call (703) 557-0613. FREE.

American College Theater Festival

Terrace Theater, Kennedy Center, 2700 F Street, NW. Mid-March to April for two weeks. College productions chosen from a regional level. Traditional and new plays as well as musicals. A different performance every night. FREE, but tickets are required (15 minutes before curtain, empty seats are made available to those without tickets). For information, call 416-8850.

U.S. Botanic Garden's Easter Flower Show

At the foot of Capitol Hill, 1st Street & Maryland Avenue, SW. 225-8333. The third week in March for four weeks. A beautiful display of lilies for the Easter season and a profusion of spring flowers, just when we need them. *OPEN 7 days 9am-5pm.* FREE. (*See also PARKS & GARDENS, Gardens.*)

Smithsonian Kite Festival

West side of the Washington Monument grounds, 17th Street & Constitution Avenue. Last Saturday in March. Co-sponsored by the Smithsonian Resident Associates and the National Air & Space Museum. Every year kite makers and fliers of all ages gather at the monument to compete. It's an exhilarating sight. Registration usually in the am. Note: Kites must be homemade and must be able to reach an altitude of 100 feet. Awards are given in a variety of categories. For information, call 357-3030. FREE.

McDonald's Capital Classics

Capitol Centre, Landover, Md. Late March. America's most prestigious high school all-star basketball game. For information, call (301) 350-3400. Admission.

Late March or Early April depending . . .

National Cherry Blossom Festival

Over a half million visitors come to see a one- to two-week display of splendor compliments of Mother Nature and Tokyo. In 1912, a variety of flowering cherry trees, numbering 3,200, were donated to America by Japan. Markers commemorate the planting of the first two trees, at the south end of 17th Street. (Ironically, cuttings from those were returned to Japan in 1952 to replace war-damaged ones in Tokyo.) Around the Tidal Basin, the white Yoshino cherry blossoms; pink Akebanos at Hains Point. The festivities begin with the lighting of the 300-year-old Japanese Lantern at the Japanese Pagoda, northwest corner of the Tidal Basin, at 6pm. Other events include the Cherry Blossom Festival Parade (see below), fireworks, and free concerts in downtown parks. For more information on the festival, call 737-2599 or 789-7000.

April

Check the March calendar for ongoing events.

The Cherry Blossom Festival Parade

Constitution Avenue from 7th to 17th Streets,

NW. First Saturday in April at 12:30pm. Man-made pageantry to accompany nature's presentation: a parade, princesses, a massed band salute to the president by 3,000 musicians, and a 21-gun salute. For information about tickets, call 728-1135.

Easter Sunrise Service
Memorial Amphitheater, Arlington National Cemetery. Easter Sunday at sunrise. For information, call 475-0856. FREE.

White House Easter Egg Roll
Enter at the southeast Gate on East Executive Avenue. Held the Monday after Easter from 10am to 2pm. For children 8 years of age and under, accompanied by an adult. The main attraction is a contest in which kids, arranged in groups by age, roll eggs across the White House lawn. Prizes for everyone. Eggs are provided; entertainment, too. For information, call 456-2200. FREE.

Imagination Celebration
Kennedy Center, 2700 F Street, NW, Terrace Theater. The month of April; call for exact dates and time. An annual performing arts festival for young people. Music, dance, opera, ballet, drama, and puppetry. Participation by some of the best national children's theater companies. Call 416-8000. FREE and moderately priced events.

Open Studio Annual
The month of April, usually for four weekends from 11am to 6pm. More than 200 artists open their private studios to the public in this popular event. Sponsored by the **Washington Project for the Arts**, which distributes maps to the studio locations at 400 7th Street, NW. For information, call 347-8304.

U.S. Army Band Concerts
See January.

Carillon Recitals
Netherlands Carillon, on the grounds of the Iwo Jima Memorial, Arlington, Va. Every Saturday in April, May, and September from 2 to 4pm; June, July and August from 6:30 to 8:30pm. The carillon was a gift from the Netherlands to the United States in appreciation of our aid during and after World War II. The concerts feature internationally renowned carillonneurs. For information, call (703) 285-2598. FREE.

Thomas Jefferson Birthday Celebration
Jefferson Memorial, south bank of the Tidal Basin. April 13 at noon. Traditional wreath-laying ceremony to celebrate the birthday of the author of the Declaration of Independence and third U.S. president. For information, call 619-7222.

C&O Canal Barge Rides
Depart from Foundry Mall, 30th & Thomas Jefferson Streets, NW, in Georgetown. 472-4376. Mid-April to mid-October. Step back in time with a ride on a mule-drawn barge up the scenic and historic Chesapeake and Ohio Canal to Great Falls, Maryland. The ride takes approximately 90 minutes each way and costumed Park Service guides tell the canal's history through stories and songs. Admission. (*See also* SIGHTSEEING, On

Your Own, *and* HISTORIC & NEW WASHINGTON, Historic Buildings & Areas.)

White House Spring Garden Tours
In mid-April, one Saturday and Sunday from 2 to 5pm. The beautiful White House gardens are open to the public. Tours include the Jacqueline Kennedy Rose Garden and the West Lawn. In bloom are daffodils, tulips, and hyacinths. Also available, tours of the public rooms. For information, call 456-2200. FREE.

C&O Canal Reunion Hike
Sometime in April (aka the Chief Justice Douglas Memorial Hike). Nearly 40 years ago, the late William O. Douglas and a large group of intrepids hiked the entire route of the C&O Canal (184.5 miles!). The purpose was to save the canal from being destroyed to make way for a highway; happily, they succeeded. Every year a different part of the canal is hiked—usually lasting the whole day. Blessedly a free shuttle service takes you back. For date, time, and details, call (301) 739-4200 or write to the sponsor, the C&O Canal Association, P.O. Box 366, Glen Echo, MD 20812. (*See also* PARKS & GARDENS, Nature Trails & Wildlife Preserves: C&O Canal National Historic Park.) FREE.

Ringling Bros. and Barnum & Bailey Circus
DC Armory, 2001 East Capitol Street. Mid-April for 2 weeks. For more than 120 years the Greatest Show on Earth has come to town and we all become children once more. Tickets may be purchased in advance. For information, call 448-4000.

Georgetown Garden Tour
Sponsored by and benefiting the Georgetown Children's House, 3224 N Street, NW. One day mid- to late April from 10:30am to 5pm. Tour approximately 13 different gardens in this beautiful historic district. Self-guided walking tour includes Evermay, Dumbarton Oaks, and Prospect House. Complimentary tea is served from noon to 4pm at the Children's House. The tour lasts at least 2 hours. For information, call 333-4953. Admission; children under age 12 free.

Old Town Tour of Homes & Gardens
Old Town, Alexandria, Va. The fourth Saturday in April from 10am to 4:30pm. A tour of some of this historic port's most elegant private homes and gardens. Part of Annual Historic Garden Week in Virginia. For information, call (703) 838-4200. Admission.

Smithsonian's Washington Craft Show
Departmental Auditorium, 14th Street & Constitution Avenue, NW. Late April for three days. An exhibit and sale of fine handcrafted objects; all works are one-of-a-kind. Media included are fiber, ceramics, glass, metal, paper, textiles, and wood. The 100 exhibits are selected by a jury of experts in the field. For information, call 357-2700. Admission.

"Wings & Things" Garber Open House
Paul E. Garber Facility, Silver Hill, Md. In late April for two days from 10am to 3pm. The once-a-year day-long chance to see the Air & Space Museum's reserve collection of air- and space-

craft in this giant hangar facility. For exact dates, call 357-2700. FREE.

William Shakespeare's Birthday
Folger Shakespeare Library, 201 East Capitol Street, SE. 544-7077. Late April, in celebration of the Bard's birth, a day filled with music, theater, food, exhibits, and children's events. Call for details. FREE.

Georgetown House Tour
One Sunday, late April, from noon to 5pm. Homes in one of the city's oldest and loveliest neighborhoods are open for viewing. Included in the price of admission is high tea, served from 2 to 6pm, at St. John's Parish Church. For information, call 338-1796.

Potomac International Regatta
Best viewing: Washington Harbor in Georgetown. Late April. A spirited showing on the Potomac, when U.S. rowing teams compete with those from Oxford and Cambridge University. For information, call 333-3838.

May

Check the April calendar for ongoing events.

Washington Cathedral Flower Mart
Washington Cathedral, Mount St. Alban, Wisconsin Avenue & Woodley Road, NW. 537-6247. First Friday and Saturday in May from 11am to 5pm. Each year saluting a different country. Flowers, herbs, and food for sale; decorating demonstrations. Proceeds benefit the church. FREE.

Filmfest, DC
In theaters across the city. The first two weeks in May. Premieres of dozens of international and American films. Check the local papers for film locations and schedules.

Sunday Polo Matches
On the field in West Potomac Park east of the Lincoln Memorial, every Sunday in May at 2pm, in June at 3pm, July to August at 4pm, September to October at 3pm. For information, call 619-7222. FREE.

Gross National Parade
Starts at M & 18th Streets, NW, and proceeds to M & Wisconsin. The first Sunday in May. More a parody than a parade, but it's great fun and the zaniest scheduled thing you might see in the capital city. Benefits the Police Boys and Girls Clubs of DC. For information, call 686-3215.

Air Force Service
Washington National Cathedral, Mount St. Alban, Wisconsin Avenue & Woodley Road, NW. The first Sunday in May at 3:30pm. The annual service commemorating the U.S. Air Force anniversary. For information, call 537-6247.

American Classic Antiques Show
At the DC Armory, 2001 East Capitol Street. Three days in early May. A celebration of Americana, country and folk art. For information, call (301) 738-1966 or, during the show, (202) 547-9215.

Marine Corps Friday Evening Parade
Marine Barracks, 8th & I Streets, SE. 433-6060.

Early May to late August, every Friday evening at 7pm. Performances by the famed Marine Band, Silent Drill Team, ceremonial guard, and Drum and Bugle Corps. Reservations must be made at least three weeks in advance to assure seating. FREE.

Goodwill Industries Embassy Tour
The second Saturday in May from noon to 5pm. A self-guided walking tour (or free shuttle bus service) of approximately six to eight embassies that are normally closed to the public. Complimentary tea and an opportunity to meet members of the media and government. Admission (tax deductible), discounts for groups of more than 25. Reserve at least two weeks in advance. For information, call 636-4225. Proceeds benefit the Davis Memorial Goodwill Industries.

Capitol Hill House & Garden Tour
The second Sunday in May from noon to 6pm. Visit some of the charmingly restored turn-of-the-century homes of this historic, renewing Washington neighborhood. Sponsored by the Capitol Hill Restoration Society. For details, call 543-0425. Admission.

Greek Spring Festival
Saints Constantine and Helen Greek Orthodox Church, 4115 16th Street, NW. Usually mid-May, Friday to Sunday, from 11am to 9pm. Greek food, music, and dancing; clowns, games, arts and crafts. For details, call 829-2910. FREE.

The Preakness
Pimlico Race Course, Northern Parkway & Belvedere Avenue, Baltimore, Md. (301) 542-9400. Third Saturday in May; post time is noon. The middle jewel of the Triple Crown. Admission. (*See also* SPORTS, Horseracing, Thoroughbred.)

Marine Corps Tuesday Evening Sunset Parades
Iwo Jima Memorial, Arlington Boulevard & Ridge Road, Arlington, Va. Late May to late August, every Tuesday evening at 7pm. The U.S. Marine Drum and Bugle Corps and Silent Drill Team perform at day's end at this moving memorial. Free shuttle bus service from Arlington Cemetery Visitors Center starting at 6pm. For information, call (202) 433-4173. FREE. (*See also* HISTORIC & NEW WASHINGTON, Statues & Monuments: Marine Corps War Memorial.)

"The American Sailor"
Washington Navy Yard, M & 9th Streets, SE. 433-2218. Late May through Labor Day, every Wednesday promptly at 9pm. Music and ceremony celebrating the navy's history and folklore. Navy Band, Sea Chanters, Ceremonial Drill Team and Guard. Reservations required at least one to three weeks in advance to assure seating. FREE.

Memorial Day Ceremonies

Amphitheatre at Arlington National Cemetery, Arlington, Va. Memorial Day at 11am, an Armed Forces Full Honor Ceremony. The placement of the presidential wreath at the Tomb of the Unknowns, memorial services at the Amphitheatre, and music by the U.S. Army Band; the president very often attends. Usually lasts 45 minutes. For information, call 475-0856. Also, at the **Vietnam Veterans Memorial** a wreath laying at 11am followed by a military band and speeches. For information, call 619-7222. FREE.

Memorial Day Jazz Festival
Oronoco Bay Park, Old Town, Alexandria, Va. Held on the federal holiday from noon to 7pm. Bring a picnic lunch and listen to live big band swing music. For information, call (703) 838-4686. FREE.

Memorial Day Weekend Concert
The U.S. Capitol, West Lawn. This special concert the Sunday of Memorial Day weekend at 8pm by the National Symphony Orchestra with an array of guest artists marks the official beginning of summer in the capital. Bring a blanket or chair and picnic. Come early to ensure a good place on the lawn. For information, call 619-7222 or 416-8100. FREE.

U.S. Navy Memorial Concerts on the Avenue
U.S. Navy Memorial, Pennsylvania Avenue & 7th Street, NW. At 8pm on Memorial Day and every Thursday and Saturday thereafter through Labor Day. Band concerts by the Navy Band (on Thursdays) and other military bands (rotating Saturdays) at the striking new Pennsylvania Avenue plaza. For information, call 433-2525. FREE.

June

Check the May listings for ongoing summer events.

Military Band Summer Concerts
Every summer evening at 8pm from Memorial Day through Labor Day, delightful concerts by the U.S. Navy Band (Mondays at the U.S. Capitol, west side; Thursdays at Navy Memorial Plaza), the U.S. Army Band (Tuesdays at the Sylvan Theater on the Washington Monument grounds; Fridays at the U.S. Capitol), the U.S. Air Force Band (Tuesdays at the U.S. Capitol; Fridays at the Sylvan Theater), and the U.S. Marine Band (Wednesdays at the U.S. Capitol; Sundays at the Sylvan Theater). On Saturdays at Navy Memorial Plaza, a rotation of the branches.

Wolf Trap Farm Park
1551 Trap Road, Vienna, Va. (703) 255-1800. The first National Park for the Performing Arts begins its season, which runs from June through September. Lovely outdoor setting with choice of covered amphitheater or lawn seating, for symphony, opera, pop concerts, ballet, musicals, and theater. Bring a picnic supper. Admission.

Summer Concert Series
Merriweather Post Pavilion, off South Entrance Road, Columbia, Md. (301) 982-1800. June through September. More than 60 concerts a season by such performers as Sting; Liza Minnelli; John Denver; Peter, Paul, and Mary; Doobie Brothers; Beach Boys; Johnny Mathis. Per-

formances rain or shine. Pavilion or lawn seating. Parking is included in price of ticket. Ticketmaster or Pavilion box office.

Carillon & Organ Concerts
National Shrine of the Immaculate Conception, 4th Street & Michigan Avenue, NE. 526-8300. June to August, every Sunday at 6pm. Recitals usually last 90 minutes. FREE. (*See also* HISTORIC & NEW WASHINGTON, Churches & Synagogues: National Shrine of the Immaculate Conception.)

Noon Hour Concerts
Enjoy a little light noon music June through August, every Tuesday at Farragut Square, and every Thursday at Pershing Park, Pennsylvania & 14th Street, NW. For information, call 619-7225. FREE.

Dupont-Kalorama Museum Walk Day
The first Monday in June. A celebration of the eight institutions located in this Dupont-Kalorama neighborhood. Family activities include demonstrations, video programs, music, historic-house tours, foods, crafts, and more. Shuttle service provided. For information, call 387-2151. FREE.

Music Under the Stars
Sylvan Theater on the Washington Monument grounds. Every Wednesday evening mid-June to end of August from 8 to 10pm. Big band sounds under the summer night sky. For information, call 619-7222. FREE.

"Ulysses" Marathon Reading
Irish Times Pub, 14 F Street, NW. 543-5433. The popular annual marathon reading of the James Joyce classic starts at 11am on June 15 and ends early morning, June 16—the days during which the novel is set.

Alexandria Red Cross Waterfront Festival
Second weekend in June. A celebration of Alexandria's historic role as a seaport. Historic ships, boat rides, children's events, ship tours, arts and crafts shows, food, entertainment, and fireworks. For information, call (703) 838-4200. Admission.

Mostly Mozart Festival
Kennedy Center for the Performing Arts. 416-8000. Late June for four days. The melodies of Wolfgang Amadeus Mozart fill the halls during this annual concert series. Admission.

Northern Virginia Antiques Show
Thomas Jefferson Center, 3501 S. 2nd Street, Arlington, Va. (301) 738-1966. The third weekend in June. A fine show featuring 130 dealers from around the country. Admission.

Children's Day
Carter Barron Amphitheatre, 16th Street & Colorado Avenue, NW. 619-7226. Last Saturday in June from 11:30am to 4:30pm. A day-long festival featuring performing arts, live music, and hands-on activities. Sponsored by the Capital Children's Museum and the National Park Service. FREE.

Festival of American Folklife
On the National Mall. End of June/early July for about ten days. An enormously popular annual event sponsored by the Smithsonian's Office of

Folklife Programs. Illustrations of American crafts by skilled artisans from all over the U.S. Demonstrations, music, everything and anything that has tradition, from quilting to coal mining. Food, arts and crafts for sale. For information, call 357-2700. FREE.

Annual Civil War Living History Weekend
Fort Ward Park and Museum, 4301 West Braddock Road, Alexandria, Va. (703) 838-4848. Late June or July. On Saturday and Sunday, an authentically outfitted and equipped Civil War military unit demonstrates Civil War camp life with drills, music, and a review of the troops. Torchlight tours of the camp on Saturday night. Admission.

Fourth of July Celebrations

The nation's capital is awash in celebrations of the Fourth of July. For details on the following events, call 619-7222.

National Archives Program
Constitution Avenue & 8th Street, NW. At 10am. The annual program featuring American music, a dramatic reading of the Declaration of Independence, and a demonstration of colonial military maneuvers on the steps of the building. FREE.

National Independence Day Parade
Down Constitution Avenue past many of the historic monuments on the Mall. Followed at 4pm by a variety of free entertainment at the Sylvan Theater on the Washington Monument grounds. FREE.

DC Free Jazz Festival
Freedom Plaza, 1300 Pennsylvania Avenue, NW. From 1pm. An annual happening downtown, with top national and international performers in concert.

National Symphony Concert
The Capitol, West Lawn. At 8pm the National Symphony performs a memorable concert, with guest artists. Bring a chair or blanket and a picnic. Come early to ensure a good place on the lawn. FREE.

Fireworks
Washington Monument grounds, 15th Street & Constitution Avenue, NW. Starts at 9:15pm and lasts for 20 minutes. It's quite a show. Bring a blanket or lawn chair.

July

Check the April, May, and June listings for ongoing summer events.

Bastille Day Waiters Race
Dominique's Restaurant, 20th Street & Pennsylvania Avenue, NW. 452-1132. July 14 from noon to 4pm. Approximately 100 waiters and waitresses (some chefs, too) carry trays with two splits of champagne and glasses from Dominique's to a block beyond the White House and back. Usually the prize is round-trip air fare and hotel expenses in Paris. FREE.

Civil War Life Reenactment
Sully Plantation, 3601 Sully Road (Route 28), near Dulles International Airport. Mid-July. Union and Confederate troop encampments; drills and skirmishes; music, dancing, and a tour of a 1794 historic home. For information, call (703) 759-5241. Admission.

Latin American Festival
At the National Mall on the Washington Monument grounds. Late July, for one week from 11am to 6:30pm. The cultural contributions of 40 Latin American countries are showcased in a lively offering of food, music, dance, and theater. For exact dates, call 966-5804 or 387-9830. FREE.

Twilight Tattoo Series
On the Ellipse, between the White House and the Washington Monument. Late July through August, every Wednesday at 7pm. The 3rd U.S. Infantry and the U.S. Army Band and Honor Guard present a re-creation of American military history from the Revolutionary War to WW II. Authentic costumes and historical music program. Bring a blanket. For information, call 696-3570. FREE.

Virginia Scottish Games
Episcopal High School Stadium & Fields, 3901 West Braddock Road, Alexandria, Va. Fourth weekend in July from 9am to 5pm. A two-day annual Celtic fair. One of the nation's largest Scottish country fairs with bagpipes, Highland dancers, national fiddling competitions, food, arts and crafts, activities. For information, call (703) 838-4200. Admission.

August

Check the May, June, and July listings for ongoing summer events.

1812 Overture
Sylvan Theater on the Washington Monument grounds. One evening in mid-August at 8pm. A patriotic concert performed by the U.S. Army Band assisted by the Salute Gun Platoon of the 3rd U.S. Infantry. For exact date, call (703) 696-3399. FREE.

Navy Band Lollipop Concert
Sylvan Theater at the Washington Monument. One evening in mid-August the U.S. Navy Band presents a special song-and-dance program geared to children of all ages. Shriner clowns give out lollipops. For exact date, call 433-2525.

Civil War Living History Day
Fort Ward Museum & Park, 4301 West Braddock Road, Alexandria, Va. One evening in mid-August. Reenactment of camp life, torchlight tours of Union and Confederate camps, artillery drills. Donations accepted. For exact date, call (703) 838-4848.

National Frisbee Festival
On the Mall. The last Saturday in August from noon to 5pm. Sponsored by the Smithsonian. The largest noncompetitive Frisbee event in the world, attracting as many as 12,000 people. Demonstrations by world-class champs (includ-

ing dogs). Workshops for people of all ages and abilities. For information, call (301) 645-5043. FREE.

Labor Day Weekend

The first Monday in September.
Annual International Children's Festival
Wolf Trap Farm Park, 1551 Trap Road, Vienna, Va. A gala three-day outdoor arts celebration for families. Activities include an array of performances and workshops of national and international groups, where children of all ages may express their creativity. For information, call (703) 642-0862. Admission.
Adams-Morgan Day Festival
In Adams-Morgan, 18th Street & Columbia Road, NW. Sunday of Labor Day weekend from noon to 10pm. An exuberant urban festival celebrating the cultural diversity of this neighborhood. International crafts, wares, and food; music, theater, and dance; an art show and children's carnival. For information, call 332-3292. FREE.
National Symphony Concert
U.S. Capitol, West Lawn. Sunday of Labor Day weekend at 8pm (rain date is Labor Day). Special program performed by the National Symphony Orchestra (it's their last outdoor concert of the season) and a variety of guest performers. Bring a chair or blanket and a picnic. Come early to ensure a good place on the lawn. For information, call 619-7222 or 416-8100. FREE.
Annual Maryland Renaissance Festival
Symphony Woods, adjacent to the Merriweather Post Pavilion, Columbia, Md. Beginning Labor Day weekend for six consecutive weekends from 10am to 6pm. Re-creation of a 16th-century autumn fair for all ages. Complete with entertainment: jugglers, minstrels, magicians, approximately 100 artisans, jousting, and fencing. Food and games including a "human" chess game. The public is encouraged to participate and come in costume. Admission; discount for seniors; ages 5 to 12 discount in advance; under age 5 free. For more information, call (301) 267-6118.

September

Check the May, June, July, and August listings for ongoing events. The Washington Redskins football season begins at RFK Stadium, 546-2222.
National Symphony
Kennedy Center for the Performing Arts, New Hampshire Avenue & Rock Creek Parkway, 254-3600. September to May, three to four concerts a week. Regular series of concerts with nationally known guest artists. Admission.
Constitution Day Commemoration
National Archives, Constitution Avenue at 8th Street, NW. On September 17, the anniversary of its signing, the Constitution of the United States is displayed in its entirety. Events of the day also include a naturalization ceremony, speakers,

and a band concert. For information, call 501 5215. FREE.
Elderfest
Freedom Plaza, 1300 Pennsylvania Avenue, NW. Mid-September. A week-long annual festival for older Americans culminates in a giant arts and crafts festival. For information, call 724-4091 FREE.
Saints Constantine and Helen Greek Orthodox Church Bazaar
4115 16th Street, NW. 829-2910. One weekend in mid-September. Greek food, crafts, and dancing at this festive and colorful fair. FREE.
Rock Creek Park Day
Visitors Information Center, 5000 Glover Road, NW. 426-6832. One day in late September from noon to dusk, festivities throughout the park in celebration of Washington's largest park, nearly 102 years young. International and national music, food, arts and crafts. Recreational and environmental activities, exhibits, and demonstrations. FREE.
Annual Tour of Homes in Old Town Alexandria
Old Town, Alexandria, Va. The last Saturday in September from 11am to 5pm. Tour approximately eight private homes of this historic part of town. All are decorated with beautiful period furnishings and most have lovely gardens to visit. Complimentary tea is served from 2:30 to 4pm. For the benefit of Alexandria Hospital. Tickets may be purchased in advance. For information, call (703) 838-4200.

October

The Smithsonian Performing Arts
October to May at various times and locations throughout the museum complex. The programs usually complement the museum—for example, the Renwick features romantic period-chamber music; the Hall of Musical Instruments has baroque concerts using some of the instruments on display. Also jazz, Big Band, gospel, pop, and ethnic. For information, call 357-2700. FREE. (Check other months for additional Smithsonian-sponsored special events.)
U.S. Army Band Fall Concerts
Bruckner Hall, Fort Myer, Arlington, Va. Every Tuesday and Thursday in October and November at 8pm. The band featuring ensembles and soloists. For information, call (703) 696-3399. FREE.
National Gallery Orchestra
National Gallery of Art, 6th Street & Constitution Avenue, NW, West Gardon Court of the West Building. 842-6941. From October through June, every Sunday at 7pm. One-hour classical concerts with symphony orchestra and guest artists. Passes are required; they are distributed beginning at 4pm on the main floor of the West Building. FREE.
Decorators' Show Houses
The month of October. Tour a Washington-area residence that has been redecorated by local

interior designers and is featured as a showcase home for one week. Proceeds benefit the National Symphony Orchestra. For information, call 416-8100. Admission.

American Discoveries Festival
Freedom Plaza, 1300 Pennsylvania Avenue, NW. The second Saturday in October. An annual festival of discovery highlighting the unique music and food of a different American city each year. For details, call 783- 0360. FREE.

Fall DC Antiques Fair
DC Armory, 2001 East Capitol Street. Mid-October for three days. More than 185 dealers from 20 states, Canada, and Europe offer centuries of goods for sale. For information, call (301) 738-1966 or, during the show, 547-9215. Admission.

Columbus Day Ceremonies
Columbus Memorial Plaza, Union Station, Massachusetts & Delaware Avenues, NE. On October 12, the Knights of Columbus conduct this traditional tribute to the discoverer of America. Speeches, music, and a wreath laying. For details, call 619-7222.

U.S. Navy Birthday Concert
DAR Constitution Hall, 18th & D Streets, NW. Mid-October. The birthday salute of the U.S. Navy Band, founded 217 years ago. The concert features entertainment for the whole family. Tickets must be picked up before the event. For information, call 433-2525. FREE.

White House Fall Garden Tours
Enter at East Gate on East Executive Avenue. One weekend in mid-October, Saturday and Sunday from 2 to 5pm. A self-guided tour of the splendid gardens and grounds of the president's house. In addition to the famed Rose Garden, fall foliage, and chrysanthemums. Music by a military band. For details, call 456-2200. FREE.

Washington International Horse Show
Capitol Centre, Largo, Md. Approximately one week in late October. One of the country's most important equestrian events. Begun in 1958, only the top 30 horses in the U.S. and Canada qualify to compete against the world's best. For information, call 840-0281; to charge tickets, call 432-0200.

Theodore Roosevelt Birthday Celebration
On Roosevelt Island in the Potomac (reached only via car; [00ab] mile north along the George Washington Memorial Parkway from downtown DC). Last weekend in October. Festivities on a lovely island named in honor of the naturalist president. For details, call (703) 285-2702. (*See also* PARKS & GARDENS, Nature Trails & Wildlife Preserves.)

November

The Washington Bullets begin their basketball season; (301) 350-3400. *See October listing for ongoing events.*

U.S. Army Band Fall Concerts
See October.

Marine Corps Marathon of the Monuments
Start: Iwo Jima Marine Corps Memorial, Arlington National Cemetery & U.S. Route 50, Arlington, Va. First Sunday in November at 9am. Anyone over 10 years of age can participate in this 26-mile, 385-yard marathon. The annual event attracts world-class runners; the course wends its way through Arlington and DC, passing all the national monuments on the way (hence the name). Over 50 awards, including oldest finisher, youngest, etc. Registration and entry fee in advance. For information, call (703) 690-3431.

U.S. Botanic Garden
At the foot of Capitol Hill, 1st Street & Maryland Avenue, SW. 225-8333. In November, one of four seasonal shows. The chrysanthemums are especially pretty. *OPEN 7 days 9am-5pm.* FREE. (*See also* PARKS & GARDENS, Gardens.)

Veteran's Day Ceremonies
At Arlington National Cemetery, Arlington, Va. (703) 695-1622. November 11 at 11am. A solemn ceremony honors the nation's war dead. A presidential wreath is laid on the Tomb of the Unknowns, often by the president himself. There is a service at the Memorial Amphitheatre. The U.S. Army Band plays a special program (usually lasts one hour). Ceremonies also at the Vietnam Veterans Memorial. For information, call 619-7222. FREE.

December

Choirs & Carols at Wolf Trap
Wolf Trap Farm Park, 1551 Trap Road, Vienna, Va. (703) 255-1934. One day in early December, usually a Sunday. An outdoor program featuring performances by local choirs and the U.S. Marine Band plus a candlelight procession. Dress warm, bring a bell, and participate in the caroling. FREE.

Scottish Christmas Walk
Old Town, Alexandria, Va. First Saturday in December at 10am. The annual parade starts at South St. Asaph Street and goes to Market Square. Under the patronage of the British ambassador; clan chieftains, bagpipe bands, Highland dancers all salute Alexandria's Scottish founders. Special events take place all over Old Town till 4pm. Antiques, food, arts and crafts, children's activities, and historic-house tours. Food and crafts sales continue through Sunday from 9am to 6pm. For information, call (703) 838-4200. FREE.

An American Holiday Celebration
DAR Constitution Hall, 18th & D Streets, NW. Two evenings in early December the U.S. Army Band presents a holiday show featuring seasonal music. Free tickets are available by mail; write to An American Holiday Celebration, P.O. Box 24074, Washington, DC 20024. Or call 692-7219. FREE.

Christmas Tree Lighting Ceremony
Market Square, 301 King Street, Old Town, Alexandria, Va. Second Monday in December at 7pm. The mayor lights the Christmas tree. Car-

olers and a visit from Santa. Bring a candle. For details, call (703) 838-4000. FREE.

Old Town Christmas Candlelight Tour
Alexandria, Va. A Friday and Saturday in mid-December from 7 to 9:30pm. Tour historic 18th- and 19th-century homes such as Ramsay House, Gadsby's Tavern Museum, the boyhood home of Robert E. Lee, the Lee-Fendall House, and the Carlyle House. Included in the tour: storytelling, music, colonial dancing, period decorations, and light refreshments. For information, call (703) 838-4200. Admission.

Nutcracker Suite
George Washington University, Lisner Auditorium, 730 21st Street, NW. 362-3606. Mid- to late December. Performances by the Washington Ballet of Tchaikovsky's Christmas gift to us all. Tickets may be purchased in advance.

People's Christmas Tree Lighting
At the west side of the U.S. Capitol. Beginning at 6pm, the second Wednesday in December, the day before the National Christmas Tree is lighted, the so-called people's tree is lighted accompanied by performances of military bands. For information, call 224-3069.

Pageant of Peace
Mid-December to January 1. On the Ellipse. The pageant starts with the lighting of the giant National Christmas Tree by the president; usually on a Thursday, two weeks before Christmas, at 5:30pm. On the Ellipse and the Mall grounds from then until New Year's are choral performances, caroling, and seasonal music nightly from 6 to 9pm. For information, call 426-6690. FREE.

"A Christmas Carol"
Ford's Theater, 511 10th Street, NW. 347-4833. Mid- to late December. Charles Dickens's holiday classic perfectly set in historic Ford's. Tickets may be purchased in advance.

U.S. Botanic Garden
At the foot of Capitol Hill, 1st Street & Maryland Avenue, SW. 225-8333. Third week in December to early January. To help dress up the Christmas season, the annual colorful display of red and white poinsettias amid a holiday display of wreaths and a 25-foot Christmas tree. *OPEN 7 days 9am-5pm. CLOSED Christmas Day.* FREE. (*See also* PARKS & GARDENS, Gardens.)

Kwanzaa Celebration
Late December. The traditional African-American celebration of the harvest. For information on events commemorating this holiday, call the Anacostia Museum, 287-3369.

Washington National Cathedral Christmas Celebration
Washington Cathedral, Mount St. Alban, Wisconsin Avenue & Woodley Road, NW. 537-6200. December 24 at 4pm, Christmas carols and seasonal choral performances at this magnificent edifice. At 10pm there is a special service. FREE.

White House Christmas Candlelight Tour
Enter at the East Gate on East Executive Avenue. 456-2200. For three evenings just after Christmas from 6 to 8pm. A self-guided tour of a candlelit White House. Military band plays holiday music in the Grand Foyer. Check well in advance for details and plan to queue up early. FREE.

New Year's Eve Celebration at the Old Post Office
The Old Post Office Building, 1100 Pennsylvania Avenue, NW. 289-4224. December 31. The annual celebration at the Pavilion at the Old Post Office Building is the class bash in DC on New Year's Eve. Live entertainment; a giant (it weighs 1,000 pounds!) postage stamp with a "love" motif is lowered from the clock tower at the stroke of midnight. FREE.

HISTORIC
&
NEW
WASHINGTON

Treasury Department Building

HISTORIC BUILDINGS & AREAS

This list covers the Washington area's most historic buildings, monuments, and houses, as well as notable structures and districts.

NOTE: Historic sites open to the public under federal government auspices are subject to changes in budget allocations, which may alter days and times of access. Always call before visiting one unless you are in the vicinity. Metro stations are included for those places open to the public.

Anderson House
2118 Massachusetts Avenue, NW. 785-2040. (Little & Brown, 1900) An elaborate Dupont Circle Beaux Arts mansion with walled entry court, built for diplomat Larz Anderson. Now headquarters and Museum of the Society of Cincinnati (Anderson was a member), founded in 1783 by descendants of a group of Revolutionary War officers. The house retains original furnishings; the museum contains portraits, swords, firearms, documents, and uniforms. A reference library on the American Revolution is also available for use. There are delightful free concerts one Saturday a month at 2:30pm, followed by tea and coffee. Call in advance for special group tours. *OPEN Tues-Sat 1-4pm. CLOSED Sun, Mon & federal holidays, except Washington's birthday. FREE. Metro: Dupont Circle.*

Anderson Cottage
3700 North Capitol Street, NW. Built in 1843, the stuccoed cottage was used by Presidents Lincoln and Van Buren as a "summer White House." Now part of the Old Soldiers Home.

Arlington House (Custis-Lee Mansion)
Arlington National Cemetery, between Lee & Sherman Drives. (703) 557-0613. (George Washington Custis, 1819) Home of, and since 1955 permanent memorial to, Robert E. Lee, who left in 1861 to command the Confederate Army, never to return. Confiscated in 1864 from his widow for nonpayment of taxes, 200 acres of it were set aside for use as a National Cemetery. (*See also* Graveyards & Tombs: Arlington National Cemetery.) It was later restored to Lee's

son, who sold it to the government in 1883 for $150,000. The fine Greek Revival house contains furnishings original to the house and other period pieces. Self-guided tours only in the summer, but special group tours may be arranged in advance, October to March. In front of the mansion, the tomb of the capital city's original planner, Pierre L'Enfant. Gaze across the Potomac from here at what was described by Lafayette as the "finest view in the world," the view of L'Enfant's Washington. *OPEN Apr-Sept, 7 days 9:30am-6pm; Oct-Mar, 7 days 9:30am-4pm. CLOSED Christmas Day. FREE. Accessible via Tourmobile. Metro: Arlington Cemetery.*

Arts & Industries Building
900 Jefferson Drive, SW. 357-1300. (Cluss & Schulze, 1880) Originally the National Museum, it was built to house the contents of 21 freight cars from 30 countries that became Smithsonian property after the 1876 Philadelphia Centennial Exposition. Its exterior, polychrome brick, with trussed sheds and iron balconies, is a spirited Victorian celebration that complements the interior Victorian collections. (*See* MUSEUMS & GALLERIES, Museums.) *Metro: Smithsonian.*

Arts Club
2017 I Street, NW. 331-7282. (Timothy Caldwell, 1802-5) Where President James Monroe and his wife, Elizabeth, lived after his inauguration in 1817 until a refurbished White House (burned by the British in 1812) was completed. Since 1916, home to the Arts Club, which also annexed the house next door. Permanent display of 18th- and 19th-century art; also rotating exhibits of contemporary art. *OPEN Tues & Thurs 10am-5pm; Wed-Fri 2-5pm; Sat 10am-2pm; Sun 1-5pm. CLOSED Mon. Metro: Foggy Bottom, Farragut West.*

The Atheneum
201 Prince Street, Alexandria, Va. (703) 548-0035. Magnificent 1850 Greek Revival building, originally the Bank of the Old Dominion, then a house of worship. It now houses the Northern Virginia Fine Arts Association and contains an art reference library and a gallery for art exhibits— held from September to June. *OPEN Wed-Sat 11am-4pm; Sun from 1pm during exhibits. CLOSED Mon, Tues & July & Aug. Donation.*

Barracks Row
8th Street, SE, from Pennsylvania Avenue to the Southeast Freeway. This area of Capitol Hill is showing renewed signs of life. The name is derived from the presence, at I Street, of the Marine Corps Barracks.

"Bernard Baruch Bench of Inspiration"
Lafayette Park, between Pennsylvania Avenue & H Street, NW. Favorite bench of Bernard M. Baruch, millionaire, financier, philanthropist, and trusted adviser to Presidents Wilson, Harding, Coolidge, Hoover, Roosevelt, Truman, and Eisenhower. Commemorated by a stone and metal marker. (*See also* PARKS & Gardens, Parks.)

Joseph Beale House
2012 Massachusetts Avenue, NW. (Glenn Brown, 1898) Austere limestone and stucco mansion in the manner of 18th-century Italy. Elaborate interior; not open to the public.

Belmont House (Eastern Star Temple)
1618 New Hampshire Avenue, NW. (Sanson, Trumbauer, 1908) This well-situated triangular building in the Dupont Circle area reflects the Gallic influence of its French architect Ernest Sanson, imported for the task. In 1937 it was sold to the Order of the Eastern Star.

Blaine Mansion
2000 Massachusetts Avenue, NW. (John Fraser, 1881) A large imposing Victorian residence, one of the first in the Dupont Circle area. Built for three-time presidential candidate James G. Blaine.

Blair House
1651-53 Pennsylvania Avenue, NW. Two fine houses, the Blair, circa 1824, and the Lee, circa 1860, purchased by the government in 1942 for $175,000 to serve as our nation's guest house. Reportedly, it was Eleanor Roosevelt's idea to create a president's guest house, complaining that visitors like Winston Churchill were turning the White House into a hotel. Kings, presidents, and ambassadors have graced the premises and no less a personage than President Harry Truman lived here from 1948 to 1952 when the White House underwent desperately needed repairs. A plaque commemorates Leslie Coffelt, the guard killed in the attempted assassination of Truman on November 1, 1950. In 1988, Blair House reopened after a long-required $8 million restoration; an historically accurate wing was added as well. *Never open to the public.*

British Embassy
3100 Massachusetts Avenue, NW. 462-1340. (Sir Edward Luytens, 1930) A red-brick and stone slice of the Empire on Embassy Row. The statue of Churchill (William McVey, 1966) stands on soil brought from his birthplace in Blenheim, England, as well as some from his mother's birthplace in Brooklyn, New York.

Brown Spangler House
120 4th Street, SE. Post-Civil War town house (ca. 1867) restored 1968. A good example of Capitol Hill-area rejuvenation.

Cairo Hotel
1615 Q Street, NW. (Thomas Franklin Schneider, 1894) Dupont Circle area. Early steel-frame residential high rise. Moorish details include carved elephants. Its shocking 165 feet resulted in strict height regulations (1910) for the District. Went condo in 1979.

The Capitol
Capitol Hill, east end of the Mall. 224-3121. L'Enfant felt the location, 88 feet above the Potomac, was "a pedestal waiting for a monument. . . ." A monument, according to Thomas Jefferson, "dedicated to the sovereignty of the people. . . ." In 1792 a design competition was held and a Dr. William Thornton won the $500 prize, and on September 18, 1793, George Washington laid the cornerstone. With the North Wing completed, Congress met for the first time in Washington in November 1800. By 1807 the South Wing was completed, but in 1814 the British put a torch to the Capitol. Restoration followed, and a wooden dome was added in 1827. In 1857 the Senate and House extensions were completed. In 1865 a double-shelled dome of cast iron was completed, and the statue *Freedom* was fittingly placed atop. It is the tallest building in DC. (*See also* SIGHTSEEING, On Your Own: The Capitol *and* The Capitol Subway, *and* RESTAURANTS, Cafeterias: The Senate Cafeteria.) *Metro: Capitol South, Union Station.*

Capitol Gatehouse
The Ellipse, Constitution Avenue at 15th Street, NW. (Charles Bulfinch, 1828) Originally on Capitol Hill; on its present site since 1880. Note the two high-water marks, dated 1877 and 1881.

The Capitol (Spring) Grotto
Capitol Grounds, northwest of the Capitol. (Frederick Law Olmsted, 1874-75) This lovely structure was built as part of the original Capitol Hill landscaping; it carried spring water. Designed by one of the creator's of New York's Central Park, it's now a municipal water facility. *Metro: Union Station, Capitol South.*

Capitol Hill Area
Immediately east of the Capitol Building, it was the direction in which the city was expected to grow. Well, that it has at present it's one of Washington's most active areas of residential restoration. The area boasts a wide variety of architectural styles. East Capitol Street is the area's main thoroughfare. (*See also* Eastern Market.)

Lafayette Square

Carlyle House
121 North Fairfax Street, Alexandria, Va. (703) 549-2997. (John Carlyle, 1752) Architecturally grand mansion built by Scottish merchant Carlyle, restored in 1976. Historically significant as the site of a meeting on April 15, 1775, between General Braddock and five Royal colonial governors in an effort to find a means "to compel the colonists to pay" for the French and Indian War. The result was the Stamp Act, fuel for the coming American Revolution. Tours by reservation. *OPEN Tues-Sat 10am-5pm; Sun noon-5pm. CLOSED Mon.* Admission.

Cedar Hill
See Frederick Douglass House.

Chamber of Commerce Building
1615 H Street, NW. (Cass Gilbert, 1925) Neoclassical building planned to further unify the architectural style of Lafayette Square.

Chesapeake and Ohio (C&O) Canal
In Georgetown, near 30th & M Streets, NW. Construction began on July 4, 1828, when John Quincy Adams turned the first spade of dirt. Not finished until 1850, it consisted of 184.5 miles of waterway with 74 lift locks, 11 stone aqueducts, 7 dams, hundreds of culverts, and a 3,117-foot tunnel, providing a safe, albeit slow, form of transport for coal, grains, lumber, food stuffs. Unfortunately, the construction of the B&O Railroad, completed in 1842, soon rendered the canal obsolete, though it continued to operate until 1924. Mule-drawn barges (*see* SIGHTSEEING, On Your Own) and innumerable opportunities for outdoor activities (*see* SPORTS, Boating *and* Fishing) keep the canal and towpath alive and well used. In 1979 it was declared a National Park (*see* PARKS & GARDENS, Nature Trails & Wildlife Preserves; *also* ANNUAL EVENTS, April).

Chinatown Friendship Archway
7th & H Streets, NW. Gateway to DC's eight-block Chinatown neighborhood, bounded by H, I, 6th to 11th streets. The colorful red, green, blue, and gold structure boasts 7,000 tile and 272 painted dragons in the Ming and Qing dynasties style. It's especially colorful at the Chinese New Year's celebration (*see* ANNUAL EVENTS, February). *Metro: Galley Place.*

City Tavern
3206 M Street, NW. Built in 1796, some of the original parts of the tavern are intact. Restored in 1961, it's now a private club.

Connecticut Avenue Apartments
2101 Connecticut Avenue, NW. When luxury apartment buildings became the rage along the avenue, this one—built in 1928—was one of the most luxurious, with seven-room apartments being the minimum.

Constitution Hall
1778 D Street, NW. (John Russell Pope, 1930) Small concert hall, whose acoustics were praised by Toscanini, once home to the National Symphony (now at Kennedy Center). Still a desirable concert venue, check the current papers for roster. Contains a Revolutionary Period Mu-

Capitol Gatehouse

seum run by the DAR (*See* MUSEUMS & GALLERIES, Museums: DAR Museum.) *Metro: Farragut West, Farragut North.*

Cooke's Row
3007-29 Q Street, NW. (Starkweather & Plowman, 1868) A charming Victorian row in predominantly Georgian Georgetown.

Cosmos Club (Townsend House)
2121 Massachusetts Avenue, NW. (Carrere & Hastings, 1900) Constructed for Mrs. Townsend, a railway tycoon's wife. It was said that because she was superstitious about new houses, she had hers built around another building's shell. Now home to a prestigious private club, which finally deigned to accept women in 1988.

Cox Row
3327-39 N Street, NW. (Col. John Cox, 1817) Though some of the five houses have been altered, a still-fine row of federal-style houses, set back from the street. Built by the man who became Georgetown's first mayor in 1823.

Dr. James Craik House
210 Duke Street, Alexandria, Va. Built circa 1790, its owner, a respected physician, was referred to in George Washington's will as "my compatriot in arms and old and intimate friend."

Custis-Lee Mansion
See Arlington House.

Decatur House
748 Jackson Place, NW. 842-0920. (Benjamin Latrobe, 1818) Federal-style town house facing Lafayette Square, where Commodore Stephen Decatur, a hero of the War of 1812, famed foe of the Barbary pirates, lived for 14 months until his death in a duel. Restored in the 1940s, the house contains period furnishings. Now part of the National Trust for Historic Preservation. Tours every half hour until 3:30pm. Group tours by reservation only. The Trust has a fine bookstore, Preservation Shop, at 1600 H Street. (*See also* SHOPPING, Specialty, Books: Special Interest.) *OPEN Tues-Sat 10am-2pm; Sun noon-4pm. CLOSED Mon, Thanksgiving, Christmas & New Year's Day.* Admission. *Metro: Farragut West.*

Denman-Hinckley House
1623 16th Street, NW. (Fuller & Wheeler, 1886)

Fine Romanesque Revival residence, built for Judge H. P. Denman.

Department of Agriculture

14th Street & Independence Avenue, SW. (Ranking, Kellogg & Crane, 1905) Begun in 1905, this building covers three city blocks. It was not completed until 1930.

Department of Commerce

14th Street between E Street & Constitution Avenue, NW. (York & Sawyer, 1932) In the Federal Triangle, housed in the Herbert Clark Hoover Building, covering an 8-acre area. When first built it was the world's largest office building within are 4,500 civil servants. In the main lobby there's a Census Clock that records the U.S. population. Groups can arrange a visit, call 377-5754. In the lower lobby is the National Aquarium (*see* PARKS & GARDENS, Zoos & Aquariums). *Metro: Federal Triangle.*

Department of Justice Building

10th Street & Constitution Avenue, NW. (Zantzinger, Borie & Medary, 1934) The office of attorney general was created in 1789; the Department of Justice in 1870. This building, filling the entire block between 9th and 10th streets, became the first permanent home for both. The FBI was here, too, until it moved to its ugly home on Pennsylvania Avenue in 1974.

Devore House

2000 24th Street, NW. (William L. Bottomly, 1931) Richly detailed limestone Louis XV-styled mansion in Kalorama area.

District (of Columbia) Building

Pennsylvania Avenue at 14th Street, NW. (Cope and Stewardson, 1908) Beaux Arts classicism, the first of its kind to be built in the Federal Triangle, to the dismay of many. On the facade, 28 8-foot-tall allegorical figures. It's the District's seat of government. *Metro: Federal Triangle.*

DC Courthouse (Old City Hall)

4th & D Streets, NW. (George Hadfield, 1820-49) Early Greek Revival; the first of the District of Columbia's government buildings. Used as a hospital during the Civil War, now the Data Processing Division of the DC Supreme Court. In front, Washington's first Lincoln memorial.

Dougal House

3259 R Street, NW. (Adams & Haskins, 1854) Lovely Victorian house in Georgetown built for artist and engraver William H. Dougal.

Frederick Douglass House (Cedar Hill)

1411 W Street, SE. 426-5961. Built circa 1856, overlooking the Anacostia River, this simple white Victorian house, the residence of ex-slave and famed abolitionist, editor, and orator Frederick Douglass in his later years, 1877-95, is now a National Historic Site. The building and much of its original furnishings have been fully restored; it's well worth a visit. There's a 30-minute film at the Visitors Center depicting Douglass's life; a half-hour tour by a costumed guide follows. From here there's a lovely view of DC. *OPEN Apr-Oct, 7 days 9am-5pm; Nov-Mar, 7 days 9am-4pm. CLOSED Christmas Day.* Donation. Accessible via Tourmobile.

Frederick Douglass Town House

316 A Street, NE. The first Washington residence (1871-77) of the famed abolitionist and editor Frederick Douglass. (*See* Frederick Douglass House.)

Dumbarton House

2715 Q Street, NW. 337-2288. Large late-Georgian-style house, one of Georgetown's oldest. Built circa 1800 (remodeled by Benjamin Latrobe, 1905), it was moved to its present site in 1915. Home to the National Society of Colonial Dames of America, it is furnished with exquisite federal-period furnishings, silver, and china. *OPEN Mon-Sat 9:30am-12:30pm. FREE;* contributions appreciated.

Dumbarton Oaks

1703 32nd Street, NW. 338-8278 (recorded information); 342-3200. The house, acquired by Mr. and Mrs. Robert Woods Bliss in 1920, the beautiful gardens (*see* PARKS & GARDENS, Gardens), and their extensive library and art collections (*see* MUSEUMS & GALLERIES, Museums) were given to Harvard University in 1940. The original federal-style house (ca. 1800) has been much altered. In 1944 the music room was the site of two international meetings, now referred to as the "Dumbarton Oaks Conference," which resulted in the agreement of principles incorporated into the Charter of the United Nations. The pre-Columbian museum is in a lovely contemporary (1963) building by famed architect Philip Johnson. Art Collection *OPEN Tues-Sun 2-5pm. CLOSED Mon.* Garden *OPEN Apr-Oct, 7 days 2-6pm; Nov-Mar, 7 days 2-5pm. CLOSED federal holidays and in inclement weather.*

Dupont Circle

N Street, NW from 15th Street to Florida Avenue, north to R Street, east on R to 15th Street, south on 15th to N Street. The elite (and westernmost) residential area of the city at the turn of the century, it was filled with Victorian mansions, many of which are gone. The area once called Millionaires Row is now basically Embassy Row. A young and diverse group of professionals are leading the area's restoration movement. Architecturally and socially interesting.

Eastern Market

7th & C Streets, SE. (Adolph Cluss, 1871) A bustling focal point of the Capitol Hill community, it's the last remaining of the brick city markets. Vendors outside purvey fresh produce and flowers. Inside are meat, fish, cheese, bread, and what have been rated as DC's very best crab cakes. In all, an old-fashioned, colorful, and aromatic treat. Best time to go: early Saturday morning. (*See also* RESTAURANTS, Breakfast/Brunch: Market Lunch.) On Sunday the market itself is closed, but antique, "junque," and crafts vendors do business outside. *OPEN Tues-Thurs 7:30am-6pm; Fri 6am-7pm; Sat 6am-6pm. CLOSED Sun & Mon. Metro: Eastern Market.*

Ecuadorian Embassy

2535 15th Street, NW. 234-7200. (George Oakley Totten, 1922) Prompted by Mrs. John B.

Henderson, Totten designed residences here in hopes of developing the Meridian Hill area for embassies.

The Ellipse

15th to 17th Streets, NW (E Street to Constitution Avenue). Between the White House and the Washington Monument. Technically President's Park South, the 54 acres, originally swampland, were fenced in and used as corrals during the Civil War. The scene of much of the Vietnam protest in the 1960s and early 1970s. Setting for the National Christmas Tree, ceremoniously lit by the president each year. (See ANNUAL EVENTS, December.)

Embassy Row

Massachusetts Avenue from Dupont Circle to Wisconsin Avenue, NW. The diplomatic missions of approximately 150 foreign governments are located in DC. Most of them are concentrated on residential streets, in lovely old mansions, though the Canadian government may have started a trend with the building of a new chancery on Pennsylvania Avenue. (See also ANNUAL EVENTS, May: Goodwill Industries Embassy Tour.)

Evermay

1623 28th Street, NW. (Nicholas King, 1801) Magnificent Georgetown residence and garden overlooking Rock Creek Park.

Federal Reserve Building

C Street between 20th & 21st Streets, NW. 452-3000. (Paul Cret, 1937) Home of America's central bank, by the architect of the Folger Library. FDR dedicated the building in 1937. The Arcadia conference—concerning decisions to help end WW II—was held here, December 1941 to January 1942. From the first to second floors is the Monumental Staircase, constructed of marble from Italy, Belgium, France, and Spain. Public guided tours lasting approximately one hour, Thursday only at 2:30pm, and guided group tours by appointment only (452-3149) on the architecture of the building include a 20-minute film "The Fed—Our Central Bank" and the boardroom. Rotating art exhibits in the lobby gallery. Building OPEN Mon-Fri 8am-7pm. CLOSED Sat & Sun. Gallery OPEN Tues-Fri 11:30am-2pm. Metro: Foggy Bottom.

Federal Trade Commission

Constitution Avenue & 6th Street, NW. (Bennet, Parsons, Frost, 1937) At the apex of the Federal Triangle. Elements of Art Deco styling predominate on the building's facade.

Federal Triangle

Between Pennsylvania Avenue, NW, and the Mall, from 4th to 15th Streets. Covering three-quarters of a mile, a planned area of huge buildings to house the offices of the federal government, built 1928-31. Consists of the Federal Trade Commission, the National Archives, the Department of Justice, the IRS, the Interstate Commerce Commission, the Department of Labor, the Post Office Department, the Department of Commerce. Construction began in 1991 on an 11-acre tract within the triangle that has been a

parking lot for 70 years. The building, which will contain a Cultural and Trade Center, will be the second-largest federal structure (the Pentagon is the largest) when completed in 1995. The nine-story L-shaped building will have an 800-by-500-foot "footprint."

Folger Shakespeare Library

See MUSEUMS & GALLERIES, Museums.

Ford's Theater

511 10th Street, NW. 426-6924. (James J. Gifford, 1863. Restored 1968: Macomber & Peter; William Haussman) The theater where, at 10:15pm on the evening of April 14, 1865, President Abraham Lincoln, attending a gala performance of Our American Cousin, was mortally wounded by John Wilkes Booth. Ford's was not used as a theater again until, accurately restored, it was reopened in 1968, once more presenting live entertainment. In the basement a Museum of Lincolniana (426-6927), including objects associated with his early years, his public career, and the presidential years. Also the clothes he wore that fateful night, the pistol that ended his life, and the flag that draped his coffin. (See also House Where Lincoln Died.) Museum OPEN 7 days 9am-5pm. Theater CLOSED Thurs noon-3:30pm & Sun 2-5pm for matinee performances. NOTE: Sometimes closed during the day due to rehearsals. Admission. Metro: Gallery Place, Metro Center.

Forrest-Marbury House

3350 M Street, NW. House of Col. Uriah Forrest. Site of a dinner party, March 29, 1791, for George Washington and the local landowners whose property would become the new federal city. The house later belonged to William Marbury of the famous Marbury vs. Madison Supreme Court case.

Fort De Russey

Rock Creek Park, Oregon & Military Roads, NW. Part of the city's Civil War defense system. Lincoln was brought here at one point when it was feared the Confederates would overrun the capital.

Fort McNair

L'Enfant Plaza, 4th & P Streets, SW. Established in 1794 as the Washington Arsenal, it's America's oldest active military post. Beautifully sited on Greenleaf Point, a mile-long peninsula at the junction of the Washington Channel and the Anacostia River, it figured in L'Enfant's first plan of the city. The original buildings were destroyed by the British in 1814. It was the site of the first U.S. penitentiary in 1826 and where the trial and execution of four of the conspirators to the Lincoln assassination took place. The red-brick Beaux Arts-styled **Army War College**, built in 1908 (now the National Defense University), is a focal point of the McKim, Mead & White architectural plan for the fort. Buildings not open to the general public. Grounds accessible 7 days dawn to dusk (ID must be presented upon entry).

Fort Myer

Arlington Boulevard & Pershing Drive, Arlington, Va. (703) 545-6700. Home base of the U.S. Army's oldest active infantry company, the 3rd U.S. Infantry. Famed as a ceremonial unit, they are the traditional guard of the Tomb of the Unknowns (formerly Tomb of the Unknown Soldier) (see also Graveyards & Tombs: Arlington National Cemetery; John F. Kennedy grave; Robert F. Kennedy grave; L'Enfant's grave; and Tomb of the Unknowns). Some of the fort's buildings are over 100 years old.

Fort Ward Park
4301 West Braddock Road, Alexandria, Va. (703) 838-4847; museum (703) 838-4848. Work on Fort Ward began September 1, 1861. It was the fifth largest fort in a chain of defense of 68 that surrounded Washington during the Civil War. It had 36 guns and 5 bastions—the northwestern one has been restored; authentic replica guns have been mounted. A replica Officer's Hut and a museum were also constructed, the latter containing an impressive collection of Civil War memorabilia. The historic 40-acre park also has picnic facilities, and during the summer months, reenactments of Civil War battles take place. Museum OPEN Tues-Sat 9am-5pm; Sun noon-5pm. CLOSED Mon, Thanksgiving & Christmas Day. Park OPEN 7 days 9am-sundown. FREE.

Foxhall House
2908 N Street, NW. (Henry Foxall, ca. 1820) Small, charming, wall-enclosed house built by prosperous Georgetown foundry owner.

Gadsby's Tavern Museum
134 North Royal Street, Alexandria, Va. (703) 838-4242. Once described as the finest public house in America; George Washington often wined and dined here, not to mention John Adams, Thomas Jefferson, and James Madison. Its two buildings, City Tavern (built before the Revolution) and City Hotel (1792), are Georgian architectural standouts. Restored in 1976, it is still an authentic colonial tavern as well as a museum of authentic furnishings and memorabilia. Half-hour tours are given on the quarter hour; also special group tours by reservation. Washington birthnight balls, begun in his time, still take place (see also ANNUAL EVENTS, February). OPEN Tues-Sat 10am-5pm; Sun 1-5pm. CLOSED Mon & Thanksgiving, Christmas & New Year's Day. Admission.

Gallaudet University
7th Street & Florida Avenue, NE. 651-5050; TDD 651-5104. Educational facilities for the deaf; founded as the National Deaf Mute College. Renamed in 1894 for the pioneer educator of the deaf, Thomas Hopkins Gallaudet. The original Victorian Gothic buildings (Vaux & Withers, ca. 1857) on grounds laid out by Frederick Law Olmsted, landscape designer of New York's Central Park. Call the Visitors Center in advance for guided tours. OPEN Mon-Fri 8:30am-5pm. CLOSED Sat & Sun. Metro: Union Station, Rhode Island Avenue.

Georgetown
West of Rock Creek Park in NW, to the Potomac River. By the time the capital was founded,

The Capitol (Spring) Grotto

Georgetown was already a flourishing port. Established in 1751 and named in honor of King George II, it was originally to consist of 60 acres of land to be divided into 80 lots. Its growth is attributed to the designation of a local warehouse as the official point of tobacco inspection. Though the port city officially became part of Washington in the 1890s, residents persist in a form of separatism, as evidenced by the nonexistence of Metro within its boundaries. Of two natures: One boasts historic houses on charming, lushly planted side streets, the other offers an astounding number of trendy and/or tacky boutiques and restaurants; the crossroads of its main streets M and Wisconsin bustles day and night.

Georgetown Market House
3276 M Street, NW. Built in 1865 on property deeded to the city in 1795 for use as a public market "forever, and for no other use, interest or purpose whatsoever." It is slated to become part of the expansion of Georgetown Park, the upscale Victorian-style shopping mall.

Georgetown Park
3222 M Street, NW (entrance also on Wisconsin Avenue, NW). 342-8180. Behind the reconstructed facades of century-old commercial warehouses is an impressive $100 million Victorian-style shopping mall with more than 100 shops. The block-long skylit roof and the interior garden indeed give this mecca for upscale shopping a parklike aura. Classical concerts daily and it's oh so special at Christmas. OPEN Mon-Fri 10am-9pm; Sat 10am-7pm; Sun noon-6pm.

Georgetown Post Office
1215 31st Street, NW. (Ammi B. Young, 1857) Built as the Port of Georgetown's Custom House, it resembles an Italian palazzo. The lobby has been extensively renovated to accommodate the post office, but if you look beyond the counters you can see seven of the original pillars. OPEN Mon-Fri 8am-5:30pm; Sat 8:30am-12:30pm. CLOSED Sun.

Government Printing Office
710 North Capitol Street, NW. 275-2091. This massive structure houses the world's largest publisher—the U.S. government. The bookstore, with a stock of over 3,000 titles, offers opportunities to buy perennial best-sellers, such as the Recorded Presidential Conversations of Richard Nixon, as well as helpful books on infant care,

diet, exercise, cooking, medicine, and more. Bookstore *OPEN Mon-Fri 8am-4pm. CLOSED Sat & Sun. Metro: Union Station.*

Gunston Hall
10709 Gunston Road (Route 1), Lorton, Va. (703) 550-9220. (William Buckland, 1758) Set above the Potomac, 20 miles from DC, is the home of George Mason, whose Virginia Declaration of Rights was the basis of the federal Bill of Rights. The house and grounds remain virtually unchanged from the days when Washington and Jefferson came to call. All furnishings are original, predating 1792, and many were Mason family pieces. The lovely gardens contain colonial-era plants only, and the English boxwood allé is the one Mason himself planted. George and his wife, Ann, are buried in the family graveyard. Barn Wharf Nature Trail, picnic tables; gift shop. Special events at various times during the year. A 17-minute orientation film precedes public guided tours given every 30 minutes. Group rates and special tours by appointment. (*See also* KIDS' WASHINGTON, Museums for Children.) *OPEN 7 days 9:30am-5pm.* Admission.

John Stoddert Haw House
2808 N Street, NW. Fine federal-period house with lovely garden.

Christian Heurich Mansion
1307 New Hampshire Avenue, NW. 785-2068. (John Granville Meyers, 1892) This turreted 31-room red-brick Victorian mansion built for immigrant German businessman and brewer Christian Heurich was the city's first fireproof residence, and the first single-family home constructed with poured concrete. The Gilded Age interior—huge marble fireplaces, stenciled walls, and mahogany woodwork—and its opulent furnishings are worth a visit. There is also a lovely garden. The library's documents, books, photos, and journals give insight into the social history of Washington. Headquarters of the Columbia Historical Society (*see also* MUSEUMS & GALLERIES, Museums). Tours for a fee. Mansion *OPEN Wed, Fri & Sat noon-4pm.* Library *OPEN Wed, Fri & Sat 10am-4pm. Metro: Dupont Circle.*

The Highlands
3825 Wisconsin Avenue, NW. (Joseph Nourse, 1817) An early 19th-century fieldstone house, one of the few remaining in Washington. Nourse built it for his son Charles and wife as a wedding present to them. Added to in 1926. Unfortunately no efforts were made to preserve the exterior. It's now the Sidwell Friends School Administration building and is not open to the public.

Hillwood Mansion
4155 Linnean Avenue, NW. 686-5807. This red-brick mansion built in 1926 was home to Mrs. Marjorie Merriweather Post, the breakfast cereal heiress, from 1955 till her death in 1973. Its 40 rooms are a veritable museum of 18th- and 19th-century Russian and French decorative arts, in a dazzling yet elegant setting. The house and gardens of this 25-acre estate provide a rare glimpse of an affluent, opulent way of life. *Two-hour individual and group tours of the house and gardens (only between 11am-3pm) by appointment only, Tues-Sat 9 & 10:30am, noon, 1:30 & 3pm (group maximum 25 people).* No children under age 12 or pets. Cafe for light fare and afternoon tea. Admission. *Metro: Van Ness.* (*See also* PARKS & GARDENS, Gardens.)

House Where Lincoln Died (Petersen House)
516 10th Street, NW. 426-6830. The house, belonging to a Swedish tailor, to which President Lincoln was carried after being shot at Ford's Theater across the street. He lingered the night and passed away at 7:22am on April 15, 1865, in a small first-floor bedroom the Petersens normally rented to lodgers. Restored in 1932. Self-guided tours. (*See also* Ford's Theater.) *OPEN 7 days 9am-5pm. CLOSED Christmas Day.* FREE. *Metro: Gallery Place, Metro Center.*

Howard Hall
607 Howard Place at Georgia Avenue, NW. Home of one of the founders of Howard University, Gen. Oliver O. Howard. Built in 1867, at the same time the first classes were held in the first university building (unfortunately it no longer stands). Now being used as one of the university's offices.

Howard Theater
620 T Street, NW. Opened in 1910. This theater, now a national historic landmark, provided a welcoming stage for black artists when segregation set up barriers they were unable to cross. Its amateur night contests were won by, among others, the then-unknown Ella Fitzgerald and Billy Eckstein; the Supremes debuted here. Sadly, it's been dark since 1970.

Howard University
2400 6th Street, NW. 806-6100. Founded by head of the Freedman's Bureau, Gen. Oliver Howard, in 1867 as an institution of learning open to all, including freed slaves. Now covering over 75 acres, it is a dominant presence in the

Capitol Lamppost

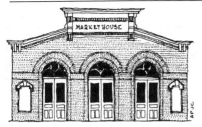

Georgetown Market House

black residential Le Droit Park area in which it is located. For a tour of the university, call 806-2900.

Inter-American Defense Board
2600 16th Street, NW. (George Oakley Totten, 1906) For obvious reasons, nicknamed the Pink Palace. All this Venetian Gothic palazzo needs is a Grand Canal.

Internal Revenue Service Building
1111 Constitution Avenue, NW. (Supervising Architect of the Treasury, 1930) Part of the Federal Triangle, limestone and granite with columns of Tennessee marble. Landscaped interior courtyards.

Interstate Commerce Commission
12th Street & Constitution Avenue, NW. (Arthur Brown, 1935) Part of the Federal Triangle. Established to regulate railroads and other carriers engaged in interstate or foreign commerce. The main entrance is rich in Art Deco architectural details.

Embassy of Iraq
1801 P Street, NW. 745-0803. (Hornblower & Marshall, 1893) Once the Boardman House; outstanding Romanesque Revival mansion.

Japanese Lantern
West Potomac Park, Independence Avenue & West Basin Drive. Carved in the 17th century, the lantern was a gift from Tokyo's governor in 1954. Located nearby, two of the original Japanese cherry trees planted in 1912. The lighting of the lantern marks the beginning of the Cherry Blossom Festival. (*See also* ANNUAL EVENTS, Late March.)

Jefferson Memorial
The Tidal Basin, south side, in West Potomac Park. 426-6822. (Architect: John Russell Pope. Sculptor: Rudolph Evans, 1943) One of the city's most beautifully situated and serene public places. Dedicated in 1943, on the 200th anniversary of Jefferson's birth, this simple circular classical white marble monument is in keeping with a style much favored by the third U.S. president, architect, scholar, political thinker. At its center, a towering 19-foot bronze portrait statue (the plaster one, in position until after WW II, is in the basement, too large to be removed intact) stands on a 6-foot pedestal. Panels are inscribed with excerpts of Jefferson's writing, including one that best sums up the man: "I have sworn

upon the altar of God eternal hostility against every form of tyranny over the mind of man." The view from the steps is magnificent, especially at night when a halo of blue light crowns the structure. Cherry blossom season bestows added beauty to the site. Park rangers give 15-minute talks several times an hour. (Ask about the mistakes in the Declaration of Independence quote.) *OPEN always. Park ranger present 7 days 8am-midnight.* Concerts on the steps in summer. FREE. Accessible via Tourmobile. *Metro: Arlington Cemetery.* IMPORTANT NOTE: Though still very accessible, the memorial will be surrounded by scaffolding for the next three to five years as experts survey every stone in the monument for a much-needed restoration project.

Kalorama
Kalorama Circle to Sheridan Circle, Columbia Road, NW. Quiet "hilltop" residential area overlooking Rock Creek Park and Massachusetts Avenue. Known for high concentration of embassies and Beaux Arts mansions.

Lafayette Square
On the west side of Lafayette Park are the row houses that were saved from demolition by President and Mrs. John F. Kennedy and completely restored under their watchful eyes (literally; it's just across from the White House) by architect John Carl Warnecke. (*See also* PARKS & GARDENS, Parks: Lafayette Park.) *Metro: McPherson Square, Farragut West.*

Laird-Dunlop House
3014 N Street, NW. (Attributed to William Lovering, 1799) In Georgetown, built for Scottish tobacco warehouse-owner John Laird. Later home to President Lincoln's oldest son, Robert, from 1915 till his death in 1926. The last remaining original Georgetown boundary marker is located in the garden.

Thomas Law House
1252 6th Street, SW. (Attributed to William Lovering, 1796) This federal-style house (aka the Honeymoon House) is one of DC's oldest re-

Howard Hall

maining residences. Listed in the National Register of Historic Places, it's now the community center for Tiber Island residents.

Le Droit Building
8th & F Streets, NW. (A. L. Barber & Co., 1875) Early Victorian elevatorless office building, presently being renovated under the auspices of the Pennsylvania Avenue Development Corporation.

Le Droit Park
North of Florida Avenue to W & 6th Streets, NW. This residential area was developed in the 1870s and is rich in local architect James McGill's designs, illustrating a variety of the period's more romantic styles (see the 400 block of U Street; its 1870s architectural integrity is maintained). A predominantly black residential area since the turn of the century, the presence of Howard University and Howard Theater make the area socially and culturally significant. Black author Paul Dunbar lived here. Listed in the National Register of Historic Places.

Robert E. Lee Boyhood Home
607 Oronoco Street, Alexandria, Va. (703) 548-8454. Built in 1795, this early federal-period house belonged to Revolutionary War hero Light Horse Harry until he died in 1818. He left behind his widow and five children, one of whom became the respected commander of the Confederate Army, Robert E. Lee. Beautifully furnished. *OPEN Mon-Sat 10am-4pm; Sun 1-4pm. Last tour at 3:30pm. CLOSED Easter Sunday, Thanksgiving Day & Dec 15-Jan 31, except by appointment. Admission.*

Thomas Simm Lee Corner
3001-9 M Street, NW. At 30th and M streets in Georgetown (also called Historic Georgetown) a row of four houses built circa 1790, restored 1955. Fine examples of late-federal-period architecture. The two houses at the corner (once a single house) belonged to Lee, twice governor of Maryland and friend of George Washington. Saved and preserved by a group of dedicated Georgetowners.

Thomas Simm Lee Corner

Lee-Fendall House
614 Oronoco Street, Alexandria, Va. (703) 548-1789. Built in 1785, Robert E. Lee family members occupied this house until 1903. Later owned by United Mine Workers' leader John L. Lewis. Period furnishings, dollhouse collections. (See also KIDS' WASHINGTON, Museums for Children.) Guided tours. *OPEN Tues-Sat 10am-4pm; Sun noon-4pm. CLOSED Sun. Occasionally closed on weekends for private events, call first. Admission.*

Lenthall Houses
612 & 614 19th Street, NW. Built circa 1800. Initially owned by John Lenthall, assistant to Benjamin Latrobe, builder of the Capitol, who was killed during its construction.

Library of Congress
1st Street & Independence Avenue, SE. 707-5000 or -5558. (Original building [the Thomas Jefferson], Smithmeyer & Pelz, 1886-97) The elaborate Italian Renaissance building just east of the Capitol is a fitting repository for a nation's library. The foyer is a splendid entry with stained-glass skylight and a monumental double marble staircase. The library itself was created by an act of Congress in 1800, but much of its original material was lost in the British burning of the Capitol in 1814. As replacement, Thomas Jefferson sold (at cost) his 6,487-volume private library to the government. (It's now in the Rare Book and Special Collection Division.) The library, purely for research, is now the world's largest, housing 75 million items covering 340 miles. Of special interest: the Gutenberg Bible (1455), early presidential manuscripts, the world's largest collection of miniature books, early Mathew Brady glass plate negatives, and last but not least the domed **Main Reading Room**, one of the world's most serene places, newly resplendent following an $81 million restoration. Needing more room over the years, two more buildings were added: the white marble **John Adams Building** (1939), and the six-story **James Madison Memorial Building** (1980)— on 46 acres, the world's largest library building. The library's card catalog itself, with approximately 20 million entries, has long been a browser's delight but is no longer being added to. Alas, technology supersedes: browsing is now done on public computer terminals, which electronically catalog the 81 million cross-referenced entries (Thomas Jefferson, the most intellectually curious man of his time, would probably be delighted). There are literary performances and chamber music concerts weekly from October to April in the Coolidge Auditorium and the Whittall Pavilion, and outdoors in the lovely Court of Neptune Fountain in summer; call for information. Conducted tours lasting 45 minutes are given Monday to Friday at 10am and 1 and 3pm. *OPEN Mon-Fri 8:30am-9:30pm; Sat & Sun 8:30am-5pm. FREE. Metro: Capitol South.*

Lincoln Memorial
The Mall, West Potomac Park, West End. 426-6896. (Sculptor: Daniel Chester French. Archi-

Library of Congress

ect: Henry Bacon, 1922) A noble and striking classical Greek temple with 36 columns meant to represent the Union at the time of Lincoln's death. In its center a seated Lincoln as the War President. The white marble statue—19 feet high by 19 feet wide. On the north wall, the 16th president's Second Inaugural Address; on the south wall, the Gettysburg Address. Above the statue the words: "In this Temple, as in the hearts of the people, for whom he saved the Union, the memory of Abraham Lincoln is enshrined forever." No statistics or descriptions can prepare you for its drama and power. In the pm the reflecting pool and the view down the Mall to the Washington Monument and Capitol are breathtaking. Looking toward Arlington you can glimpse the eternal flame at the Kennedy grave. *OPEN always. Park Service ranger in attendance 8am-midnight, except Christmas Day. FREE. Metro: Foggy Bottom, Arlington Cemetery.* IMPORTANT NOTE: Though still very much accessible, the memorial will be surrounded by scaffolding for the next three to five years as experts survey and seek methods to repair the damage caused by pollution, acid rain, and overzealous cleaning.

The Lindens
2401 Kalorama Road, NW. Built in 1754 (Robert Hooper) in Danvers, Massachusetts! Rescued and moved to DC in sections in 1934 by Mr. and Mrs. George Maurice Morris. When Mrs. Morris died in 1982 the fine 18th-century Georgian frame house was sold to pay taxes due, and the interior period treasures of the Lindens were sold at auction.

Logan Circle Historic District
Vermont & Rhode Island Avenues, NW. Encir-cled by Victorian residences built between 1875 and 1900, when the area was highly fashionable. Falling on hard times over several decades of this century, it is now an active restoration area, attracting a racial mix of middle- to high-income professionals.

Lothrop Mansion
2001 Connecticut Avenue, NW. (Joseph Hornblower & James Rush Marshall, 1901) Where Connecticut and Florida avenues intersect. This 40-room limestone mansion belonged to dry-goods merchant Alvin Mason Lothrop of Woodward & Lothrop, then became part of the Russian embassy complex.

Loughboro-Patterson House
3039-41 M Street, NW. On Georgetown's main street. Built circa 1805, it was beautifully and carefully restored in 1963. The current tenant is the Junior League Shop of Washington.

Lover's Lane
30th & R Streets, NW. The divider between Montrose Park and Dumbarton Oaks Gardens.

Mackall-Worthington House
1686 34th Street, NW. Built in 1820, when this was "out of town." Lovely garden.

Dolley Madison House
Madison Place & H Street, NW. Where the widow of the president lived until her death in 1849; it was the center of Washington social life during her residence.

The Mall
Part of Pierre L'Enfant's plan for this grand city was a "vast esplanade" at its center, linking the Capitol and the Potomac River. But by the 1860s the Mall was crisscrossed by railroad tracks, a cattle depot was erected near the base of the uncompleted Washington Monument, and the stench of the Washington Canal's sewage hung over it all. In the early 1900s the McMillan Commission made recommendations to Congress that would help make the Mall the noble greensward L'Enfant had envisioned. Today, its 2 miles encompass the Smithsonian's museum buildings; the memorials to Washington, Lincoln, and Jefferson; and the Constitution Gardens with the Vietnam Memorial. In spring, the Tidal Basin's cherry blossoms dazzle; in summer, people fly kites, play Frisbee, picnic, and attend festivals; in West Potomac Park (the Mall's west end) they even play polo.

The Maples House
619 D Street, SE. (William Lovering, 1795) Still attractive despite additions, this fine house was once owned by Francis Scott Key, author of the national anthem. Since 1937, it has housed the Friendship House Association.

Marbury House
3307 N Street, NW. Built in 1812 by William Marbury, it was the rectory of nearby St. John's Episcopal Church. Bought by JFK as a present for his wife, Jacqueline, following the birth of their daughter, Caroline. Their next house was the big white one on Pennsylvania Avenue. A plaque across the street on 3302 is from the members of the press to its occupants.

Marine Barracks/Marine Commandant's House

8th & I Streets, SE. (703) 545-6700. (George Hadfield, 1805. Additions 1901: Hornblower & Marshall) In the Capitol Hill area. This is the service's oldest post. The commandant's house is the only remaining original building and has been in continuous use since built. The brick barracks surround an interior courtyard/parade ground. Site of sunset parade and band concerts on Friday nights in summer (see ANNUAL EVENTS, May). Metro: Eastern Market, Potomac Avenue.

John Marshall House

1801 F Street, NW. (Tench Ringgold, 1825) This beautiful house has had a series of prominent residents, including Presidents Madison and Van Buren.

McCormick Apartments

1785 Massachusetts Avenue, NW. (Jules Henri de Sibour, 1917) Once the most spacious (11,000 square feet!) and desirable apartments in Washington. Now headquarters of the National Trust for Historic Preservation.

Memorial Amphitheater

Arlington National Cemetery, adjoining the Tomb of the Unknowns. (Carrere & Hastings, 1920) In the architectural tradition of a Greek theater, with a capacity of 5,000, it serves as a memorial to the U.S. Army, Navy and Marine Corps. The Trophy Room is a repository for decorations bestowed by other nations on the Unknown Soldier. Nearby is the mast from the USS Maine, rallying point in the Spanish-American War. Site of Memorial and Veteran's Day observances. (See also ANNUAL EVENTS, May and November.)

Meridian House International

1630 Crescent Place, NW. (John Russell Pope, 1915) Opposite Meridian Hill Park. Built for Irwin Laughlin, who was the U.S. ambassador to Spain at the time. The house is richly embellished; the pollarded trees are striking. Since 1961 it's been home to Meridian House International, a nonprofit foundation dedicated to fostering international cooperation. OPEN Mon-Fri 1-4pm. CLOSED Sat & Sun. Metro: Woodley Park/Zoo. (See also MUSEUMS & GALLERIES, Museums.)

Mount Vernon

(703) 780-2000. In Virginia, 16 miles from downtown Washington, is one of America's most historic sites. Home of George Washington from 1754 to 1799, the mansion is a mid-Georgian jewel, enlarged from the one-and-a-half-story farmhouse of his youth by Washington himself. Fourteen rooms are open for viewing, furnished with original and period pieces. Also open are nine outer service buildings that housed domestic servants and the cottage industries of this successful plantation. A museum contains personal possessions of the Washingtons. From the two-story piazza, the sweeping view of the Potomac and rural Maryland beyond will lead you to agree with Washington, who wrote: "No estate

in United America is more pleasantly situated than Mount Vernon." There are more than 30 acres on which to stroll and explore. A tomb containing the remains of George and his wife Martha, is on the grounds. Mount Vernon is owned and maintained by the Mount Vernon Ladies' Association, founded in 1853 to purchase, preserve, and restore the home of America's first leader for the public benefit. There are no guided tours but a free map is available. Free parking. OPEN Mar-Oct, 7 days 9am-5pm; Nov-Feb, 7 days 9am-4pm. (See also SIGHTSEEING, River Trips.) Modest admission charge. Accessible via Tourmobile or Metrobus.

Municipal Center Building

300 Indiana Avenue, NW. (Nathan C. Wyeth, 1941) Houses offices of local government including the Metropolitan Police Department. Facing the interior courtyard (out of public view) are brightly colored ceramic friezes that decorate the building. Cast-aluminum entranceway doors are Art Deco gems.

The National Archives

Constitution Avenue at 8th Street, NW. 501-5000. (John Russell Pope, 1935) Fittingly inscribed on a statue out front is: "What is past is prologue." Part of the Federal Triangle, the purely classical structure with 72 Corinthian columns contains the original Declaration of Independence, the Constitution of the United States, and the Bill of Rights. Previously kept in the Library of Congress (except during WW II, when they were transferred to Fort Knox, Kentucky, for safekeeping), since 1952 they have been on display to the public in helium-filled bronze cases under filtered lights. (The Declaration is considerably faded due to exposure to sunlight in the 19th century.) At night the entire display is electronically lowered into a bomb- and fireproof vault 20 feet below the Exhibition Hall. The Exhibition Hall OPEN Apr 1-Labor Day, 7 days 10am-9pm; the day after Labor Day-Mar 31, 7 days 10am-5:30pm. CLOSED Christmas Day. (See also SIGHTSEEING, On Your Own.) FREE. Metro: Federal Triangle.

The National Gallery of Art, West Building

Constitution Avenue & 6th Street, NW. 737-4215. (John Russell Pope, 1941) Repository of the nation's finest art collection. The neoclassical Pantheon-like building, complete with majestic rotunda, fountains, and light courts, is by the architect of the Jefferson Memorial. An underground concourse connects it to the modern East Wing. (See also Modern Architecture and MUSEUMS & GALLERIES, Museums.)

National Theater

1321 Pennsylvania Avenue, NW. 628-6161. A grand old theater constructed in 1885 (on the site of six previous theater buildings) and given a much-needed restoration in 1982-84, which is still going strong. A key part of the revitalization of Pennsylvania Avenue. Features mainly megamusicals, check the Washington Post for current attractions. Metro: Federal Triangle, Metro Center.

Octagon House

Octagon House

1799 New York Avenue, NW. 638-3105. (Dr. William Thornton, 1798-1800) A graceful and unusual example of federal-period residence architecture. The elegant simplicity of the interior and its furnishings provides a glimpse of life in the capital city in the early 1800s. It was built as a winter town house for Col. John Taylor III, a wealthy Virginia planter and horse breeder. The house was occupied by President Madison and his wife while the White House, burned by the British in 1814, was being rebuilt. The Treaty of Ghent, ending the War of 1812, was signed here on February 17, 1815. Restored and maintained by the American Institute of Architects. Tours are given every half hour. *OPEN Tues-Fri 10am-4pm; Sat & Sun noon-4pm. CLOSED Mon & Thanksgiving, Christmas, New Year's Day. FREE;* donation suggested. *Metro: Farragut West.*

Old Anacostia

Martin Luther King Avenue to 15th Street, Good Hope Road to U Street, SW. Originally called Uniontown, residential development began in 1854. Now a black residential area with many homogeneous groupings of late-19th-century buildings. NOTE: Good Hope Road was John Wilkes Booth's escape route following his shooting of President Lincoln. (*See also* MUSEUMS & GALLERIES, Museums: Anacostia Museum.)

Old Executive Office Building (EOB)

1700 Pennsylvania Avenue, NW. 395-5895. (Alfred B. Mullett, 1875-88) A flamboyant French Second Empire celebration with 553 rooms, 14-foot-high ceilings, 2 miles of corridors, 900 Doric columns, and enough architectural detail to exhaust the eye. Originally the State, War, and Navy Building, it was the world's largest government building when finished. Now it houses the Executive Office and White House staffs. Harry Truman called this "the greatest monstrosity in America," yet he was one of the few who didn't want it torn down. Recently restored, the jewel is the three-story former War Department Library; see it! Guided tours *Sat only, 9am-noon.* Reservations must be made three to four weeks in advance. FREE. *Metro: Farragut West.*

Old North Building

Georgetown University, 37th & O Streets, NW. 687-0100. Built in 1795, it's the oldest and the only original building of America's oldest Catholic university still standing. In 1797, George Washington addressed the students. Restored and rededicated in 1984. Call in advance to arrange a tour of the campus. *OPEN 7 days 8am-5pm.*

Old Patent Office Building

8th Street between F & G Streets, NW. (William Parker Elliot, 1836-67) One of the oldest public buildings in Washington as well as one of the largest and finest Greek Revival structures in America. Originally home to the Interior Department as well as the Patent Office, at one time it had on its premises such government possessions as Ben Franklin's printing press, George Washington's furniture, and the Declaration of Independence, not to mention thousands of models by hopeful inventors. Utilized as barracks, hospital, and morgue during the Civil War; site of Abraham Lincoln's second Inaugural Ball, March 6, 1865; now permanent home to the Smithsonian's National Portrait Gallery and National Collection of Fine Arts (*see* MUSEUMS & GALLERIES, Museums). The Lincoln Gallery, "the greatest room in Washington," measures 264 by 63 feet; 32 pillars support its vaulted ceiling. There's also a wonderful cafeteria (*see* RESTAURANTS, Cafeterias: Patent Pending). *Metro: Gallery Place.*

Old Pension Building

5th & G Streets, NW. 272-2448. (Maj. Gen. Montgomery Meigs, 1883) Architecturally inspired by no less than Rome's 16th-century Farnese Palace, this fireproof building was nicknamed "Meigs' Old Red Barn." It was used to disburse pension funds to Union Army veterans of the Civil War. In the 1880s, its huge central court with eight 76-foot-high—the world's largest—Corinthian columns was used for presidential inaugural balls (those of FDR, Nixon, Carter, Reagan, and Bush were also here). Since 1980, it has housed the National Building Museum, which commemorates architecture, construction, and building craftsmen. (*See* MUSEUMS & GALLERIES, Museums.) *OPEN Mon-Sat 10am-4pm; Sun noon-4pm. Tours of the building are Mon-Fri at 12:30pm; Sat & Sun 12:30 & 1pm.* For group tours, call 272-2877. Exhibition galleries, gift shop. *Metro: Judiciary Square.*

Old Post Office Building

12th Street & Pennsylvania Avenue, NW. 523-5691. (W. Edbrooke, 1899) A Romanesque Revival landmark on the Federal Triangle, with distinctive 315-foot clock tower (the third highest structure in the city) and magnificent interior sky-lit courtyard. Saved from the wrecker's ball

Old Executive Office Building

(mainly through the efforts of the late Nancy Hanks, head of the National Endowment for the Arts, 1969 to 1977) and restored (Arthur Cotton Moore, 1983), now an inviting multiuse complex of commercial space, shops, restaurants, and federal cultural offices. The East Atrium, an addition opened in 1992, contains additional retail shops, a food court, and a theater to feature the 50-minute film "Washington: American City!" to be shown every hour. (*See also* SIGHTSEEING, Viewpoints: Old Post Office Clock Tower *and* On Your Own: The Pavilion at the Old Post Office.) *Metro: Federal Triangle.*

Old Soldiers' Home
3700 North Capitol Street, NW. (B. S. Alexander, 1852) America's oldest old soldiers' home, founded in 1851. Abraham Lincoln preferred to spend summer nights here when the stench from the garbage-ridden Washington Canal drove him from the White House. (*See also* Anderson Cottage.)

Old Stone House
3051 M Street, NW. 426-6851. (Christopher Layman, 1765) Located on Georgetown's bustling main street, this pre-Revolutionary residence, the oldest building extant in the District of Columbia, is furnished with household items typical of a late-18th-century middle-class dwelling. Layman was a cabinetmaker. A garden blooms with fruit trees and seasonal blossoms. Now a National Historic Site, six rooms are open to the public, and there are demonstrations of spinning, quilting, and daily domestic chores by a costumed staff. Group tours by appointment. *OPEN Wed-Sun 8am-4:30pm. CLOSED Mon & Tues, Thanksgiving, Christmas & New Year's Day.* FREE.

Old Town
Alexandria, Va. Alexandria is the Washington area's oldest surviving town. Settled in 1732, it became a tobacco shipping port and was part of the District of Columbia until it was returned to Virginia in 1846. Much of the past is retained, especially in Old Town, where historic residences and commercial structures exist side by side with charming boutiques and chic dining

choices. Easily accessible from Washington via car, Metro, or the #11 Metrobus from Pennsylvania Avenue & 12th Street. (*See also* BASIC INFORMATION, Information Centers: Ramsay House Visitors Center.)

Organization of American States
17th Street & Constitution Avenue, NW. 458-3000. (Albert Kelsey & Paul Cret, 1910) Formerly known as the Pan American Union. Striking Beaux Arts building utilizing white Georgian marble and black Andean granite. The Hall of Americas—with its barrel-vaulted ceilings and Tiffany chandeliers—is where state dinners are held. Guided tours lasting half an hour start in the lobby from 9am to 4:30pm. Large groups should reserve in advance. (*See also* PARKS & GARDENS, Gardens: The Aztec Garden, *and* MUSEUMS & GALLERIES, Museums: Art Museum of the Americas.) *OPEN Tues-Sat 10am-5pm. CLOSED Sun & Mon. Metro: Farragut West.*

Thomas Nelson Page House
1759 R Street, NW. (McKim, Mead & White, 1897) Federal Revival for famous Southern author by famous Northern architects.

Peirce Mill
Rock Creek Park, 2311 Tilden Street near Beach Drive. 426-6908. The 19th century comes alive at this old-fashioned water-powered flour mill, the last remaining of the eight once located in Rock Creek Park. It began operation in 1829 and ceased in 1897 until the 1930s. Contrary to the usual, the water turned the wheel from below. The three pairs of millstones are the originals. Informal tours are given throughout the day; the mill is once again used to grind corn and wheat Saturday and Sunday between noon and 2pm. Group tours must reserve in advance. *OPEN Wed-Sun 8am-4:30pm. CLOSED Mon & Tues, Thanksgiving, Christmas & New Year's Day.* FREE.

Pennsylvania Avenue
Washington's main artery, it runs from the Capitol to the White House—it's the route of the inaugural parade—and continues into Georgetown. For the last decade it has been undergoing a dramatic redevelopment, initially spurred by President Kennedy, who felt "America's Main Street" had become much less than it should or could be (wouldn't he be pleased with its reincarnation). The Pennsylvania Avenue Development Corporation (PADC) oversees the plan, which when completed will provide over 1,700 residential units, retail space and offices, 1,500 hotel rooms, and welcoming parks and plazas. (*See also* Old Post Office Building *and* Willard InterContinental Hotel.)

Philadelphia Row
124-154 11th Street, SW. (Charles Gessford, ca. 1866) A lovely row said to have been built by Gessford to humor his wife, homesick for Philadelphia.

Pomander Walk
Volta Place, between 33rd & 34th Streets, NW. Hard to believe this charming alley (ca. 1885) was ever a slum.

Old Stone House

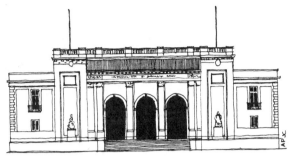

Organization of American States Building

Post Office
Massachusetts Avenue & North Capitol Street, NE. (Graham & Burnham, 1914) Architecturally complements Union Station, currently undergoing a much-needed restoration. *Metro: Union Station.*

Potomac Masonic Lodge #75
1058 Jefferson Street, NW. Small building in Georgetown built in 1810 as a Masonic Lodge Hall. Now an architect's office.

Prospect House
3508 Prospect Street, NW. Situated for a lovely view of the Potomac (hence the name). Built in 1788 by James Maccubbin Lingan, a War of Independence patriot. The first Secretary of Defense James Forrestal's residence at the time of his suicide. Later used as "President's Guest House" when Truman was occupying Blair House; guests included the Shah of Iran. Private residence.

Quality Hill
3425 Prospect Street, NW. Fine spacious house in a fine neighborhood, built by John Thomson Mason, nephew of George Mason, 1798.

Ramsay House Visitors Center
221 King Street, Alexandria, Va. (703) 832-4200. (ca. 1724; restored 1956) This charming residence, the first in Alexandria, was moved from Dumfries, Virginia, in 1794 by barge. Home of William Ramsay, Scottish merchant and Alexandria's first citizen and Lord Mayor. Now houses the Alexandria Tourist Council, which presents a 13-minute color film orientation. (*See also* BASIC INFORMATION, Information Centers.) *OPEN 7 days 9am-5pm.*

Renwick Gallery
Pennsylvania Avenue at 17th Street, NW. 357-1300. (James Renwick, Jr., 1859-61) French Second Empire by architect of New York's St. Patrick's Cathedral. Built by financier art collector William Wilson Corcoran to house his collection but seized by the government for use by the Quartermaster Corps during the Civil War. Reclaimed by the owner in 1869, it housed his collection until it was moved to its present location in 1897. This building is now a Smithsonian museum dedicated to American decorative arts and crafts. (*See also* MUSEUMS & GALLERIES, Museums: Corcoran Gallery of Art *and* Renwick Gallery of the National Museum of American Art.)

Riggs House
3038 N Street, NW. (Romulus Riggs, 1816) Small, harmonious federal-style house in Georgetown. Residents have included Abe Lincoln's stepmother and more recently former New York governor W. Averell Harriman.

Riggs National Bank
9th & F Streets, NW. (James G. Hill, 1891) A noteworthy commercial building now a landmark. Reminiscent of Adler & Sullivan's Auditorium Building in Chicago.

Rosedale
3501 Newark Street, NW. (Uriah Forrest, 1793) Built by the owner as a summer retreat. Originally on 990 acres, the typical 18th-century farmhouse soon became his full-time residence. Both George Washington and L'Enfant are rumored to have slept here.

Russian (formerly Soviet) Embassy
1115 16th Street, NW. (Nathan C. Wyeth, 1909.) Built by sleeping-car tycoon George M. Pullman, one of America's early leading capitalists, it became the property of the Russian government in 1913. Note what were, during the cold war years, controversial high-frequency antennas on the roof.

Scott Circle
Intersection of Massachusetts & Rhode Island Avenues & 16th Street, NW. Much smaller than originally planned by L'Enfant, and modified by Andrew Ellicot. The statue of Gen. Winfield Scott is by Henry Kirke Brown.

Scott-Grant House
3238 R Street, NW. Built by A. V. Scott in 1858. General Grant spent the summer after the Civil War here.

Sewall-Belmont House
144 Constitution Avenue, NE. 546-1210. Capitol Hill town house built by Robert Sewall in 1800 and owned by his family for 123 years. From 1801 to 1812, the house was rented to Secretary of the Treasury Albert Gallatin. In 1814, the only resistance the British encountered on the way to burn the Capitol came from the patriots at this

site; in punishment, the house was set afire. It was repaired and, through the years, has been greatly altered, displaying a potpourri of styles. Now National Women's Party Headquarters. Interesting furnishings include a rolltop desk belonging to Susan B. Anthony, also exhibits dedicated to the women's rights movement, especially the Suffrage and ERA campaigns. Reserve for groups. *OPEN Tues-Fri 10am-3pm; Sat & Sun noon-4pm; weekend schedule on holidays. CLOSED Mon, Thanksgiving, Christmas & New Year's Day. Metro: Capitol South, Union Station.*

Sheridan Circle
Massachusetts Avenue & 23rd Street, NW. Elegant early 20th-century mansions characterize this formal Kalorama-area circle (originally Decatur Circle) with its statue of Union Civil War hero General Sheridan (by Gutzon Borglum) at its center.

Smith Row
3255-63 N Street, NW. (Walter and Clement Smith, 1815) A full row of nearly identical classic federal houses.

Smithsonian Institution Building
1000 Jefferson Drive, between 9th & 12th Streets, SW. 357-2700. (James Renwick, 1849) The castle, as it is best known, is the oldest building of the Smithsonian Institution and one of America's finest Gothic Revival structures (by the architect of New York's St. Patrick's Cathedral). Its reddish color and irregular shape made up of turrets, parapets, spires, and towers make it immediately recognizable, a welcome anachronism in an orderly city. It houses the Smithsonian Visitors Information Center and the Crypt Room, holding the tomb of the institution's benefactor, James Smithson. It also houses the headquarters of the Woodrow Wilson International Center for Scholars. (*See also* MUSEUMS & GALLERIES, Museums.) *OPEN 7 days 9am-5:30pm.*

John Philip Sousa Birthplace
636 G Street, SE. Built in 1844. The boyhood home of America's "March King," composer, and the best-known band master of the U.S. Marine Corps, which is headquartered at nearby Marine Barracks.

Stabler-Leadbeater Apothecary Shop
107 South Fairfax Street, Alexandria, Va. (703) 836-3713. Founded in 1792 by Edward Stabler, a Quaker preacher and Alexandria's first librarian. It was a favored meeting place where Alexandrians received their mail and waited for the Georgetown ferry. It functioned until 1933. The furnishings are original and the pharmacy, now a museum, looks as it did when George Washington, Robert E. Lee, Daniel Webster, and John Calhoun came to shop. Documents include an 1802 request from Mrs. Washington at Mount Vernon for "a quart bottle of his [Mr. Stabler's] best castor oil. . . ." An adjacent antique shop, operated by the Landmarks Society, helps maintain the museum. *OPEN Mon-Sat 10am-4pm. CLOSED Sun. FREE.*

Stabler-Leadbeater Apothecary Shop

Benjamin Stoddert House
3400 Prospect Avenue, NW (aka Halcyon House). Stoddert, America's first secretary of the navy, built his elegant federal house in 1787. Much altered.

The Supreme Court of the United States
1st Street & Maryland Avenue, NE. 479-3030. (Cass Gilbert, Jr., 1935) Three million dollars worth of marble was used to construct this imposing neoclassical building, the first permanent house of the nation's highest tribunal, guardian of the Constitution, which met first in 1790 in New York, then the country's capital. Few American institutions are as steeped in tradition: the annual "term" commences the first Monday in October and continues until the end of June, each session opens at 10am with the crier's chant ("Oyez! Oyez! Oyez!"), the nine black-robed justices are seated in a row with the chief justice at the center, recess is 3pm on days of oral arguments, which start at 10am and include a noon to 1pm break for lunch. One tradition was broken in 1981 when Sandra Day O'Connor became the first female member of the high court. Mondays are usually "decision" days and they are popular. You may tour the building (not the courtroom) on your own. Sessions are open to the public on a first-come, first-served basis (limited seating). When court is not in session there are free lectures every hour on the half hour from 9:30am to 3:30pm. No reservations are necessary. There is a great ground-floor cafeteria open to the public for breakfast and lunch (*see* RESTAURANTS, Cafeterias), as well as exhibits, a

ilm, and a gift shop. Building *OPEN Mon-Fri 9am-4:30pm. CLOSED Sat, Sun, holidays. FREE. Metro: Capitol South, Union Station.*

The Surratt House
604 H Street, NW. Located in Washington's Chinatown. Marked by a historic plaque, it's the boardinghouse where, in 1865, John Wilkes Booth, Mary Surratt and her son, a boarder named Lewis Paine, and others conspired to assassinate President Lincoln. Paine and Mary Surratt were hanged.

William Howard Taft House
2215 Wyoming Avenue, NW. This Kalorama-area Greek Revival structure, built in 1904, was home to the former president during his tenure as Chief Justice of the Supreme Court, 1921-30, and to his widow until her death in 1944. Now the Syrian embassy.

Temple of the Scottish Rite
1733 16th Street, NW. 232-3579. (John Russell Pope, 1910) The monumental headquarters of the Supreme Council of the Southern Jurisdiction of the 33rd Degree of the Ancient and Accepted Scottish Rite of Free Masonry. Designed after the Mausoleum of Halicarnassus, 350 B.C., one of the wonders of the ancient world. The steps are flanked by two carved limestone sphinxes, Wisdom and Power (Alexander Weinman), the interior is filled with neoclassical designs and Masonic regalia and artifacts. It is also the oldest public library in DC, open to the public since 1880. The main collection is on freemasonry. Tours lasting approximately one hour are available at any time. *OPEN Mon-Fri 8am-2pm. CLOSED Sat & Sun. FREE.*

3017 N Street
Built in 1794. Jacqueline Kennedy resided here for one year following her husband's assassination in 1963. Complaining of curiosity seekers, she sold the house and moved to a high-rise on New York's Fifth Avenue.

Thomas Circle
Massachusetts Avenue & 14th Street, NW. One of the 15 large circles envisioned by the L'Enfant Plan. It is a bustling intersection that a statue of Maj. Gen. George H. Thomas (John Quincy Adams Ward, 1879) oversees.

Treasury Department Building
15th Street & Pennsylvania Avenue, NW, 20220. 566-2000. (Robert Mills, Thomas U. Walter, Ammi B. Young, Isaiah Rogers, Alfred Bult Mullet, 1838-69) This impressive Greek Revival building, covering 5 acres, is the capital's third

oldest. The site, chosen by Andrew Jackson, has a fatal flaw—it destroyed L'Enfant's carefully planned vista of the White House from the Capitol. During WW II the basement vaults were ready to receive President Roosevelt in case of an air attack. The vast Treasury Department includes the Internal Revenue Service; the Mint; the Bureau of Engraving and Printing; the Bureau of Alcohol, Tobacco and Firearms; Customs; and the Secret Service. There is a tour every other Saturday at 10, 10:20 & 10:40am; write for reservations very well in advance, call 343-9136 Monday to Friday for information. *OPEN Tues-Sat 9:30am-3:30pm. CLOSED Mon & federal holidays. FREE. Metro: McPherson Square, Metro Center.*

Trolley Waiting Stations
Capitol Grounds, east side. Built circa 1876, designed by Frederick Law Olmsted, these graceful iron waiting stations were served by the horse-drawn trolleys.

Tudor Place
1644 31st Street, NW. 965-0400. (Dr. William Thornton, 1816) This federal-period Georgetown mansion, by the original designer of the Capitol, is considered an architectural masterpiece. Until 1983, the house was successively occupied by descendants of the man for whom it was built, Thomas Peter, a wealthy Scottish tobacco merchant married to Martha Parke Custis, a granddaughter of Martha Washington. The historic house and its contents, including original furnishings, silver, china, portraits, photos, and books, and the lovely formal garden may now be visited by the public with advance reservations. *Tours Thurs, Fri & Sat at 10 & 11:30am, 1 & 2:30pm by appointment only. Admission.*

Turkish Embassy
1606 23rd Street, NW. (George Oakley Totten, Jr., 1914) Edward H. Everett, for whom this imposing Sheridan Circle mansion was built, became a millionaire from his invention: the bottle cap! A mixture of classical and idiosyncratic by a versatile architect. Occupied by the Turkish government since 1932.

Twin Oaks
3225 Woodley Road, NW. (Allen Kenway, 1888) Characteristic of the Cleveland Park area's late-19th-century private estates. Where many, including President Cleveland, had summer retreats.

Union Station
50 Massachusetts Avenue, NE. 371-9441. (Dan-

The Supreme Court of the United States

iel H. Burnham, 1908. Restoration 1988: Harry Weese & Assocs; design, Benjamin Thompson & Assocs) Grand Beaux Arts architecture by Burnham, one of the people who helped popularize it at the Columbia Exposition, Chicago, 1893. When built it was the largest train station in the world. The exterior has a ceremonial air, the grand-scale interior is monumental, and since its ambitious restoration following years of neglect, and its reincarnation as a shopping/dining/entertainment complex, it has taken on a splendid new life as the quintessential urban agora. Now, in addition to being a fitting gateway to the capital city for those arriving by train, it is also a destination in and of itself. *Metro: Union Station.*

Vice President's House
Massachusetts Avenue & 34th Street, NW. You were wondering where he lived? It's on the grounds of the Naval Observatory, but it's not open to the public.

Volta Bureau
1537 35th Street, NW. 337-5220. (Peabody & Stearns, 1893) Endowed by Alexander Graham Bell, this research and information center contains one of the most comprehensive archives on the subject of deafness. A 13-year-old Helen Keller attended the ground-breaking ceremony.

Wadsworth House
1801 Massachusetts Avenue, NW. This triangular brick mansion, built in 1903, by Herbert and Martha Wadsworth, it was one of the first Beaux Arts residences in the Dupont Circle area. It now houses the Sulgrave Club, a prestigious private club for women.

Walsh-McLean House
2020 Massachusetts Avenue, NW. 775-5200. (Henry Andersen, 1903) When built by Irish immigrant Thomas Walsh, who struck it rich in the Colorado gold fields, it was the Dupont Circle area's most expensive residence. Indeed, the pediment of the front entrance contained a piece of pure gold. His daughter Evalyn married Edward Beale McLean, whose family owned the *Washington Post.* They were also the owners of the fabled Hope Diamond. Purchased in 1952 by Indonesia for their embassy. Outside are two Balinese "demons" carved from volcanic rock.

Warder Totten House
2633 16th Street, NW. (H. H. Richardson, 1885. Renovated 1902, George Oakley Totten, Jr.) Constructed on K Street (1500 block) for Benjamin Warder, architect Totten bought the shell in 1902 and reconstructed it as his own residence. Now part of Antioch College.

Washington Canoe Club
3700 K Street, NW, near Key Bridge. A Chinese-inspired building constructed at the turn of the century. Viewed from across the river you can forget where and when you are.

Washington Club
15 Dupont Circle, NW. (Stanford White, 1902) Patterson House, interesting white marble Renaissance palazzo built for the publisher of the *Washington Times Herald.* In 1927 it was temporary home to President Coolidge and his wife while the White House was having a new roof put on. It was here that the chief executive welcomed aviator-hero Charles Lindbergh following his solo transatlantic flight. Now a private women's club.

Washington Monument
The Mall, Constitution Avenue at 15th Street, NW. 426-6839. (Robert Mills, 1836) The 555 foot, 5⅛-inch-high marble obelisk at the center of the Mall is the tallest masonry structure in the world. Designed initially as a more ornate tribute to America's first president, it almost didn't make it this far. The cornerstone was laid in 1848, but lack of funds and the impending Civil War halted construction until 1876. A difference in the shading of the marble (visible approximately 150 feet up) used upon resumption clearly delineates the initial construction from the later. It was opened to the public in 1888. Reached by elevator in 70 seconds (the original was steam-powered and took a lot longer), the pinnacle provides a wonderful panoramic view of the city, even more striking at night. From April to early September daily, and on weekends the rest of the year, there are "walk-down" tours for the energetic who wish to descend via the stairs. *OPEN Apr 1-Labor Day, 7 days 8am-midnight; balance of year, 7 days 9am-5pm. CLOSED Christmas Day.* Note: Be prepared to wait on very long lines for daylight entry during peak visiting seasons. Accessible via Tourmobile. FREE. *Metro: Federal Triangle, Smithsonian.*

Wheatley Houses
3041-43 N Street, NW (Francis Wheatley, 1859) Lovely pair of twin (actually mirror-image) Victorian town houses.

Wheat Row
Harbor Square, 1313-21 4th Street, SW. (Attributed to William Lovering, 1793) The chosen few. Exemplary federal houses selected for preservation, incorporated in the Southwest Urban Renewal Area.

The White House
1600 Pennsylvania Avenue, NW. (James Hoban, 1800) Though he chose the site and approved the design for the "Presidents' Palace," George Washington never lived in the White House. The first residents were John and Abigail Adams in 1800, though it was still unfinished (it's been oft reported that Mrs. Adams hung her wash in the East Room). Burned by the British in 1814, only the walls remained and it had to be rebuilt. Modernizations have kept step with the times, but during the Truman administration it was suggested that tradition alone kept the mansion standing, and while the Trumans moved across the street to Blair House, the entire structure was strengthened. It was First Lady Jacqueline Kennedy who set out to make the White House the most beautiful residence in America. The house has 54 rooms and 16 baths, not counting offices! It is surely the most visited house in America. Renamed the White House by President Theodore Roosevelt, it is stately yet in some ways quite homey; it's uniquely American for the

people to be able to visit the house where the chief executive of the country resides with his family and works with his staff. (For tour information, see SIGHTSEEING, On Your Own.) *Metro: McPherson Square.*

Villard InterContinental Hotel
Pennsylvania Avenue & 14th Street, NW. (Henry J. Hardenbergh, 1901) By the architect of New York's Plaza Hotel, this hotel was always a popular choice, even of presidents. Restored as part of the Pennsylvania Avenue Redevelopment Plan, with a major addition (Hardy Holzman Pfeiffer Associates) that is a series of architectural echoes of the original. (*See also* HOTELS, Deluxe.) *Metro: Federal Triangle.*

Woodrow Wilson House
2340 S Street, NW. 673-4034. (Waddy B. Wood, 1915) Washington's only presidential house museum. This lovely brick Georgian Revival residence in the Embassy Row area became home to President Wilson and his second wife, Edith Bolling Galt, following his second term. On February 3, 1924, Wilson died here. Furnished with personal and professional mementos; small gift shop. There are 45-minute guided tours throughout the day (last tour at 3pm). Group tours by appointment. *OPEN Tues-Sun 10am-4pm. CLOSED Mon, Thanksgiving, Christmas & New Year's Day.* Admission. *Metro: Dupont Circle.*

Winder Building
604 17th Street, NW. (William H. Winderin, 1848.) First of the inexpensive speculative office buildings earmarked for federal use in DC. It was also one of the first to use central heating.

Woodlawn Plantation
Mount Vernon, Va. (703) 780-4000. (Dr. William Thornton, 1805) Fourteen miles south of Washington, DC, originally part of Mount Vernon, it was bequeathed by George Washington to his adopted daughter, Nellie Parke Custis, and his nephew, Lawrence Lewis. An elegant Georgian mansion, beautiful furnishings, lovely restored grounds and gardens provide insight into 19th-century plantation life (*see also* PARKS & GARDENS, Gardens). Tours every half hour. Of interest for children, too. Well-stocked gift shop. *OPEN 7 days 9:30am-4:30pm. CLOSED Thanksgiving, Christmas & New Year's Day.* Admission. A combination entry also includes Pope-Leighey House (*see* Modern Architecture). Group tours by appointment only.

Woodward Apartments
2311 Connecticut Avenue, NW. (Harding and Upman, 1913) Kalorama-area apartment building with elaborate detailing.

STATUES & MONUMENTS

Alexandria Confederate Memorial
Pierce & South Washington Streets, Alexandria, Va. (Casper Buberl, 1889) Facing south; a sensitive memorial to comrades lost in a lost war.

General Jose Gervasio Artigas
Constitution Avenue & 18th Street, NW. (Juan M. Blanes, 1950) Artigas (1764-1850), Uruguayan national hero; bronze replica of one in Uruguay.

The Arts of Peace
Rock Creek Parkway Entrance, West Potomac Park. (James Earl Fraser, 1949) Two 17-foot bronze neoclassical statues, Music and Harvest (on the left) and Aspiration and Literature (on the right), were designed in 1925 but not cast until 1949 in Italy, where they were "mercury gilded" as a gift from that country. The 36 stars represent the states at the Civil War's end.

The Arts of War
Entrance to the Arlington Memorial Bridge, West Potomac Park. (Leo Friedlander, 1949) Valor on the left, Sacrifice on the right. Note that both are depicted as women.

Francis Asbury
16th & Mt. Pleasant Streets, NW. (Henry Augustus Lukeman, 1924) The pioneer Methodist bishop, captured in a life-size equestrian statue. In his right hand a Bible with his fingers between the pages.

Aztec Fountain
Organization of the American States courtyard, Constitution Avenue & 17th Street, NW. (Gertrude Vanderbilt Whitney, 1910) Eight-foot-tall red-stone fountain in glass-roofed courtyard. Decorated with figures and hieroglyphics of early south-of-the-border civilizations. (*See also* PARKS & GARDENS, Gardens: The Aztec Garden.)

Commodore John Barry
Franklin Park, 14th Street between I & K Streets, NW. (Edward P. Casey, 1914) Irish-American naval hero of the American Revolution.

Peacock Alley, Willard Hotel

Bartholdi Fountain
Independence Avenue & 1st Street, SW. (Frederic Auguste Bartholdi, 1876) By the sculptor of the Statue of Liberty, this cast-iron bronze-coated fountain was bought by the U.S. for $6,000 after its prize-winning exhibition at the 1876 Philadelphia Centennial Exhibition. It provided one of the earliest public displays of electrical illumination. It has recently been lovingly restored.

Mary McLeod Bethune Memorial
Lincoln Park, East Capitol & 12th Streets, NE. (Robert Berks, 1974) Bronze tribute to the daughter of freed slaves and founder of the National Council of Negro Women, Inc. The children are symbolic of her dedication to young people, to whom she bequeathed the legacy seen inscribed on the pedestal. Her cane was a gift from FDR, to whom she was an adviser on minority affairs.

Sir William Blackstone
Constitution Avenue & 3rd Street, NW. (Paul Wayland Bartlett, 1920) In his left hand his legal Commentaries, used as reference by those who drafted the U.S. Constitution. Brought from England and erected in 1943.

Simón Bolívar
18th & C Streets. (Felix W. de Weldon, 1959) South America's George Washington, donated by the government of Venezuela.

Boy Scout Memorial
The Ellipse, 15th Street between Constitution Avenue & E Street. (Donald DeLue, 1964) The 12-foot-tall neoclassical figures are representations of American Manhood and Womanhood, with a contemporary scout. Odd.

James Buchanan
Meridian Hill Park, 16th Street & Florida Avenue, NW. (Hans Schuler, 1930) Bronze, marble, and granite memorial to the 15th president of the U.S.

The Burghers of Calais
Hirshhorn Museum & Sculpture Garden, Jefferson Drive & 7th Street, NW. (Francois Auguste Rene Rodin, 1886) The six townsmen of Calais who surrendered themselves to the forces of England's King Edward III to save their town. One of Rodin's most powerful pieces.

Edmund Burke
Massachusetts Avenue & 11th Street, NW. (J. Howard Thomas, 1922) English statesman Burke, a supporter of the American colonies in Parliament, fittingly honored in America's capital. Donated by a British organization.

Butt-Millet Memorial Fountain
The Ellipse. (Daniel Chester French, 1913) Erected by their friends as a memorial to Major Archibald Wallingham Butt and Francis Davis Millet, both of whom perished on the *Titanic* after each gave his life jacket to a woman passenger.

Rear Admiral Richard Evelyn Byrd
Avenue of Heroes, approach to Arlington National Cemetery. "Upon the bright globe he carved his signature of courage." Byrd, explorer of Antarctica and the first man to fly over both the north and south poles, in a determined and stoic pose.

Sir Winston Churchill
British Embassy, 3100 Massachusetts Avenue NW. (William M. McVey, 1966) Nine-foot bronze statue of the former prime minister of Great Britain. His two familiar trademarks: the V for victory sign, and in his left hand the ever-present cigar. Poised between the street and the garden, with one foot on British "soil," the other on American (from his mother's birthplace in Brooklyn). A time capsule placed beneath the statue will be opened in 2063, the 100th anniversary of Churchill's honorary U.S. citizenship.

Columbus Memorial Fountain
Union Station Plaza, Massachusetts & Delaware Avenues, NE. (Lorado Taft, 1912) A richly embellished fountain dedicated to America's discoverer. Figures on either side of the explorer represent the old and new worlds. The three flag-poles are symbolic of Columbus's three ships.

Confederate Memorial
Arlington National Cemetery, Jackson Circle near McPherson Avenue. (Moses Ezekiel, 1914) In the Confederate section of the cemetery (magnanimously permitted by Congress in 1900), a moving monument to those who died for the South. The sculptor was a Confederate veteran.

The Court of Neptune Fountain
Library of Congress, 1st Street between Independence Avenue & East Capitol Street, SE. (Roland Hinton Perry, 1897) Lavish grottolike bronze and granite fountain reminiscent of Rome's Trevi. A 12-foot Neptune is central.

Dante
Meridian Hill Park, 16th Street & Florida Avenue, NW. (Ettore Ximenes, 1920) In the Italian Renaissance half of the park, an 11½ foot statue of the Florentine poet and scholar. (*See also* PARKS & GARDENS, Parks: Meridian Hill Park.)

Joseph Darlington Fountain
Judiciary Square, 5th & D Streets, NW. (Carl Paul Jenne Wein, 1923) This memorial fountain honored a prominent member of the Washington Bar Association. The nymph's nudity scandalized some of Darlington's Baptist co-religionists.

The Discus Thrower
Kelly Park, Virginia Avenue & 21st Street, NW. Copy of the famed Greek statue by Myron (450 b.c.). In gratitude from the Italian people for the return of their ancient Roman copy of the statue seized by the Germans during WW II.

The Downing Urn
Adjacent to the Smithsonian Institution Building, 1000 Jefferson Drive, SW. (Designer: Calvert Vaux. Sculptor: Robert E. Launitz, 1856) Andrew Jackson Downing was commissioned in 1850 to design the Mall the result became America's first landscaped city park. The 37-year-old landscape architect was killed in a boating accident in 1852. The Mall's design reverted to L'Enfant's original 1791 plan in 1930. The white marble urn is a tribute to Downing from friend and partner Calvert Vaux.

Dupont Memorial
Dupont Circle, Massachusetts & Connecticut Avenues, NW. (Daniel Chester French, 1921) Memorial fountain dedicated to Rear Adm. Samuel Francis Dupont, Union naval hero of the Civil War.

Albert Einstein
National Academy of Sciences, 2101 Constitution Avenue, NW. (Robert Berks, 1979) Three times larger than life a melancholy portrait of the famed scientist. Set on a base depicting the stars in the sky on the day of the dedication, April 22, 1979, if you stand at its very center your voice echoes back to you. Close by is the Vietnam Memorial; people come here to reflect. It's also a place for kids to climb.

Emancipation Monument
Lincoln Park, East Capitol & 11th Streets, NE. (Thomas Ball, 1876) Clasped in Lincoln's right hand, the Emancipation Proclamation (January 1, 1863); his left hand appears to bid a kneeling unshackled slave to rise. Also depicted: chains, fetters, a whipping post, and whip. Erected with funds contributed solely by newly freed men and women to the memory of their emancipator. Dedicated on the 11th anniversary of Lincoln's assassination.

Robert Emmet
Massachusetts Avenue & 24th Street, NW. (Jerome Connor, 1917) Sculpted by an Irishman, the Irish patriot, on a pedestal of emerald-green Brazilian granite, is depicted as he was upon hearing the British sentence of death.

John Ericson Memorial
West Potomac Park, Independence Avenue & Ohio Drive, SW. (James Earl Fraser, 1926) Granite tribute to Swedish-American inventor. Financed by Americans of Scandinavian descent.

Admiral David G. Farragut
Farragut Square, K Street between 16th & 17th Streets. (Vinnie Ream Hoxie, 1881) Ten-foot portrait statue of bold naval Civil War hero and first Admiral of the Navy, David ("Damn the torpedoes! Full speed ahead!") Farragut. Cast from the bronze propeller of his ship, the USS *Hartford*, by famed woman sculptor.

First Division Monument
President's Park South, State Place & 17th Street, NW. (Daniel Chester French, 1924) An 80-foot-tall monument to those of the First Division "who gave their lives in the World War. . . ." Atop, a gilded bronze Victory.

Benjamin Franklin
Pennsylvania Avenue at 10th Street, NW. (Jacques Jouvenal, 1889) The American statesman in marble, depicted at Versailles. Donated by Stilson Hutchins, founder of the *Washington Post*.

Freedom
Atop the Capitol dome. (Thomas Crawford, 1863) This 19½-foot statue of a woman as the embodiment of freedom was erected December 2, 1863, with a ceremony designed to provide inspiration for the dispirited Union troops.

Albert Gallatin
Treasury Building, Pennsylvania Avenue & 15th Street, NW. (James Earl Fraser, 1947) Secretary of the treasury under Thomas Jefferson, negotiator of the Treaty of Ghent, congressman, senator, American minister to Great Britain and France.

Edward Miner Gallaudet
Gallaudet College, Florida Avenue & 7th Street, NE. (Peter Lazzari, 1969) Son of the founder of America's first school for the deaf.

Thomas Hopkins Gallaudet
Gallaudet College, Florida Avenue & 7th Street, NE. (Daniel Chester French, 1888) Lovely bronze memorial to Thomas Hopkins Gallaudet, the country's pioneer educator of the deaf. Captured, with first student Alice Cogswell, at a moment of learning—the letter *A*.

President James Abram Garfield
1st Street & Maryland Avenue, SW. (John Quincy Adams Ward, 1887) Garfield, like Lincoln, was born in a log cabin; also like Lincoln, he was assassinated. President for only three months when he was shot on July 2, 1881; he died on September 19.

Samuel Gompers Memorial
Massachusetts Avenue & 10th Street, NW. (Robert I. Aitkin, 1933) Bronze memorial to the founder and president of the American Federation of Labor. Favored by climbing children.

Grant Memorial
The East Mall at 1st Street, SW. (Henry Merwin Shrady, 1922) This bronze and marble memorial is the most expensive ever funded by the government, as well as the most extensive (252 feet wide by 71 feet deep). At its center a 17-foot 2-inch tall equestrian statue of General Grant lauded for its authenticity, as are the two groupings, Artillery and Cavalry, flanking it. The sculptor devoted 20 years of his life to the monumental undertaking but, sadly, died two weeks before its dedication on April 27, 1922.

Major General Nathaniel Greene
Stanton Square, Maryland & Massachusetts Avenues, NE. (Henry Kirke Brown, 1877) In a city blessed with innumerable equestrian statues, this is considered one of the best, now firmly secured after having been toppled by a windstorm in 1930. In 1774, Green rose from private to brigadier general in one year!

Samuel Hahnemann
Scott Circle, Massachusetts Avenue & 16th Street, NW. (Charles Henry Niehaus, 1900) German physician and researcher (1775-1843) responsible for the beginnings of homeopathic medicine.

Captain Nathan Hale
Department of Justice, Constitution Avenue between 9th & 10th Streets, NW. (Bela Lyon Pratt, 1915) Revolutionary War hero. Posing as a schoolteacher, Hale was captured behind British lines. Carved in the statue beneath his bound feet: "I only regret I have but one life to lose for

my country," his heroic last words before being executed.

Alexander Hamilton
Department of Treasury Building, south entrance. (James Earl Fraser, 1923) Elegant bronze portrait statue of the first secretary of the treasury was funded by a still-anonymous donor.

The Hiker
Avenue of Heroes, approach to Arlington National Cemetery. (Theodora Alice Ruggles Kitson, 1965) An 8-foot bronze memorial to Spanish-American War veterans.

Iwo Jima
See Marine Corps War Memorial.

Major General Andrew Jackson
Lafayette Park, Pennsylvania Avenue between Jackson & Madison Places, NW. (Clark Mills, 1853) Jackson reviewing his troops at the Battle of New Orleans during the War of 1812. The first equestrian statue cast in America. Around the base are cannons captured from the Spanish by Jackson at Pensacola, Florida. It's the only non-Revolutionary War tribute in the park.

Joan of Arc
Meridian Hill Park, 16th Street & Florida Avenue, NW. (Paul Dubois, 1922) Replica of the one at Rheims Cathedral in France, a gift from the women of that country.

John Paul Jones
West Potomac Park, Independence Avenue & 17th Street, SW. (Charles Henry Niehaus, 1912) The Revolutionary War naval hero in bronze; his famous words "Surrender? I have not yet begun to fight!" appear on the rear. Sadly, he died in poverty in Paris, 1792.

Major General Philip Kearney
Arlington National Cemetery, at Lee, Miegs & Wilson Drives. (Edward Clark Potter, 1914) Seemingly in motion, this fine equestrian statue honors a colorful and brave soldier who, it is reported, rode into battle, the reins of his mount in his teeth, waving his right arm for his men to follow. He had lost his left arm in the Mexican War.

Robert F. Kennedy
Department of Justice, courtyard, 10th Street between Constitution & Pennsylvania Avenues, NW. (Robert Berks, 1969) A bronze bust of RFK. It stands on a marble pedestal, which, like the life of the late attorney general and senator, was left uncompleted.

Thaddeus Kosciuszko
Lafayette Park, Pennsylvania Avenue between Jackson & Madison Places, NW. (Antoni Popiel, 1910) Polish patriot and freedom fighter. Major contributions to the American Revolutionary War effort were his fortifications at Saratoga and West Point, New York.

Major General Marquis de Lafayette
Lafayette Park, Pennsylvania Avenue between Jackson & Madison Places, NW. (Jean Alexandre Joseph Falquiere & Marius Jean Antonin Mercie, 1891) The famed French general depicted petitioning the French National Assembly for aid to help America's war for independence.

Lafayette himself served Washington at Valley Forge. Located in the southeast corner of the park—where it doesn't block the view of Andrew Jackson from the White House.

Abe Lincoln, Rail Joiner
Department of the Interior, C Street between 18th and 19th Streets, NW. (Louis Slobodkin, 1940) A young lanky Lincoln. A contrast to the man he grew into.

Major General John A. Logan
Logan Circle, Vermont Avenue, 13th & P Streets, NW. (Franklin Simmons, 1901) An elaborate bronze equestrian memorial to Union Army general, three-term senator, and the man who conceived of Memorial Day, first set aside May 30, 1868.

Henry Wadsworth Longfellow
Connecticut Avenue & M Street, NW. (Thomas Ball & William Couper, 1909) The celebrated American poet in bronze.

Martin Luther
Thomas Circle, Massachusetts Avenue & 14th Street, NW. (E. Reitshel, 1884) Leader of the Protestant Reformation in bronze.

Guglielmo Marconi
16th & Lamont Streets, NW. (Attilio Piccirilli, 1941) A bust of the inventor of radio, behind it a gilded bronze Art Deco figure of a woman, symbolic of his achievement.

Marine Corps War Memorial (Iwo Jima)
Arlington Boulevard & Ridge Road (just north of Arlington Cemetery), Arlington, Va. (Felix W. de Welden, 1954) A moment in time captured as memorial to those who perished as U.S. Marines. During WW II, after five days of battle, six marines fought their way up Mount Suribachi on Iwo Jima island and, using a piece of pipe as a pole, raised the American flag. The Joe Rosenthal photograph capturing the event won the Pulitzer Prize (1945) and became the inspiration for this 100-ton bronze memorial to valor. Three of the survivors posed, the others were done from photos. The flag is raised daily at 8am and lowered at sunset. The memorial is also the scene of outdoor concerts every Tuesday in summer. (*See* ANNUAL EVENTS, May.) *Metro: Arlington Cemetery.*

John Marshall
The Capitol, West Terrace. (William Wetmore Story, 1884) The famed Federalist and prominent chief justice of the Supreme Court, 1801-35, seated, in bronze. By the son of one of his associate justices. A twin statue from the same mold stands outside the Philadelphia Museum of Art.

Major General George B. McClellan
Connecticut Avenue & Columbia Road, NW. (Frederick MacMonnies, 1907) Nine-foot bronze statue of the Civil War commander of the Army of the Potomac. On the pedestal, escutcheons honoring his battles. Exhibited in Paris in 1906, before being sent here.

Brigadier General James B. McPherson
McPherson Square, 15th Street between K & P Streets, NW. (Louis T. Rebisso, 1876) Civil War

general who was part of Sherman's march to the sea; he was killed during the Battle of Atlanta. The bronze equestrian statue is cast from a cannon captured there.

Andrew W. Mellon Memorial Fountain
Intersection Constitution & Pennsylvania Avenues, NW. (Eggers & Higgins, 1952) In front of financier Mellon's gift to the nation, the National Gallery of Art. The three-tiered fountain decorated with signs of the zodiac (Sidney Waugh, sculptor) was inspired by one in Genoa, Italy.

The National Law Enforcement Officers Memorial
Judiciary Square, E Street between 4th & 5th Streets, NW. (Architect: Davis Buckley; landscape architect: James Urban; bronze lions: Ray Kaskey, 1991) This landscaped memorial is an affecting and fitting tribute to the thousands of law-enforcement officers who have died in the line of duty. Two low, curving marble walls are inscribed with the names of the fallen, beginning with the earliest known, Robert Forsyth, a U.S. Marshall killed in 1794 while serving a warrant. At the extremities of the walls are exquisitely executed bronze lions, symbolic representations of valor. With its terraced pool, an alley of linden trees, and plenty of spaces to sit, it's a serene and welcoming space.

Nuns of the Battlefield
Rhode Island Avenue & M Street, NW. (Jerome Conner, 1924) A large bronze relief honoring nuns who volunteered to tend the Civil War's wounded in hospitals and on the battlefield.

Peace Monument
Pennsylvania Avenue & 1st Street, NW. (Franklin Simmons, 1877) America weeps on the shoulders of History. Inscription on the book: "They died that their country might live." Originally called Navy Monument.

Penguin Fountain
Walter Reed Army Medical Center, 16th Street & Alaska Avenue, NW. A charming fountain dedicated in 1935 boasts four 2½-foot-high penguins.

Brigadier General Albert Pike
3rd & D Streets, NW. (Gaetano Trentanove, 1901) The only monument to a Confederate general in Washington, DC.

Prodigal Son
Washington Cathedral, Mount St. Alban, Wisconsin & Cathedral Avenues, NW. (Heinz Warneke, 1961) Within the Bishops' Gardens formal rose garden, the biblical lesson depicted in granite.

Puck Fountain
Folger Shakespeare Library, East Capitol & 2nd Streets, SE. (Brenda Putnam, 1932) Poised in front of a narrow fountain, Shakespeare's prankster from A Midsummer Night's Dream. One of his lines is inscribed beneath him.

Brigadier General Count Casimir Pulaski
Pennsylvania Avenue & 13th Street, NW. (Albert R. Ross, 1910) One of the courageous foreigners who helped Americans win their Revolutionary War, Pulaski is depicted here in his Polish marshal's uniform.

Major General Comte Jean de Rochambeau
Lafayette Park, Pennsylvania Avenue between Jackson & Madison Places, NW. (J. J. Fernand Homar, 1902) Heroic bronze tribute to the commander of the 5,500-strong Royal French Expeditionary Force (1780).

Franklin Delano Roosevelt Memorial
Pennsylvania Avenue near 9th Street, NW. Rather amazing in this city of statues and monuments, this small marble stone has been the city's only memorial to FDR. Thirty-seven years ago Congress authorized a memorial to be built at the Tidal Basin between the Jefferson and Lincoln memorials, but ground breaking did not take place until 1991. The impressive $48 million memorial should be completed in 1995.

Theodore Roosevelt Memorial
Theodore Roosevelt Island, Potomac River, between Key & Roosevelt Bridges. (Paul Manship, 1967) The 26th U.S. president and early conservationist in a familiar pose. Fittingly memorialized by a 17-foot-tall bronze statue on an island set aside as a nature and wildlife preserve. (See also PARKS & GARDENS, Nature Trails & Wildlife Preserves: Theodore Roosevelt Island.)

St. Jerome the Priest
1359 Monroe Street, NE. (Ivan Mestrovic, 1954) An intense characterization of the learned priest by a protégé of Rodin. The lessons obviously took.

Father Godfrey Schilling
Franciscan Monastery, 14th & Quincy Streets, NE. (F. C. Shrady, 1955) The founder of the Order of St. Francis in America. In his hand, a replica of the church he built.

Lieutenant General Winfield Scott
Scott Circle, Massachusetts & Rhode Island Avenues, NW. (Henry Kirke Brown, 1874) Cast from a cannon Scott captured during the Mexican War. Controversy surrounded the choice of mount portrayed. A mare, Scott's favorite, was thought unsuitable by the family. They preferred a stallion. The result is a "compromise" horse.

Second Division Memorial
The Ellipse, Constitution Avenue near 17th Street, NW. (James Earle Fraser, 1936) Constructed initially to memorialize the Division's dead in WW I, two additions honor the dead of WW II and the Korean conflict. The gilded sword is a symbolic impediment to the German advance on Paris.

Settlers of the District of Columbia Memorial
Ellipse, 15th Street between Constitution Avenue & E Street, NW. (Carl Mose, 1936) A simple monument dedicated to the 18 landowners whose property became the nation's capital.

Olive Risley Seward
601 North Carolina Avenue, SE. (John Cavanaugh, 1971) Adjacent to Seward Square. Lead statue of foster daughter of Secretary of State William H. Seward. Said to have been an idealized portrait of a Victorian lady since no photo of the subject was known to exist.

Sheridan Statue
Sheridan Circle, Massachusetts Avenue & 23rd Street, NW. (Gutzon Borglum, 1909) Eleven-foot-tall bronze Philip H. Sheridan, Civil War Union cavalry leader, and his horse Rienzi, renamed Winchester after the victorious battle the statue commemorates.

General William Tecumseh Sherman
15th Street & Pennsylvania Avenue, NW. (Carl Rohl-Smith & others, 1903) An elaborate memorial to the Union Army general on the spot where he reviewed returning troops in 1865. The sculptor died in 1900 leaving the work to be finished by a series of other sculptors.

Taras Shevchenko
P Street between 22nd & 23rd Streets, NW. (Leo Mul, 1964) A monument to the Ukrainian poet, hero to the Ukrainian people.

Sphinxes
Scottish Rite Temple, 1733 16th Street, NW. (Alexander A. Weinman, 1915) Wisdom on the right, Power on the left. Each is 7 feet tall, carved from a single piece of solid limestone.

Major General Friedrich Wilhelm von Steuben
Lafayette Park, Pennsylvania Avenue between Jackson & Madison Places, NW. (Albert Jeagers, 1910) A veteran of the Seven Years' War, he brought from Prussia techniques of organization, administration, and military training that in 1778 helped the Americans become a formidable fighting force.

Oscar S. Strauss Memorial Fountain
14th Street between Constitution & Pennsylvania Avenues, NW. (Alexander A. Weinman, 1947) A bronze and marble tribute to a man who was one of this country's first career diplomats, as well as a statesman and author.

Taft Bell Tower
Capitol Grounds, Constitution, New Jersey & Louisiana Avenues, NW. (Sculptor: Wheeler Williams. Architect: Douglas W. Orr, 1959) Senator Robert A. Taft, son of our 27th president. "Mr. Republican," congressman, senator 1938-53, staunch foe of FDR's New Deal. Electronically set to chime on the quarter hour and toll the hour, daily, from 8am to 8pm. Manually rung on special occasions.

Temperance Fountain
Pennsylvania Avenue & 7th Street, NW. An eccentric bronze and granite water fountain presented to the city in 1882 by temperance crusader Dr. Henry D. Cogswell, who apparently gave one to any city that would accept it. This is one of the few remaining.

Major General H. Thomas
Thomas Circle, Massachusetts Avenue & 14th Street, NW. (John Quincy Adams Ward, 1879) Union Army Civil War hero on horseback. One of the best by famed American sculptor.

Three Fightingmen
Vietnam Veterans Memorial, Constitution Gardens. (Frederick Hart, 1984) A realistic bronze sculpture of three U.S. servicemen in combat in Vietnam, it was erected in answer to the criticism

Temperance Fountain

that the memorial itself was too abstract. (*See* Vietnam Veterans Memorial.)

Titanic Memorial
Washington Channel Park, 4th & P Streets, SW. (Gertrude Vanderbilt Whitney, 1931) An 18-foot-tall granite figure stands as memorial to those lost when the "unsinkable" British luxury ship sank, April 15, 1912, during its maiden voyage. Ironically, the sculptor's brother, Alfred Gwynne Vanderbilt, perished in the sinking of the *Lusitania* in 1915.

U.S. Navy Memorial
701 Pennsylvania Avenue, NW. (703) 524-0830. Just across the avenue from the National Archives. A living memorial dedicated to all who have served in the U.S. Navy. The plaza with an amphitheater—on its floor an etching of the world's oceans—for Navy Band concerts (Memorial Day to Labor Day) is enhanced by fountains and pools. A Visitors Center containing a Ship's Store, a 30-minute film on our Navy's history, and an interactive video display. Also here "The Homecoming," a life-like 7-foot sailor in bronze by Stanley Bleinfeld.

Vietnam Veterans Memorial
Constitution Gardens, Constitution Avenue between 17th and 21st Streets. On 2 acres, dedicated in 1982, a memorial to the Americans who died in the Vietnam War between 1961 and 1975. The horizontal landscape design by 21-year-old Maya Ying Lin—chosen from over 1,400 entries in a national competition—consists of two 200-foot-long walls that are inscribed with the names of those Americans who perished in the war. Its color—black—and its trenchlike appearance initially drew criticism from some. Others feel it's a fitting metaphor. A statue has been added to quiet those who felt it too abstract. Still to come a statue honoring the women who served in Vietnam. (*See also* SIGHTSEEING, On Your Own.)

Major General Artemus Ward
Ward Circle, Massachusetts & Nebraska Avenues, NW. (Leonard Crunelle, 1938) A member

f the Continental Congress from Massachuetts, he was honored by his alma mater, Harard.

Lieutenant General George Washington
Washington Circle, Pennsylvania Avenue at the intersection of New Hampshire, 23rd & K Streets, NW. (Clark Mills, 1860) The horse is spooked, but Washington is serene as he leads the surprise attack on the British at Princeton and Trenton.

Lieutenant General George Washington
Washington Cathedral, Mount St. Alban, Wisconsin & Cathedral Avenues, NW. (Herbert Hazeltine, 1959) A gilded bronze statue of a young Washington on horseback. Note the horse's glass eyes.

Daniel Webster
Scott Circle, Massachusetts Avenue & 16th Street, NW. (Gaetano Trentanove, 1900) American orator, statesman, and staunch defender of the Union.

John Wesley
Wesley Theological Seminary, 4400 Massachusetts Avenue, NW. (Arthur George Walker, 1961) A gentle tribute to the founder of the Methodist church. The original stands at Wesley Chapel, Bristol, England.

John Witherspoon
connecticut Avenue & N Street, NW. (William Couper, 1909) The Scotsman, a signer of the Declaration of Independence, who dedicated himself to public service and the Presbyterian church in America.

CHURCHES & SYNAGOGUES

Adas Israel Synagogue Landmark
3rd & G Streets, NW. 789-0900; (301) 881-0100. Washington's oldest synagogue building, dedi-

Adas Israel Synagogue Landmark

All Souls' Unitarian Church

cated in 1876 with President Grant in attendance. It housed the city's second-oldest Jewish congregation until 1908. Saved from demolition and moved from 6th and G Streets, NW, to its present site in 1969, it was beautifully restored. Now in the National Register of Historic Places. In the lower level, the Albert & Lillian Small Jewish Museum, containing the Jewish Historical Society's library, archives, and artifacts. Museum *OPEN Sun-Thurs 11am-3pm & by appointment.* FREE. *Metro: Foggy Bottom.*

All Souls' Unitarian Church
16th Street & Harvard Square, NW. 332-5266. (Coolidge & Shattuck, 1924) Built at a cost of $1 million, in what was then one of DC's best residential areas. Patterned after London's St. Martin-in-the-Fields (James Gibbs). Sunday services 11am (Ethical dialogue 9:45am). *OPEN Tues-Fri 9am-10pm; Sun till 3pm.*

Capitol Hill United Methodist Church
5th Street and Pennsylvania Avenue, SE. 546-1000. (A. Hensel Fink, 1966) Built on the site of the birthplace of late FBI director J. Edgar Hoover. The J. Edgar Hoover window, which appears to be three-dimensional, symbolizes Hope, Justice, Courage, Wisdom, Faith, Education, Purity, and Temperance. Mr. W. E. Bliss donated the window in Hoover's honor because of his help following the kidnapping of a family member. Sunday service 11am. *OPEN Mon-Fri 10am-4pm.*

Christ Church (Episcopal)
620 G Street, SE. 547-9300. (Benjamin H. Latrobe, 1805) This lovely, albeit altered, Gothic Revival church in Capitol Hill area counts among its former parishioners Presidents Adams, Mad-

ison, and Monroe. Circumstantial evidence indicates Jefferson attended as well. John Philip Sousa was married here. Sunday services 8:30 and 11am. *OPEN Mon-Fri 10am-4pm.*

Christ Church (Episcopal)
118 North Washington Street, Alexandria, Va. (703) 549-1450. (James Wren, 1767-73) Charming Georgian country church where George Washington regularly worshiped (pew #60), so did Robert E. Lee (pew #46). It has been traditional for the president to attend services here on the Sunday closest to George Washington's birthday. (*See also* Graveyards & Tombs.) An informal tour on Sunday from 2:30 to 4pm. Sunday services 8, 9 & 11:15am. *OPEN Mon-Sat 9:30am-4pm; Sun till 4:30pm.*

Christ Episcopal Church
31st & O Streets, NW. 333-6677. (Henry Laws, 1885) A small-scale Gothic cathedral houses this congregation founded in 1817. One former parishioner was Francis Scott Key, who penned our national anthem. Sunday services 8, 9, and 11am; from June to September at 8 and 10am.

The Church of the Pilgrims (Presbyterian)
2201 P Street, NW. 387-6612. (Benjamin Flournoy, 1929-30) A landmark church on the edge of the Dupont Circle neighborhood. Repository of the last pipe Ernest Skinner pipe organ made. Sunday service 11am. *OPEN Sun-Fri 9am-5pm; Sat 9am-1pm.*

Ebenezer United Methodist Church
4th & D Streets, SE. 544-1415. On this site in 1838, a small building became the first school for blacks in Washington. The present Richardson-Romanesque church building dates from 1897 and is an integral part of the Capitol Hill community. Sunday service 11am. *OPEN Mon-Fri 10am-3pm.*

Epiphany Episcopal Church
1317 G Street, NW. 347-2635. A graceful Gothic church in the downtown area, built in 1873.

Christ Church

Lovely stained-glass windows. Sunday service 8 and 11am. *OPEN 7 days 8am-5pm.*

Foundry United Methodist Church
16th & P Streets, NW. 332-4010. (Appleton P Clark, 1903-4) Founded by Henry Foxhall, Georgetown foundry owner. Still a large, active congregation. Sunday services 9:30 and 11am.

The Franciscan Monastery
Mount St. Sepulchre, 1400 Quincy Street, NE. 526-6800. (Aristides Leonori, 1899) The Byzantine church building and the grounds offer opportunities for a religious pilgrimage without leaving the city. Beneath the church are Roman-like catacombs, in the garden a reconstruction of the grotto at Lourdes as well as Holy Land shrines. Even from a secular standpoint the grounds are lovely (*see also* PARKS & GARDENS, Gardens). Free half-hour tour leaves from the lobby every hour on the hour between 9am and 4pm (except at noon); Sunday every 15 minutes from 1 to 4:30pm. Sunday services 7, 8:30, and 10:30am and noon. *OPEN 7 days 9am-4pm.*

Friends Meeting of Washington
2111 Florida Avenue, NW. 483-3310. (Walter H. Price, 1930) Quaker simplicity in stone, thoughtful inscription on sundial. The only Quaker meetinghouse in DC, it was built for President Hoover so that he could have a place to worship. Mrs. Hoover decorated the parlor. Lovely garden. Groups should call in advance. Meetings Sunday 9, 10, and 11am. *OPEN Mon-Fri 8am-4pm; Sun 8:30am-1pm. CLOSED Sat.* Metro: Dupont Circle.

Georgetown Presbyterian Church
3115 P Street, NE. 338-1644. The congregation moved to this church in 1873. Sunday service 11am.

Grace Episcopal Church
1041 Wisconsin Avenue, NW. 333-7100. Charming Gothic Revival mission church built in 1866 as a place for C&O canal boatmen to worship. Sunday services from September to June at 9 and 11am; July and August at 8:30 and 10am.

Grace Reformed Church
15th & O Streets, NW. 387-3131. (Sanctuary: Abner Ritcher, 1903. Sunday school: Paul Pelz, 1903) Teddy Roosevelt was a member of this 104-year-old congregation and he attended services here as vice president and president (1901-9). He also laid the cornerstone of the present church building, which contains Teddy memorabilia. Eisenhower and Nixon were also members of the congregation at one time. Sunday service 11am, Wednesday at noon.

Holy Trinity Parish (Roman Catholic)
36th Street between N & O Streets, NW. 337-2840. (Duffy, 1851) Greek Revival church building replaced original Holy Trinity parish in 1851. Recently renovated, it's the oldest standing Catholic church in DC. Restored pure Skinner organ that was originally designed for the Library of Congress. Sunday services 7, 8, 9:15, and 11:30am; 1 and 5:30pm. *OPEN Mon-Fri 9am-5pm.*

Islamic Center

2551 Massachusetts Avenue, NW. 332-8343. (Mario Rossi, 1955) On Embassy Row, an authentic Middle Eastern mosque designed in Egypt. From the graceful 160-foot-tall minaret five times a day Muslims are called to prayer. The center consists of a mosque and reference library on Islamic religion. Appropriate dress required (remove shoes). Reserve at the information office for group tours. *OPEN 7 days 10am-5pm. (Muslims may come at any time to pray.) Metro: Dupont Circle.*

Luther Place Memorial Church (Lutheran)

1226 Vermont Avenue, NW. 667-1377. (Judson York, 1870. Addition 1952: L. M. Leisenring) On Thomas Circle. Red sandstone neo-Gothic church built in thanksgiving for the Civil War's end. Sunday services 8:30 and 11am. *OPEN Mon-Fri 9am-5pm. Metro: McPherson Square.*

Metropolitan African Methodist Episcopal Church

1518 M Street, NW. 331-1426. (Samuel T. Morsell, 1886) A Victorian Gothic church (aka National Cathedral of African Methodism) with main sanctuary on the second floor. One of the city's oldest and most influential black congregations. The funeral service for abolitionist Frederick Douglass was held here. Sunday services 8 and 11am. *Metro: Farragut North, McPherson Square.*

Mt. Zion United Methodist Church

1334 29th Street, NW. 234-0148. The oldest black church in Washington DC; the congregation dates back to 1814. This building dates from 1876. Sunday service 11am; in summer at 10am.

National City Christian Church (Disciples of Christ)

14th Street & Massachusetts Avenue, NW. 232-0323. (John Russell Pope, 1930. Addition 1954: Leon Chatelain, Jr.) Beautifully situated on Thomas Circle. Former presidents James Garfield and Lyndon Johnson were parishioners. Very pretty stained glass. Guided tours upon request. Sunday service 11am. *OPEN Mon-Fri 8:30am-5pm. Metro: McPherson Square.*

Metropolitan African Methodist

Episcopal Church

National Shrine of the Immaculate Conception

4th Street & Michigan Avenue, NE. 526-8300. This is the largest Roman Catholic church in America, the seventh largest in the world. Dedicated to the Virgin Mary November 1959. Huge and elaborate, built of stone, brick, and tile in a Byzantine-Romanesque style with 56 different chapels, a wealth of mosaics, statues, works of art, stained-glass windows. The 329-foot bell tower contains a 56-bell French Paccard carillon (dedicated in 1964), the heaviest bell weighing 7,200 pounds. Concerts every Sunday from September to May at 2:30pm (*see also* ANNUAL EVENTS, June: Carillon & Organ Concerts). Guided tours in summer Monday to Saturday from 9am to 4pm; Sunday at 1:30, 2:30, 3, 3:30, and 4pm. Cafeteria, gift shop. Sunday services 7:30, 9, and 10:30am; noon, 1:30 (in Latin), and 4:30pm. *OPEN 7 days 9am-5pm. Metro: Brookland-CUA.*

New York Avenue Presbyterian Church

1313 New York Avenue, NW. 393-3700. This congregation was founded in 1793. Their first church building was erected in 1859, where President Lincoln and his family were parishioners during the Civil War. The present Georgian-style building, which contains two Tiffany windows, was built in 1951. In the Lincoln Parlor, the original handwritten draft of what would eventually become the Emancipation Proclamation. Sunday services 9 and 11am. *OPEN Tues-Fri 9am-5pm; Mon, Sat & Sun 9am-1pm.*

Oak Hill Chapel

Oak Hill Cemetery, 30th & R Streets, NW. (James Renwick, 1850) Simple, small Gothic Revival stone chapel by architect of the Smithsonian Castle and New York's St. Patrick's Cathedral. (*See also* Graveyards & Tombs: Oak Hill Cemetery.)

Old Presbyterian Meeting House

321 South Fairfax Street, Alexandria, Va. (703) 549-6670. A somber Presbyterian church, built in 1774 by Alexandria's Scottish founders. Site of

memorial services for George Washington (the snow was too deep to get to Christ Church, where Washington was a parishioner). In the cemetery, the tomb of the Revolutionary War's Unknown Soldier. Sunday service 11am. *OPEN Mon-Fri 8:30am-4:30pm.*

Pohick Episcopal Church
9301 Richmond Highway, Lorton, Va. (703) 550-9449. Known as Mount Vernon's parish church, it was completed in 1774 (James Wren and William West). George Washington drew up the original plans and George Mason finished the church after the original engineer died; they were also vestrymen. It was used as a stable during the Civil War, by both North and South, and the interior was destroyed. It was restored sometime during the 1950s. Over 500 families are part of a very active congregation. Sunday services 8, 9:15, and 11am; in summer at 8 and 10am. *OPEN 7 days 8:30am-4:30pm.*

St. Alban's Episcopal Church
Mount St. Alban, Massachusetts & Wisconsin Avenues, NW. 363-8286. Consecrated in 1855, the original parish church was of wood; in 1926 it was enlarged and stone-encased. Located on the National Cathedral Close. Sunday services from September to May at 8, 9:15, and 11am; June to August at 8 and 10:30am. *OPEN Mon-Fri 8:30am-4:30pm.*

St. John's Church (Episcopal)
16th & H Streets, NW. 347-8766. (Benjamin H. Latrobe, 1816. Remodeled 1883: James Renwick) On Lafayette Square, opposite the White House. Attended by President Madison and his wife, Dolley, and every subsequent president at least once in his term. The president's pew is #54. Free organ recitals from October to July, every Wednesday at noon (except during Lent). Reserve for group tours. Sunday services 8, 9, and 11am; in French at 4pm. *OPEN Mon-Thurs 9am-5pm; Fri 9am-4pm.*

St. John's Episcopal Church
Potomac & O Streets, NW. 338-1796. (Dr. William Thornton, 1809) DC's second oldest Episcopal church, by the Capitol's original designer. Still lovely, though oft modified (greatly in 1870 by Starkweather & Plowman). The congregation was founded in 1796. The Chapel of the Carpenter is particularly nice. Sunday services 8, 9, and 11am; in summer at 8 and 10am. *OPEN Mon-Fri 9am-4:30pm.*

St. Mark's Episcopal Church
3rd & A Streets, SE. 543 0053. (T. Buckler Chequier, 1888) Brick Gothic Revival church with timber roof and an active congregation. Was frequented by the late president Lyndon B. Johnson. Listed in the National Register of Historic Places. Sunday services 9 and 11am. *OPEN Mon-Fri 9am-5pm.*

St. Mary's Church (Roman Catholic)
727 5th Street, NW. 289-7770. (E. F. Baldwin, 1891) German Gothic church built by German Catholics. Saturday service 5pm; Sunday services 10am, 1 and 7:30pm.

National Shrine of the Immaculate Conception

St. Mary's Episcopal Church
728 23rd Street, NW. 333-3985. (James Renwick, 1887) Renwick's red-brick Gothic parish church is a beauty. The second of the city's Episcopal churches built for a black congregation (now racially mixed). The stained-glass windows are standouts; three are from France, the other is Tiffany. The congregation is justifiably proud of their church. Listed in the National Register of Historic Places. Sunday services 11am; from June to September at 10am. *OPEN Mon-Fri 9am-3:30pm.*

St. Matthew's Cathedral (Roman Catholic)
1725 Rhode Island Avenue, NW. 347-3215. (Heins & LaFarge, 1899) This is the church John F. Kennedy attended while president, and it was the site of his funeral mass. Inscription carved in the marble floor: "Here rested the remains of President Kennedy at the requiem Mass November 25, 1963, before their removal to Arlington, where they lie in expectation of a heavenly resurrection." Lovely mosaics and white marble altar. Sunday mass 12:10 and 5:30pm; in Spanish at 6:30pm. *OPEN 7 days 9am-8:30pm. Metro: Dupont Circle.*

St. Paul's Episcopal Church (Rock Creek Parish)
Rock Creek Cemetery, Rock Creek Church & Webster Hoads, NW. 726-2080. Located near the center of the cemetery. Founded in 1712; the original chapel, built of wood circa 1775, was DC's first church. The 18-inch-thick walls are still intact though the interior, destroyed by fire in 1921, is a restoration. Beautiful stained-glass windows. Sunday services 8, 9:30, and 11am; from the end of June to the end of September at 8 and 10am. *OPEN Mon-Fri 9am-3pm by appointment. (See also Graveyards & Tombs: Rock Creek Cemetery.)*

St. Thomas Episcopal Church
18th Street between P & Q Streets, NW. An arsonist destroyed this Dupont Circle-area Gothic church building in 1970. The parish house is the site of worship now.

Temple of the Church of Jesus Christ of Latter-Day Saints
9900 Stoneybrook Drive, Kensington, Md. Temple: (301) 588-0650; Visitors Center: (301) 587-0144. (Keith W. Wilcox, 1974) One of the Washington area's most visible structures. The spire rises 288 feet above the ground; atop is an 18-foot-tall, 2-ton gilded bronze statue of the angel Moroni. The temple is closed to everyone but church members but on the grounds is the Washington Temple Visitors Center, which provides films, photos, and literature on the temple. Visitors Center *OPEN 7 days 10am-10pm.*

Temple Micah/St. Augustine's Episcopal Church
600 M Street, SW. Temple Micah: 554-3099; St. Augustine's: 554-3222. In the Southwest Renewal Area. The Southwest Hebrew Congregation, organized in 1963, shares the premises with St. Augustine's Episcopal Church. The same sanctuary (with slight modifications for each) is used by both congregations on their respective Sabbaths. Friday service 8pm. Sunday service from June to September at 10:30am; from September to May at 9 and 11am. *OPEN Mon-Fri 9am-3pm.*

United Church
1920 G Street, NW. 331-1495. Remnant of ethnic German community that resided in the area in the late 19th century. Sunday service 11am; in German 1st and 3rd Sunday of every month at 9:30am. *OPEN Mon-Fri 9am-2:30pm.*

Washington Hebrew Congregation
Massachusetts Avenue & Macomb Street, NW. 362-7100. (F. Wallace Dixon, 1955) Chartered in 1852, this is Washington's oldest and largest Jewish congregation. The cornerstone of the present temple contains a stone from the Wall of Agrippa, one of Jerusalem's defensive walls 2,000 years ago. Friday services 8:30pm; Saturday services 10:30am. *OPEN Mon-Fri 9am-5pm.*

Washington National Cathedral (Episcopal)
Mount St. Alban, Wisconsin Avenue & Woodley Road, NW. 537-6200. (Vaughn, Bodley, 1907. Frohman, Robb and Little, 1922. Completion Goodwin & Beckett, supervising architects, 1990) Widely known as the National Cathedral; officially it's the Cathedral Church of St. Peter and St. Paul. The foundation stone was laid in 1907 with President Theodore Roosevelt doing the ground breaking; the first sections were opened in 1912, yet this magnificent Gothic cathedral remained unfinished until 1990. The remaining construction—two towers costing $12 million—took seven years to finish. The cathedral is now the world's sixth largest. The top of the Gloria in Excelsis Tower, 676 feet above sea level, is the highest point in Washington. The interior of this vast traditionally constructed medieval (albeit 20th-century) Gothic church is powerful. Also on the 57-acre close are three schools, a college, and St. Alban's Parish Church. Herb Cottage, one of the oldest buildings on the close, was built originally to house the baptistry; it's now a gift shop. (*See also* PARKS & GARDENS, Gardens: Washington Cathedral Close.) Free tours lasting 45 minutes, Monday to Saturday from 10am to 3pm, Sunday from 12:30 to 2pm. Free concerts year-round; carillons Saturday at 4:30pm; bells Sunday at 12:15pm; organ recitals Sunday at 5pm. Visitors Center, book and gift shop. Sunday services 8, 9, 10, and 11am and 4pm. Lovely views of Washington from Pilgrim's Observation Gallery *OPEN Mon-Sat 10am-4pm; Sun noon-3:15pm.* Main floor *OPEN 7 days 10am-4:30pm.* Chapel of the Good Shepherd *OPEN 24 hours. Metro:* Woodley Park-Zoo.

GRAVEYARDS & TOMBS

Adams Memorial
Rock Creek Cemetery, Rock Creek Church Road & Webster Street, NW, Section E. (Sculptor: Augustus Saint-Gaudens. Architect: Stanford White, 1890) In 1888, historian-educator Henry Adams commissioned his friend Augustus Saint-Gaudens, the leading sculptor of the period, to memorialize his wife, Marian, who had committed suicide in 1885 at age 42. The result, considered one of Gaudens's finest works, which he entitled *The Peace of God* (though no inscription appears), is more often and more appropriately referred to as *Grief.* One can't help but be moved —by the statue, by the setting. In 1918, at the foot of the statue, Henry Adams was buried beside his wife. The graves are unmarked.

Arlington National Cemetery
Arlington, Va. (202) 692-0931. Now 612 acres, it is the third largest of the 109 national cemeteries but the most famed. In 1864, 200 acres were acquired by the Union as a final resting place for

Washington Cathedral (Completed)

Adams Memorial

its fallen. The Custis mansion at the crest of the hill was the residence of Robert E. Lee until he joined the Confederacy; it and the surrounding acreage were bought by the government at public auction for use as a burial ground following tax default by the Lees. (*See also* Historic Buildings & Areas: Arlington House.) Interment is available to all armed services personnel who die on active duty, Medal of Honor winners, and retired members of military with wives and children who die as minors. But also resting here are two Italians and a German who died of natural causes as prisoners of war in the U.S. The graves of JFK, RFK, President Taft, Robert Todd Lincoln, Gen. John J. Pershing, prizefighter Joe Louis, astronaut Virgil (Gus) Grissom, William Jennings Bryan, and Medgar Evers are also here. There are 26 different approved headstone symbols used to indicate the religion of the 201,000 interred. Among that number are 7,725 unknowns, mainly from the Civil War, and the remains of the seven Challenger crewmembers. (*See also* John F. Kennedy Grave, Robert F. Kennedy Grave, L'Enfant's Grave, *and* Tomb of the Unknowns.) Tourmobiles leave from the Visitors Center for a one-hour tour that visits the Kennedy graves, the Tomb of the Unknowns, and Arlington House. Fee charged, lower for children ages 2 to 11. No autos are permitted on

grounds. *OPEN Apr-Sept, 7 days 8am-7pm; Oct-Mar, 7 days 8am-5pm. Metro: Arlington Cemetery.*

Arsenal Monument
Congressional Cemetery, 18th & E Streets, SE. (Leo Flannery, 1867) A 20-foot-high obelisk; atop, a weeping female. Buried beneath, the 21 women who died in the explosion in the Washington Arsenal on June 18, 1864.

Christ Church Graveyard
Christ Church, North Washington & Cameron Streets, Alexandria, Va. This 18th-century cemetery was Alexandria's principal burial ground until 1809. Unusual are the carved slate headstones on the graves of Capt. George Mumford and Isaac Pierce, more common in New England than this area. The first burial was in 1772 and the last in 1885.

Congressional Cemetery
18th & E Streets, SE. 543-0539. Established in 1807, a portion of it was set aside in 1816 for interment of members of Congress. (*See also* Latrobe Cenotaphs.) Among those buried here: architects Thornton, Hadley, and Mills; Elbridge Gerry, a vice president of the U.S.; John Philip Sousa, the "March King"; and Push-Ma-Ta-Ha, a Choctaw Indian chief who served under Andrew Jackson and whose epitaph reads "Let the big guns boom over me." *OPEN 7 days dawn till dusk.* Go to the gatekeeper's office for information and maps (not available on Sunday). *Office OPEN 8am-5pm for research.*

Glenwood Cemetery
2219 Lincoln Road, NE. 667-1016. A rural cemetery on 90 acres chartered July 27, 1854. Contains many ornate Victorian gravestones and monuments. See especially the Benjamin C. Grenup monument, which records the first death in line of duty of a DC fireman, and "the child in the rocker," Teresina Vasco, dead of burns, age 2. Cemetery *OPEN 7 days dawn to dusk.* Office *OPEN Mon-Fri 9:30am-3:30pm.*

John F. Kennedy Grave
Arlington National Cemetery, Fort Meyers, Va. (John Carl Warnecke, 1966) Off Sheridan Drive, on the slope of the hill below Arlington House. A granite walkway leads to the final resting place of John Fitzgerald Kennedy, 34th president of the U.S. Defined by a low wall inscribed with quotes from his inaugural address (1960). The grave area with its eternal flame is a familiar sight

Arlington House, Arlington National Cemetery

even to those who have never before visited it. Cape Cod fieldstones cover the simple grave area, with plain slate markers for the late president, his infant son, and stillborn daughter. The landscaped setting is serene and beautiful. *OPEN Apr-Sept, 7 days 8am-7pm; Oct-Mar, 7 days 8am-5pm.*

Robert F. Kennedy Grave
Arlington National Cemetery, Fort Meyers, Va. Assassinated in 1968; close to his brother in life and now in death. *OPEN Apr-Sept, 7 days 8am-7pm; Oct-Mar, 7 days 8am-5pm.*

Latrobe Cenotaphs
Congressional Cemetery, 18th & E Streets, SE. 543-0539. In the original northeastern section of the "first national cemetery" are these 4½-foot-tall sandstone memorials under which lie congressmen who died between 1807 and 1877. Designed by noted architect of the period, Benjamin Henry Latrobe, the memorials fell out of fashion following a speech by Massachusetts senator George Hoar. He exclaimed that "the prospect of being buried beneath one of the cenotaphs added new terror to death." (*See also* Congressional Cemetery.)

L'Enfant's Grave
Arlington National Cemetery, Fort Meyers, Va. Though his plan was rejected and he died penniless and alone, the city of Washington you see today is essentially the one L'Enfant envisioned. Originally interred at Green Hill, Maryland, he—like his plan—was once again accepted. Now he lies where the vista of his Washington is unsurpassed.

Mt. Zion Cemetery
27th & Q Streets, NW. 234-0148. Established in 1843 by the Female Union Band Society, a group of freed slaves. In the late 19th century it served the Georgetown area, then approximately 40 percent black. *OPEN 24 hours a day, 7 days a week.*

Oak Hill Cemetery
30th & R Streets, NW. 337-2835. (Gatehouse: George F. de la Roche, 1850) Named for a grove of giant oaks, this 12½-acre, parklike cemetery was founded in 1849; the land and gatehouse were gifts of William Wilson Corcoran. Buried here are Lincoln's secretary of war, Edwin Stanton, and John Howard Payne, composer of "Home Sweet Home." The Victorian monuments

Oak Hill Cemetery Gatehouse

and tombs offer a very personal insight into another time. *OPEN Mon-Fri 9am-4:30pm. CLOSED Sat, Sun & holidays.*

Rock Creek Cemetery
Rock Creek Church Road & Webster Street, NW. 829-0585. The first burial ground in what is now DC. Established in 1719, it is situated on 68 acres of rolling terrain, on one of the District's highest elevations. Natural beauty, tasteful landscaping, and monuments by Augustus Saint-Gaudens, Gutzon Borglum, and William Ordway Partridge make it a nice place to visit (interments continue, so you may arrange to stay). *OPEN 7 days 7:30am-7pm.*

Tomb of the Unknowns
Arlington Memorial Amphitheater Plaza, Arlington National Cemetery, Fort Meyers, Va. 692-0931. (Thomas Hudson Jones, 1931) Formerly known as the Tomb of the Unknown Soldier. "Here rests in honored glory an American soldier known but to God." He was brought home from the WW I battlefield at Chalons-sur-Maine, France. Later, an unknown American serviceman from WW II, one from the Korean War, and more recently (1984) one from the Vietnam War were also interred in the plaza. The allegorical figures in relief represent Victory, Peace, and the American Soldier. Watched over always by a lone sentinel from the 3rd Infantry, who paces with precision in front of the tomb. There is an impressive ceremony at the change of the guard: April to October every half hour between 8am and 7pm; November to March every hour on the hour, 8am to 5pm.

Van Ness Mausoleum
Oak Hill Cemetery, 30th & R Streets, NW. (George Hadfield, 1833) On the cemetery hill a tomb inspired by the Roman Forum's Temple of Vesta.

MODERN ARCHITECTURE

So far, with a few exceptions, Washington's track record in this area has not been good. Part of the "problem" for architects is the legal height constraints.

American Institute of Architects Headquarters
1735 New York Avenue, NW. (The Architects Collaborative, 1973) Surrounds Octagon House; the modern building provides an interesting contrast to the older building. In the lobby and on the second floor are exhibits of art pertaining to architecture. The bookstore (626-7474) is devoted to architecture and design. *OPEN Mon-Fri 8:30am-5pm.*

Arena Stage & Kreeger Theater
6th & Maine Streets, SW. 488-3300. (Harry Weese & Associates, 1961; 1970) In the Southwest Urban Renewal Area. The Arena is an imaginatively designed concrete theater-in-the-round, well used and used well, it's one of the nation's most vital and innovative. Seats 800. The

Kreeger has a proscenium stage and seats 500. The third part of the complex is the 150-seat Old Vat Room, a cabaret-style theater.

Canadian Embassy
Pennsylvania Avenue, NW. 682-1740. (Arthur Erickson, 1989) Across the street from the National Gallery of Art, on a prominent piece of real estate no where near Embassy Row. Built of unpolished Canadian marble in a mix of classicism and modernism, which is not quite seamless. Set on an attractive plaza with reflecting pool. There is also a small gallery showing the work of Canadian artists *OPEN Mon-Fri 9am-5pm.*

Canal Square
1054 31st Street, NW. (Arthur Cotton Moore & Associate, 1970) In Georgetown, one of the town's first mixed-use complexes, incorporates old C&O canalside warehouses.

Central Intelligence Agency (CIA)
Langley, Va. Telling you where it is located is simply a point of information. Barely visible from the road, it houses 12,000 employees. They can enter, you can't—unless you have official business.

Department of Housing and Urban Development
451 7th Street, SW. (Marcel Breuer and Herbert Beckhard, Nolen-Swinburne & Associates, 1968) The curved design, typical of Breuer, provides an attractive form as well as the most light to the most people.

Dulles Airport
Chantilly, Va. (Eero Saarinen, 1962) Considered by many to be a landmark of 20th-century design. It was the first airport built primarily for jet traffic (i.e., long runways) and it just may be the nation's most aesthetically beautiful airport. It is also the least busy, due to its location, 26 miles from downtown DC. Huge glass-enclosed lobby; observation deck on the south concourse offers a serene spot for great views.

Euram Building
21 Dupont Circle, NW. (Hartman Cox, 1970) Striking eight-story brick-and-glass structure considered one of the more "imaginative" modern buildings. Pleasant interior courtyard.

James Forrestal Building (Federal Office Building No. 5)
Independence Avenue & 10th Street, SW. 586-5000. (Curtis & Davis, 1970) Composed of three buildings. The first floor of the 660-foot-long main building starts 30 feet above the street, providing entrance to the 10th Street Mall and allowing a view of the Smithsonian Castle's tower. Public document room for pamphlets and reports. *OPEN Mon-Fri 8:30am-4pm.*

Freedom Plaza
Pennsylvania Avenue between 13th & 14th Streets, NW. (Venturi, Rauch & Scott Brown, 1980) A rather sterile urban plaza containing a walk-on map of L'Enfant's plan of the city carved in light marble and dark granite. Perceptions of the city by visitors as diverse as Alexander Graham Bell and Mark Twain, over a 200-year period, are inscribed in multihued marble. They, and the ability to see clearly what L'Enfant envisioned, are the chief pluses. Head straight for that nearby little oasis, Pershing Park, with its welcoming pool (skating rink in winter), snack kiosk, and tables and chairs. *Metro: Federal Triangle.*

Hart Senate Office Building
Constitution Avenue & 2nd Street, NE. (John Carl Warnecke & Associates, 1983) Located between the classical Everett Dirksen Senate Office Building and the historic old Sewell-Belmont House is the most expensive federal office building in history—$138 million. Known widely as the SOB, the nine-story stark white building has a 3-inch-thick marble veneer, a 100-foot-high atrium, room for 50 senators and their staffs—it also has a host of critics.

Hirshhorn Museum & Sculpture Garden
Independence Avenue & 8th Street, SW. 357-1300. (Skidmore, Owings & Merrill, 1974) The first true modern architecture to be built on the Mall. When completed, the cylindrical concrete building (doughnut to some) with no exterior windows and sunken sculpture garden caused some controversy, but not so the magnificent art collection, nor the air-conditioning system, reported to be DC's best. (*See* MUSEUMS & GALLERIES, Museums.)

J. Edgar Hoover FBI Building
Pennsylvania Avenue at 10th Street, NW. 324-3000. (C. F. Murphy Associates, 1975) The Chicago architects were no doubt constrained by this city's height restrictions, not to mention the agency's security conditions. Four years to design and eight years to build, at a cost of $126 million (they didn't want anything elaborate). Fascinating tours lasting one hour leave every 15 minutes. Groups must reserve. *OPEN Mon-Fri 8:45am-4:15pm. CLOSED Sat, Sun & holidays.* (*See also* SIGHTSEEING, On Your Own: The FBI.) *FREE. Metro: Federal Triangle.*

Hubert Humphrey Federal Office Building
Independence Avenue, SW, between 2nd & 3rd Streets. (Marcel Breuer & Herbert Beckhard, 1976) A six-story rectangle set on an urban plaza. Light wells provide daylight for inside offices. The building's core contains an exhaust

James Forrestal Building

Kennedy Center for the Performing Arts

shaft from the Interstate Highway, which runs beneath. Houses the Department of Health and Human Services.

International Monetary Fund (IMF) Visitors Center
19th & G Streets, NW. 623-6869. (Vincent G. Kling & Partners; Clas, Riggs, Owens & Ramos, 1973) This addition to the world bank complex boasts a huge and spectacular interior court-yard that contains a bi-level plaza for special events. Art shows, permanent exhibits on the functions of the IMF, crafts exhibitions, and films by the International Cine Club. Reading room and bookstore. *OPEN Mon-Fri 9:30am-6pm. Metro: Farragut West.*

Kennedy Center for the Performing Arts
New Hampshire Avenue & F Street, NW at Rock Creek Parkway. 467-4600. (Edward Durell Stone, 1971) A grand cultural resource perched on the Potomac, its debut put Washington firmly on the cultural map. In 1958, President Eisenhower signed a bill authorizing the creation of a national center for the performing arts. It received funding in President Kennedy's administration, and it opened September 8, 1971, as a living memorial to the slain young president. Home to the National Symphony Orchestra, under the baton of Mstislav Rostropovich, and the Washington Opera. Its theaters (the Eisenhower, the Opera House, Concert Hall, Terrace Theater, Theater Lab, and the American Film Institute Theater) present a high caliber variety of music, dance, opera, theater, and film. The Grand Foyer, 60 feet high, 630 feet long, is one of the world's largest rooms; in it, a rough-hewn bronze bust of JFK. The Hall of States flies flags of all U.S. states and territories; the Hall of Nations, the flags of all nations recognized by the U.S. There are information desks situated in each of the halls. Accessible via Tourmobile. (*See also* SIGHTSEEING, Viewpoints *and* On Your Own, *and* ENTERTAINMENT.)

Martin Luther King Memorial Library
901 G Street, NW. 727-1111. (Office of Ludwig Mies Van der Rohe, 1972) This black steel-and-glass box, aka New DC Central Library, is the only Miesian building in Washington. The main branch of Washington's public library system. There's a black studies division and the largest compilation in existence of material on the history of our nation's capital. Free film programs throughout the year. Exhibits in the gallery. *OPEN Mon-Thurs 9am-9pm; Fri & Sat 9am-5:30pm; Sun 1-5pm; summer hours may vary. Metro: Gallery Place, Metro Center.*

David Lloyd Kreeger House
2401 Foxhall Road, NW. (Phillip Johnson & Richard Foster, 1967) Admirable contemporary residence.

L'Enfant Plaza
L'Enfant Plaza, SW, south of Independence Avenue. (I. M. Pei & Partners and Araldo Cussuta, 1965. Hotel and office building: Vlastimil Koubek, 1970-73) At the southern end of the Mall between 7th and 9th streets, SW, what was the centerpiece of the Southwest Urban Renewal Area in the 60s. A modern complex in an area dominated by government buildings, with offices, 160 underground shops, restaurants, a theater, and the Loew's L'Enfant Plaza Hotel (*see* Hotels, Expensive). *Metro: L'Enfant Plaza.*

Longfellow Building
1741 Rhode Island Avenue, NW. (William Lescaze, 1940) Known as the city's first modern office building, and one of the first to construct a separate core for service equipment.

Market Square
701-801 Pennsylvania Avenue, NW. (Hartman-Cox, 1991) A classy $150 million neoclassic set of twin semicircular towers containing offices and 210 residential units, attracting an interesting mix of urban dwellers. Toward a Pennsylvania Avenue neighborhood. Faces onto Navy Memorial.

Metropolitan Square
655 15th Street, NW. (Vlastimil Koubek, 1983) The facade of the National Metropolitan Bank was integrated into this retail/office complex. The Secret Service was aghast because upper level floors gave a too-clear view of the White House.

National Air & Space Museum
Independence Avenue at 6th Street, SW. 357-1300. (Hellmuth, Obata & Kassabaum, 1976) The largest museum of the Smithsonian Institution. It took five years to construct but was finished on time and under budget for America's 200th birthday. The 680-foot, pink-hued Tennessee marble and glass structure with its giant bays was designed to showcase the massive exhibits. It has understandably become one of the world's most heavily visited museums. (*See also* MUSEUMS & GALLERIES, Museums.) *Metro. L'Enfant Plaza.*

National Gallery of Art, East Building
Constitution Avenue & 4th Street. 737-4215. (I. M. Pei, 1978) Built where Pennsylvania Avenue and the Mall converge, forming a trapezoid the shape the architect used to define and execute the design of this absolute knockout of a building. The exterior marble is identical in color and

texture to the classical West Building; the interior is enhanced by pyramidal skylights and marble floors that follow through on the triangle pattern. Interesting concourse-level restaurant area complete with prismatic skylights and cascade connects this to the older West Building. Don't miss! (*See also* MUSEUMS & GALLERIES, Museums.)

National Permanent Building
Pennsylvania Avenue & 18th Street, NW. (Hartman-Cox, 1977) At the time, a welcome departure from the bland boxlike architecture prevalent in downtown. Exposed air-conditioning ducts, pipes, and concrete support columns give visual interest to most, annoy others. Winner of the National Award of Honor from the American Institute of Architects.

Office of Thrift Supervision
1700 G Street, NW. 906-6000. (Max Urban & Associates, 1977) Formerly Federal Home Loan Bank Board. This building represents a departure from the usual sterile government architecture. The innovative design creates an urban area for relaxing around a pond in the summer and ice skating in winter. The shops and activities add liveliness to a still relatively deserted area. *OPEN Mon-Fri 8:45am-5:15pm.*

Pope-Leighey House
Woodlawn Plantation, 900 Richmond Highway, Mount Vernon, Va. (703) 780-3264. (Frank Lloyd Wright, 1941) Fourteen miles south of Washington. An attempt at a well-designed house for the person of modest means, described as a "usonian" house featuring heated concrete-slab floors. It was moved to this site, which closely resembles its original surroundings in Falls Church, in 1964 after being threatened with extinction by the building of a highway. (*See also* PARKS & GARDENS, Gardens: Woodlawn Plantation Gardens.) Last informal tour at 4pm. *OPEN 7 days 9:30am-4:30pm & by appointment.* (*See also* Woodlawn Plantation.) Admission.

Sedgwick Gardens Apartments
3726 Connecticut Avenue, NW. (M. Mesrobian, 1932) This once fashionable apartment block is distinguished by an elaborate Art Deco marquee.

Simmons House
316 9th Street, SE. (Thomas B. Simmons, 1967) In this area of active renovation, an interesting contemporary house.

Southwest Redevelopment Area
Along Independence Avenue from 12th to 3rd Streets, south to C Street, east to South Capitol Street, south to the waterfront. Covering approximately 560 acres, this massive government-sponsored urban renewal project, begun in 1953, includes residential and commercial complexes, among them L'Enfant Plaza, Tiber Island, and Carrollsburg Square, as well as the Arena Stage/Kreeger Theater buildings. One solution to the problem of a city's decaying areas, though some saw it as too drastic.

Techworld Plaza
9th Street & New York Avenue, NW. Close by the Washington Convention Center, Washington's largest mixed-use complex with offices, a technological conference and exhibition center, the Tech 2000 Museum (*see* MUSEUMS & GALLERIES, Museums), and the 801-room Ramada Renaissance Techworld Hotel.

Tiber Island
429 N Street, SW. (Keyes, Lethbridge, and Condon, 1965) Part of Southwest Urban Renewal Area. Four eight-story apartment high-rises and 85 town houses, two and three stories, in a well-designed setting.

Town Center Plaza
1100 block of 6th Street, SW. (I. M. Pei Associates, 1962) Well-designed apartment development in urban renewal area.

Stephen Trentman House
1350 27th Street, NW. (Hugh Newell Jacobsen, 1968) Contemporary Georgetown house suits its neighbors and neighborhood.

2000 Pennsylvania Avenue Complex
2000 Pennsylvania Avenue, NW. (John Carl Warnecke with Hellmuth Obata and Kassabaum, 1983) A modern high rise grew behind the facades of a strip of 19th-century buildings known locally as Red Lion Row. This solution to the problem of old and new co-existing is called "facadism" by some, "facadectomy" by others.

Washington Convention Center
900 9th Street, NW. 371-4200 (recording of events); 789-1600. (Welton Beckett Associates, Gray and West and H.D. Nottingham, 1983) Two blocks long—with 350,000 square feet of exhibition space—it is one of the nation's largest and most modern convention centers. The center is a major component in the revitalization of DC's old downtown. *Metro: Metro Center, Gallery Place.*

Washington Harbor
3000 K Street, NW. (Arthur Cotton Moore, 1986) A $200 million commercial, residential, and retail complex perched on the Potomac's edge in Georgetown. This postmodern exercise in excess, with columns, turrets, domes, and bays to spare, and a riverfront plaza with a monumental fountain, has become a popular attraction. A prominent tenant is the Sequoia restaurant (*see* RESTAURANTS, Rooms with a View) with its terraced outdoor seating, where a drink at the outdoor bar in season is a perfect way and place to end the day. Also, don't miss J. Seward Johnson's startling outdoor sculptures.

The Watergate
2500, 2600, 2700 Virginia Avenue, NW; 600 & 700 New Hampshire Avenue, NW. (Luigi Moretti, 1964-72) In Foggy Bottom, this series of sweeping curves is a total-environment contemporary complex: residential units, shops (DC's best bakery, *see* SHOPPING, Food, Baked Goods: Watergate Pastry Shop), restaurants, offices, health club, hotel. Site of the break-in of the Democratic National Committee, which led to the breakdown of the Nixon administration. Kennedy Center is a neighbor. This is a rich neighborhood. *Metro: Foggy Bottom.*

Woodson High School
55th & Eads Streets, NE. (McLeod, Ferrara &

Ensign, 1972) DC's first contemporary high-rise high school.

OUTDOOR ARTWORK & SCULPTURE

Adam
East Potomac Park. (Alexander Liberman, 1969) A 28-foot-tall, red-painted steel abstract sculpture.

Ascension
George Washington University Campus, 21st Street between G & H Streets, NW. (Rudolph A. Heintze, 1967) Twenty feet of stainless-steel rectangles of various sizes, on a 4-foot granite base. The sculptor aimed for "the union of space and object."

Australian Seal
Australian Embassy, 1601 Massachusetts Avenue, NW. (Thomas Bass, 1969) A 5-foot by 8-foot artistic rendering of Australia's official seal in bronze.

The Awakening
Hains Point, East Potomac Park. (J. Seward Johnson, 1980.) Originally part of a temporary outdoor art exhibition, the half-buried metal giant, who appears to be struggling to rise out of the ground, has remained to startle and delight, albeit he has been "injured" in a couple of traffic mishaps.

Cubi XI
Universal North Building, 1875 Connecticut Avenue, NW. (David Smith, 1964) Highly polished chrome, nickel, and steel on a marble pedestal. Precarious power.

Eurythmy
Swiss Embassy, 2900 Cathedral Avenue, NW. (Andr[0082] Ramseyer, 1955) A fluid bronze abstract by Swiss sculptor.

Family Tree of Hope
Rock Creek Park, 16th & Kennedy Streets, NW. (Dennis Stroy, Jr., 1974) A primitive representation of a black family, carved from a red oak tree.

The Gwenfritz
National Museum of American History, 14th Street & Constitution Avenue, NW. (Alexander Calder, 1969) Named for its donor, the 40-foot, black-painted steel stabile was fabricated in France.

The Habitat
2020 Connecticut Avenue, NW. (Alfredo Halequa, 1968) Polished white reinforced fiberglass forms.

Infinity
National Museum of American History, Madison Drive. (Jose de Rivera, 1967) The city's first abstract work commissioned by the federal government. Representing time and technology, the mirrorlike stainless-steel, three-dimensional figure eight completes a revolution every six minutes.

Netherlands Carillon
North of Arlington National Cemetery off Marshall Highway. (Joost W. C. Boks, E. Van den Grinten,

Lucker Paul Konig, 1960) Presented to America by the Netherlands in gratitude for WW II aid. Each of the carillon's 49 bells is engraved with words and art signifying the area that donated it. Two bronze panthers guard the tower. Recitals during the summer.

Noyes Armillary Sphere
Meridian Hill Park, 16th Street & Florida Avenue, NW. (Carl Paul Jenne Wein, 1931) A bronze-and-copper version of an ancient astrological instrument.

Orbit
Swiss Embassy, 2900 Cathedral Avenue, NW. (Walter Linck, 1972) An 18-foot-tall, burnished steel contemporary sculpture reminiscent of a musical clef. The wind and a small motor propel the piece.

The Prophet
Venezuelan Embassy, 2445 Massachusetts Avenue, NW. (Harry Abend, 1960) A bronze abstract piece by a Polish-born Venezuelan artist.

Three Red Lines
National Museum of American History, Madison Drive & 12th Street, NW. (George Rickey, 1969) Moving painted stainless-steel vertical blades by a student of Calder.

Trylon of Freedom
Federal District Courthouse, Constitution Avenue between 3rd & 4th Streets, NW. (Carl Paul Jenne Wein, 1954) The three branches of the American government—Judicial, Executive, and Legislative—are represented symbolically on each of the three sides.

BRIDGES

Arlington Memorial Bridge
Between Lincoln Memorial and the main gate of Arlington Cemetery. (McKim, Mead & White, 1926-32) Recommended by the McMillan Commission, 1901. Built with a draw span, replacing a wooden one, it connects Washington to Virginia (north to south) symbolically linking the Lincoln Memorial to the Custis-Lee House as well as providing access to Arlington National Cemetery (see Graveyards & Tombs). Considered one of America's finest bridges. Wonderfully peaceful views from here.

Cabin John Aqueduct Bridge
Cabin John, Md. (Montgomery C. Meigs, 1859) Washington's municipal water supply arrives via this aqueduct, which until this century was the world's largest single masonry arch at 220 feet.

Calvert Street Bridge
Calvert Street & Connecticut Avenue, NW, over Rock Creek. (Paul P. Cret, 1935) Graceful limestone bridge spans Rock Creek Valley, 120 feet below. Pylon sculpture depict modes of travel: air, water, rail, and roadway.

Dumbarton "Buffalo" Bridge
Across Rock Creek Parkway at 23rd & Q Streets. (Glenn & Bedford Brown, 1914) Concrete span built like a Roman aqueduct. Four 7-foot-tall

bronze buffaloes stand at the approaches (sculptor: A. Phemister Proctor). On each side of the bridge, carved sandstone Indian heads.

St. Alban's Bridge
35th & Garfield Streets, NW. (Walter Dodd Ramberg, 1961) Interesting design, wooden per donor's stipulation.

Taft Bridge
Connecticut Avenue, NW. (Edward Pierce Casey, 1897-1906) One of the first in America to be constructed of precast concrete, it was originally known as Million Dollar Bridge. Lining each side, Ernest C. Baerstow's Eagle Lampposts. Renamed for William Howard Taft in 1930.

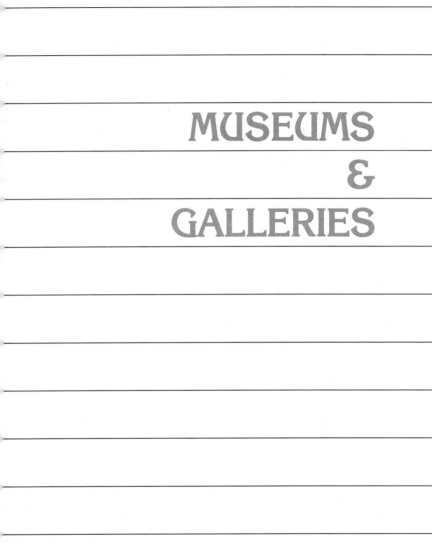

MUSEUMS
&
GALLERIES

Arts & Industries Building (Smithsonian)

MUSEUMS

For information about any of the Smithsonian Institution museums, call 357-2700 (hearing impaired, Tdd 357-1729) between 9am and 5pm. Dial-a-museum, 357-2020, is a 24-hour-a-day recorded information number for current Smithsonian special programs, exhibits, lectures, films. Smithsonian museums are open every day of the year (except December 25) from 10am to 5:30pm. Summer hour extensions are determined annually.

The Smithsonian Visitor Information Center is located in the Castle (the Smithsonian Institution Building). There you can begin your visit with an orientation (contrary to most people's mistaken impression, the Smithsonian is not one building but rather a complex of 16 museums and the National Zoo) via video technology, film, displays, and lectures (foreign language as well).

The Institution can help plan your trip with their free previsit packet. Write to the Smithsonian Visitor Information Center, Washington, Dc 20560.

See also Historic & New Washington *for historic buildings with museum collections.*

Anacostia Museum (Smithsonian)
1901 Fort Place, SE. 287-3369. This museum, located in the historic Anacostia section of DC, opened its doors in 1967 as the first federally funded neighborhood museum in America. Changing exhibits and programs related to African-American history and culture. There is a resource center for African-American studies and frequent special programs, lectures, and concerts for adults and children. Their new location adjoins a wooded area with picnic tables, benches, and grills provided by the National Park Service for those who wish to combine the museum tour with a picnic. Guided tours by appointment only Monday to Friday at 10am, 11am, and 1pm. *OPEN 7 days 10am-5pm. CLOSED Christmas Day.* FREE.

Armed Forces Medical Museum
Armed Forces Institute of Pathology, Walter Reed Army Medical Center Building, No. 54, 6825 16th Street, NW. 576-2418 (recorded information); 576-2341. (Weekend access to museum is through the Georgia Avenue & Elder Street gate.) Free parking in front of museum.

The Army Medical Museum, founded in 1862, contains specimens representing practically all diseases that affect man as well as medical history pertaining to the Civil War and the Lincoln and Garfield assassinations. Extensive collections of antique medical, surgical, and diagnostic instruments, including the world's most comprehensive collection of microscopes. Exhibits pertaining to pathology are highlighted, many not suitable for the squeamish. Instruction and materials are available for research purposes. Group guided tours must reserve in advance; call 576-2348, weekends 576-2800. *OPEN Mon-Fri 9:30am-4:30pm; Sat & Sun, most holidays 11:30am-4:30pm. CLOSED Thanksgiving, Christmas & New Year's.* FREE. *Metro: Tacoma Park, Silver Spring.*

Art Museum of the Americas
201 18th Street, NW. 458-6016. (Formerly the Museum of Modern Art of Latin America.) The first museum in the U.S. completely devoted to contemporary Latin American and Caribbean art. Paintings, sculpture, prints, drawings, graphics. Guided group tours by appointment. *OPEN Tues-Sat 10am-5pm. CLOSED Sun, Mon & holidays.* The gallery for temporary exhibits is housed in the main OAS building at 17th and Constitution Avenues, NW. *OPEN Mon-Fri 9am-5pm. CLOSED Sat & Sun.* FREE. *Metro: Farragut West.*

Arts and Industries Building (Smithsonian)
On the Mall, 900 Jefferson Drive, SW. 357-2700. Used for James Garfield's inaugural ball in 1889, it's the Smithsonian's second-oldest building. There is a new Experimental Gallery that features changing multi-cultural exhibitions in the arts, humanities, and sciences; and interactive exhibitions in the physical and natural sciences. In 1995, this building is to become the site of a National African-American Museum. For the moment, it continues to house one of the most extensive collections of Victorian Americana in an authentic setting. Call for update. A well-stocked gift shop; a theater for performances and films. *OPEN 7 days 10am-5:30pm.* FREE. *Metro: Smithsonian.*

Barney Studio House (Smithsonian)
2306 Massachusetts Avenue, NW. 357-3111. On fashionable Sheridan Circle, the turn-of-the-century residence, studio, and salon of socially

prominent painter Alice Pike Barney. Planned by its owner as "a meeting place for wit and wisdom, genius and talent." On view are original furnishings and watercolors by Mrs. Barney, who studied with Whistler in Paris. The house and its contents were donated to the Smithsonian in 1960; it is curated by the National Museum of American Art. Call 357-3111, Monday to Friday from 9am to 5pm, to arrange for a free guided tour. *OPEN by appointment only. CLOSED July-Sept. Metro: Dupont Circle, Q Street exit.*

B'nai B'rith Klutznick Museum
1640 Rhode Island Avenue, NW. 857-6583. Founded in 1956, this is the leading institution of Jewish art and history in the nation's capital. More than 500 ceremonial objects, folk art, and antiquities related to Jewish religion and culture spanning 20 centuries, including a collection of ancient Judaic coins, silver spice boxes, and hand-embroidered Torah wrappers. Changing exhibits illustrate subjects from archaeology to modern art and Jewish sports heroes. B'nai B'rith history, lectures, films. Maintains a National Jewish Visitors Center. Group tours by appointment. Special arrangements for foreign language. Museum shop (closes at 4:30pm) for original art, gifts, and books. *OPEN Sun-Fri 10am-5pm. CLOSED Sat, legal & Jewish holidays. FREE; $1 donation suggested. Metro: Farragut North, L Street exit.*

Center for African, Near Eastern and Asian Cultures (Smithsonian)
See The Quadrangle.

Columbia Historical Society
1307 New Hampshire Avenue, NW. 785-2068. The Christian Heurich residence, a baronial mansion just off Dupont Circle, is the headquarters of the society, a 100-year-old organization devoted to collecting, preserving, and teaching the history of the nation's capital. Its research collection includes more than 100,000 photographs and 30,000 books. There are pay tours of the mansion with its original furnishings between noon and 3:15pm. (*See also* HISTORIC & NEW WASHINGTON, Historic Buildings & Areas: Christian Heurich Mansion.) Membership available. Library *OPEN Wed, Fri & Sat 10am-4pm.* House *OPEN Wed, Thurs, Fri & Sat noon-4pm.* Admission. *Metro: Dupont Circle, Circle exit.*

Corcoran Gallery of Art
17th Street & New York Avenue, NW. 638-3211. Founded in 1859 by philanthropist William Wilson Corcoran, the collection represents an amazing historic and stylistic survey of American

art: from 18th-century portraits, Hudson River School, Western landscapes, late-19th-century American Impressionism, Ashcan School to contemporary modern art including the experimental and avant-garde. European paintings and tapestries plus the reconstructed original Grand Salon from the Hotel d'Orsay in Paris. The Corcoran School of Art housed in the north wing of the building promotes and encourages "American genius." Gallery shop; special events (*see also* ANNUAL EVENTS, February); lectures. Chamber music concert series: Eight or nine concerts in the fall and spring feature the Takacs String Quartet and Cleveland Quartet using original instruments from the Corcoran's collections. Tickets may be bought in a subscription series or before the performances. Reserve two weeks in advance for group tours. *OPEN Tues-Sun 10am-4:30pm; Thurs 10am-9pm. CLOSED Mon & national holidays. FREE. Metro: Farragut West.*

DAR Museum
1776 D Street, NW. 628-1776. Maintained by the National Society Daughters of the American Revolution, female descendants of those who fought the War of Independence; and housed in Memorial Continental Hall. Gallery exhibits from the museum's extensive decorative arts collection and 33 state period room settings, representing regional American styles, contain an impressive collection of furniture, paintings, ceramics, silver, costumes, textiles, and artifacts from the Revolutionary War and early federal periods. Guided and special subject tours of the period rooms available Monday to Friday from 10am to 3pm, Sunday from 1 to 5pm. For further information, call 879-3254. *OPEN Mon-Fri 8:30am-4pm; Sun 1-5pm. CLOSED Sat & federal holidays, the Sun & Mon of 3-day weekends, and the second & third weeks of Apr. FREE. Metro: Farragut West, Farragut North.*

Dumbarton Oaks Collection
1703 32nd Street, NW. 338-8278 (recorded information); 342-3200. Mr. and Mrs. Robert Woods Bliss acquired the house (built in 1800, though greatly altered) and the magnificent gardens (*see also* PARKS & GARDENS, Gardens) in 1920. In 1940 they gave Dumbarton Oaks and their collections to Harvard University. The Byzantine Collection: objects from major centers of the East Roman, or Byzantine, Empire; some examples of classical and Western medieval art as well. The pre-Columbian Collection, housed in a modern pavilion designed by Philip Johnson, covers the major cultures of Central and South America from their origin to the first half of the

Corcoran Gallery of Art

16th century. Gift shop. (*See also* HISTORIC & NEW WASHINGTON, Historic Buildings & Areas.) *OPEN Tues-Sun 2-5pm. CLOSED Mon.* Gardens *OPEN 7 days 2-6pm.* Admission; senior citizens free on Wednesday.

Dupont-Kalorama Museum Consortium
Formed in 1983 by the owners of seven museums housed in former residences located in the northwest residential neighborhoods of Dupont Circle and Kalorama. The Consortium sponsors an ongoing series of activities and tours throughout the year (*see* ANNUAL EVENTS, June). A stroll through this historic district, coupled with a visit to at least one of the museums, will acquaint you with a genteel aspect of historic Washington. Each of the following members of the consortium is listed alphabetically in this chapter: Fonda del Sol Visual Arts Center; Historical Society of Washington, DC; Meridian House International; Phillips Collection; The Textile Museum. Anderson House and Woodrow Wilson House are described in HISTORIC & NEW WASHINGTON, Historic Buildings & Areas.

Folger Shakespeare Library
201 East Capitol Street, SE. 544-4600. A private institution administered by Amherst College. The handsome "modern" exterior (Paul Cret, 1932) belies its Elizabethan interior, which includes a full-size Elizabethan theater that is in use from October to May for performances by the Shakespeare Theater at the Folger. (*See* ENTERTAINMENT, Theaters.) Its magnificent collections include the world's finest Shakespeare library (including 82 copies of the 1623 First Folio edition of Mr. Shakespeare's *Comedies, Histories and Tragedies*); rare books and manuscripts from the European Renaissance. It is also the greatest repository of printed material of the English Renaissance outside Great Britain. (Collections open to scholars only.) There are lectures, seminars, poetry readings, and a concert series, featuring Renaissance music played on original instruments by the Folger Consort. Wonderful shop for gifts and books. Membership available. Walk-in tours Monday to Friday at 11am, noon, and 1pm. Group tours with reservations, call 544-7077. *OPEN Mon-Sat 10am-4pm. CLOSED Sun & all federal holidays.* FREE. *Metro: Capitol South.*

Fonda del Sol Visual Arts Center
2112 R Street, NW. 483-2777. A bilingual community museum founded in 1973. Housed in a historic former residence, the permanent collection contains Santos, pre-Columbian, folk, and contemporary Hispanic, North American, and Latin American art. There are also changing exhibits, concerts, lectures, poetry readings, and more. It's a vibrant visual art and media center. *OPEN Tues-Sat 12:30-5:30pm. CLOSED Sun & Mon.* In summer, *Wed-Sat 1-6pm. CLOSED Sun-Tues.* FREE. *Metro: Dupont Circle.*

The Freer Gallery of Art (Smithsonian)
On the Mall, Jefferson Drive & 12th Street, SW. 357-2700. Described by John La Farge as "a place to go and wash your eyes." Founded by railroad-car manufacturer Charles Lang Freer who donated his superb art collection to the country in 1906. The gray Italian Renaissance-style building (1923) contains one of America's finest collections of Asian art (the 26,000 objects are shown on a rotating basis): paintings, drawings, bronzes, pottery, porcelain, jade, sculpture, scrolls, and screens. The museum also houses works by late-19th- and early-20th-century American artists including the world's largest collection of work by James A. McNeill Whistler, a good friend of Freer's, as well as paintings by Winslow Homer, Thomas Wilmer Dewing, D. W. Tryon, and John Singer Sargent. Don't miss the Peacock Room, a Whistler interior design, opulent and fascinating, brought from London. The library contains over 50,000 books and periodicals on art topics relating to the collections. Group tours by appointment. Gift shop (357-1432) open till 4:30pm. *OPEN 7 days 10am-5:30pm. CLOSED Christmas Day.* FREE. *Metro: Smithsonian.*

Hirshhorn Museum and Sculpture Garden (Smithsonian)
On the Mall, Independence Avenue at 7th Street, SW. 357-2700. Distinctive and controversial building (*see also* HISTORIC & NEW WASHINGTON, Modern Architecture) houses a remarkable collection of 19th- and 20th-century American and European painting and sculpture, bequeathed to the American government by Joseph Hirshhorn, a Latvian immigrant who became a uranium millionaire. The primary focus is on modern American art: Ashcan School, Abstract Expressionism, Pop, Minimal, New Realist. Well represented are Hopper, Sloan, Shahn, Soyer, Kline, Rivers, de Kooning, Gorky, Pollock. Highlights of the extensive sculpture collection: Rodin's *Burghers of Calais, Tribute to Balzac,* Giacometti's *Dog.* The largest public collection of Moore's works as well as bronze reliefs by Matisse, and pieces by Brancusi, Calder, Degas, Daumier, Noguchi, Nevelson, and more. Monumental works are in the plaza and garden. The permanent collection is on the second and third floors; loan exhibits, focusing on the newest trends in modern art, are on the lower level. It's breathtaking. For information on films and lectures, call 357-3280 and 357-3030, respectively. Tours of the permanent collection Monday to Saturday at 10:30am, noon, and 1:30pm; Sunday at noon, 1:30, and 2:30pm from the plaza-level information desk. Group tours and special sculpture tours for the blind must be arranged two weeks in advance; call 357-3235. Museum shop, 357-1429. *OPEN 7 days 10am-5:30pm.* FREE. *Metro: L'Enfant Plaza.*

Holography World
Techworld Plaza, 800 K Street, NW. 408-1833. A branch of the Art, Science, and Technology Institute, this space features a changing international exhibition of holographic art, as well as demonstrations and examples of application. Guided 20-minute tour (last tour at 5:30pm) will acquaint you with holography. Group tours by

appointment. Gift shop for holographic artwork, as well as calculators and other small gift items with holograms. Seminars and workshops available. There is a permanent exhibition of 70 holograms at the institute at 2018 R Street, NW. *OPEN Mon-Fri 11am-6pm.* Admission charge, lower for children under age 12. *Metro: Gallery Place.*

Interior Department Museum
Interior Building, C Street between 18th & 19th Streets, NW. 208-4743. Exhibits seek to explain and dramatize the activities of the Department of the Interior, which is responsible for most nationally owned public land and natural resources as well as American Indian affairs. Paintings, lifelike dioramas with historic themes, original documents and exhibits. Good authentic Indian crafts shop not affiliated with the museum but also housed in the Interior Building (*Mon-Fri 8:30am-4:30pm*). For additional information, call 208-4056. Museum *OPEN Mon-Fri 8am-4pm. CLOSED Sat, Sun & holidays.* FREE. *Metro: Farragut West.*

Marine Corps Museum
Washington Navy Yard, Building #58, 9th & M Streets, SE. 433-3839. Art and personal papers by or relating to the history of the marines, with emphasis on the Vietnam War. Artifacts and exhibits, from 1775 to present. Guided tours Monday to Friday; arrange in advance. *OPEN Mon-Fri 10am-4pm (in summer, Fri 6-8pm as well); Sat 10am-5pm; Sun noon-4pm.* FREE. *Metro: Eastern Market.*

Meridian House International
1624 & 1630 Crescent Place, NW. 667-6800. Housed in two elegant classical mansions designed by John Russell Pope on a 2-acre site, Meridian House was founded to promote intercultural understanding through exchanges of people, ideas, and the arts. Exhibitions, lectures, and concerts give visitors an opportunity for understanding other cultures. Lovely gardens. Guided tours for groups, call 939-5558 in advance. FREE. *Metro: Dupont Circle, Q Street exit.*

National Air and Space Museum (Smithsonian)
On the Mall, Independence Avenue between 4th & 7th Streets, SW. 357-2700. Testimony to the nation's fascination with flight it's been the top tourist attraction on the Mall since opening in 1976. The Smithsonian's aeronautical collection began in 1876 with a group of Chinese kites presented to it following the Philadelphia Centennial Exhibition. Today, original objects illustrating the history of aviation and space exploration include the Wright Brothers' 1903 *Flyer*, Lindbergh's *Spirit of St. Louis*, the Friendship 7 and Apollo 11 command modules, and missiles, rockets, engines, propellers, and instruments. Visitors may enter a Skylab Workshop, touch a moon rock, view films related to flight on a giant screen. Other fascinating devices and exhibits celebrate the concept, drama, and excitement of flight. In the Langley Theater (first floor) four films a day on aviation and space, on a screen five stories high! An art collection includes paintings with air-and-space-related themes. A 40,000-volume library is available for historical research, call 357-3133 for an appointment. Cafeteria on first level. Museum shop and Planetarium, a large shop with flight-related items. Free public tours from Gallery 100 daily at 10:15am and 1pm. Group tours by appointment, Tuesday to Friday at 10:15 and 11:30am, call 357-1400. *OPEN 7 days 10am-5:30pm.* FREE. (*See also* KIDS' WASHINGTON, Museums for Children: Paul E. Garber Facility.) *Metro: L'Enfant Plaza.*

The National Building Museum
Located in the Old Pension Building, 401 F Street, NW. 272-2448. A magnificent old building, for years ridiculed as a huge white elephant, was saved from the wrecker's ball and since 1985 has served as a museum that celebrates all aspects of building, including architecture, engineering, building crafts, and urban planning. It is dedicated to documenting and informing through its data bank and exhibits. But the museum is upstaged by its own building: Its central court is the city's largest indoor space with eight of the largest Corinthian columns in the world—measuring 76 feet high by 25 feet in diameter. A permanent exhibit, "Washington: Symbol and City," chronicles how Washington, DC, evolved, addressing the social, economic, and political forces that have shaped the city over its 200-year history. It's a perfect orientation to the city. The exhibition includes two models created by the Senate Park Commission in 1901, one showing the Mall and downtown, the other showing plans for the area's redevelopment. The models of well-known landmarks intended to "show" through touch what they look like, as well as Braille and audiotape descriptions, are designed for the blind and visually impaired. Tours of the building Monday to Friday at 12:30pm; Saturday, Sunday, and holidays at 12:30 and 1:30pm. Once a month, September through June, there are free noontime concerts. Good museum gift and bookshop. Membership available. *OPEN Mon-Sat 10am-4pm; Sun noon-4pm. CLOSED Thanksgiving, Christmas & New Year's Day.* FREE. (*See also* HISTORIC & NEW WASHINGTON, Historic Buildings & Areas: Old Pension Building.) *Metro: Judiciary Square.*

National Gallery of Art, East Building (Smithsonian)
On the Mall, Constitution Avenue at 4th Street, NW. 737-4215. Built to house the overflow of art treasures from the West Building (*see below*), the building itself is a work of art. (*See* HISTORIC & NEW WASHINGTON, Modern Architecture.) In the light-filled interior court, a 920-pound Calder mobile, three stories high, 76 feet across; one of the last and largest he ever created, it would seem to belong nowhere but here. Introductory tours to the building collections: Monday to Friday at 11:30am, Saturday at 11am, Sunday at 2 and 4pm from the ground-floor lobby. Free Sunday lecture at 4pm in the auditorium. Group tours reserve in advance. Bookshop on concourse

National Building Museum (Old Pension Building)

level, near the Buffet/Cascades. Also Terrace Cafe (*see* RESTAURANTS, Inexpensive Lunch). *OPEN Mon-Sat 10am-5pm; Sun noon-9pm. CLOSED Christmas & New Year's Day. FREE. Metro: Judiciary Square, Federal Center, Archives.*

National Gallery of Art, West Building (Smithsonian)
On the Mall, Constitution Avenue & 6th Street, NW. 737-4215. One of the world's finest museums with outstanding collections of European and American paintings, sculpture, and graphic arts beginning with the 13th century. Especially strong in Italian art (including Leonardo da Vinci's only work outside Europe), Rembrandt, Vermeer, and the French Impressionists. Frequent special events. Introductory tours to the collection Monday to Friday at 1:30 and 3pm, Saturday at 3pm, Sunday at 1 and 3pm from the rotunda. Special tours, with a different subject every week, Tuesday to Sunday, also from the rotunda; call for information. Free Sunday concerts (except in summer) at 7pm; tickets are distributed at 4pm in the West Building Art Information Room; first-come seating to ticket holders at 6pm. Superb bookstore, two restaurants. (*See also* HISTORIC & NEW WASHINGTON, Historic Buildings & Areas.) *OPEN Mon-Sat 10am-5pm; Sun 11am-6pm. CLOSED Christmas & New Year's Day. FREE. Metro: Judiciary Square, Federal Center West, Archives.*

National Geographic Society
Explorer's Hall, 17th & M Streets, NW. 857-7000 or -7588. A 1,100-pound illuminated free-standing globe, 11 feet in diameter; exhibits relating to exploration and research. The library provides information on remote corners of the world. Copies of every issue of the magazine. *OPEN Mon-Fri 9am-5pm; Sat & holidays 9am-5pm; Sun 10am-5pm. CLOSED Christmas Day. FREE. Metro: Farragut North, L Street exit.*

National Museum of African Art (Smithsonian)
950 Independence Avenue, SW. 357-2700. Formerly located on Capitol Hill and ensconced in the Quadrangle Complex behind the Smithsonian Castle, the museum is the only one in the nation devoted to the visual arts of sub-Sahara

Africa. The collection contains over 6,000 objects including woven textiles. Temporary exhibits of a thematic or regional nature as well as related lectures, performances, story telling, and programs for teachers. *OPEN 7 days 10am-5pm. FREE. Metro: Smithsonian.*

National Museum of American Art (Smithsonian)
Old Patent Office Building, 8th & G Streets, NW. 357-2700. America's oldest national art collection has its first permanent home; it shares quarters with the National Portrait Gallery in the Old Patent Office Building (*see also* HISTORIC & NEW WASHINGTON, Historic Buildings & Areas). Over 30,000 works offer a panorama of American painting, sculpture, graphic art, and photographs from the 18th century to the present. Major holdings include Gilbert Stuart portraits and George Catlin's Indian paintings. Free public tours from Monday to Friday at noon, Saturday and Sunday at 2pm, from the lobby. Group tours daily from 10am to 2pm by reservation, call 357-3111. Museum shop; Patent Pending cafeteria (*see* RESTAURANTS, Cafeterias) and a lovely courtyard for outdoor picnics. *OPEN 7 days 10am-5:30pm. FREE. Metro: Gallery Place.* (*See also* Barney Studio Museum *and* Renwick Gallery.)

National Museum of American History (Smithsonian)
On the Mall, 14th Street & Constitution Avenue, NW. 357-2700. (Formerly the Museum of History and Technology.) Exhibits highlight the nation's scientific, cultural, political, and technological developments. It's an extremely popular museum. Among the permanent exhibits: the development of electricity and communications (displaying Edison's light bulb and Bell's first telephone), money and medals, large ceramics and glass collections. The Graphic Arts Division demonstrates both fine arts and newspaper printing and reporting. There are the lively Halls of Transportation and Underwater Exploration; the First Ladies' Hall with gowns worn by former presidents' wives; the Bradford Doll House; Flag Hall, with the original Star-Spangled Banner. Dorothy's ruby slippers, the Fonz's leather jacket, and Archie Bunker's armchair are among

visitors' favorite attractions. For group tours, call 357-1481. Cafeteria, snack bar, gift shop. The ine Smithsonian bookstore, devoted to Ameri-ana. OPEN 7 days 10am-5:30pm. FREE. Metro: Federal Triangle, Smithsonian.

National Museum of Natural History (Smithsonian)
On the Mall, 10th Street & Constitution Avenue, NW. 357-2700. Devoted to man and his natural surroundings from prehistoric times to the present. Objects in the large (over 120 million items) and diverse collections include dinosaur skeletons, a mounted African bush elephant, and the 45.5-carat Hope Diamond. Dioramas explore the daily lives of African, Asian, and Pacific cultures. Exhibits devoted to the evolution, history, and culture of American Indians and Eskimos. A living coral reef, an insect zoo, naturalist center, and the Discovery Room. (See also KIDS' WASHINGTON, Museums for Children.) Restaurant, gift shop. For group tours and special program information, call 357-2747; adult tours should be arranged a month in advance, call 357-1756. OPEN 7 days 10am-5:30pm. FREE. Metro: Smithsonian, Federal Triangle.

National Museum of Women in the Arts
13th Street & New York Avenue, NW. 783-5000. Opened April 1987, this is the first major museum in the world honoring the achievements of women artists—past, present, and future. Exhibitions highlighting important historical periods and movements. Comprehensive library, advanced study center for students of art. The museum is housed in an elegant Renaissance Revival building. Membership available. Cafe open Monday to Friday from 11:30am to 2:30pm. Museum shop with books, tapes, postcards on women and by women artists. OPEN Mon-Sat 10am-5pm; Sun noon-5pm. FREE.

National Portrait Gallery (Smithsonian)
Old Patent Office Building, 8th & F Streets, NW. 357-2700. In 1857, Congress commissioned George Peter Alexander Healy to paint a series of presidential portraits for the White House. But it was not until 1962 that Congress formally created "a free public museum for the exhibition and study of portraiture and statuary depicting men and women who have made significant contributions to the history, development, and culture of the people of the United States." In addition to the permanent collection of over 500 portraits (including the Gilbert Stuart portrait of George Washington), special exhibits highlight specific historical themes and personalities. Excellent education department: tours, lectures, films. Housed in the Old Patent Office Building (see also HISTORIC & NEW WASHINGTON, Historic Buildings & Areas). Museum shop. Patent Pending cafeteria (see RESTAURANTS, Cafeterias) and a lovely courtyard for picnics. Tours Monday to Friday from 10am to 3pm; Saturday and Sunday at 11:30am and by request at 1pm—for information, call 357-2920. OPEN 7 days 10am-5:30pm. FREE. Metro: Gallery Place.

Navy Mem
Washington
Streets, SE.
manufacturing
600 feet long.
5,000) include
bilia, pictures; t
Constitution. Out
Anacostia River,
played. OPEN Mor
summer); Sat, Su
CLOSED Thanksgiv
New Year's Day. FRE   market.

The Phillips Collecti
1600 21st Street at Q S ...et, NW. 387-0961 (recording); 387-2151. Opened in 1921 by Duncan Phillips in the family home; it was the first U.S. museum devoted to modern art and its sources. Housed in a Georgian Revival mansion, designed by Hornblower and Marshall (1897), and an annex (1960), it's a comfortable, intimate setting in which to appreciate masterworks of 19th- and 20th-century American and European paintings and sculpture, including the largest collection of Bonnard in America. Also here, Renoir's Luncheon of the Boating Party as well as works by Picasso, Braque, Cézanne, Daumier, Klee, Rothko, O'Keeffe, Prendergast, Soutine, Dove, Marin, Rouault, Calder. Also selected earlier works by Goya, Delacroix, El Greco. To enhance appreciation of the permanent collection, there are six to eight temporary exhibits a year. Since 1941 there have been free Sunday afternoon concerts in the paneled music room from September to May at 5pm. Year-round introductory walk-in tours every Wednesday and Saturday at 2pm. "Gallery Talks," lasting 30 to 40 minutes, the first and third Thursday of the month at 12:30; and the booklet "A Child's Adventure into the Artist's World of Color," to aid parents and school-age children touring together. Group tours by appointment, call 387-7390. The petit cafe serves lunch and light fare, Tuesday to Saturday from 10:45am to 4:15pm and Sunday from 2 to 6:15pm. Fine book and gift shop (667-6106). Membership available. OPEN Tues-Sat 10am-5pm; Sun 2-7pm. CLOSED Mon, July 4, Labor Day, Thanksgiving, Christmas & New Year's Day. Weekdays FREE, suggested contribution; weekends, admission fee. Metro: Dupont Circle, Q Street exit.

The Quadrangle (Smithsonian)
On the southern quadrangle of the Mall bordered by the Freer, the Castle, the Arts & Industries Building, and Independence Avenue. 357-2700. Known more formally as the Center for Africa, Near Eastern, and Asian Cultures, the 4-acre site consisting of two underground pavilions housing two museums: the National Museum of African Art (formerly located on Capitol Hill) and the Arthur M. Sackler Gallery of Asian and Near Eastern Art. The surrounding Enid A. Haupt Garden features pools, fountains, antique garden furniture; its walkways link the National Mall with Independence Avenue.

84

Renwick Gallery of the
American Art (Smith
Pennsylvania Av
2700. Origina
tion, the J
saved
nat

...National Museum of ...sonian)

...nue at 17th Street, NW. 357-
...home to the Corcoran art collec-
...mes Renwick-designed building was
...from demolition to become, in 1972, a
...nal showcase for contemporary and historic
American creativity in design, crafts, and the
decorative arts. The Grand Salon and Octagon
Room are restored with late-19th-century furnishings. Special exhibits, including arts and
crafts of other countries. Films, lectures, crafts
demonstrations. Prearranged group tours Monday through Thursday from 10am to 1pm, call
357-2531. Gift shop carries extensive selection
of craft books. *OPEN 7 days 10am-5:30pm.*
FREE. *Metro: Farragut North, Farragut West.*

Arthur M. Sackler Gallery (Smithsonian)
1050 Independence Avenue, SW. 357-2700.
Opened in 1957, this museum, located in the
Quadrangle Complex behind the Smithsonian
Castle, is devoted to Asian art from ancient times
to the present. Included in the permanent col-
lection are Chinese, Japanese, Near Eastern,
South and Southeast Asian art. *OPEN 7 days
10am-5:30pm. CLOSED Christmas Day.* FREE.
Metro: Smithsonian, Mall exit.

Lillian and Albert Small Jewish Museum
3rd & G Streets, NW. 789-0900; (301) 881-0100.
The Adas Israel Synagogue, dedicated in 1876,
was the first building erected in Washington to
serve as a Jewish house of worship. A guided
tour of the museum includes the restored second floor of the sanctuary and exhibits depicting
the Washington Jewish community. (*See also*
HISTORIC & NEW WASHINGTON, Churches &
Synagogues: Adas Israel Synagogue Landmark.) *OPEN Sun-Thurs 11am-3pm; Fri by appointment only. CLOSED Sat & Jewish holidays.*
FREE. *Metro: Judiciary Square, F Street exit.*

Smithsonian Institution Building
On the Mall, 1000 Jefferson Drive, SW. 357-2700
(TDD 357-1729). The James Renwick "Castle"
(*see also* HISTORIC & NEW WASHINGTON, Historic Buildings & Areas), the first of the Smithsonian's buildings, officially became a public museum in 1858 when the "National Cabinet of

Renwick Gallery (Smithsonian)

Curiosities" was transferred here from the Patent
Office. Now houses the Visitors Information Center (in the Great Hall), administrative offices, and
the Woodrow Wilson International Center for
Scholars. The Crypt Room contains the tomb of
James Smithson, an English scientist who had
never visited America but who bequeathed the
funds to establish the Smithsonian Institution in
1846. Devoted to public education, research,
and national service in the arts, science, and
history, it is the world's largest museum
complex—with 16 museums (all but two, the
Cooper-Hewitt and the National Museum of the
American Indian in New York, are located in
Washington) and the National Zoo. Often referred to as the nation's attic, the catalog of
objects—approximately 137 million—increases
at the rate of a million a year. Throughout the
year the permanent and changing exhibits are
augmented with special programs, lectures,
concerts, and performances. Don't miss sam-
pling and savoring at least part of this repository
of America's cultural, technological, and scientific heritage. Each of the Smithsonian museums
listed below is described separately in this section, organized alphabetically.

Anacostia Museum
Arts and Industries Building
Barney Studio House
The Freer Gallery of Art
Hirshhorn Museum and Sculpture Garden
National Air and Space Museum
National Gallery of Art (West & East Wings)
National Museum of African Art
National Museum of American Art
National Museum of American History
National Museum of Natural History
National Portrait Gallery
Renwick Gallery
Sackler Gallery

OPEN 7 days 10am-5:30pm. FREE. *Metro:
Smithsonian.*

Tech 2000
Techworld Plaza, 800 K Street, NW. 842-0500.
Get ready for high-tech adventure with a glimpse
into the 21st century at this museum (designed
by Edwin Schlossberg) dedicated to interactive
multimedia—essentially a joining of video images, computer processing, sound, and text.
Buffs of every age are intrigued and involved,
and it's easy to spend the whole day. Most popular: Virtual Reality, where your image is pro-
jected onto a huge screen putting you in contact
with the video images you are watching—your
body movements setting the scene. Group tours
by appointment. *OPEN Tues-Sun 11am-5pm.*
Admission charge, lower for students, seniors,
and children under 12. *Metro: Gallery Place.*

The Textile Museum
2320 S Street, NW. 667-0441. Founded in 1925
by private collector George Hewitt Myers.
Housed in two former Kalorama residences (one
by John Russell Pope, architect of the Jefferson
Memorial), exhibitions draw on strengths of the
permanent collection of more than 15,000 pieces

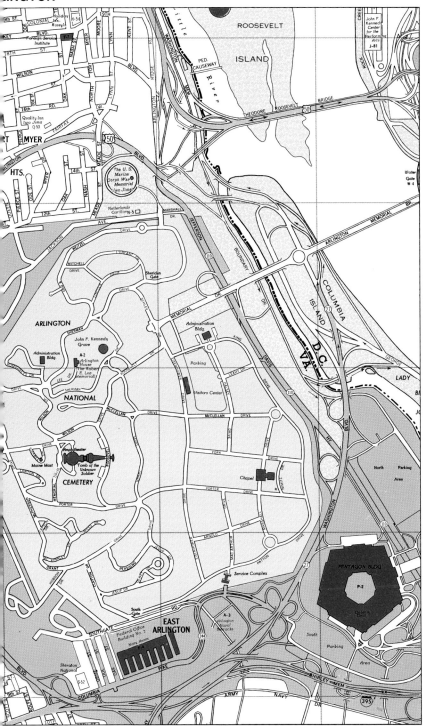

WHITE HOUSE AND CAPITOL

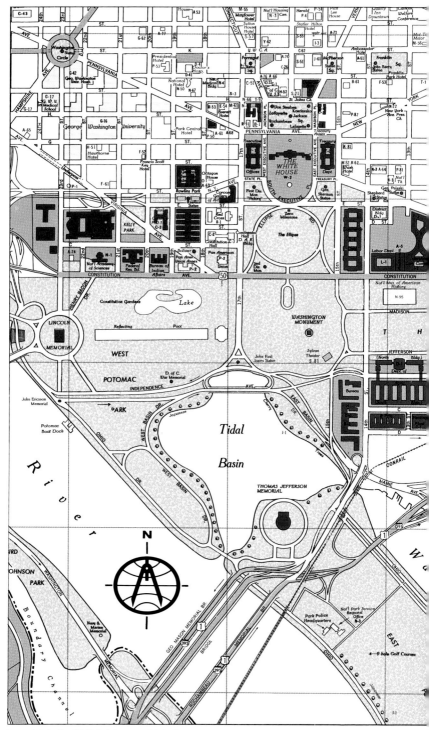

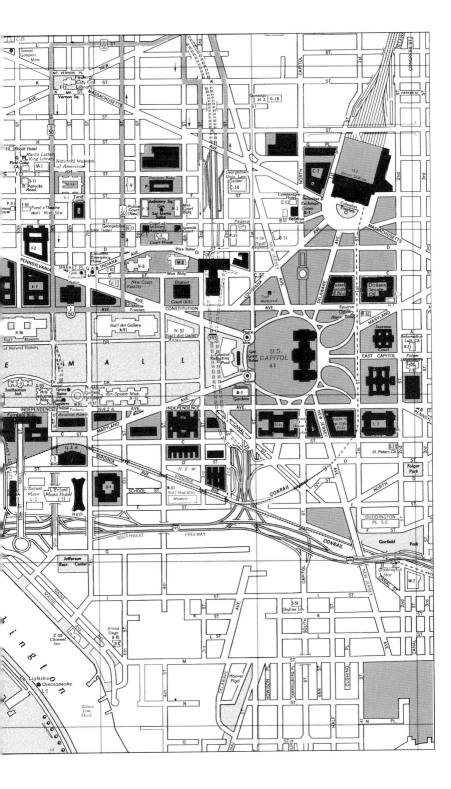

GEORGETOWN AND ZOO

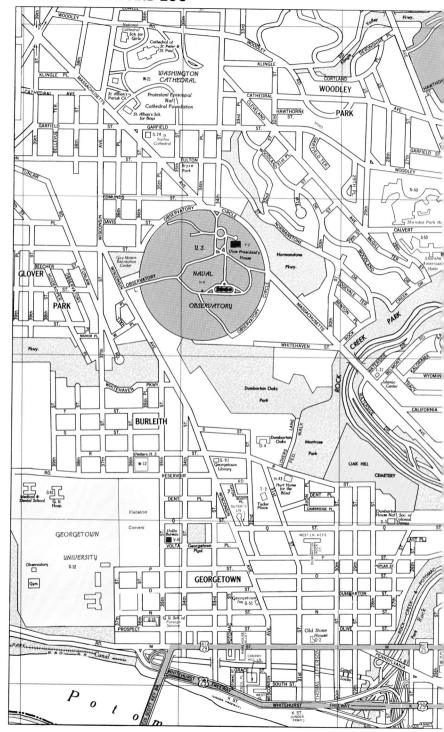

M System Map

metro

Legend

● Red Line
○ Orange Li
● Blue Line
○ Green Lin
  Yellow Lir

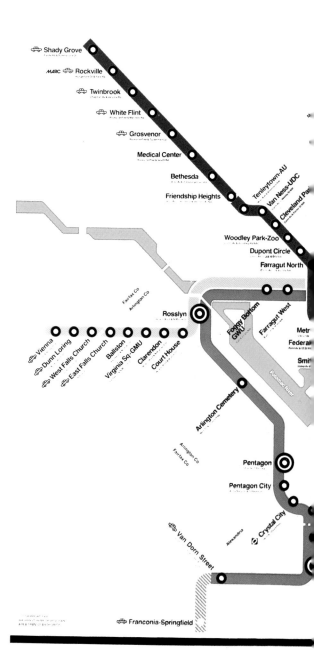

Shady Grove

MARC Rockville

Twinbrook

White Flint

Grosvenor

Medical Center

Bethesda

Friendship Heights

Tenleytown-AU

Van Ness-UDC

Cleveland Pa

Woodley Park-Zoo

Dupont Circle

Farragut North

Fairfax Co
Arlington Co

Rosslyn

Foggy Bottom
GMU

Farragut West

Metr

Federa

Smi

Vienna

Dunn Loring

West Falls Church

East Falls Church

Ballston

Virginia Sq-GMU

Clarendon

Court House

Potomac River

Arlington Cemetery

Arlington Co
Fairfax Co

Pentagon

Pentagon City

Crystal City

Alexandria

Van Dorn Street

Franconia-Springfield

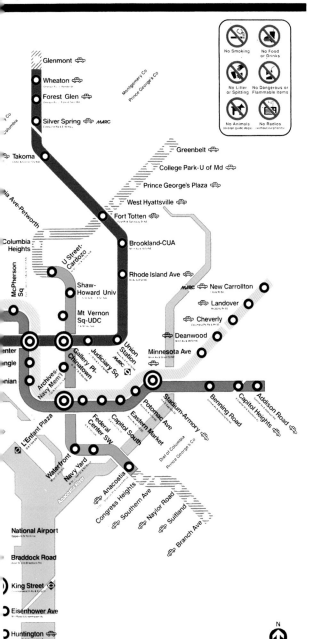

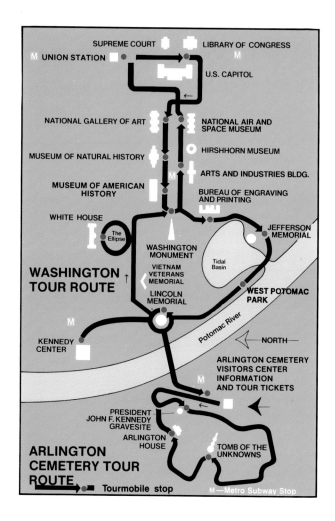

Tourmobile® Sightseeing

(Authorized by the United States Department of the Interior, National Park Service.)

See page 23 for more information.

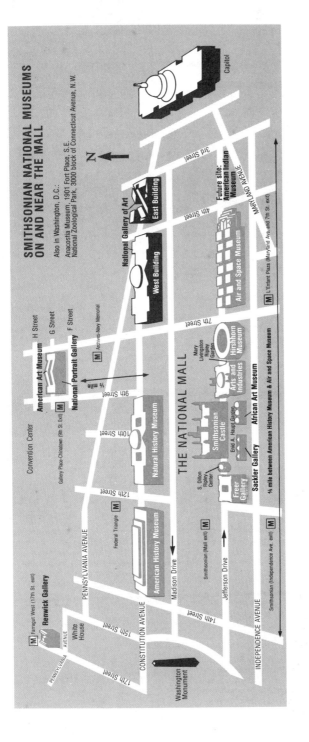

SMITHSONIAN NATIONAL MUSEUMS ON AND NEAR THE MALL

Also in Washington, D.C.:
Anacostia Museum, 1901 Fort Place, S.E.
National Zoological Park, 3000 block of Connecticut Avenue, N.W.

N

Capitol

East Building

National Gallery of Art

West Building

Future site:
American Indian Museum

Air and Space Museum

MARYLAND AVENUE

M L'Enfant Plaza (Maryland Ave. and 7th St. exit)

3rd Street

4th Street

7th Street

American Art Museum   H Street

G Street

National Portrait Gallery   F Street

M Archives–Navy Memorial

M Gallery Place-Chinatown (9th St. Exit)

Convention Center

9th Street

¼ mile

Natural History Museum

10th Street

THE NATIONAL MALL

Mary Livingston Ripley Garden

Hirshhorn Museum

Arts and Industries

African Art Museum

Smithsonian Castle

Enid A. Haupt Garden

Sackler Gallery

S. Dillon Ripley Center

Freer Gallery

¼ mile between American History Museum & Air and Space Museum

12th Street

M Federal Triangle

American History Museum

Madison Drive

M Smithsonian (Mall exit)

Jefferson Drive

PENNSYLVANIA AVENUE

INDEPENDENCE AVENUE

M Smithsonian (Independence Ave. exit)

14th Street

M Farragut West (17th St. exit)

Renwick Gallery

White House

PENNSYLVANIA AVENUE

15th Street

CONSTITUTION AVENUE

17th Street

Washington Monument

providing an overview of man's creative achievements in the textile arts and insights into the historical and cultural context in which they were made. Emphasis is on Oriental carpets, from 12th-century fragments to 20th-century rugs; Near and Middle Eastern and Peruvian textiles. Six to seven shows a year include contemporary work. Walk-in tours available September through June, Saturday and Sunday from 1 to 3pm. Group tours Tuesday, Wednesday, and Friday by appointment only; call 667-0441. Lectures, demonstrations, and workshops complement exhibitions. Research library; museum shop for books and textiles. *OPEN Mon-Sat 10am-5pm; Sun 1-5pm. CLOSED public holidays.* Donation suggested. *Metro: Dupont Circle.*

United States Holocaust Museum
On Raoul Wallenberg Place, on the Mall, between 14th & 15th Streets, SW. Under congressional charter, this national museum, to be completed in 1993, will memorialize the 6 million Jews and millions of other victims of Nazism who perished in the Holocaust. There will be one permanent and two changing exhibits to tell the story of what happened through oral histories, artifacts, photos, film, and documents. A computer-based Learning Center, a solemn Hall of Remembrance, and a Children's Wall, to commemorate the 1.5 million children who perished, will make up the complex. *Metro: Smithsonian.*

GALLERIES

In the last few years, an arts-roots revitalization process has been going on in a once-thriving, then decaying, downtown area of Washington. "Alternative space" galleries began to crop up, and now, in the vicinity of 7th & D Streets, NW, a full-fledged arts community has developed. The high concentration of galleries, and the experimental nature of many of them, makes this an interesting area in which to browse. Metro: Gallery Place.

NOTE: *The "art scene" slows during June, July, and August. Gallery hours and weeks may be shorter, and in many cases "never in August" is the case. In general, call for summer hours.*

Aaron Gallery
1717 Connecticut Avenue, NW. 234-3311. Contemporary American paintings, works on paper, sculpture, and installations by American and European artists. *OPEN Mon noon-6pm; Tues-Sat 10am-6pm; Sun by appointment.*

Adams Davidson Galleries
3233 P Street, NW. 965-3800. *The gallery for 19th- and early-20th-century American painting.* Specializes in Hudson River School and Luminist paintings. Mary Cassatt, Frederic Church, Thomas Cole, William Glackens, Childe Hassam, Winslow Homer, Paul Manship, John Singer Sargent. *OPEN Tues-Fri 10am-5pm; Sat noon-6pm.*

David Adamson Gallery
406 7th Street, NW. 628-0257. Graphics, paintings, and drawings. Richard Adams, Jennifer Berringer, Nancy Depew, Helen Frederick, Hugh Kepets, Sherry Sanabria. *OPEN Tues-F. 10:30am-4:30pm; Sat 10:30am-5pm.*

Addison/Ripley Gallery
9 Hillyer Court, NW. 328-2332. Contemporary paintings, drawings, and sculpture. Alan Campbell, Dickson Carrol, Pat Fox, Greg Hannan, Wo. Kahn, Val Lewton, Michael Smallwood, Lee Weis. *OPEN Tues-Sat 11am-5pm.*

Alex Gallery
2106 R Street, NW. 667-2599. Contemporary painting, sculpture, and drawings. Representational, figurative, impressionist, abstract, and expressionist by national and international artists. *OPEN Tues-Sat 11am-5pm & by appointment.*

Americana West Gallery
1630 Connecticut Avenue NW. 265-1630. Contemporary painting, pottery, and sculpture by Southwestern artists. American Indian art and artifacts. *OPEN Mon-Fri 11am-7pm; Sat 11am-6pm; Sun noon-5pm.*

Anton Gallery
2108 R Street, NW. 328-0828. Contemporary American painting and sculpture with an emphasis on DC-area artists. Rob Barnard, Lisa Batemen, Bruce Burris, Annella Frank, David Frye, Betsy Packard, Tony Sheeder, Morris Yarowsky. *OPEN Tues-Sat noon-5pm.*

Art Barn Gallery
Rock Creek Park, 2401 Tilden Street, NW. 244-2482. Nonprofit alternative gallery features local artists. Fine art exhibitions; cultural arts programs for visual artists and poets. Classes and demonstrations, call for information. *OPEN Wed-Sat 10am-5pm; Sun noon-5pm.*

Atlantic Gallery
1055 Thomas Jefferson Street, NW. 337-2299. Traditional paintings and prints, mainly marine and hunting scenes. *OPEN Mon-Sat 10am-6pm; Sun 1-5pm.*

Franz Bader Gallery & Bookstore
1500 K Street, NW. Gallery 393-6111. Washington's first private art gallery. (Bader is known as the dean of DC's art dealers—he gave Grandma Moses her first show. Bader retired in 1985, selling the gallery to Wretha Hanson.) Contemporary art, including sculpture and paintings and works on paper by local as well as national and international artists. Peter Milton, Michael Platt, John Winslow, William Calfee, Simon Gouverneur, John Van Alstine, Gary Goldberg, Harry Nadler, Paul Suttman, F. L. Wall. *OPEN Tues-Sat 10am-5pm.*

Baumgartner Gallery
2016 R Street, NW. 232-6320. Specializes in works by Hundertwasser, Arik Brauer, and contemporary American artists. *OPEN Tues-Sat 11am-6pm.*

Bird-in-the-Hand Gallery & Bookstore
323 7th Street, SE. 543-0744. Contemporary artists and printmakers. Books on art, architecture, textiles, and photography. Heather Bentz, Mar-

aret O'Donnell Correia, Ester Fe Espejo, Kathleen Geier, Betty MacDonald, Penelope Mayer, Adrienne Mayor, Dale Osterle, Alan Scherr, Barbara Bickley Stephens, Isabelle Tokumaru, Jane Wallace. *OPEN Tues-Sun 11am-5pm.*

Brody's Gallery
706 21st Street, NW. 462-4747. Contemporary painting, sculpture, drawings, prints, and photography. *OPEN Tues-Sat 11am-5:30pm or by appointment.*

Robert Brown Contemporary Art
2005 New Hampshire Avenue, NW. 822-8737. Contemporary American and European works of art. *OPEN Tues-Sat 11am-5pm.*

Carega Foxley Leach Gallery
1732 Connecticut Avenue, NW. 462-8462. International and American contemporary painting, drawing, sculpture; limited print selection. *OPEN Mon-Fri 10am-3pm.*

Susan Conway Carroll Gallery
1058 Thomas Jefferson Place, NW. 333-4082. Early American paintings, late-19th-century American art and 20th-century American and international art. *OPEN Tues-Sat 11am-5pm.*

Capitol East Graphics
600 E Street, SE. 547-8246. Original works on paper. Emphasis is on graphics. Many fine European and American printmakers are represented; sculptors, too. *OPEN Tues-Sun by appointment.*

Capricorn Galleries
4849 Rugby Avenue, Bethesda, Md. (301) 657-3477. Twentieth-century American realism: paintings, prints, drawings, and sculpture. Ned Bittinger, Robert Brawley, Robin Freedenfeld, June Mihalik, Dana Winslow, Jon Hunt, William Haney, Roger Medearis, Brad Clever, Charles Jarboe, Ed Gordon, Jeremiah Stermer, Stephen Kozar, Karen Horn, Mary Etta Thorn. *OPEN Tues-Sat 10am-5pm & 7-9pm (call first); Sun 1-5pm.*

Jackie Chalkley Gallery & Jackie Chalkley at the Willard Collection
Foxhall Square, 3301 New Mexico Avenue, NW; 686-8884. And 1455 Pennsylvania Avenue, NW, Suite 130; 638-3060. Also *Chevy Chase Plaza, 5301 Wisconsin Avenue, NW, 537-6100. Fine handcrafted clothing, jewelry, and accessories. Contemporary decorative arts for the home: porcelain, stoneware, blown glass, fiber hangings, wood, handmade paper, baskets, metal. *OPEN Mon-Sat 10am-5:30pm; *evening Sunday hours, call for exact times.*

Kathleen Ewing Gallery
1609 Connecticut Avenue, NW. 328-0955. Specializes in 19th-, early-20th-century, and contemporary photography. Contemporary photographers include Steven Szabo, Mark Power, Aubrey Bodine. *OPEN Wed-Sat noon-6pm.*

Fonda del Sol
2112 R Street, NW. 483-2777. Alternative space gallery and arts center showcases the art and cultures of the Americas Hispanic, African American, and Native American. Film and video workshop. Monthly shows. The only DC gallery to show video on a regularly scheduled basis. *OPEN Tues-Sat 12:30-5:30pm.*

Foundry Gallery
9 Hillyer Court, NW. 387-0203. Artist-owned gallery. Contemporary art in a variety of media; primarily Washington-area artists. Julie Bloos, Frank Cappello, Jessica Danen, Char Gardner, Aurelio Grisanty, Josephine Haden, Katheryn M. Henneberry, Mary Virginia Langston, Shawn McPartland, Randy Michener, Betty Murchison, Patricia Natirbov, Jay Orbeck, Louise Spindel, Barbara Sweet, Bob Tiemann, Elizabeth C. Vail, Afaf Zurayk. *OPEN Tues-Sat 11am-5pm; Sun 1-5pm.*

Foxhall Gallery
3301 New Mexico Avenue, NW. 966-7144. Contemporary art. Bryn Craig, Yrjo Edelmann, Joel Jaecks, Ed Knippers, Dean Larson, Jacques Maroger, Jim McVicker, John Olsen, David Zuccarini. *OPEN Mon-Sat 10am- 5pm.*

Galerie Lareuse
2820 Pennsylvania Avenue, NW. 333-5704. Works by 20th-century masters. Georges Braque, Bernard de Buffet, Mary Cassatt, Marc Chagall, Wassily Kandinsky, Ferdinand Léger, Henri Matisse, Joan Miró, Pablo Picasso, Camille Pissaro, Pierre-Auguste Renoir, Georges Rouault, Henri de Toulouse-Lautrec. *OPEN Tues-Sat 11am-6pm; Sun noon-6pm.*

Gallery 4
115 South Columbus Street, Alexandria, Va. (703) 548-4600. Contemporary American prints, watercolors, paintings, sculpture. William Dunlap, Gorden Mortensen, Katherine Steiger, Hilda Thorpe, and others. *OPEN Tues-Sat 10am-5pm.*

Gallery K
2010 R Street, NW. 234-0339. Contemporary figurative and surrealist art by American and international artists. Jo Rango, John Herne, Jacques Poli, Maureen McCabe. Washington artists, too, including Lani Irwin, Susan Abbott, Wayne Paige, Catherine Batza, Ed Ahlstrom. *OPEN Tues-Sat 11am-6pm.*

Gallery 10 Ltd.
1519 Connecticut Avenue, NW, 2nd floor. 232-3326. Artist-owned gallery. Exhibition of contemporary art and sculpture, sometimes around a theme. *OPEN Tues-Sat 11am-5pm.*

Georgetown Gallery of Art
3235 P Street, NW. 333-6308. Alexander Calder, Marc Chagall, Honoré Daumier, R. C. Gorman, Rockwell Kent, Reginald Marsh, Henry Moore, Pablo Picasso. *OPEN Tues-Sat 11am-5pm & by appointment.*

Glass Gallery
4720 Hampden Lane, Bethesda, Md. (301) 657-3478. Contemporary studio glass, with emphasis on nonfunctional pieces. *OPEN Tues-Sat 11am-5pm.*

Govinda Gallery
1227 34th Street, NW. 333-1180. Imaginative and unusual art forms; European and American "visionary art"—figurative work with a fantastic, magical element; book illustrations by British illustrators; figurative work by new contemporary

artists. Photographers Christopher Makos and Michael Halsbrand. *OPEN Tues-Sat 11am-5pm.*

Guarisco Gallery
2828 Pennsylvania Avenue, NW. 333-8533. Nineteenth and early-20th-century European, British, and American paintings and watercolors. *OPEN Mon-Fri 10am-5:30pm; Sat 10am-5pm.*

Jane Haslem
2025 Hillyer Place, NW. 232-4644. Twentieth-century American paintings, prints, and works on paper. *OPEN Wed-Sat noon-6pm.*

Henri Gallery
1500 21st Street, NW, 3rd & 4th floors. 659-9313. Avant-garde abstract painting and sculpture. *OPEN Tues-Sat 11am-6pm; Sun 2-6pm.*

Howard University Gallery
College of Fine Arts, 2455 6th Street, NW, 1st floor. 806-5416. Rotating exhibitions of traditional African art from the permanent collection; also contemporary black art. *OPEN Mon-Fri 9:30am-4:30pm. FREE.*

Jones Troyer Fitzpatrick
1614 20th Street, NW. 328-7189. Contemporary art and photography. Zeke Berman, Barbara Crane, William de Looper, Claudia DeMonte, Mary Beth Edelson, Susan Eder, John Gossage, Marianne LaRoche, Ed McGowin, Tom Mullany, Lawley Paisley-Jones, Denise Ward-Brown, Mindy Weisel. *OPEN Wed-Sat 11am-5pm.*

Kimberly Gallery
1621 21st Street, NW. Contemporary Latin American artists. *OPEN Mon-Sat 11am-6pm.*

Kornblatt Gallery
406 7th Street, NW. 638-7657. Contemporary paintings, sculpture, prints, works on paper, architectural installations. *OPEN Tues-Sat 10:30am-5:30pm.*

Mickelson Gallery
707 G Street, NW. 628-1734. Contemporary printmakers and sculptors: Anthony Gross, Norman Ackroyd, Fairfield Porter, David Aronson, Peter Rockwell, Susan Litsios, Anne Shreve. Strong collection of M. C. Escher and George Bellows prints. *OPEN Mon-Fri 10am-5pm; Sat 10am-3pm.*

Middendorf Gallery
2009 Columbia Road, NW. 462-2009. Nineteenth- and 20th-century American art and modern masters. Represents William Christianberry, Joseph White, Yuriko Yamaguchi, Ralston Crawford. A broad contemporary print inventory as well as paintings, drawings, sculpture, and vintage and contemporary photography. *OPEN Tues-Fri 11am-6pm; Sat 11am 5pm.*

Ann O'Brien
2114 R Street, NW. 265-9697. Contemporary two- and three-dimensional art. *OPEN Tues-Sat 11:30am- 5:30pm.*

Old Print Gallery
1220 31st Street, NW. 965-1818. Original American prints of the 18th and 19th centuries. American genre, historical, political; maps, too. Museum-quality framing. *OPEN Mon-Sat 10am-5:45pm.*

Osuna
1919 Q Street, NW. 296-1963. Old masters, 19th century and selected contemporary American painting, drawing, sculpture. Ann Truit, Tor Downing, Manon Cleary, Rebecca Davenport, Ann Purcell, Cita Scott. Also Latin American art 16th century to contemporary. *OPEN Tues-Sat 10am-5pm.*

Pensler Gallery
2029 Q Street, NW. 328-9190. Nineteenth- and 20th-century American and European paintings and drawings. *OPEN Tues-Sat 10am-5pm & by appointment.*

Andrea Ruggieri Gallery
2030 R Street, NW. 265-6191. Contemporary American and international artists; all media. *OPEN Tues-Sat 11am-5:30pm.*

Shogun
1083 Wisconsin Avenue, NW, 2nd floor. 965-5454. Eighteenth-, 19th-, 20th-century Japanese woodblock prints including such masters as Kuniyoshi, Kunisada, Hiroshige, Hasui, and others; also a large collection of contemporary Japanese print artists. Books on Japanese prints and posters available. Museum framing and appraisals. *OPEN Wed-Sat 11am-6pm & by appointment.*

Mary Singer Gallery
2920 44th Place, NW. 363-6785. Contemporary prints, sculpture, and paintings. Carolyn Brady, Louisa Chase, Sonia Delaunay, Helen Frankenthaler, Nancy Graves, David Hockney, Robert Motherwell, Robert Rauschenberg, Antoni Tapies. *By appointment only.*

Spectrum Gallery, Inc.
1132 29th Street, NW. 333-0954. Artist-run cooperative. Paintings, sculpture, prints, pottery, jewelry. Spectrum Gift Collection includes small items. *OPEN Tues-Sat 11am-6pm; Sun 2-5pm.*

St. Lukes Gallery
1715 Q Street, NW. 328-2424. Seventeenth- to late-19th-century European old masters: paintings, prints, and drawings. Giovanni Batista Caraccio, Hendrik Goltzius, Cornelius Johnson, Nicolaes Maes, Giambattista Piranesi, Rembrandt van Rijn. *OPEN Tues-Sat 11am-5pm.*

Studio Gallery
2108 R Street, NW. 232-8734. Contemporary paintings, sculpture, graphics, photography, and mixed media. *OPEN Tues-Sat 11am-5pm.*

Taggert & Jorgensen Gallery
3241 P Street, NW. 298-7676. Nineteenth- and 20th-century American paintings. Childe Hassam, Winslow Homer, Maurice Prendergast, John Singer Sargent. *OPEN Mon-Sat 11am-5pm & by appointment.*

Tartt Gallery
2017 Q Street, NW. 332-5652. Nineteenth- and 20th-century photography; contemporary outsider art. *OPEN Tues-Sat 11am-5pm.*

Touchstone Gallery
2009 R Street, NW. 797-7278. Changing shows by artist-owners of this co-op in various media and styles. Pottery, graphics, painting, sculp-

ure, photography. *OPEN Tues-Sat 11am-5pm; Sun noon-5pm.*

Trocadero Arts of Asia
1501 Connecticut Avenue, NW. 234-5656. Furniture, porcelain, and sculpture—primarily 14th-to 18th-century Chinese. Selection of oriental rugs and woven objects downstairs. *OPEN Tues-Sat 10:30am-6pm.*

Veerhoff Galleries
1604 17th Street, NW. 387-2322. Eighteenth-, 19th-, and 20th-century American and European prints including Audubon, Nast, Homer, Piranesi. Work of contemporary American realist painters. Framing as well. Full restoration service. *OPEN Tues-Fri 11am-7pm; Sat 10am-6pm.*

Venable-Neslage Gallery
1803 Connecticut Avenue, NW. 462-1800. This gallery, established in 1892, is now the exclusive representative of Frederick H. McDuff, featuring paintings, silk-screen prints of this contemporary American Impressionist. Also paintings by Jerry Weers, Beverly Erschell, Bill Rolig, Clifford Bailey, Herman Raymond, and sculpture by Meg Egeberg, Donna Dobberfuhl, David Breeden. *OPEN Tues-Sat 10am-6pm; Sun noon-6pm.*

Washington Printmaker Gallery
2106 R Street, NW. Contemporary prints. *OPEN Tues-Sat 11am-5pm.*

Zenith Gallery
417 7th Street, NW. 783-2963. Artists' complex—contemporary work, experimental and innovative, in a variety of media. Painting, sculpture, crafts, and neon. Mostly local, some national artists. *OPEN Mon-Fri 10am-6pm; Sat 11am-6pm; Sun noon-4pm.*

PARKS & GARDENS

Meridian Hill Park

The parks and gardens of the nation's capital and nearby sections of Virginia and Maryland are under the supervision of the National Park Service. They publish a monthly calendar of events, Kiosk, which includes theater, concerts, bikes, and boat trips. You may obtain a copy by writing to National Capital Parks, Public Affairs Office, 1100 Ohio Drive, SW, Washington, DC 20242; or by calling 619-7225.

Dial-a-Park, 619-7275, gives recorded information on current park activities and events in the Washington area. Use it to help you plan your day.

PARKS

Anacostia Park
Between South Capitol Street & Benning Road, SE. From Capitol Hill via the John Phillip Sousa Bridge. Extending 8 miles along the Anacostia River, covering a total of 1,355 acres. It contains Kenilworth Aquatic Gardens (see Gardens); a recreation center, 767-7345, with roller skating and community and educational activities; a bird sanctuary; and boat rental facilities. Also a swimming pool, playgrounds, tennis courts, horseshoe pitches, shuffleboard. Picnic facilities. Rest rooms. Parking. OPEN year-round 7 days sunrise to sundown.

Battery-Kemble Park
Chain Bridge Road between Nebraska Avenue & MacArthur Boulevard, NW. 426-6834. Close to the Potomac River, a small serene park, ⅛ mile wide by one mile long. People come here to enjoy the evidence of the changing seasons. There's Japanese honeysuckle, flowering dogwood, yellow poplar trees, and sycamore, maple, beech, and Virginia pine. Also contains a historic ruin: a two-gun battery position dating from the Civil War. The hilly terrain makes it popular for sledding in snowy winters. For summer

pleasures, there are picnic facilities, including grills. Rest rooms. Parking. OPEN year-round 7 days sunrise to sundown.

Dumbarton Oaks Park
Accessible only by foot: via Lover's Lane from M Street (east of M & R Streets, NW). 426-6834. These 27 serene acres of woods and meadows have been called "America's smallest national wilderness park." Its special attraction: wild flowers. Every spring a rainbow of color bursts forth— crocus, forsythia, narcissus, primrose, hyacinth, daffodil, wild orchids, azalea, and forget-me-nots. Runner-up in the beauty contest: autumn for the fall foliage. Picnic tables. OPEN year-round 7 days sunrise to sundown.

Dupont Circle Park
At the intersection of Connecticut, New Hampshire & Massachusetts Avenues, NW. The largest of Washington's circle parks. Popular for sunning, sitting, and listening to impromptu entertainment (day and night).

East Potomac Park
South of Independence Avenue and east of the Tidal Basin. Ohio Drive, SW. A man-made peninsula between the Washington Channel and the Potomac River; 327 acres with a one-way perimeter road bordered by cherry trees—later-blooming by about two weeks than the ones in the Tidal Basin (see West Potomac Park); these have pink blossoms. At the southern tip, Hains Point, a favorite spot to catch a cool breeze—or take the kids, there's a playground (Visitors Center, National Park Service headquarters). Here, too, is an intriguing piece of outdoor sculpture called Awakening (see HISTORIC & NEW WASHINGTON, Outdoor Artwork & Sculpture). Free outdoor swimming pool, tennis courts, golf course, miniature golf, boat rentals (see SPORTS). Picnic tables. The 5-mile waterside perimeter road is popular with walkers and joggers. Benches offer opportunities to sit and watch the boats go by. Snack bar. Rest rooms. Parking.

Ellipse
See President's Park

Farragut Square
Connecticut Avenue & K Street, NW. Admiral Farragut in the center. A pretty and, because of its location, very popular little urban park. Scheduled noontime concerts in summer.

Fort Dupont Park
At Randall Circle, SE. 426-7723. On 400 acres. The site of a Civil War defense fortification, which is now the park's boundary on the east. Community/Nature Center, indoor skating rink, basketball and softball facilities (*see* SPORTS). Free concerts in summer.

Glover-Archbold Parkway
From MacArthur Boulevard & Canal Road, NW, to Van Ness Street & Wisconsin Avenue, NW. Adjacent to Georgetown University. Approximately 100 acres given in 1924 by Charles C. Glover and Ann Archbold, with the express wish it be maintained in its natural state for the pleasure of birds and people—and so it is. Within are a tract of virgin beechwoods, a profusion of wild flowers; a bird sanctuary that makes it a good "watching" spot. A nature trail starts at 44th Street and Reservoir Road and crisscrosses the Foundry Branch stream for the length of the park (2 miles). There are also picnic areas. *OPEN year-round 7 days sunrise to sundown.*

The Great Falls of the Potomac
Great Falls Tavern, 11710 MacArthur Boulevard, Potomac, Md. (301) 299-3613. Located on either side of the Potomac; approximately 15 miles northwest of downtown DC; part in Virginia, part in Maryland. Maryland side: Information Center, the Great Falls Tavern, founded 1830, now restored and containing historical exhibits; rest rooms; parking. FREE. Center *OPEN year-round, Wed-Sun 9am-5pm.* Best for fall foliage. Bike and canoe rental (*see* SPORTS). Virginia side: Visitors Center, 9200 Old Dominion Drive, (703) 285-2965; photo exhibits and films and better views of the 76-foot cascading waterfalls; 4 miles of nature trails; picnic facilities with fire grills; the remains of the Potomac Canal designed by George Washington, used by boats to avoid the falls; guided walks and hikes on weekends; rest rooms. Admission fee on daily, weekly, or yearly basis. Center *OPEN year-round 7 days 9am-5pm.*

Lady Bird Johnson Park
Adjacent to George Washington Memorial Parkway. On an island in the Potomac (access only via footbridge from a parking lot on the Virginia shore). Within DC, though reached via Virginia. Previously known as Columbia Island (man-made); it's long and narrow—approximately 1¼ miles long, and 1,000 feet at its widest. Dedicated, in 1968, in recognition of Mrs. Johnson's efforts to beautify America. Oak, maple, and 2,700 dogwoods, and in spring a million daffodils—quite a sight! At the south end of the park, Lyndon Baines Johnson Memorial Grove. *OPEN 7 days 8am-sundown.*

Lyndon Baines Johnson Memorial Grove
Lady Bird Johnson Park, south end. A 15-acre grove planted in honor of LBJ contains several hundred white pine trees, flowering dogwood, azaleas, and rhododendrons. In it, a monolith of pink Texas granite. There is one mile of bike and walk trails through the grove. (Sociological note: Once picked by *Washingtonian* magazine as DC's "best lunchtime necking spot.")

Kalorama Park
Columbia & Kalorama Roads, NW. 673-7606. Lovely and lively small park in the transitional Kalorama-Adams-Morgan area. Scene of Adams-Morgan Day Festival (*see* ANNUAL EVENTS, Labor Day Weekend).

Kelly Park
Virginia Avenue & 21st Street, NW. Attractive park with a copy of the famed Greek statue, the *Discus Thrower*. Popular for alfresco lunches in summer.

Lafayette Park
Between Pennsylvania Avenue & H Street, NW. Befitting its location across from America's most famous house, this is one of Washington's prettiest parks. Tall bald cypress trees (equipped with lightning rods); Norwegian maples; American and English elms; red, white, and yellow oak; Southern magnolia. Its name notwithstanding, the statue of Andrew Jackson is central, with Lafayette in support (*see* HISTORIC & NEW WASHINGTON, Statues & Monuments: Major General Andrew Jackson). Favored by financier Bernard Baruch in the 1930s, "his" bench is duly commemorated. Popular with protesters, footsore tourists, pigeon feeders, chess and checkers players, and people watchers. *Metro: McPherson Square, Farragut West.*

Lincoln Park
East Capitol & 11th Streets, NW. During the Civil War, a camp and hospital area for Union Army soldiers. The 7-acre park was formally dedicated in 1876, in memory of the slain president. It contains magnolia and chestnut trees, the Emancipation monument as well as a tribute to Mary McLeod Bethune (*see* HISTORIC & NEW WASHINGTON, Statues & Monuments). In 1974, game tables, tot lots, and play sculptures were added.

Meridian Hill Park
Between 15th & 16th, Euclid & W Streets, NW. The 12 acres on which the park is situated were acquired in 1910 but not opened as a park until 1936. It is a magnificent example of formal garden design. Only 20 blocks from the White House, but you could be in Europe. The upper part was designed in the style of a formal French garden; the lower in the manner of an Italian Renaissance garden. Terraces, a broad stairway, promenades, cascading waterfalls—all man-made—enhance the natural topography. Dogwood, cherry, and azalea bloom in spring, and there are lovely views of the city from here. The black community in which it is located refers to it as Malcolm X Park. It has fallen on hard times and is best visited in daylight with a friend.

Montrose Park

R Street between 30th & 31st Streets, NW. 426-6827. Once part of the Dumbarton Oaks estate. Just a few blocks from Georgetown's bustle, bounded on the north by Rock Creek Park, it's 16 acres of mainly rugged wooded terrain. Popular for Sunday strolling and picnicking (there are tables); tennis, too (see SPORTS). The western boundary is Lover's Lane, an old cobblestoned path (to Baltimore in the 18th century) apparently conducive to romance. Also, there is a glorious rose garden. Rest rooms. OPEN year-round 7 days sunrise to sundown.

Pershing Park

Pennsylvania Avenue between 14th & 15th Streets, NW. This 1981 addition to the rehabilitation of Pennsylvania Avenue, a tribute to Gen. John J. Pershing, is a popular retreat in any season. The central waterfall-fed pool becomes a public skating rink in winter; in summer, outdoor tables and a food kiosk beckon. (See also SPORTS, Skating: Ice Skating.)

Potomac Park

See East Potomac Park and West Potomac Park.

President's Park

The White House grounds, 1600 Pennsylvania Avenue, NW. Eighteen acres, south of the White House, containing 80 varieties of trees. It has become traditional for the family of every president (since John Quincy Adams) to plant trees on the lawns. The magnolia near the South Portico was brought from Tennessee by Andrew Jackson; there is also one planted by FDR. There is a white oak from the Kentucky birthplace of Lincoln and a giant sequoia selected by Richard Nixon. The Rose Garden, adjoining the press office, gained fame as a retreat during the Carter campaign for reelection. The East Garden, renamed the Jacqueline Kennedy Rose Garden by President and Mrs. Johnson, is intended for the first lady's use. The Children's Garden—donated by President Johnson and family—has a goldfish pool. Grounds and gardens OPEN only three weekends a year—one in spring, one in fall, one in December, as well as for the Annual Easter Egg Roll (see ANNUAL EVENTS, April, October, and December). Other times of the year you can only gaze through the fence. Major trees and shrubs have markers.

Rawlins

E Street between 18th & 19th Streets, NW. A jewel of an urban park, not to be missed when its magnolias are in bloom. Concerts and puppet shows in warm weather.

Rock Creek Park

Visitor Information Center, 5000 Glover Road, NW. 426-6832. Former home to the Algonquin Indians, now an oasis within the city. The District's largest and finest park encompassing approximately 1,800 acres (4 miles long, with an average one mile width). It was purchased by Congress in 1890 to be set aside for the public enjoyment. (Another 2,700 acres, Rock Creek Regional Park, falls within Montgomery County, Md.) It's a tranquil haven of hills and valleys,

ravines, fields, and near-virgin forests; the 12-mile creek itself is unfortunately polluted (no swimming, wading, or fishing). The area is of great geological interest, as well as exhibiting glorious natural beauty—wild flowers are in bloom much of the year, though in greatest profusion April and May. The park also contains Fort De Russy and Pierce Mill (see HISTORIC & NEW WASHINGTON, Historic Buildings & Areas), and Joaquin Miller Cabin. There are numerous picnic sites, many of which contain fireplaces. Some have to be reserved, and all need permits. Contact the Department of Recreation, 3149 16th Street, NW, 20010, or call 673-7646. Picnic kits containing game equipment are also loaned free of charge but with a $25 deposit and $5 late fee. Opportunities for hiking—15 miles of trails as well as a 10-mile drive with many scenic vista stops. Bike paths—obtain map from the Rock Creek Nature Center (5200 Glover Road, 426-6829) or Park Headquarters. In addition, Beach Drive between Joyce and Broad Branch roads is closed to vehicular traffic from 7am Saturday to 7pm Sunday. A parcourse, jogging path, horseback riding, tennis, golf (see also SPORTS); the Carter Barron Amphitheater (16th Street and Colorado Avenue, NW, 829-3200) provides 4,000 outdoor seats for a variety of entertainment in summer. Two not-so-tranquil roadways traverse the park avoid rush hours. Rest rooms; parking lots. The park is OPEN year-round 7 days sunrise to sundown.

West Potomac Park

Along the Potomac River up to the Lincoln Memorial, surrounding the Tidal Basin (426-6821). Together with East Potomac Park, it comprises approximately 700 acres. In it you'll find the Lincoln and Jefferson memorials, the DC War Memorial, and the Tidal Basin, where in spring one of America's major extravaganzas takes place, courtesy of Mother Nature: the cherry blossoms (see ANNUAL EVENTS, Late March or Early April). Paddleboats may be rented in season. Also located here are Constitution Gardens and the Vietnam Veterans Memorial (see also Gardens, and SIGHTSEEING, On Your Own, respectively). Accessible via Tourmobile.

GARDENS

The Aztec Garden

OAS Building, 17th Street & Constitution Avenue, NW. 458-3000. Islands of water lilies float in a blue-tiled pool, watched over by a statue of Xochipilli, the Aztec god of flowers. In the patio a variety of tropical trees and shrubs including the Peace Tree, planted by President William Howard Taft in 1910. Forty-five-minute guided tours by reservation. OPEN Mon-Fri 9:30am-5pm. FREE.

Brookside Botanical Gardens

Wheaton Regional Park, 1500 Glenallan Avenue, Wheaton, Md. (301) 949-8230. A public garden on 35 acres (Maryland's largest) with a wonderful conservatory complete with small stream. Also an Azalea Garden (mid-May), a Rose Garden (June), and a Fragrance Garden. The Trial Garden for innovations. Seasonal displays. OPEN year-round 7 days 9am-5pm. CLOSED Christmas Day. FREE.

Constitution Gardens
West Potomac Park, north side of the Lincoln Memorial Reflecting Pool. Along Constitution Avenue between 21st & 17th Streets, NW. Dedicated in 1976. A natural setting with a wonderful 7½-acre lake, in the center of which is a serene one-acre island (reached via footbridge) inhabited by mallard ducks and turtles. Also here, the Signers Memorial saluting those who signed the Declaration of Independence. There are about 14 acres of open meadow where one may picnic. Over 5,000 plants have been planted. The Vietnam Veterans Memorial comprises the far western corner of the gardens. (See also SIGHTSEEING, On Your Own.)

Dumbarton Oaks Garden
Garden entrance: R Street between 31st & 32nd Streets, NW. 342-3212. In the heart of Georgetown, 16 acres of breathtakingly beautiful formal gardens on the grounds of this estate named for the oaks that surrounded the mansion. It is truly a garden for all seasons. Forsythia Hill blooms golden, late March or early April, and the secluded Lover's Lane Pool is everyone's "secret" spot. There's a formal Rose Garden, a towering bamboo stand, an English country garden, and so much more. A must visit! No picnics, pets, bikes, or—heaven forbid—radios, only peace. Twenty-foot-high holly bushes act as sentinels at the entrance to the house. Group tours must reserve, call 342-3212. (See also HISTORIC & NEW WASHINGTON, Historic Buildings & Areas, and MUSEUMS & GALLERIES, Museums.) Garden OPEN Apr-Oct, 7 days 2-6pm; Nov-Mar, 7 days 2-5pm. CLOSED federal holidays and in inclement weather. Admission, senior citizens and children under age 12 free. Free for all from November to March.

The Franciscan Monastery
1400 Quincy Street, NW. 526-6800. A tranquil oasis on 40 acres. Daffs in the spring, lilies at Easter, roses in summer; beautifully arranged and maintained. Amid the blossoms, replicas of Holy Land shrines. Tours conducted Monday to Saturday from 9am to 4pm, every hour on the hour; Sunday every 15 minutes from 1 to 4:30pm. OPEN year-round 7 days 8:30am-sundown. (See also HISTORIC & NEW WASHINGTON, Churches & Synagogues.) FREE; donations accepted.

Hillwood
4155 Linnean Avenue, NW. 686-5807. Designed for heiress Marjorie Merriweather Post by Perry Wheeler, planner of the White House Rose Garden, these formal gardens contain more than 3,500 varieties of plants and trees. Among Hillwood's delights are a complete Japanese garden with bridges, a waterfall and stone lanterns, a rose garden, some ivy clipped from Buckingham Palace, and a boxwood tree from Mount Vernon. The greenhouses contain over 5,000 orchids. OPEN Mon, Wed-Sat 10:30am-3:30pm. CLOSED Sun & Tues. Tours by reservation only. No children under age 12. Admission. Cafe on premises, reservations suggested. (See also HISTORIC & NEW WASHINGTON, Historic Buildings & Areas: Hillwood Mansion.)

Kahlil Gibran Memorial Garden
On Massachusetts Avenue, just opposite the British Embassy. Dedicated to the famed Lebanese poet and philosopher, it is a serene environment for reflection.

Kenilworth Aquatic Gardens
Anacostia Park, Anacostia Avenue at Douglass Street, SE. 426-6905. A magnificent collection of exotic, often giant, flowering aquatic plants on part of the original marshland that became Anacostia Park. The gardens were begun in the 1880s by a government clerk, W. B. Shaw, who planted some white water lilies he brought from his native Maine to plant on his property on the shore of the river. Shaw's garden grew and was purchased by the federal government in 1938; now administered by the National Capital Parks System. More than 100,000 water plants contained on 11 acres of ponds, among them rare lotuses and water lilies including the Egyptian lotus, said to be Cleopatra's favorite blossom. Insect, bird, small wild animal, and plant life are abundant (more abundant than people). Best time to visit: mid-June, when over 70 varieties of day-blooming tropical water lilies put in an appearance. The lotus is best seen from July to early August. Early in the day is best as the blossoms close in the heat of the day (and for safety reasons as well). There are picnic tables and a playground. Every weekend at 9 and 11am and 1 and 3pm, a park naturalist conducts tours along the natural footpaths and among the aquatic pools. Assemble in area adjacent to the parking area. Visitors Center OPEN 7 days 8am-3:30pm. Park OPEN year-round 7 days 7am-sundown (approximately 5:30pm in winter, 9pm in summer). CLOSED Christmas Day. FREE. Metro: Deanwood.

Tulip Library
South of Independence Avenue & East Basin Drive, NW, near the Tidal Basin Boating Center. Over 13,000 tulips! There are 95 beds, each with a different variety of tulip. After the tulips have put in their appearance, seasonals are planted.

U.S. Botanic Garden
1st Street & Maryland Avenue, SW, at the foot of Capitol Hill. 225-7099 (recorded information); 225-8333. Within the glass and aluminum conservatory are extensive collections of azalea (90 varieties, usually in winter), lilies at Easter, cacti, citrus, and cycad (12 varieties of the survivor from prehistoric times); orchids year-round; 300 varieties of chrysanthemums in November; poinsettias in December. A permanent display of tropical and subtropical plants. There is also an exotic jungle and a tropical rain forest. From mid-

May to September the summer terrace outside is glorious with hanging baskets and annuals, and the successive seasonal displays are a treat. Guided group tours by reservation Monday to Friday. *OPEN year-round 7 days 9am-5pm (till 9pm June-Aug). CLOSED Christmas Day. FREE. Metro: Federal Center.*

Washington Cathedral Close
Washington Cathedral, Wisconsin & Massachusetts Avenues, NW. 537-6200. The cathedral, which occupies 57 acres on a hilltop, has a walled medieval garden—the Bishop's Garden—with orchids, boxwood, magnolias, herbs, and flowers. Special: the Herb Garden, small and fragrant; in front, the Herb Cottage, where you may purchase herbs, honey, sachets—the proceeds go to the maintenance of the cathedral grounds. (*See also* ANNUAL EVENTS, May: Washington Cathedral Flower Mart.) The greenhouse raises (and sells) rare herbs. There is also a wooded path, a rose garden, and the mysterious Glastonbury Thorn tree from England, which, according to legend, blooms only on Christmas Day and when royalty visits—and so it did, when Elizabeth II visited, as princess in 1951, as queen in 1957, and again in Prince Charles's presence in 1981 (would we lie?). Garden *OPEN 7 days sunrise to sundown.* Herb Cottage *OPEN Mon-Fri 9:30am-5pm; Sat 9am-5pm; Sun noon-4:30pm.* Greenhouse *OPEN Mon-Sat 9am-5pm; Sun 10am-5pm.* Cathedral Sunday services at 8, 9, 10, 11am, and 4pm. *Metro: Woodley Park-Zoo.* (*See also* HISTORIC & NEW WASHINGTON, Churches & Synagogues: Washington National Cathedral.)

Woodlawn Plantation Gardens
9000 Richmond Highway (Route 1), Mount Vernon, Va. (703) 780-4000. A jewel of a setting overlooking the Potomac and Mount Vernon. Once part of Mount Vernon, its 2,000 acres were given by George Washington to his foster daughter Nellie Custis (Martha Washington's daughter) as a wedding present. It is famed for its 18th- and 19th-century rose gardens; May is the best month to visit. There are two meandering nature trails, each about a mile long, and parterres, geometrically designed gardens with walkways, as well as Frank Lloyd Wright's Pope-Leighey House (*see also* HISTORIC & NEW WASHINGTON, Historic Buildings & Areas *and* Modern Architecture.) *OPEN year-round 7 days 9:30am-4:30pm. CLOSED Thanksgiving, Christmas & New Year's Day.* Admission; lower for senior citizens.

ZOOS & AQUARIUMS

The National Aquarium
U.S. Department of Commerce Building, 14th & Constitution Avenue, NW, lower lobby. 377-2825. Established in 1873, it's the nation's oldest aquarium (in its present site since 1932). There are 50 tanks containing over 200 species of salt and fresh water fish, including piranha (understandably in their own tank), shark, eel, and Japanese carp; also some endangered species. Now operated by the National Aquarium Society; membership available, proceeds go to maintaining the aquarium, and it entitles you to free classes, a bi-monthly newsletter, and discounts in some area pet stores. Group tours available. *OPEN year-round 7 days 9am-5pm. CLOSED Christmas Day.* Admission. *Metro: Federal Triangle.*

The National Zoological Park
Main Entrance: 3001 Connecticut Avenue, NW, west of Calvert Street. Other entrances: Harvard & Adams Mill Roads, NW; Beach Drive in Rock Creek Park. Information Desk in the lobby of the Education Building. 673-4800 (recorded information); 673-4717. Under the auspices of the Smithsonian Institution, it was begun when they acquired a herd of buffalo circa 1890; it has since become one of the world's finest zoos. On 165 acres—much of it natural habitat exhibits—live nearly 5,000 animals representing 500 species, many of which are endangered. Until his death, it was home to the original "Smokey the Bear," who bore the scars of the forest fire from which he was rescued. The most popular attraction since their arrival in 1972 (a much publicized gift from the People's Republic of China) are Ling Ling and Hsing Hsing, the Western Hemisphere's only Giant Pandas (attempts to breed them have been, sadly, unsuccessful). Close behind in popularity are the rare blue-eyed white Bengal tigers from India and the Atlas lions, no longer found in the wild. Other unusual species you will find here are the golden marmoset, Eld's deer, and the bald eagle. Feeding times are always fun: The pandas are fed at 11am and 3pm; training and feeding sessions for the elephants are at 11:30am; seal and sea lion training sessions alternate, also at 11:30am. When you enter, follow the zoo's main trail, Olmstead Walk, branching off it are trails leading to the various exhibits. In addition to the pandas, and Lion- Tiger Hill, don't miss the Great Ape House, the Reptile House, and the new Invertebrate Exhibit. Wear comfortable shoes; strollers are available for rental at the Information Desk in the Education Building. NOTE: Much of what you purchase during the day—from food to postcards to tees—provide revenue for FONZ (Friends of the National Zoo), modern-day Noahs working today to conserve wildlife for tomorrow. Of special interest to children are three Discovery Rooms—Zoolab, Birdlab, and Herplab—which feature films, games, puzzles, activity boxes, things (tusks, bones, etc.); Herplab has live animals. (*See also* KIDS' WASHINGTON, Zoos & Animal Preserves.) Group tours by reservation, call 673-4955 at least two weeks in advance. There are plenty of food and beverage facilities as well as picnic facilities (no fires). Although accessible from the bike path in Rock Creek Park, bike riding is prohibited within the zoo. Caveat: Limited space for parking (for a

ee). Grounds *OPEN May 1-Sept 15, 7 days 8am-8pm; Sept 16-Apr 30, 7 days 8am-6pm.* Buildings *OPEN May 1-Sept 15, 7 days 9am-5pm; Sept 16-Apr 30, 7 days 9am-4:30pm.* CLOSED *Christmas Day.* Birdlab, Herplab, and Zoolab *OPEN Fri 10am-1pm; Sat & Sun 10am-2pm. FREE. Metro: Woodley Park-Zoo.*

NATURE TRAILS & WILDLIFE PRESERVES

The C&O Canal National Historic Park
From M & 30th Streets in Georgetown to Cumberland, Md. Covering a distance of 184½ miles. Pick up the towpath, where in the 19th century mules toted that barge (mainly filled with coal), and walk the route at least to Great Falls. (The late Chief Justice of the Supreme Court, William O. Douglas, in his 70s, used to hike the entire route, *see* ANNUAL EVENTS, April: C&O Canal Reunion Hike.) Passing en route interesting plant life, humans on bikes (passing you), and a variety of birds and wildlife, including beaver, fox, raccoon, muskrat, and woodchuck. You may also picnic, fish, or boat along the Canal (*see* SPORTS, Boating *and* Fishing). For nonwalkers, present-day barges tote visitors (*see* SIGHTSEEING, On Your Own: C&O Canal Barge Ride).

National Arboretum
24th & R Streets, NE. 475-4815. Established by Congress in 1927, administered by the U.S. Department of Agriculture mainly for research and educational purposes. But visitors to the 444-acre arboretum (planned but not formal) will be amply rewarded—mainly by Mother Nature. The arboretum, located 2 miles northeast of the Capitol, was placed on the National Register of Historic Places in 1973. It contains the National Bonsai Collection and the Japanese Garden, a gift from the Nippon Bonsai Association of Japan to commemorate America's Bicentennial (it's worth $4.5 million!). Thirty-four species of the miniatures are represented by 53 trees, ranging in age from 30 to 350 years. Other highlights: the Herbarium (500,000 dried plants all grown in the National Herb Garden); the Gotelli Dwarf Conifer Collection, one of the world's finest; and the new Carl Buchheister National Bird Garden. Spring here is particularly dazzling. Late March to early April the camellias, magnolias, and the first pear trees bloom. Late April to May the most extensive plantings of azaleas in America—over 70,000—plus dogwood, rhododendrons, quince, daffodils, mountain laurel, peonies, elephant ear magnolia. Because it's in an intermediate climatic zone, trees and shrubs from a wide range of climatic situations are able to grow. There are marvelous views to be had of the Capitol, the Washington Monument, and the Anacostia River. Paths wind through groupings of ornamental cherry and crab apple trees, day lilies, hollies, and box woods. A nature trail, ponds, a stream, and 9 miles of hard surface for biking

complete the picture. You may also drive 9.5 miles of roadway through the facility. In the Great Meadow, a classical design utilizing 22 sandstone columns discarded when the Capitol was enlarged in 1959. You will be tempted but no picnicking or picking is permitted. There are lectures, classes, workshops, films, walks. Group tours by advance reservations, call 475-4815 (for 10 or more). Parking, rest rooms, and rain shelters. Arboretum *OPEN year-round Mon-Fri 8am-5pm; Sat, Sun & holidays 10am-5pm.* CLOSED *Christmas Day.* National Bonsai Collection *OPEN 7 days 10am-2:30pm.* Information Center & Administration Building *OPEN Mon-Fri 8am- 4:30pm. FREE. Metro: Stadium-Armory.*

Rock Creek Nature Center
Rock Creek Park, 5200 Glover Road, ¼ mile south of Military & Oregon Roads, NW. 426-6829. Run by the National Park Service for educational purposes, with activities geared to both adults and children. There are exhibits, live animals, insects, a working beehive. In the auditorium, a small planetarium with shows for children Saturday and Sunday at 1pm, for adults at 4pm; also films, slide shows, a self-guided trail (approximately ¼ mile long), guided nature walks every Saturday and Sunday at 3pm. Bookstore with nature-related books. *OPEN year-round Tues-Sun 9am-5pm.* CLOSED *Mon. FREE.*

Theodore Roosevelt Island
In the Potomac between Key & Roosevelt Bridges; access via pedestrian footbridge from a parking lot on the Virginia side of the Potomac, off the northbound lane of the George Washington Memorial Parkway. (703) 285-2600. A gift from the Theodore Roosevelt Memorial Association. The island, one mile long, half a mile wide, and so close to DC, contains 88 acres of dense forest, marshland, swamp, and rocky seashore. It provides a serene natural environment for small wildlife—and visiting humans. There are 2½ miles of nature trails; you may picnic albeit there are no picnic facilities. The monument to the 26th president, a naturalist and early conservationist, contains a 17-foot bronze statue (*see* HISTORIC & NEW WASHINGTON, Statues & Monuments: Theodore Roosevelt Memorial). Administered by the National Park Service; there are guided tours Saturday and Sunday by park rangers (times vary, so call 285-2598 for further information). Groups by advance reservation only. Nearby Little Island accessible only by boat. *OPEN year-round 7 days 9:30am- sundown. FREE.*

BIRDWATCHING

There are approximately 180 species of birds living in the DC area. Many more pass through during migratory periods.
Audubon Naturalist Society
8940 Jones Mill Road, Chevy Chase, Md. (301) 652-9188. Voice of the Naturalist, a recorded weekly message for birdwatchers, (301) 652-

1088. Guided bird walks, usually held once a week; a variety of parks are covered in DC, Maryland, and Virginia. Walks can last from 3 hours to a whole day. Reserve in advance. Early October to late November from noon to 5pm are open house times for feature films, guided tours—of the house and grounds—and various outdoor activities. Membership available. FREE.

The C&O Canal

From M & 30th Streets in Georgetown to Cumberland, Md. For information, call the Great Falls Tavern Museum, (301) 299-3613. On the migratory route, therefore good birdwatching: whippoorwills, barred owls, redstarts, wood ducks, black-billed cuckoos, wood thrushes, water fowl. Call for information on organized bird walks.

Glover-Archbold Parkway

From MacArthur Boulevard & Canal Road, NW to Van Ness Street & Wisconsin Avenue, NW Over 150 species of birds have been sighted including pileated woodpecker, red-shouldered hawk, and the barred owl.

Rock Creek Park

5200 Glover Road, NW. DC's largest park has 150 species, 30 of which are residents, and offers opportunities to spot white-throated sparrows, blue jays, cardinals, woodpeckers, mallards, ducks, owls (great horned, barred, screech, and whet), swifts, turkey vultures, red-tailed hawks, chimney swifts, and whippoorwills. The Nature Center gives bird walks on an irregular basis; for information, call 426-6829.

KIDS'
WASHINGTON

Ling Ling, the Giant Panda

SEEING WASHINGTON

Here are some fun things to do with kids in and around Washington. For more traditional attractions, see also SIGHTSEEING and HISTORIC & NEW WASHINGTON for the traditional sights of the nation's capital and ANNUAL EVENTS for parades, fairs, and festivals—many of which are FREE.

For up-to-the-minute scheduling of activities and entertainments for children in DC, check the Weekend section of the Washington Post.

Chesapeake & Potomac Telephone Co.
1710 H Street, NW. 392-4580. See the work centers, switchboard, and assistance operators on the job, with a brief explanation of how it all works. For ages 10 and up. Groups only by appointment (it is possible for an individual to join a group if one is scheduled); call two weeks in advance. FREE. *Metro: Farragut North.*

Hard Rock Cafe
999 E Street, NW. 737-7625. Kids are mad for these musical museums cum restaurant located in every major city. They don't mind waiting to get in (you might) to see the rock 'n' roll memorabilia set against a backdrop of deafening music while munching on burgers or sipping a shake. Don't expect to leave without buying the ubiquitous sweatshirt or some other logo merchandise from the gift shop. *OPEN 7 days 11am-2am. Metro: Gallery Place.*

Old Stone House
3051 M Street, NW. 426-6851. This is a wonderfully accessible site, a pocket of serenity in the midst of Georgetown's hustle and bustle. It is the oldest surviving residence in DC, built in 1764 by cabinetmaker Christopher Laymen. The home is furnished with things typical of the 18th century. The staff, wearing period costumes, goes through daily chores of colonial life and gives demonstrations of spinning and quilting. There is

a lovely English-style garden to wander around in. Groups must reserve in advance. *OPEN Wed-Sun 8am- 4:30pm. CLOSED Mon, Tues & all federal holidays.* FREE.

Paddle Boats
Tidal Basin Boathouse, 15th Street & Maine Avenue, SW. 484-0206. Rental of two-person paddleboats is fun way to spend the afternoon after you've seen the monuments up close. *OPEN Apr-Oct 7 days.*

Pierce Mill
Rock Creek Park, 2375 Tilden Street near Beach Drive, NW. 426-6908. Visit this fascinating restored mill, which dates back to 1820. It's the last of the original eight mills that were located here, utilizing the power generated by the waters of Rock Creek; three pairs of the original millstones remain. The mill is once again being used to grind corn and wheat every Saturday and Sunday from noon to 2:30pm and the products made from the grains are sold as well. Ongoing tours throughout the day. There are special programs for groups of children, ages 7-12; to arrange call three weeks in advance. *OPEN Wed-Sun 8am-4:30pm. CLOSED Thanksgiving, Christmas, New Year's Day & federal holidays.* FREE. (*See also* HISTORIC & NEW WASHINGTON, Historic Buildings & Areas.)

Smithsonian Carousel
On the Mall, near the Smithsonian Castle, Constitution Avenue & 10th Street. A three-minute whirl on the 50- year-old carousel is a perfect mini respite from touring. *OPEN May-Sept (weather permitting), Mon-Fri 10:30am-4pm; Sat & Sun 10:30am-5:30pm. Nominal fee. Metro: Smithsonian, Mall exit.*

Uncle Beazley
National Museum of Natural History, Madison Drive & 10th Street, NW. One of nine originally sculpted by Louis Paul Jones for the Sinclair Refining Company Pavilion at the 1964 New York World's Fair, this 25-foot dinosaur—Triceratops, to be exact—took up residence on the Mall in 1967. The name comes from a TV program in which this particular model played a role. Have a climb! *Metro: Smithsonian, Federal Triangle.*

Washington Cathedral Children's Chapel
Mount St. Alban, Wisconsin Avenue & Woodley Road, NW. 537-6200. Within the massive recently completed cathedral, a chapel scaled in size for young people. The Scientists and Technicians Window, presented to the church by astronauts of Apollo 11, has a piece of moon rock embedded in it. The window also shows the moon and sun orbits and commemorates the flights to the moon. While here don't miss the view from the Observation Gallery, where the 70 windows afford faraway views of the Potomac Valley and the Blue Ridge Mountains and close-up views of the facade's gargoyles and grotesques. *OPEN 7 days 10am-4:30pm.* FREE. *Metro: Woodley Park-Zoo.*

Washington DC Post Office
900 Brentwood Road, NE. 636-1208. Mail delivery demystified. Follow the letter from pickup to

Uncle Beazley

delivery how it's sorted, culled, canceled, and delivered. For children ages 8 and up, by appointment. Call the Communications Office 24 hours in advance of planned visit. *Available Tues-Fri.* FREE. *Metro: Rhode Island.*

The Washington Post
1150 15th Street, NW. 334-7969. Get a glimpse of the presses and newsrooms; in their museum see different methods of printing old and new; and a brief history of the award-winning newspaper. One-hour public tours, starting from the lobby, for fifth grade or ages 11 and up. Maximum number per group is 40. *By appointment only, Mon & Thurs only, every hour on the hour, 10am-3pm.* Call or write in advance for reservations. FREE. *Metro: McPherson Square, Farragut North.*

MUSEUMS FOR CHILDREN

Also included are general museums with special attractions for children.

Arts & Industries Building
On the Mall, 900 Jefferson Drive, SW. 357-1300. In a wonderful Victorian building, a new Experimental Gallery, with changing hands-on exhibits in the physical and natural sciences. Also special: The Discovery Theater for pantomime, puppets, and special programs to introduce children to the performing arts. *OPEN 7 days 10am-5:30pm. CLOSED Christmas Day.* FREE. *Metro: Smithsonian.*

Capital Children's Museum
800 3rd Street, NE. 638-5437 (recording); 543-8600. A museum especially for kids that gives them a chance to experience the exhibits by taking part in them: try on costumes or make paper flowers in the Mexico exhibit; play shopkeeper in a store with tins of food, grains, and soap; slide down a fire pole; feed and pet Rosie the goat; and take apart simple machines to see how they work. The City Room is a city scaled down to kids' size, complete with manholes and a city bus. There's a sign language exhibit and a Braille typewriter; a printing exhibit to make prints. A Communications Room will interest high schoolers, with TV and radio station control panels to manipulate. There's also a talking computer. In all, a full range of experiences. Snack bar; in summer bring a picnic (benches are set up on the grounds). Group visits Monday to Friday at 10 and 11:30am and 1pm (it is possible for a single child to join up with a group if you

arrive at one of those times). *OPEN 7 days 10am-5pm. CLOSED holidays.* Admission; lower for kids. *Metro: Union Station.*

Discovery Room
Museum of Natural History, 10th Street & Constitution Avenue, NW. 357-2695. A special exhibit to encourage visitors to use all their senses to explore objects. Things to touch, look at, and smell that are made of animal, vegetable, or mineral material. Sit down and examine boxes filled with things (all labeled in bold, black letters) from the world of natural history and anthropology, like animal teeth, pelts and skulls, seashells, plants, pine cones. There are plenty of volunteers to answer questions. School group tours Monday to Thursday from 10 to 11:30am during the school year; reserve in advance. Children under age 12 must be accompanied by an adult. *OPEN Mon-Fri noon-2:30pm; Sat & Sun 10:30am-3:30pm. CLOSED Christmas Day.* A ticket is required on weekends, holidays, and in the summer months—obtain at the Mall reception desk. FREE. *Metro: Smithsonian, Federal Triangle.*

Paul E. Garber Facility
3904 Old Silver Hill Road, Suitland, Md. (202) 357-1400. Best for flight buffs. Two huge no-frills bare-bones warehouses used by the Smithsonian as a preservation, restoration, and storage facility for historically significant aircraft, spacecraft, models, and engines not currently on display at the National Air & Space Museum. The only way to see it is to take a tour, which lasts between 2 and 3 hours (or plan to go during their annual open house, usually the last weekend in April; *see* ANNUAL EVENTS, April). You must call (Monday to Friday, 9am to 3:15pm) to reserve for the tour at least two weeks in advance. Tours *Mon-Fri at 10am; Sat & Sun at 10am & 1pm.* Note: There is no heating in winter and no air-conditioning in summer, so dress accordingly. FREE.

Gunston Hall
George Mason Plantation, Lorton, Va. (703) 550-9220. George Mason is famed as the father of the American Bill of Rights and his elegant colonial mansion, now administered by the National Society of Colonial Dames of America, offers an opportunity to see a slice of colonial life. There are sheep on the grounds of the 550-acre plantation, as well as beautiful gardens and the nature trail where you may encounter deer and wild turkeys. In March there is a Kite Festival, free for children under age 16; in May, on George Mason Day, there are reenactments of plantation life with costumed participants; and in early December, an antique car show takes place on the grounds. In the basement, a special Touch-It Museum, for school groups only, where children may touch and handle reproductions of 18th-century items. Costumes to try on, too. Best for grades three to five. By advance reservation. *OPEN 7 days 9:30am-5pm. CLOSED Thanksgiving, Christmas & New Year's Day.* Admission; discount for children under age 16.

Holography World

Techworld Plaza, 800 K Street, NW. 408-1833. A changing international exhibition of holographic art. There are guided 20-minute tours (last tour at 5:30pm) to acquaint you with this fascinating technique using lasers. There is a gift shop for items utilizing holograms. OPEN Mon-Fri 11am-6pm. Admission charge, lower for children under age 12. Metro: Gallery Place. (See also Tech 2000, located in the same building complex.)

Lee-Fendall House

614 Oronoco Street, Alexandria, Va. (703) 548-1789. On the third floor of this historic 1785 house is a collection of dollhouses that date from 1875 (most with the original furniture) to the finest ones made today. There are miniature churches, garden houses, banks, and a mill. While there take a tour of the whole house and learn about old ways of doing such simple things as how to use a button hook and other period tools. Groups should book in advance. OPEN Tues-Sat 10am-4pm; Sun noon-4pm. CLOSED Mon. Occasionally closed on weekends for private events, call first. Admission; lower for children.

NASA/Goddard Space Flight Center

Route 495 to exit 22A North, Greenbelt, Md. (301) 286-8981. A guided tour of this facility, available Wednesday through Friday at 2:30pm, takes you to see the tracking center, with its sophisticated computer and communication technology, and spacecraft control rooms. In addition to the five full-scale rockets (one is 92 feet high) on view in the garden, you can see a lunar vehicle, and on the first and third Sunday of every month, from 1 to 2pm, watch small test rockets being launched. Visitors Center OPEN Wed-Sun 10am-4pm. CLOSED Mon & Tues, Thanksgiving, Christmas & New Year's Day. FREE.

National Air & Space Museum

On the Mall, Independence Avenue between 4th & 7th Streets, SW. 357-2700. Spirits will soar from the moment you enter this museum and see the dazzling array of flying machines and spacecraft: missiles, rockets, propellers, engines, models, instruments, uniforms, and insignias. Everything here is special but don't miss the Wright Brothers' 1903 flyer, Lindbergh's Spirit of St. Louis, and the Apollo 11 command module. "Flight Over Mars" gives a view of the Martian landscape; "Descent" to Venus puts you in a spaceship cockpit circa 2150; puppets illustrate how and why planes fly. Look inside an engine, touch a moon rock, walk through a Skylab workshop, help set the design requirements for aircraft of the future; watch a film about flight on a five-story-tall screen! The Einstein Planetarium transports you to faraway galaxies with daily shows. Tours of the museum's highlights from Gallery 100, seven days, 10:15am and 1pm; meet at the Information Desk. Group tours by appointment, call 357-1400, Monday to Friday, from 9:30am to 3:15pm. Three museum shops

for flight-related items and a restaurant on the first floor. OPEN 7 days 10am-5:30pm. CLOSED Christmas Day. FREE (there is a nominal fee for films and planetarium shows). Metro: L'Enfant Plaza. (See also Paul E. Garber Facility.)

The National Building Museum

401 F Street, NW. 272-2448. Temporary and changing exhibits focus on construction, engineering, architectural design, environmental and urban planning. The permanent exhibit, "Washington: Symbol and City," is an interactive exhibition designed so that blind and visually impaired visitors may "see" through touch the nation's capital it's fascinating. School-age children may attend classes and workshops on bridge construction, land use, and how buildings are able to stand. Hard-hat tours of construction sites are also available, call 272-2448. The building itself, with its enormous Great Hall and eight huge columns, is worth the visit. Interesting museum shop. OPEN Mon-Sat 10am-4pm; Sun noon-4pm. CLOSED Thanksgiving, Christmas & New Year's Day. FREE. Metro: Judiciary Square.

National Capital Trolley Museum

Bonifant Road, Wheaton, Md. (301) 384-6088. Sixteen miles from DC. A collection of old European and American streetcars and trams, including a Sweeper 07 (1889) that was in service till 1962 to maintain the DC-area trolley system in snowy weather. There are gaily-decorated German trolleys and Austrian cars with measuring sticks (your fare was determined by your height!). A model railroad operates every day from 1 to 5pm; there's also a 20-minute pay trolley ride through the surrounding fields with narration by a staff member. On the third Sunday in April and September there's a Trolley Car Parade. Groups call in advance. OPEN July & Aug, Wed noon-4pm, Sat & Sun noon-5pm; balance of the year Sat & Sun only; last trolley leaves ½ hour before closing. CLOSED Christmas & New Year's Day. FREE.

National Geographic Society Explorer's Hall

17th & M Streets, NW. 857-7000 (recording). Among the permanent exhibits of interest to children is an interactive display called "Geographica: A New Look at the World," where they may learn about the physical world as well as about the customs of the people inhabiting it. Also explore an illuminated 1,100-pound, freestanding world globe, 11 feet in diameter, with a "narrator" who will take you on an adventure of learning. There are films and narratives dealing with expeditions and discoveries throughout the day. Frequently changing special exhibits. Group tours by appointment, call 857-7689. OPEN Mon-Sat & holidays 9am-5pm; Sun 10am-5pm. FREE. Metro: Farragut North.

National Portrait Gallery

8th & F Streets, NW. 357-2920. Hundreds of portraits of famous Americans and all of our past presidents in the Hall of Presidents. Interesting life masks of Lincoln show how much he aged during his presidential term. Walk-in guided tours available daily from 10am to 3pm; groups must reserve in advance. Suitable for ages 9 and up; call for special programs geared to school-age children. *OPEN 7 days 10am-5:30pm. CLOSED Christmas Day. FREE. Metro: Gallery Place, 9th Street exit.*

New Hampshire Attic

DAR Museum, 1776 D Street, NW. 879-3254. Within the museum devoted to decorative and fine arts is a delightful collection of mainly hand-made dolls, games, toys, and children's furniture from the late 18th and 19th centuries. Some of the dolls are made from rags, corncobs, papier-mâché, china, or wood. Guided tours (the only way to visit the attic) between 10am and 2:30pm; Sunday between 1 and 5pm. Group tours by appointment. Also, don't miss "Touch of Independence," a hands-on exhibition with reproductions of items from the Revolutionary period to the late 19th century. Gift shop. DAR Museum *OPEN Mon-Fri 8:30am-4pm; Sun 1-5pm. CLOSED Sat & holidays. FREE. Metro: Farragut West, Farragut North.*

The Phillips Collection

1600 21st Street, NW. 387-0961 (recording); 387-2151. This, the nation's oldest museum of modern art, has an impressive series of children's programs. Special: "A Parent-Child Guide, A Child's Adventure into the Artist's World of Color," a workbook designed for ages 6-12 with sections on drawing and viewing, is designed for adults and children to use together. There is a mailing list so you can keep abreast of family workshops. Terrific museum store and cafe. Membership available. *OPEN Tues-Sat 10am-5pm.* Weekdays FREE, suggested contributions accepted; weekends admission fee. *Metro: Dupont Circle, Q Street exit.*

Tech 2000

Techworld Plaza, 800 K Street, NW. 842-0500. High-tech adventure in this museum dedicated to interactive multimedia a joining of video imaging, computers, sound, and text (like Nintendo, which you probably have at home). There are 70 programs at various terminals and kids can "get behind" the wheel of a car, learn about famous paintings, take a simulated luge ride, or "play" with a rock band. In all it's fascinating for those who are computer literate, as well as the novice. There are more than a dozen exhibits specifically geared to children. Group tours by appointment. *OPEN Tues-Sun 11am-5pm.* Admission charge lower for students, seniors, and children under age 12. *Metro: Gallery Place. (See also* Holography World, *located in the same complex.)*

Washington Doll House & Toy Museum

5236 44th Street, NW. 244-0024. A museum since 1975; antique dollhouses, dolls, toys, and games—mostly Victorian but some from other periods—all from the Flora Gill Jacobs collection. Replicas of Mount Vernon, the Capitol, Noah's ark; an old-fashioned schoolroom; a mil-

liner's shop; a circus; a fully furnished 12-room dollhouse with every detail of family life miniaturized. There are also very special seasonal exhibitions. Birthday parties may be arranged in the charming Edwardian Tea Room (*see also* Children's Parties). Two gift shops for books, toys, and dollhouses, and all the accessories to furnish and accessorize them, as well as the raw materials to build one yourself. Group tours by appointment. *OPEN Tues-Sat 10am-5pm; Sun noon-5pm. CLOSED Mon, Thanksgiving, Christmas & New Year's Day.* Admission; lower for senior citizens and children. *Metro: Friendship Heights.*

ZOOS & ANIMAL PRESERVES

The National Aquarium

U.S. Department of Commerce Building, 14th Street & Constitution Avenue, NW (downstairs). 377-2825. Established in 1873, it is the nation's oldest public aquarium (and it looks it). Designed to entertain and educate so that you can take a self-guided tour of the 70 exhibits with over 1,200 species of salt and fresh water fish. The Touch Tank allows children to handle live sea creatures. Feeding times are fun times to visit: Sharks eat Monday, Wednesday, and Saturday at 2pm; the piranhas are fed Tuesday, Thursday, and Sunday at 2pm. The Department of Commerce Cafeteria is open to the public Monday to Friday from 8:30am to 2pm. Aquarium *OPEN year-round 7 days 9am-5pm.* Nominal admission. *Metro: Federal Triangle.*

The National Zoological Park

Main Entrance: 3000 block of Connecticut Avenue, NW, west of Calvert Street. Others: Harvard & Adams Mill Roads, NW; Beach Drive in Rock Creek Park. Information Desk is in the lobby of the Education Building. 673-4800 (recorded information); 673-4717. Until his death, this was home to the original Smokey the Bear, who bore the scars of the forest fire from which he was rescued. The Western Hemisphere's only giant pandas, Ling Ling and Hsing Hsing, gifts from the Chinese government, are the zoo's most popular residents. The best and most fun time to see them is when they are fed—11am and 3pm. Training sessions (which include feeding) for elephants at 11:30am; seal and sea lion training sessions alternate, also at 11:30am. For group tours and reservations, call 673-4955. Seven food and beverage facilities as well as picnic facilities (no fires). Note: Limited parking (for a fee). Rest rooms. Stroller rental available; no bikes or skateboards. Grounds *OPEN May 1-Sept 15, 7 days 8am-8pm; Sept 16-Apr 30, 7 days 8am-6pm.* Buildings *OPEN May 1-Sept 15, 7 days 9am-6pm; Sept 16-Apr 30, 7 days 9am-4:30pm. CLOSED Christmas Day. FREE. Metro: Woodley Park-Zoo.*

Within the National Zoo are the following special events and activities for children:

Birdlab

National Zoo Birdhouse. On the Valley Trail. Anything a child might want to know about birds where they live, what they eat. "Learning boxes" filled with things to examine, books, bird information file, and plenty of volunteers to answer questions. You can even try on a "bird wing." OPEN Fri 10am- 1pm; Sat & Sun 10am-2pm; other days for groups by appointment. FREE.

Herplab

National Zoo Reptile House. Geared to children ages 6 and up. Activity boxes with eggs, bones, and snake skin—all to be touched. Learning through games, question-and-answer cards, and, most exciting of all, an opportunity to touch live animals. Add your own observational data to an ongoing experiment involving lizards that change color. Educational and fascinating. OPEN Fri 10am-1pm; Sat & Sun 10am-2pm. FREE.

Zoolab

National Zoo Education Building, Connecticut Avenue entrance. Children are able to explore and discover by touching nests, skulls, feathers, antlers, reptile and bird eggs. "Learning boxes" contain objects to examine. Volunteers are available to answer questions. OPEN Fri 10am-1pm; Sat & Sun 10am-2pm. FREE.

Oxon Hill Farm

South Capitol Street to Indian Head Highway (exit 3A on Capitol Beltway), Oxon Hill Road, Oxon Hill, Md. (301) 839-1177. A turn-of-the-century working farm showing how life was then. The "family" goes through the daily tasks of sewing, milking, harvesting, sheep shearing, carding and spinning, and more (the demonstrations are seasonal). There is plenty of livestock to pet: cows, horses, sheep, goats, and even pigs. Self-guided nature trail of the surrounding woods and a picnic area. A horse-drawn wagon ride may be arranged in advance. For guided tours, call (301) 839-1176—reserve one month in advance. OPEN 7 days 8:30am-5pm. CLOSED Thanksgiving, Christmas & New Year's Day. FREE.

Rock Creek Nature Center

Rock Creek Park, 5200 Glover Road, NW. 426-6829. Every Saturday and Sunday there are guided nature walks at 3pm. Nature films and slides at 2pm. Group tours by appointment. OPEN Oct-May, Tues-Sun 9am-5pm. CLOSED Mon. OPEN June-Sept, 7 days. FREE.

Turkey Run Farm

Beltway, Route 495 to exit 13, McLean, Va. (703) 442-7557. See how a lower-income colonial homestead of the 1770s was run. A costumed "family" goes through daily tasks of animal care, log splitting, gardening, sewing, cooking. There is a hog pen, chickens, cows, horses, and other livestock. The home is a one-room cabin. For guided tours or for large groups, call or write at least two months in advance. Special events scheduled third weekend of every month. Picnic

area. OPEN Apr-Dec, Wed-Sun 10am-4:30pm. CLOSED Mon, Tues & Jan-Mar. Admission; lower for seniors and children under age 12.

PLAYGROUNDS

For location of the playground nearest you, call 673-7660.

Benning-Stoddert Recreation Center

East Capitol Street & Stoddert Place, SE. See-saws, jumping boards, slides. Picnic facilities. Playing fields.

Cabin John Regional Park

7400 Tuckerman Lane, Rockville, Md. (301) 299-4555. A 525-acre park. Swings, slides, and the usual playground fare. Ride on the miniature train at the playground every day in the summer. Picnic areas. Ball fields. Ice skating, too. (See also SPORTS, Skating: Ice Skating.)

Garfield Park

New Jersey Avenue & E Street, SE. Capitol Hill. Swings, slides, climbing structures, and a grassy area to play on. Picnic facilities.

Hains Point

Ohio Drive, SW, below the Tidal Basin. Brightly colored metal climbing structures and at the tip of the point the wonderful buried giant of a sculpture (The Awakening) are the main attractions.

Kalorama Playground

19th Street & Columbia Road, NW. Lots of grass and the usuals.

John F. Kennedy Recreation Center

7th & P Streets, NW. 673-7614. Two play areas, connected by a tunnel.

Watkins-Buchanan Recreation Center

13th & E Streets, SE. 724-4468. Cable spider-web; pyramid with slides, seesaw, and rolling log. Sand surface.

CHILDREN'S SHOPPING

Borders Book Shop for Kids

11520A Rockville Pike, Rockville, Md. (301) 816-1067. This huge book emporium's separate annex for children's books stocks over 18,000 titles! AE, MC, V. OPEN Mon-Sat 9am-9pm; Sun noon-8pm.

Cheshire Cat Children's Book Store

5512 Connecticut Avenue, NW. 244-3956. The city's first—and still considered the best—bookstore completely devoted to children's books. Highly regarded not only for the stock but also for a series of special events in spring and fall: story telling, sing-alongs, poetry readings, and meet-the-author parties. Sign up for their newsletter and keep informed of the schedule. Mail and phone orders. MC, V. OPEN Mon-Sat.

Georgetown Zoo

Georgetown Park, 3222 M Street, NW. 338-4182. Although located in a mall, it's a very personally run toy store where the age and interests of your child are considered in helping you choose the perfect toy. AE, MC, V. *OPEN 7 days.*

Granny's Place
303 Cameron Street, Alexandria, Va. (703) 549-0119. All the traditional toys to make one feel safe and secure. Steiff stuffed animals, Creative Playthings, Raggedy Ann and Andy, Madame Alexander dolls, rocking horses. Good summer sales. AE, DC, MC, V. *OPEN 7 days.*

Imagination Station Children's Bookstore
4524 Lee Highway, Arlington, Va. (703) 522-2047. Every subject imaginable is covered in the stock of this shop catering to the early years—infant to age 12. Picture books, reference, language, nature and science, history and adventure. Also audio and video tapes. MC, V. *OPEN Mon-Sat 10am-6pm; Sun 11am-4pm.*

John Davy Toys
301 Cameron Street, Alexandria, Va. (703) 683-0079. A kid's delight. Kites, books, little and big toys, games, stuffed animals, miniatures from around the world. AE, MC, V. *OPEN 7 days.*

Kids' Closet
1226 Connecticut Avenue, NW; 429-9247. And *1990 K Street, NW; 466-5589. Colorful shop carries a complete line of children's wear, newborn to size 14. OshKosh, Bullfrog, Absorba, Carters, Christian Dior, Izod. Good selection of toys and accessories, too. AE, MC, V. *OPEN Mon-Sat. *CLOSED Sat.*

Kid's Stuff
5615 39th Street, NW. 244-2221. High-quality, gently-worn children's clothing on consignment. Toys, furniture, strollers; maternity clothing, too. No credit cards. *OPEN Mon-Sat. CLOSED Sat in July & Aug.*

Lowen's Toy Store
9201 Wisconsin Avenue, Bethesda, Md. (301) 652-1289. Great selection of toys, games, books, dolls, and more. Great annual sale every September (for *very* early Christmas shopping). AE, MC, V. *OPEN Mon-Sat.*

Maybe Baby
2603 P Street, NW. 342-8725. This Georgetown charmer features decorative furnishings and art for children. It's an imaginative and highly personal collection of tees, quilts, chairs, bibelots, and Western-motif clothes and accessories. Much is handmade, some is antique or collectible. Highly browsable. AE, MC, V. *OPEN Mon-Sat 11am-7pm.*

National Air & Space Museum Shop
Independence Avenue between 4th & 7th Streets, SW. 357-1387. Heavy on airplane and rocket models. Model kits. Science fiction books. AE, MC, V. *OPEN 7 days.*

National Museum of American History
Constitution Avenue & 14th Street, NW. 357-1528. The children's shop has model ships, dolls, animals, books, coloring books, and items related to the current exhibit. AE, MC, V. *OPEN 7 days.*

Natural History Museum Shop
10th Street & Constitution Avenue, NW. 357-1536. A wide range of items for sale. Toys, models, jewelry, crafts, mineral specimens, postcards, posters, models of prehistoric animals, and stuffed animals—all from different areas of the world. Prints of photos of American Indians taken by Edward Curtis. AE, MC, V. *OPEN 7 days.*

The Red Balloon
1073 Wisconsin Avenue, NW. 965-1200. Imported games, puzzles, and tiny toys with prices to match; stuffed animals, too. Original wooden handmade toys; Thinker Tapes Imagination Kits. AE, MC, V. *OPEN 7 days.*

F.A.O. Schwarz
Georgetown Park, M Street & Wisconsin Avenue, NW. 342-2285. Mall branch of the internationally known New York toy emporium features much that is opulent for the affluent: life-sized stuffed animals, dolls, rocking horses, and miniature powered autos—as well as highly affordable novelties, dolls, kites, and toys. AE, CB, DC, MC, V. *OPEN 7 days.*

Traditions for Children
1533 Wisconsin Avenue, NW. 625-0616. Clothing for children by Flapdoodles, Bravo, Izzy, Cory, and more, plus jewelry, accessories, charming clocks, music boxes, and an inviting friendly atmosphere are reasons enough to visit this Georgetown shop. AE, MC, V. *OPEN Mon-Sat 11am-7pm.*

Why Not?
200 King Street, Alexandria, Va. (703) 548-2080. Girls' clothing infant to preteen; boys' clothing infant to size 7. Children's books and toys, too. All in a spacious, colorful, fun environment. AE, MC, V. *OPEN 7 days.*

CHILDREN'S ENTERTAINMENT

Adventure Theater
Glen Echo Park, Goldsboro Road & MacArthur Boulevard, Glen Echo, Md. (301) 320-5331 (between 10am and 5pm). Music, dance, puppets, plays. Autograph collecting after each performance. For ages 4 to teens. Reservations advisable. Group rates. Fall classes. Shows year-round, on weekends, at 1:30 and 3:30pm. Admission.

Children's Theatre of Arlington
2700 South Lang Street, Arlington, Va. (703) 548-1154. Musicals and plays for kids. Three productions a year. Ages 5 to 14. Reserve for groups. Place and time vary, usually on weekends. Admission; free in summer.

Child's Play
WPFW (89.3 FM), 702 H Street, NW, 20001. 783-3100. An entertaining one-hour program for children ages 4 to 7. Standard stories are acted out but with a twist (reformed witches, for example). After the program, children are invited to phone in and talk to the characters (783-3104). Airs every Saturday at 8am. Phone or write for broadcast schedule.

DC Department of Recreation
3149 16th Street, NW. 673-7663; Dial-an-Event: 673-7671. Caravan and Young People's Theater. Traveling troupes of marionettes; original material (usually ecologically oriented). Performers are all 8 to 18 years old. Performs at recreation centers throughout DC. Summer only. Call for time and place. FREE.

King's Dominion
Route 30 & Route 95, Doswell, Va. (703) 941-8286; (804) 876-5000. Only 75 miles from DC, one of the largest theme parks north of Florida: 1,300 acres. Six different theme areas including International Street with shops and restaurants, Olde Virginia, and Safari Land, which can be seen by monorail. Over 42 rides. Hanna-Barbera characters like the Scooby Doo and Yogi Bear may be seen throughout the park. Parking for a fee. OPEN June-Labor Day, 7 days; Apr-May & Sept-mid-Oct, Sat & Sun only. Call for hours. Admission; children under age 2 free.

Library Theater
7210 Hidden Creek Road, Bethesda, Md. (301) 320-0093; (202) 291-4800. Musical theater for elementary- school kids; stories from children's literature using comedy, dance, and drama. Audience participation. Shows usually last one hour. Wednesday performances throughout the school year at 10am, locations in Maryland, Virginia, and DC. In summer, Monday to Friday morning performances in DC public libraries. Call for more information. Admission.

Pavilion at the Old Post Office
1100 Pennsylvania Avenue, NW. 289-4224. Concerts and other entertainment designed especially for kids. Year-round, the third Saturday of the month noon-4pm. FREE.

Programs for Children & Youth
Kennedy Center, Washington, DC, 20566. An ongoing series of high-quality performances, rehearsals, and lecture/demonstrations for young people, families, and teachers. Drama classes for students in grades 5 to 12 and artistic training opportunities for high school instrumentalists are available. Preperformance events for general public and professional development opportunities for teachers. For information, write to them or call 416-8800.

Rock Creek Nature Center
Rock Creek Park, 5200 Glover Road. 426-6829. Free planetarium shows Saturday and Sunday only, for children ages 4 to 7 (accompanied by a parent) at 1pm; for ages 7 and up at 4pm. Free tickets available half an hour before the show; no seating after it starts. Group tours by appointment. OPEN year-round, Tues-Sun 9am-5pm. CLOSED Mon. FREE.

Smithsonian Discovery Theater
Arts & Industries Building, 900 Jefferson Drive, SW. 357-1500. Live theater and puppet performances that last about an hour. A different show every month, October to May. Ages 4 to 14. Reservations are highly recommended; groups must reserve in advance. Shows Tuesday to Friday at 10 and 11:30am; Saturday at 11:30am and 1pm.

Admission; lower for children and groups. Call first to verify place of performance.

CHILDREN'S PARTIES

The Birthday Baker
(301) 460-3191. Beverly and Nina Kobrinetz give parents a kids' party alternative. They'll come to the party and show the kids how to make their own party fare: pretzels, pizza, cake, doughnuts. Bread in different shapes: dinosaurs, turtles, and other animals. Also cooking classes for kids. Call for information. At least two weeks' notice is needed.

Chuck E. Cheese's Pizza Time Theater
13807 Outlet Drive, Silver Spring, Md; (301) 890-6767. And 516 North Frederick Avenue, Gaithersburg, Md; 869-9010. Also 6803 Richmond Highway, Alexandria, Va, 660-6800. About 20 minutes from DC. A carnival of a pizza parlor with several different rooms including a game room with over 20 video games and a room for younger kids with dimestore rides—the birthday child gets five game tokens, each guest gets two. Balloons for everyone. For every four persons, a large pizza of their choice and a pitcher of soda pop. A free "mini" pizza for the birthday child. Package includes hats, napkins, tablecloths, and plates. The Pizza Time Players sing "Happy Birthday" and Chuck E. Cheese (a huge mouse) wanders around during the party. For all ages. Call at least one month in advance.

Edwardian Tea Room
Washington Doll House & Toy Museum, 5236 44th Street, NW. 244-0024. The party (for 12 to 20 children) takes place in the Edwardian Tea Room, which resembles an old-fashioned ice-cream parlor. Festivities start with a tour of the museum, followed by refreshments and games in the museum, 2 hours in all. The birthday child receives a special book. Call at least one month in advance.

FOR PARENTS

General

Directory of Public Schools
District of Columbia Public School System, 415 12th Street, NW, Washington, DC 20004. 724-4044. A listing of all the public schools in DC, elementary to high school. Included are numbers to call for special, vocational, and other programs available through the school system.

Day Camps (Summer)

There are many summer camp programs (day and sleep away) throughout the DC, Maryland, and Virginia areas. The American Camping Association issues the "Parent's Guide," a catalog of camps in the DC, Delaware, and Virginia areas (other regions are available). It is categorized by region and activities. Each camp is reviewed for health and safety standards. For more information, call (301) 484-1409.

Department of Recreation
Programs are offered in photography, dance, gymnastics, film, baseball, basketball, and tennis. For information regarding day camp programs, call the appropriate number:
DC: 673-7660
Alexandria: (703) 838-4343
Arlington: (703) 358-4747
Montgomery County: (301) 217-6880
Prince George's County: (301) 699-2407

Nursery Schools and Kindergartens

DC Government, Licensing Office
614 H Street, NW. 727-7226. You may obtain a listing of over 200 nursery schools and day-care centers in the DC area. All are licensed and grouped according to the area.

Preschool Programs
Kenilworth Elementary, 44th & Nash Streets, NE. 724-4528. They will provide information on preschool programs in DC schools. Ages 4 to 6.

SCOUTS

Boy Scouts of America
990 Wisconsin Avenue, Bethesda, Md. (301) 530-9360. Call for information about becoming a Boy Scout in DC, Maryland, and northern Virginia.

Girl Scout Council of the Nation's Capital
2233 Wisconsin Avenue, NW. 337-4300. Call for information about becoming a Girl Scout in DC, parts of Maryland, and Virginia. There is also a retail shop located in the building for uniforms, badges, equipment.

SPORTS

Robert F. Kennedy Stadium

LARGE-SCREEN VIEWING

The next best thing to being there in person is watching a sports event on a really big color screen. Many bars and restaurants that cater to a sporting clientele now have 7-foot-wide Tv screens for your viewing pleasure. Two of the most popular are:

Champions
1206 Wisconsin Avenue (tucked in from the street). 965-4005. Team pennants mark the spot —the hot spot. A bi-level singles' bar with plenty of athletes and their supporters. Sports memorabilia, festooned with baseball cards. Monday night football is big here. Chili, stuffed potato skins, cornish hen—all named for sports teams and themes. Crowded bar scene. *OPEN Sun-Thurs till 2am; Fri & Sat till 3am.*

Poor Robert's
3419 Connecticut Avenue, NW. 363-1839. Satellite sports transmissions on a 5-foot screen at the 86-foot bar (the longest in Washington). Italian cooking and seafood till 12:30am. No cover; no minimum. AE, CB, MC, V. *OPEN 7 days till 2am.*

GENERAL INFORMATION

For information regarding activities or sports facilities in the area's parks.

Dial-a-Park
619-727. A recorded announcement of events in DC parks.

Office of Recreation Information
673-7660

National Capital Parks
619-7222

Northern Virginia Regional Parks
(703) 352-5900

SPORTS STADIUMS

Oriole Park at Camden Yards
Baltimore, Md. (410) 685-9800.

Capitol Centre
1 Harry S. Truman Drive, Landover, Md. (301) 432-0200.

Robert F. Kennedy Stadium/Stadium Armory Complex
East Capitol & 22nd Street, SE. 547-9077.

ANNUAL SPORTING EVENTS

May

Kemper Open Golf Tournament
Congressional Country Club, Bethesda, Md. (301) 469-2000 or -3737 (for Kemper Open only).

The Preakness
Pimlico Race Course, Baltimore, Md. (301) 542-9400. Third Saturday in May.

June

President's Cup Regatta
On the Potomac. Best vantage point: Hains Point in East Potomac Park.

November

Washington International Horse Show
Capitol Centre. (301) 350-3400.
Marine Corps Marathon of the Monuments
Throughout DC.

TICKET AGENTS

It is always best to call the stadium where the event is taking place for information.

Orioles Baseball Store & Ticket Outlet
914 17th Street, NW. 296-2473. Tickets, schedules, and everything you have ever wanted to know about the Baltimore team (now adopted as Washington's hometown team). Direct bus service from the shop to about 40 games a season. Hats, tees, jerseys, and jackets emblazoned with the team logo. MC, V. *OPEN Mon-Fri 9am-6pm; Sat 10am-2pm.*

Ticketmaster
432-0200. Purchase tickets by phone for area sports and entertainment events. AF, MC, V.

TICKETplace
See ENTERTAINMENT, Tickets.

Ticketron
432-0200. At Woodward & Lothrop, Tower Records, Warner Theater, selected Sears stores, and other locations throughout the DC area. AE, MC, V.

Top Centre Tickets
2000 Pennsylvania Avenue, NW. 452-9040. Their specialty: sporting events and concerts. Mail-order, phone, and walk-in. Ticket and limo pack-

ages. Cash, check, and AE, MC, V. Top seats for theatrical events at Kennedy Center, National, Warner, Ford's, Folger, and Arena. *OPEN Mon-Fri 9am-5pm.*

SPORTS DIRECTORY

Archery

The DC Department of Recreation sponsors programs in archery at the following centers:
Friendship Recreation Center
45th & Van Ness Streets, NW. 282-2198.
Hardy Recreation Center
45th & Q Streets, NW. 282-2190.
Hearst Recreation Center
37th & Tilden Streets, NW. 282-2207.
Kenilworth Parkside
4300 Anacostia Avenue, NE. 727-5440.
Palisades Recreation Center
Dana Street & Sherrier Place, NW. 282-2186.
Stoddert Playground
39th & Calvert Streets, NW. 282-2193.
Woodson Jr. Recreation Center
Minnesota Avenue & Grant Street, NE. 727-5426.

Baseball

DC doesn't have a team of its own since losing the Washington Senators to Texas in 1971, but there's an alternative for baseball fans. The Baltimore Orioles play at Baltimore's Oriole Park at Camden Yards. For information about tickets, call (410) 685-9800.

The baseball season begins around the first week in April and continues through mid-October. Call the stadium for specific game or ticket information, check local newspapers, or write to Ticket Office, Baltimore Orioles, 333 West Camden Street, Baltimore, MD 21201.

Public Baseball Diamonds

There are diamonds located throughout the DC area. For information on permits and reservations, call the Department of Recreation at 673-7660.

Basketball

DC's professional basketball team is the Washington Bullets. Home court for the Bullets is the Capitol Centre (Landover, Md, 350-3400). The season starts in October and can run into June.

Some of the best college basketball in the country is played in Washington. In addition to top-ranking Georgetown and Maryland, there is American University, George Washington University, and the University of the District of Columbia.

Public Basketball Courts

For the location of the indoor or outdoor court nearest you, call the Department of Recreation, 673-7660.

National Capital YMCA
1711 Rhode Island Avenue, NW. 862-9622. Indoor gym with basketball facilities. Members only. Call for more information.

Bicycling

There are 15 miles of bike paths from the Virginia side of the Memorial Bridge through Alexandria to Mount Vernon. Also the towpath along the C&O Canal runs 184.5 miles from Georgetown to Cumberland, Maryland. In Rock Creek Park, Beach Drive is closed to traffic year-round, Friday 7pm to Sunday 7am, from Broad Branch Road to Joyce Road (east to west) and from Picnic Grove #10 to West Beach Drive (north to south). The favorite route seems to be the loop around East Potomac Park past the Lincoln Memorial and the Tidal Basin to Hains Point.

Metro's Bike-on-Rail program enables riders to take their bicycles on the last car of any train after 7pm Monday through Friday and all day Saturday, Sunday, and holidays (except July 4). Call 962-1116 in order to obtain the required permit.

For additional information about bicycling, call Dial-a-Park, 619-7275, or contact one of the following:
Potomac Area Council of the American Youth Hostels
P.O. Box 28607, Washington, DC 20038. 783-4943. A prime source of information. They have maps, guidebooks, bike routes in DC, and plan overnight bike trips. Junior and senior memberships available. *OPEN Mon-Sat 10am-6pm.*
Washington Area Bicyclist Association
1819 H Street, NW. 872-9830. Anything and everything you may need. Every available bike map of the DC area; atlas of bike routes. "Pedal Pool," a commuting service for the cyclist—a guide will show you the best way to get to work and back, or just to get around. They publish and sell the *Greater Washington Area Bicycle Atlas*, which covers bicycle trips into Maryland, Virginia, Delaware, and Pennsylvania. *OPEN Tues 10am-10pm; Wed & Thurs 1-6pm, but call anytime.*
Washington Women Outdoors
Box 345, Riverdale, Md. (301) 864-3070. They organize weekend bike trips, hiking and backpacking, water sports, rock climbing, and cross-country skiing. Membership available. *OPEN Mon-Fri 9-11am.*

Bicycle Rental & Instruction

Big Wheel Bikes
315 7th Street, SE; 543-1600. And 1034 33rd Street, NW; 337-0254. Also 2 Prince Street, Alexandria, Va, (703) 739-2300; and 6917 Arlington Road, Bethesda, Md, (301) 652-0192. Rents three- and ten-speed bikes, mountain bikes, small bikes for kids. Deposit or picture ID required. *OPEN year-round 7 days.*
Fletcher's Boat House
4940 Canal Road, NW. 244-0461. Rents mainly single-speed, some three-speed, and small

bikes for kids. ID required. Under age 16 must be accompanied by an adult. Hours vary with the season, so call ahead. *OPEN Mar-Nov 7 days.*

Metropolis Bike & Scooter Inc.
709 8th Street, SE. 543-8900. Rents three-, five-, and ten-speed bikes, also smaller bikes for children. Under age 16 must be accompanied by an adult. ID and deposit required. MC, V can be used for rentals ($10 minimum). *OPEN year-round 7 days (hours vary).*

Swain's Lock
Two miles above Great Falls, Md, on the canal. (301) 299-9006. Rents three-speed and smaller bikes for children. ID required. *OPEN Mar-Nov, 7 days 9am-dusk.*

Thompson's Boat Center
Rock Creek Parkway & Virginia Avenue, NW. 333-4861. Rents one-speed touring bikes. Under age 18 must be accompanied by an adult. ID and deposit required. *OPEN Mar-Nov, 7 days 7am-6pm.*

Billiards

The Department of Recreation sponsors programs in billiards throughout the DC area. For information, call 673-7679.

Boating

Fletcher's Boat House
4940 Canal Road, NW. 244-0461. Rowboats and canoes. Must be over age 16. ID required. Hours vary with the season, so call ahead. *OPEN Mar-Nov 7 days.*

Jack's Boats
35th & K Streets, NW. 337-9642. Rowboats and canoes. Under age 18 must be accompanied by an adult. ID required. *OPEN Apr-mid-Nov, 7 days 9am-dusk.*

Swain's Lock
Swain's Lock Road on C&O Canal, 2 miles north of Great Falls, Md. (301) 299-9006. Canoes. ID required. *OPEN Mar-Nov, 7 days 9am-sundown.*

Thompson's Boat Center
Rock Creek Parkway & Virginia Avenue, NW. 333-4861. Canoes, rowboats, sailboats, and rowing sculls. Under age 18 must be accompanied by an adult. Deposit and ID required. *OPEN Mar-Oct, 7 days 7am-8pm.*

Tidal Basin Boat House
15th Street & Maine Avenue, SW. 484-0206. Paddleboats for rent on the Tidal Basin. Two people per boat. Under age 16 must be accompanied by an adult. *OPEN Apr-Oct 7 days.*

Bowling

Bowl America, Inc.
Thirteen locations throughout the DC area. For the location nearest you, call (703) 941-6300.

Bowling Instruction
Contact the Department of Recreation, 673-7660, for information on the program nearest you.

Boxing

Major boxing events are held at Capitol Centre. For details and event information, call 350-3400. The Department of Recreation sponsors programs in boxing at many recreation facilities; for information, call 673-3519.

Boxing Equipment
The best and the oldest wholesaler of equipment to professional boxers and rings is Everlast. The following locations carry full lines.

Alperstein Bros.
8121 Piney Branch Road, Silver Spring, Md. (301) 585-1160.

Irving's Sport Shop
1111 20th Street, NW. 466-8830. Also suburban locations.

Cricket

Washington Cricket League
Contact Lloyd Conyers (301) 949-0838, for information about the league. Games are played Saturday and Sunday at West Potomac Park, Hyattsville, and College Park from 1pm to dusk, April 15 through September. Practices are from 5:30pm in Hyattsville and College Park. (Anyone can use the pitch when the league isn't using it, but you must obtain a reservation and a permit from the Department of Recreation, 767-8363.)

Fishing

You must have a license to fish in fresh water in Maryland and Virginia. Also, you have to have a license if you are not a resident of the county in which you are fishing. Licenses are not needed to fish in DC, but be sure to check what the boundaries are. You can do so by contacting any of the following:

Call the Maryland Department of Natural Resources, (301) 855-1748, or the Virginia Commission of Game and Inland Fisheries, (804) 367-1000; or write to Maryland Wildlife Administration, Tawes State Office Building, Annapolis, MD 21401, or Virginia's Commission of Game and Inland Fisheries, P.O. Box 11104, Richmond, VA 23230-1104.

Best places: Potomac Tidal Basin; around the bridges connecting DC to Virginia (great for largemouth bass); upper Potomac from Seneca to Harpers Ferry; the C&O Canal from Great Falls to Seneca.

Flying

In order to fly in DC you must have a single- or multi-engine license.

Hinson Airways, Inc.
Baltimore-Washington International Airport. (301) 859-4210. Cessna pilot center. Single- and twin-engine planes. Private pilot license all ratings. Flight and ground training school with audio/visual training. FAA approved.

Suburban Air Service
Suburban Airport, Laurel, Md. (301) 953-2293.
Single-engine planes. Flight training and ground
school. Private, commercial, or instrument ratings. FAA approved.

Football

*DC's professional football team is the Washing-
ton Redskins. They play eight regular season
games September to December at Robert F.
Kennedy Stadium, East Capitol Street, SE, 546-
2222. Tickets are sold on a seasonal basis, and
are very hard to get. Preseason (August) game
tickets, sold on a game-to-game basis, are eas-
ier to obtain. The pro-football season extends
from early September through December. College football is extremely popular, culminating in
the Bowl games on New Year's Day.*

*For ticket and game information, check the
newspaper or call the stadium.*

Public Football Fields

*For the location of the field and program nearest
you, contact the Department of Recreation, 673-
7660.*

Frisbee

*Mastered Frisbee and golf? Now try Frisbee-golf.
Like golf, there are 18 "holes"; unlike golf, there
are baskets attached to tall poles and trees. And
just to make things difficult, the course runs
through the woods. You can play anytime from
sunup to sundown. BYO Frisbee. These parks
have courses:*
Bull Run Regional Park, Va.
(703) 631-0550. Seven days.
**Pohick Bay Regional Park Fairfax County,
Va.**
(703) 339-6100.

Golf

Instruction

East Potomac Park Golf Course
East Potomac Park, Hains Point. 554-7660. PGA
professional instruction. Private or group. By appointment. Putting green for practice.
Rocky Gorge Four Seasons Golf Fairway
Route 29 & Old Columbia Road, Laurel, Md.
(301) 725-0888. Professional instruction. Group
or private. By appointment.

Practice Ranges

East Potomac Park Driving Range
East Potomac Park, Hains Point. 863-9011. Year-
round practice range. Free putting green. Lessons. Club rental.
Rocky Gorge Four Seasons Golf Fairway
Route 29 & Old Columbia Road, Laurel, Md.
(301) 725-0888. Year-round. Putting green.

Public Courses

*There are approximately 70 golfing facilities in
the DC and suburban area.*

Bowie Golf & Country Club (semi-private)
Bowie, Md. (301) 262-8141. 6,316 yards.
Bretton Woods
Germantown, Md. (301) 948-5405. 6,663 yards.
East Potomac Golf Course
East Potomac Park, Hains Point. 554-7660. 6,800
yards. Miniature golf, too.
Lake Arbor Country Club
Largo, Md. (301) 336-7771. 6,530 yards.
Marlborough Country Club (semi-private)
Upper Marlboro, Md. (301) 952-1300. 6,170
yards.
Needwood Golf Course
6724 Needwood Road, Derwood, Md. (301)
948-1075. 6,369 yards.
Patuxent Greens (semi-private)
Laurel, Md. (301) 776-5533. 6,201 yards.
Redgate Municipal Golf Course
14500 Avery Road, Rockville, Md. (301) 340-
2404. 6,400 yards.
Reston Golf Course
Sunrise Valley, Reston, Va. (703) 620-9333.
6,480 yards.
Robin Dale Country Club (semi-private)
Brandywine, Md. (301) 372-8855. 6,342 yards.
Rock Creek Park Public Golf Course
Rock Creek Park, NW. 882-7332. 4,715 yards.
South Wales
Jeffersonton, Va. (703) 451-1344. 7,077 yards.
Twin Shields
Dunkirk, Md. (301) 855-8228. 6,050 yards.
University of Maryland
College Park, Md. (301) 403-4299. 6,675 yards.

Private Courses

Argyle
Layhill Road, Silver Spring, Md. (301) 598-6042.
6,188 yards.
Army-Navy
Arlington, Va. (703) 521-6800. 6,534 and 2,876
yards, Arlington; 6,800 yards, Fairfax.
Bethesda
Bethesda, Md. (301) 365-1703. 6,536 yards.
Brooke Manor
Norbeck, Md. (301) 924-2070. 6,661 yards.
Burning Tree
Bethesda, Md. (301) 365-2588. 6,662 yards.
Cedar Crest
Centreville, Va. (703) 631-9226. 6,572 yards.
Chantilly
Centreville, Va. (703) 631-9562. 7,248 yards.
Chevy Chase
Chevy Chase, Md. (301) 652-4100. 6,184 yards.
Columbia
Chevy Chase, Md. (301) 951-5050. 6,082 yards.
Congressional
Bethesda, Md. (301) 469-2001. 6,422 and 6,195
yards.
Country Club of Fairfax
Fairfax, Va. (703) 273-3445. 6,420 yards.
Crofton
Crofton, Md. (202) 261-0119; (301) 721-3111.
6,700 yards.
Evergreen
Haymarket, Va. (703) 471-7309. 7,020 yards.

Fauquier Springs
Warrenton, Va. (703) 347-4209. 6,200 yards.
Germantown Country Club
Germantown, Md. (301) 428-2130. 6,200 yards.
Hidden Creek Country Club
Reston, Va. (703) 437-5222. 6,450 yards.
Hobbit's Glen
Columbia, Md. (301) 730-5980. 6,734 yards.
Indian Spring
Silver Spring, Md. (301) 871-6000. 6,232 and 5,652 yards.
International
Fairfax, Va. (703) 968-7070. 6,600 yards.
Kenwood
Bethesda, Md. (301) 320-3605. 5,843 yards.
Lakewood
Rockville, Md. (301) 762-9074. 6,375 yards.
Loudoun Golf & Country Club
Purcellville, Va. (703) 338-7705. 6,200 yards.
Manor
Rockville, Md. (301) 929-1131. 6,132 yards.
Montgomery
Laytonsville, Md. (301) 948-5330. 6,302 yards.
Montgomery Village
Gaithersburg, Md. (301) 948-6204. 6,678 yards.
Norbeck
Rockville, Md. (301) 774-7700. 6,418 yards.
Potomac Valley
Poolesville, Md. (301) 428-8143. 6,478 yards.
Prince George's
Mitchelville, Md. (301) 249-6104. 6,195 yards.
River Bend
Great Falls, Va. (703) 759-2640. 6,243 yards.
Springfield
Springfield, Va. (703) 451-8338. 6,475 yards.
Washington Golf & Country Club
Arlington, Va. (703) 524-4600. 5,846 yards.
Westwood
Vienna, Va. (703) 938-2593. 6,405 yards.
Woodmont
Rockville, Md. (301) 762-6801. 6,365 and 6,496 yards.

Gymnastics

The Department of Recreation sponsors programs in gymnastics throughout the DC area. For information, call 673-7660.

Handball

For the location of the handball court nearest you, contact the Department of Recreation, 673-7660.
National Capital YMCA
1711 Rhode Island Avenue, NW. 862-9622. Six handball courts. Membership required. Call for further information.

Hiking

Check Kiosk, the monthly newsletter of Washington-area events published by the Na-

tional Park Service, for outdoor treks. You can be put on their mailing list by calling 619-7222. For current park events, call Dial-a-Park, 619-7275. The following organizations sponsor many hikes throughout the year.
Potomac Appalachian Trail Club: 638-5306.
Rock Creek Nature Center: 426-6975.
Sierra Club: 547-2326.

Hockey

Washington has one professional hockey team, the Washington Capitals. They skate at the Capitol Centre, (301) 350-3400, and the season runs from October to early April.

Horseracing

Harness

Delmarva Downs
Route 589, Berlin, Md. (301) 641-0600. Season: June to September. Post time: Wednesday to Saturday, 7:10pm; Sunday, 6:20pm. The Club House, facing the track right on the finish line, for elegant dining. Admission discount for large groups. Call the track for information on transportation.
Rosecroft Raceway
6336 Rosecroft Drive, Oxon Hill, Md. (301) 567-4000. Season: January 12 to December 21. Post time: Wednesday to Saturday, 7:30pm; Sunday, 6:30pm. The Club House, overlooking the track, offers elegant dining. Custom Tours bus service from DC; for information, call (301) 350-3172.

Thoroughbred

Laurel Race Course
Route 1, Laurel, Md. (301) 725-0400. Season: January to mid-March, July 4 to third week in August, and October to December. Post time: Monday to Saturday, 1pm. The elegant Terrace Dining Room overlooks the track; smaller dining room with closed-circuit TV. Home of the Budweiser International, mid-October. Discounts for senior citizens and large groups. Gray Line bus service from DC; for information, call 289-1995.
Pimlico Race Course
Northern Parkway & Belvedere Avenue, Baltimore, Md. (301) 542-9400; (800) 638-3811. Season: Mid-March to June and September to October. Post time: Tuesday, Thursday to Saturday, and holidays, 1pm. Home of the Preakness, held on the third Saturday in May; post time is noon (*see also* ANNUAL EVENTS, May). Discounts for large groups. Terrace Dining Room overlooks the track; closed-circuit TV, too. Gray Line bus service from DC; for information, call 479-5900.
Timonium Race Course
Fairgrounds, Timonium, Md. (301) 252-0200. Season: late summer. Post time: Monday to Saturday, 1pm. Dining room with closed-circuit TV.

Gray Line bus service from DC; for information call 289-1995.

Lacrosse

Washington Lacrosse Club
Contact Chip Veise at (301) 946-7600 or (301) 984-0843. Member of the Central Atlantic Lacrosse League. They play on the Mall between the Lincoln Memorial and the Washington Monument, Sunday afternoons from March to June. Anyone can join, but they prefer experienced players. Some high school and college participation. Call for additional club information; Mr. Veise will refer you to the club nearest you.

Polo

National Capital Parks Polo Association—Lincoln Mall Club
362-3095; 426-6841 (in case of inclement weather to find out if they are playing). Season: April through July and Labor Day to end of October. They play every Sunday at approximately 3pm—at 2pm in October—in West Potomac Park across from the Lincoln Memorial. Free general admission and high-priced box seats (privilege for patron membership). Call for more information on the polo scene throughout the area.

Racquetball

See also Tennis.
Annandale Courts Royal
4317 Ravensworth Road, Annandale, Va. (703) 256-6600. Three racquetball courts. Membership and court fee. Also complete fitness center. *OPEN 7 days 6am-midnight.*
Arlington Courts Royal
1122 Kirkwood Road, Arlington, Va. (703) 522-1702. Eight racquetball courts. Saunas, steam room. Nursery. Membership and court fee. *OPEN Mon-Thurs 6am-11pm; Fri 6am-10pm; Sat 6am-8pm; Sun 6am-9pm.*
Aspen Hill Racquet Club & Fitness Center
14501 Homecrest Road, Silver Spring, Md. (301) 598-5200. Eight racquetball courts. Steam room, weight room, exercise bikes, treadmill. Members only. *OPEN 7 days 6am-midnight.*
Bethesda Sport & Health Club
4400 Montgomery Avenue, Bethesda, Md. (301) 656-9570. Seven racquetball courts. Swimming pool, sauna and steam rooms, whirlpool, indoor track, full fitness center. Members and guests only. *OPEN Sun-Fri 6am-11pm; Sat 6am-8pm.*
Big Vanilla Racquet Club
1209 Ritchie Highway, Arnold, Md. (301) 544-0800. One racquetball court. Whirlpool, sauna. Membership and court fee. *OPEN Mon-Fri 7am-11am; Sat & Sun 7am-9pm.*
Bowie Racquet & Fitness Club
100 Whitemarsh Park Drive, Bowie, Md. (301) 262-4553. Four racquetball courts. Sauna, steam room, outdoor swimming pool. Indoor

soccer. Bar and lounge. Membership and court fee. *OPEN 7 days 9am-midnight.*
Capital Courts Racquet & Fitness Club
308 Glenn Drive, Sterling, Va. (703) 430-0666. Eight racquetball courts. Supervised Nautilus, tanning booths, sauna, free weights, aerobics, rowing machines, tennis, karate. Nursery. Members only. *OPEN Mon-Fri 6am-midnight; Sat & Sun 8am-10pm.*
Chestnut Forks Tennis Club
Route 605, Warrenton, Va. (703) 347-0823. Two racquetball courts. Sauna, exercise room. Members only. *OPEN Sun-Fri 7am-11pm; Sat 9am-6pm.*
Chevy Chase Athletic Club
5454 Wisconsin Avenue, Chevy Chase, Md. (301) 656-8834. Three racquetball courts. *OPEN Mon-Fri 6am-10:30pm; Sat & Sun 8am-8pm.*
Columbia Athletic Club
5435 Beaverkill Road, Columbia Md. (301) 730-6744. Six racquetball courts, two squash courts. Pro shop; whirlpool, weight room, sauna, exercise room, indoor track, Nautilus, circuit weight training; four indoor tennis courts. Nursery. Membership and court fee. *OPEN Mon-Fri 6am-11pm; Sat & Sun 6am-10pm.*
Courts Royal Rockville
11650 Nebel Street, Rockville, Md. (301) 770-0707. Ten racquetball courts. Nautilus, free weights, aerobics, steam room, sauna, whirlpool, exercise room. Membership and court fee. *OPEN Mon-Thurs 6am-11pm; Fri 6am-10pm; Sat 7am-6pm; Sun 7am-9pm.*
Courts Royal Springfield
5505 Cherokee Avenue, Alexandria, Va. (703) 941-4848. Five racquetball courts. Sauna, whirlpool, steam room; exercise equipment. Members only. *OPEN Mon-Thurs 6am-10pm; Fri 6am-9pm; Sat 8am-6pm; Sun 8am-4pm.*
Devil's Reach
1401 Devil's Reach Road, Woodbridge, Va. (703) 491-4126. Three racquetball courts. Sauna and steam. Membership and court fee. *OPEN 7 days 6am-10pm.*
Fairfax Racquet Club
9860 Lee Highway, Fairfax, Va. (703) 273-9276. Six racquetball courts. Sauna. Membership and court fee. *OPEN 7 days 6am-11:30pm.*
Laurel Racquet & Health Club
204 Fort Meade Road, at Routes 197 & 198, Laurel, Md. (301) 953-1414. Ten racquetball courts. Sauna and steam room. Membership. *OPEN Mon-Fri 6:30am-11pm; Sat 8:30am-6:30pm; Sun 8:30am-8pm.*
Loudoun Racquet & Fitness Club
131 Fort Evans Road, Leesburg, Va. (703) 777-7505. Two racquetball courts. Swimming pool, sauna. Membership and court fee. *OPEN Sun-Fri 8am-11pm; Sat 8am-7pm.*
Mt. Vernon Health & Racquet Club
7950 Audubon Avenue, Alexandria, Va. (703) 360-7300. Four racquetball courts. Sauna. Nursery. Membership. *OPEN Mon-Sat 6am-11pm; Sun 8am-8pm.*

National Capital YMCA
1711 Rhode Island Avenue, NW. 862-9622. Six racquetball courts. Weights, swimming pool, gym, whirlpool, steam, indoor track. Members only. *OPEN Mon-Fri 6am-10:30pm; Sat 8am-7pm; Sun 11am-6pm (closed Sun during the summer).*

Player's Club
17043 Downing Street, Gaithersburg, Md. (301) 840-1920. Three racquetball courts. Sauna, steam room, swimming pool, aerobics, weights, karate. Members only. *OPEN Mon-Fri 9am-midnight; Sat & Sun 8am-6pm.*

Regency Sport & Health Club
1800 Old Meadow Road, McLean, Va. (703) 656-6550. Three racquetball/five squash courts; four swimming pools, sauna, steam room, exercise room, whirlpool, massage. Members only. *OPEN Mon-Fri 6am-11pm; Sat & Sun 7am-10pm.*

Reston Athletic Club
1800 Michael Faraday Court, Reston, Va. (703) 437-1402. Six racquetball courts. Fitness center. Members only. *OPEN Mon-Fri 6am-midnight; Sat 7am-7pm; Sun 7am-10pm.*

Skyline Club
5115 Leesburg Pike, Falls Church, Va. (703) 820-4100. Four racquetball courts. Exercise room, steam room, sauna, swimming pool, whirlpool, exercise classes. *OPEN Mon-Fri 6am-11pm; Sat & Sun 7am-7pm.*

The Sporting Club
8250 Greensboro Drive, McLean, Va. (703) 442-9150. Seventeen racquetball courts, four squash courts. Indoor and outdoor swimming pools, track, basketball and volleyball courts, sauna, steam room, whirlpool, Nautilus. Nursery. Over 115 classes, including dance, aerobics, fencing, scuba certification, water babies. Members only. *OPEN Mon-Fri 6am-10pm; Sat & Sun 8am-8pm.*

Supreme Sports Club
7080 Deepage Drive, Columbia, Md. (301) 596-2733. Twelve racquetball courts. Whirlpool, two saunas. Nursery. Membership and some court fees. *OPEN Mon-Thurs 6am-11pm; Fri 6am-9pm; Sat & Sun 7am-5pm.*

Tenley Sport & Health Club
4000 Wisconsin Avenue, NW. 362-8000. Four racquetball/two squash courts. Indoor pool; full fitness center, Nautilus, free weights, aerobics, steam room, whirlpool, massage; indoor track. *OPEN Mon-Fri 6am-10pm; Sat & Sun 8am-8pm.*

Wakefield Recreation Center
8100 Braddock Road, Annandale, Va. (703) 321-7080. Four racquetball courts. Swimming pool. *OPEN 7 days 6am-10pm.*

White Oak Courts Royal
11313 Lockwood Drive, Silver Spring, Md. (301) 593-7626. Six racquetball courts; racquetball clinics. Aerobics, free weights, volleyball, handball, karate, weight training; fitness counseling. Steam room, sauna, exercise room. Members only. *OPEN Mon-Thurs 6am-11pm; Fri 6am-10pm; Sat 8am-6pm; Sun 7am-8pm.*

Riding

The following area organizations cater to the riding enthusiast:

Capitol Hill Equestrian Society
Contact Mary Flower, (703) 751-9375.

Double S Stables
Off 95, exit 7A, Md. (301) 372-8914. English and Western saddle. Rental by the hour; 85 acres of trails to ride. *Year-round.*

Great Falls Horse Center
Arnon Chapel Road, Great Falls, Va. (703) 759-3400. No rentals. Instruction in English saddle. For ages 8 and up. Sessions throughout the year. Indoor arena. Boarding facilities. Shows every six weeks. The Fairfax County Recreation Department sponsors a program through the Horse Center; get in touch with them first, (703) 246-5550, and it will be cheaper. *Year-round.*

Meadowbrook Stables
8200 Meadowbrook Lane, Chevy Chase, Md. (301) 589-9026. English saddle instruction for ages 8 and up. Courses in stable management and instructor training. Five arenas. Access to Rock Creek Park. Boarding facilities. No rentals.

Merrymount Equitation Center
Frank Tippett Road, Upper Marlboro, Md. (301) 868-2109. Instruction only in English saddle. Private and group lessons. Boarding facilities and tack shop. Shows. Certification program.

Rock Creek Park Horse Center
Military & Glover Roads, NW. 362-0117. The only facility for riding in DC. Great for beginners. Guided group rides through the park (ages 12 and up). Three indoor arenas. English saddle instruction, ages 8 and up, group and individual. Therapeutic riding for the handicapped. Summer camp for children ages 8 to 16. *Year-round. CLOSED Mon.*

Trail Riders for Today
For information on TROT, call Barbara Cannizzo at (301) 253-4659.

Wheaton Park Stables
1101 Glenallen Avenue, Wheaton, Md. (301) 622-3311. English saddle. Escorted trail rides every Sunday. Ages 8 and up. Group and private instruction in balance seat; summer camp. Three arenas, one of which is indoor. Good for beginners. Boarding facilities. *Year-round.*

Rugby

Potomac Rugby Union
Call Matt Godek at (703) 280-5540; he can help anyone who wants to play rugby with a club and will direct you to the club convenient to your location. There are approximately 40 clubs within the Union including five for women. Seasons are September to November and March to May. They play every Saturday at 1pm. Two fields in DC are at 15th Street and Independence Avenue and at 22nd Street and Independence Avenue. The best clubs: Northern Virginia (NOVA), Club Sudamericano de Rugby, Washington

ugby, and the Maryland Old Boys. There is
ome university participation, too. *Call Mon-Fri
0:30am-5pm.*

Running & Jogging

*opular outdoor places for running and jogging
)C'ers include Rock Creek Park—south of the
"oological Park starting at Cathedral Avenue.
*long its 1.5-mile track there are 18 calisthenic
tations with "how to" signs for each exercise.
*lso, George Washington Parkway beyond Al-
*xandria, Hains Point, and the C&O Canal. To
nd the location of the outdoor track nearest you,
:all the National Park Service, 619-7222.*

National Capital YMCA
711 Rhode Island Avenue, NW. 862-9622. In-
loor track—10 laps outside or 21 inside equal
one mile. Membership required. Call for further
nformation.

Sailing (Rental & Instruction)

Annapolis Bay Charters
7210 Edgewood Road, Bert Jabins Yacht Yard,
Annapolis, Md. (301) 261-1815; (301) 269-1776.
/acht rentals for any length of time. Midweek
:harters. They will provide a captain and provi-
sions if requested. *OPEN year-round.*

The Annapolis Sailing School
501 Sixth Street, Eastport, Md. (301) 267-7205;
301) 261-1947. The oldest in the country. Sail-
ng instruction, beginner to advanced. Courses
n coastal navigation, cruising (not to mention
now to pump water out of a hull). Leads to cer-
:ification. Group basis. Daily rental on sailboats.
OPEN Mar-Oct.

C & C Charters Maryland
Mears Point Marina, Grasonville, Md. (800) 638-
0426. Rentals from a large fleet of yachts, sailboats, and motorboats. On-hand training for basic boating. Mechanic on duty seven days.
OPEN Apr-Nov.

Chesapeake Bay Boating Report
(301) 260-0505

The Chesapeake Sailing School
Port Annapolis Marina, Annapolis, Md. (800)
776-0012. Mainly instructional, but they do rent
sailboats on a daily basis. Courses offered April
to November, for ages 6 and up. Instruction in
beginning sailing to racing, cruising, and navigation. *OPEN Apr-Nov.*

Learning Annex of Washington
3333 Connecticut Avenue, NW. 966-9606.
Sixteen-hour basic sailing course, taught in Annapolis, plus an all-day sail on the Chesapeake.
Call for additional information and brochure.

The Mariner Sailing School
Belle Haven Marina, south of Alexandria, Va.
(703) 768-0018. Rentals of sunfish and catamarans. Ten-hour sailing course for adults is conducted on a 19-foot racing sloop. The youth
course (ages 8 to 15) lasts five days. They also
offer private instruction, advanced classes, and
windsurfing instruction and rentals.

North-East-Wind (N.E.W.) Charters
306 2nd Street, Annapolis, Md. (301) 267-6333.
Rentals by the hour or the full day from a large
fleet of sailboats and small outboard run-
abouts.

Pier Seven
Route 2, Edgewater, Md. (301) 261-4555. Rent-
als of speedboats, sailboats, and catamarans.
OPEN Apr-Oct.

United States Coast Guard Auxiliary
2100 2nd Street, SW. 267-1077. Boating Safety
Hotline (800) 368-5647. Classroom instruction
only, for basic boating skills, seamanship, and
safety measures. Group classes of 6 to 13 lessons, fall and spring. Call for additional information.

Washington Sailing Marina
Dangerfield Island, Alexandria, Va. (703) 548-
9027. Rentals of sailboats. Large selection of
rigged boats. You should have substantial sailing experience. Sailing classes for adults and
kids, private and group. For kids: sailing camps
with focus on racing. Also, windsurfing. Call for
brochure.

Scuba Diving

National Diving Center
4932 Wisconsin Avenue, NW. 363-6123. Scuba
diving, beginner to advanced. CPR and underwater photography are also taught. No more
than eight in a group; taught in swimming pools.
Certification programs.

Skating

Ice Skating

*There is skating on the C&O Canal, but call the
National Park Service, 299-2026, to find out if
there has been a hard freeze.*

Cabin John Ice Skating Rink
10610 Westlake Drive, Bethesda, Md. (301) 365-
0585 (recording); (301) 365-2246 or -0465. Two
enclosed rinks. Skate rental. Lockers. Snack bar.
Group and private instruction. *OPEN year-round
7 days—call for general session hours.* Admission.

Fairfax Ice Arena
3779 Pickett Road, Fairfax, Va. (703) 323-1132.
Indoor rink. Skate rental. Pro shop. Instruction,
group or private. *OPEN year-round 7 days.* Admission.

Fort Dupont Ice Skating Arena
37th Street & Ely Place, SE. 581-0199. Indoor
rink. Skate rental. Hockey October to November,
Monday and Wednesday. Group and individual
lessons. Call for general session hours. *OPEN
Sept-May, 7 days.* Admission.

Mount Vernon District Park Ice Rink
2017 Belle View Boulevard, Mount Vernon, Va.
(703) 768-3223. Indoor arena. Skate rental. Pro
shop. Instruction, group or private. *OPEN year-
round 7 days.* Admission.

National Sculpture Garden Ice Skating Rink
9th Street & Constitution Avenue, SW. 371-5342.
On the Mall, in front of the National Archives, an

outdoor rink. Skate rental and sharpening (deposit required). Pro shop. Instruction, group or private. *OPEN Dec-early Mar, Mon-Thurs 11am-9:30pm; Fri 11am-11:30pm; Sat & holidays 9am-11:30pm; Sun 9am-9:30pm.* Admission.

Pershing Park Ice Rink
Pennsylvania Avenue & 15th Street, NW. 737-6938. Small but utterly charming outdoor rink across from the Willard Hotel. Skate rental. Moonlight sessions are often a weekend feature. Call for hours. *OPEN Dec-early Mar 7 days.* Admission.

Wheaton Ice Rink
Arcola & Orebaugh Avenues, Wheaton, Md. (301) 649-2703. Covered outdoor rink. Skate rental. Group instruction. *OPEN Oct-Mar, 7 days.* Admission.

Roller Skating

Beach Drive in Rock Creek Park is closed to traffic on Sunday from 9am to 5pm for bicycling and roller skating.

L & M Streets between 17th & 20th Streets has become a favored course for city skaters.

Soccer

For the location of the field and program nearest you, contact the Department of Recreation, 673-7660.

Softball

For the location of the softball field nearest you, call the Department of Recreation, 673-7660. They also sponsor leagues.

Squash

Arlington Y Tennis & Squash Club
3400 North 13th Street, Arlington, Va. (703) 522-1700. Two courts. *OPEN 7 days 6am-1am.*

Bethesda Sport & Health Club
4400 Montgomery Avenue, Bethesda, Md. (301) 656-9570. Two squash courts; pros on premises. Restaurant. Members only. *OPEN Sun-Fri 6am-11pm; Sat 6am-8pm.*

Capitol Hill Squash Club
214 D Street, SE. 547-2255. Eight courts. *OPEN Mon-Thurs 7am-11pm; Fri 7am-10pm; Sat & Sun 8:30am-6:30pm.*

Chevy Chase Athletic Club
5454 Wisconsin Avenue, Chevy Chase, Md. (301) 656-8834. Two courts. *OPEN Mon-Fri 6am-10:30pm; Sat & Sun 8am-8pm.*

City Sports
Lafayette Center, 1120 20th Street, NW. 659-9570. Nine courts. Fitness center, free weights, aerobics. *OPEN Mon-Thurs 6:30am-11pm; Fri 6:30am-9pm; Sat & Sun 9am-6pm.*

Columbia Athletic Club
5435 Beaverkill Road, Columbia, Md. (301) 730-6744. Two courts. *OPEN Mon-Fri 6am-11pm; Sat & Sun 6am-10pm.*

National Capital YMCA
1711 Rhode Island Avenue, NW. 862-9622. Four courts. Members only. Call for hours.

Sporting Club
8250 Greensboro Drive, McLean, Va. (703) 442-9150. Four courts. Members only. *OPEN Mon-F 6am-10pm; Sat & Sun 8am-8pm.*

Wakefield Recreation Center
8100 Braddock Road, Annandale, Va. (703) 321-7080. One court. *OPEN 7 days 6am-10pm*

Swimming

The DC Department of Recreation offers free public swimming, water sports competition, and instruction. For any questions or information, call the Aquatics Program Office at 576-6436.

Public Swimming Pools

Outdoor pools are open June through August. Indoor pools are open year-round.

Outdoor

Anacostia
Anacostia Park between 11th Street & Pennsylvania Avenue Bridges, SE.

Banneker
2500 Georgia Avenue, NW.

Barry Farms
1223 Sumner Road, SE.

Benning Park
53rd & Fitch Street, SE.

Douglass
19th Street & Stanton Terrace, SE.

East Potomac
East Potomac Park & Ohio Drive, SW.

Fort Dupont
Ridge Road & Burns Street, SE.

Fort Stanton
18th & Erie Streets, SE.

Francis
25th & N Streets, NW.

Georgetown
34th Street & Volta Place, NW.

Kelly Miller
49th & Brooks Streets, NE.

Kenilworth-Parkside
Ord Street & Anacostia Avenue, SE.

Langdon Park
2901 20th Street, NE.

McKinley
Lincoln Road & Seaton Place, NE.

Oxon Run
4th Street & Mississippi Avenue, SE.

Randall
South Capitol & I Streets, SW.

Rosedale
17th & Gales Streets, NE.

Takoma
4th & Van Buren Streets, NW.

Upshur
14th Street & Arkansas Avenue, NW.

Indoor

Capitol East Natatorium
635 North Carolina Avenue, SE. 724-4495, -4496, or -4497.

C Center for Therapeutic Recreation
3030 G Street, SE. 767-7460. For handicapped
only.

Dunbar
1301 New Jersey Avenue, NW. 673-7744.

Fort Lincoln
31st Street & Fort Lincoln Drive, NE. 576-6135,
ext 32.

Mamie D. Lee Therapeutic Recreation
100 Gallatin Street, NE. 576-6877.

Marie H. Reed Learning Center
2200 Champlain Street, NW. 673-7771.

Sharpe Health
13th Street between Upshur & Allison Streets,
NW. 576-6394. For handicapped only.

Shaw Junior High School
10th & R Streets, NW. 673-7720.

Washington Highland
8th & Yuma Streets, SE. 767-7449.

Wilson Senior High School
Nebraska Avenue & Chesapeake Street, NW.
282-2216.

Woodson Senior High School
55th & Eads Streets, NE. 727-4499.

Pools: Membership

*Contact the YMCA at 862-9690 for information
on their swimming facilities in the DC area.*

*If you're stuck in the city during the summer,
relief from the heat is possible. The following District hotels have outdoor swimming pools with
summer memberships (both individual and family) available. In most cases other amenities such
as health club facilities are included. Fees vary
widely; call for details.*

Loew's L'Enfant Plaza
480 L'Enfant Plaza East, SW. 484-1000.

Omni Shoreham
2500 Calvert Street, NW. 234-0700.

Quality Hotel Central
1900 Connecticut Avenue, NW. 332-9300.

Sheraton Washington Hotel
2660 Woodley Road, NW. 328-2000.

Washington Hilton Hotel and Towers
1919 Connecticut Avenue, NW. 483-4100.

Washington Plaza Hotel
10 Thomas Circle, Massachusetts & Vermont Avenues, NW. 842-1300.

Tennis

*In order to play on a public tennis court in DC
you must have a permit. You can obtain one
by calling 673-7646, or by sending a self-
addressed, stamped envelope to Permit Section, DC Department of Recreation, 3149 16th
Street, NW, Washington, DC 20010.*

Public Courts

Anacostia
East of Anacostia River between 11th Street &
Pennsylvania Avenue Bridges, SE. Nine lighted
courts.

Arboretum
24th Street & Rand Place, NE. Two courts.

Backus
South Dakota Avenue & Hamilton Street, NE.
One lighted court.

Bald Eagle
Martin Luther King Avenue & Joliet Street, SE.
Two lighted courts.

Banneker
9th & Euclid Streets, NW. Eight courts.

Barry Farms
1230 Sumner Road, SE. One lighted court.

Benning Park
53rd & Fitch Streets, SE. Two lighted courts.

Benning Stoddert
Burns & C Streets, SE. Four lighted courts.

Brentwood Park
6th Street & Brentwood Parkway, NE. One court.

Chevy Chase
41st & Livingston Streets, NW. Two courts.

Congress Heights
Alabama Avenue & Randle Place, SE. Three
courts.

Deanwood
49th & Nash Streets, NE. Two lighted courts.

Douglass Community Center
19th Street & Stanton Terrace, SE. One lighted
court.

Dunbar
1st & O Streets, NW. Three lighted courts.

Edgewood
3rd & Evarts Streets, NE. Two courts.

Evans
5600 East Capitol Street, NE. Two courts.

Fairfax
1400 41st Street, SE. One court.

Fort Lincoln
Fort Lincoln Drive, NE. Eight lighted courts.

Fort Stanton
18th & Erie Streets, SE. Three lighted courts.

Fort Stevens
13th & Van Buren Streets, NW. Four courts.

Francis
24th & N Streets, NW. Four courts (two lighted).

Friendship
45th & Van Ness Streets, NW. Two courts.

Friendship-Oxon Run
Livingston & South Capitol Streets, SE. Two
courts.

Garfield
3rd & 9th Streets, SE. Two lighted courts.

Georgetown
33rd Street & Volta Place, NW. Two courts.

Hardy
45th & Q Streets, NW. Two courts.

Hearst
37th & Tilden Streets, NW. Three courts.

Hillcrest
32nd & Denver Streets, SE. Four courts.

Hine
7th Street & Pennsylvania Avenue, SE. Two
courts.

Jefferson
8th & H Streets, SW. Five lighted courts.

Kelly Miller
49th & Brooks Streets, NE. Three courts.

Kenilworth-Parkside
4300 Anacostia Avenue, NE. Four lighted courts.
King-Greenleaf
2nd & N Streets, SW. Two lighted courts.
Lafayette
33rd & Quesada Streets, NW. Four lighted courts.
Langdon Park
20th & Franklin Streets, NE. Four lighted courts.
Langley-Eckington
Lincoln Road & T Street, NE. Two courts.
Langston
26th Street & Benning Road, NE. Three courts.
Lansburgh Park
K Street & Delaware Avenue, SW. Two lighted courts.
Montrose Park
30th & R Streets, NW. Four clay courts.
Newark Street
Newark Street at 39th Street, NW. Three courts.
Oxon Run
7th Street & Mississippi Avenue, SE. Four courts.
Palisades
Dana & Sherrier Streets, NW. Three courts.
Rabaut
2nd & Peabody Streets, NW. Two courts.
Randall
South Capitol & I Streets, SW. Three lighted courts.
Raymond
10th Street & Spring Road, NW. Two courts.
Reed
18th Street & California Avenue, NW. Two lighted courts.
Rosedale
17th & Gales Streets, NE. Two courts.
Rose Park
26th & O Streets, NW. Three courts.
Shaw
10th Street & Rhode Island Avenue, NW. Two lighted courts.
South Grounds
15th & Constitution Streets, NW. Two clay courts.
Taft
18th & Otis Streets, NE. Five courts.
Takoma
3rd & Van Buren Streets, NW. Six lighted courts.
Turkey Thicket
10th Street & Michigan Avenue, NE. Eight lighted courts.
Washington Highland
8th & Yuma Streets, SE. Two lighted courts.

Other

Arlington Y Tennis & Squash Club
3400 North 13th Street, Arlington, Va. (703) 522-1700. Eight indoor courts. Members only. *OPEN Mon-Fri 6am-10pm; Sat 8am-6pm; Sun 8am-8pm.*
Aspen Hill Racquet Club
14501 Homecrest Road, Silver Spring, Md. (301) 598-5200. Thirteen clay outdoor, six indoor tennis courts. Members only. *OPEN 7 days 6am-midnight.*

Bethesda Sport & Health Club
4400 Montgomery Avenue, Bethesda, Md. (30⁷ 656-9570. Three outdoor tennis courts; three ir door. Members and guests only. *OPEN Sun-F 6am-11pm; Sat 6am-8pm.*
Big Vanilla Racquet Club
1209 Ritchie Highway, Arnold, Md. (301) 54⁄ 0800. Six indoor courts. *OPEN 7 days 6am-1am*
Bowie Racquet & Fitness Club
100 Whitemarsh Park Drive, Bowie, Md. (301 262-4553. Three indoor, four outdoor courts *OPEN Mon-Fri 6:30am-11pm; Sat 8:30am 6:30pm; Sun 8:30am-9pm.*
Cabin John Indoor Tennis Courts
7801 Democracy Boulevard, Bethesda, Md (301) 365-2440. Six indoor courts. *OPEN mid Sept-May, 7 days 6am-midnight; in summer hours vary.*
Capitol Courts Racquet & Fitness Club
308 Glenn Drive, Sterling, Va. (703) 430-0666 Two outdoor tennis courts; eight racquetba courts. Nautilus; free weights; aerobics. Mem bers only. *OPEN Mon-Fri 6am-midnight; Sat & Sun 8am-10pm.*
Chestnut Forks Tennis Club
Route 605, Warrenton, Va. (703) 347-0823. Fou indoor, two outdoor courts. Members only. *OPEN Mon-Fri 7am-11pm; Sat 9am-6pm; Sun 10am 10pm.*
Cosca Regional Park Indoor Tennis Center
11000 Thrift Road, Clinton, Md. (301) 868-6462 Six outdoor hard, four indoor courts. *OPEN 7 days 9am-11pm.*
Courts Royal Annandale
4317 Ravensworth Road, Annandale, Va. (703) 256-6600. Five indoor courts. Members only. *OPEN Mon- Thurs 6am-11pm; Fri 6am-9pm; Sat & Sun 7am-9pm.*
Devil's Reach Sport & Health Club
1401 Devil's Reach Road, Woodbridge, Va. (703) 491-4126. Six indoor courts, three tennis, three racquetball. *OPEN 7 days 6am-10pm.*
East Potomac Tennis
1090 Ohio Drive, SW. 554-5962. Twenty-three outdoor (ten clay), five indoor. *OPEN 7 days 6:45am-10:30pm.* (Indoor courts open till midnight in the winter.)
Fairfax Racquet Club
9860 Lee Highway, Fairfax, Va. (703) 273-9276. Six indoor, four outdoor (under a bubble in winter). *OPEN 7 days 6am-11:30pm.*
Four Seasons Tennis Club
3010 Williams Drive, Merrifield, Va. (703) 573-5105. Ten indoor courts. *OPEN 7 days 6am-11pm.*
Loudoun Racquet & Fitness Club
131 Fort Evans Road, Leesburg, Va. (703) 777-7505. Six indoor tennis courts. *OPEN Sun-Fri 8am-11pm; Sat 8am-7pm.*
Manassas Racquet Club
8709 Quarry Road, Manassas, Va. (703) 830-2139. Three indoor, three outdoor courts. Members only. *OPEN Mon-Fri 6:30am-11pm; Sat & Sun 8am-8pm.*

McLean Racquet & Health Club
472 Chain Bridge Road, McLean, Va. (703)
356-3300. Five indoor courts. Members only.
OPEN Mon-Fri 6am-11pm; Sat & Sun 7am-10pm.

Mount Vernon Health & Racquet Club
7950 Audubon Avenue, Alexandria, Va. (703)
360-7300. Five indoor courts. OPEN Mon-Sat
6am-11pm; Sun 8am-8pm.

Quince Orchard Swim & Tennis Club
16601 Roundabout Drive, Gaithersburg, Md.
(301) 948-3116. Four indoor courts. Indoor
swimming pool. OPEN 7 days 6am-10pm or
11pm.

Regency Sport & Health Club
1800 Old Meadow Road, McLean, Va. (703)
790-5292. Indoors: ten hard, two clay; outdoors:
four hard, six clay. Members only. OPEN Mon-Fri
6am-11pm; Sat & Sun 7am-10pm.

Reston Athletic Club
1800 Michael Faraday Court, Reston, Va. (703)
437-1402. Four indoor tennis courts. Members
only. OPEN Mon-Fri 6am-midnight; Sat 7am-
7pm; Sun 7am-10pm.

Skyline Clubs
5115 Leesburg Pike, Falls Church, Va. (703)
820-4100. Five indoor tennis courts; four racquetball courts. Indoor swimming pool; sauna;
whirlpool; massage. OPEN Mon-Fri 6am-10pm;
Sat & Sun 7am-7pm.

Wakefield Recreation Center
8100 Braddock Road, Annandale, Va. (703)
321-7080. Ten outdoor tennis courts; four racquetball courts (court fee 6 to 10pm only). Gym;
outdoor fitness trail. Indoor swimming pool.
OPEN 7 days 6am-10pm.

Watkins Regional Park Indoor Tennis Center
301 Watkins Park Drive, Upper Marlboro, Md.
(301) 249-9325. Four outdoor, five indoor/
outdoor. OPEN 7 days 9am-11pm.

**Wheaton Regional Park Indoor Tennis
Center**
Orebaugh & Arcola Avenues, Wheaton, Md.
(301) 649-4049. Six indoor courts. OPEN 7 days
5am-1am.

Volleyball

Contact the Department of Recreation for the location of the court nearest you. You must obtain
a reservation and permit to play on a public court
by calling 673-7646. They can also give you information on their leagues.

Yoga

For information on yoga programs, contact the
Department of Recreation, 673-7660.

Washington DC Babaji Yoga Sangam
6918 6th Street, NW. 726-5608. Group instruction on posture, relaxation, pranayama (scientific breathing), meditation. Two-hour class on
Thursday evenings.

ENTERTAINMENT

Ford's Theater

No longer thought of as a try-out town, DC's Kennedy Center, National, and Warner theaters attract Broadway-caliber shows as well as the best of the major national and international performers, including the Metropolitan Opera Company, Britain's Royal Ballet, American Ballet Theatre, and the Stuttgart among others. In addition, unique cultural resources such as the Arena Stage, the Folger Theater, and Wolf Trap Farm Park draw local crowds.

For what is current in entertainment, check the Washington Post Weekend *section on Friday, and the* City Paper, *available free in many shops and cafes every Thursday.*

TICKETS

Many theaters have their own Charge-a-Ticket number. Call the individual theater box office for the number.

TICKETplace
F Street Plaza between 12th and 13th Streets, NW. (Note: A move is in the offing; call first if you are coming a great distance.) Call T.I.C.K.E.T.S (842-5387) beginning at 11am to find out what shows are available. Tickets are for same-day performances at half price as well as full-price tickets in advance. (Tickets for Sunday performances are sold on Saturday.) For shows at many DC theaters, including Arena Stage, Ford's and National Theater, and Kennedy Center; it's also a Ticketmaster outlet for concerts and sports events. Cash only for half- price tickets; AE, MC, V for full price. The booth is a project of those nice folks at the Cultural Alliance of Greater Washington. *OPEN Tues-Fri noon-4pm; Sat 11am-5pm. CLOSED Sun & Mon.*

Ticketmaster
432-0200. Purchase tickets by phone for area entertainment and sports events. AE, MC, V.

Ticketron
432-0200. At Woodward & Lothrop, Tower Records, Warner Theater, selected Sears stores,

and many other locations throughout the DC area. Tickets for theatrical, musical, and sporting events. AE, MC, V.

WGMS Ticket-Exchange Service
Radio station WGMS (570 AM, 103.5 FM) will help you sell or exchange tickets you cannot use. Call (301) 468-1800 Monday through Friday from 9am to noon with the information about the event and the ticket price, and they will announce it with your phone number that day between 3 and 4:30pm. If you are looking for tickets, call (202) 484-8587 for ticket availability.

THEATERS (MAJOR & COMMUNITY)

Alden Theatre
1234 Ingleside Avenue, McLean, Va. (703) 790-9223.

Arena Stage
6th Street & Maine Avenue, SW. 488-3300.

Arlington Players
2700 South Lang Street, Arlington, Va. (703) 549-1063.

dc space
7th & E Streets, NW. 347-4960.

Fairlington Players
2700 South Lang Street, Arlington, Va. (703) 683-0502.

The Folger Shakespeare Theater
450 7th Street. 393-2700.

Ford's Theater
511 10th Street, NW. 347-4833.

Gala Hispanic Theatre
1625 Park Road, NW. 234-7174.

Glenmont Players
Glenmont Methodist Church, 12901 Dalewood Drive, Wheaton, Md. (301) 946-5578 or -7399.

Greenbelt Cultural Arts Center
129 Centerway Road, Greenbelt, Md. (301) 441-8770.

Hartke Theatre
The Catholic University of America, Harewood Road, NE. 319-5367.

Horizons Theatre
1602-A Beekman Place, NW. 265-6574.

The Kennedy Center for the Performing Arts
2700 F Street, NW; 467-4600. Concert Hall, Eisenhower Theater, and Opera House 254-3770; Terrace Theater 254-9895.

Kreeger
Arena Stage, 6th Street & Maine Avenue, SW. 488-3300.

Lubber Run Amphitheater
North Columbus & North 2nd Streets, Arlington, Va. (703) 358-6960.

Montgomery Players Playhouse
2101 Quince Orchard Boulevard, Gaithersburg, Md. (301) 977-5751.

Mount Vernon Players
Mount Vernon United Methodist Church, 900 Massachusetts Avenue, NW. 347-9620.

The National Archives Theater
1321 Pennsylvania Avenue, NW. 347-0365.
The National Theater
1321 North Pennsylvania Avenue, NW. 628-6161.
The Olney Theatre
Olney Sandy Spring Road, Route 108, Olney, Md. (301) 924-3400.
Port City Playhouse
Alexandria, Va. (703) 838-9303.
Prince George's Public Playhouse
5445 Landover Road, Hyattsville, Md. (301) 277-1711.
The Rep Inc.
601 13th Street, NW. 483-1052.
Reston Community Center Theater
2310 Colts Neck Road, Reston, Va. (703) 476-4500.
Rockville Little Theatre Group
Rockville Center, Rockville, Md. (301) 340-1417.
Roundhouse Theatre
12210 Bushey Drive, Silver Spring, Md. (301) 468-4234.
Silver Spring Stage
10145 Colesville Road, Silver Spring, Md. (301) 593-6036.
Smithsonian Performing Arts
Throughout the museum complex. 357-1500.
Source Theatre Company
1809 14th Street, NW. 462-1073.
Springfield Community Theatre
6320 Hanover Avenue, Springfield, Va. (703) 455-6077.
Studio Theatre
1333 P Street, NW. 332-3300.
The Sylvan Theater
Washington Monument grounds. 619-7222.
Takoma Theater
6833 4th Street, NW. 291-8060.
Touchstone
1556 Burton Court, McLean, Va. (301) 893-6806.
Trapier Theater
St. Alban's School for Boys, Massachusetts & Wisconsin Avenues, NW. 537-6537.
Trinity Theater
36th & O Streets, NW. 965-4680.
Vault Theatre
1789 Columbia Road, NW. 462-1073.
Warner Theater
513 13th Street, NW. 626-1050.
Washington Project for the Arts
400 7th Street, NW. 347-8304.
Wolf Trap Farm Park
1551 Trap Road, Vienna, Va. (703) 255-1800.
Woolly Mammoth Theatre Co.
1317 G Street, NW. 393-3939.

DINNER THEATERS

Burn Brae
15029 Blackburn Road, Burtonsville, Md. (301) 384-5800.

Colony 7
On the corner of Route 32 off 295, Annapolis Junction, Md. (301) 725-6431.
Harlequin
1330 Gude Drive, Rockville, Md. (301) 340-8515.
Hayloft
10501 Balls Ford Road, Manassas, Va. (703) 368-3666.
Lazy Susan
Route 1, Woodbridge, Va. (703) 494-6311.
Petrucci's
312 Main Street, Laurel, Md. (301) 470-3436.
Toby's
Columbia, Md. (301) 596-6161.
West End Dinner Theater
4615 Duke Street, Alexandria, Va. (703) 370-2500.

DANCE

Glen Echo Dance Theatre
Spanish Ballroom, MacArthur Boulevard & Goldsboro Road, Glen Echo, Md. (301) 229-6022. Season: *June-Aug.*
Kennedy Center Opera House
2700 F Street, NW. 476-4619. Visiting companies such as the American Ballet Theatre, Dance Theatre of Harlem, Joffrey Ballet, Royal Danish Ballet, Elliot Feld Ballet, and many more. Season: *Dec-June.*
Lisner Auditorium
George Washington University, 21st & H Streets, NW. 994-6800. Home base for the Washington Ballet. Season: *Oct-Mar.*
Wolf Trap Farm Park
1551 Trap Road, Vienna, Va. (703) 255-1860; (301) 341-WOLF; (202) 432-0200. Joffrey Ballet and American Dance Machine, among others. Season: *Early June-early Sept.*

OPERA

Kennedy Center Opera House
2700 F Street, NW. 467-4600. The Metropolitan Opera in April and the Washington Opera (416-7800) in November. *Nov-May.*
Victorian Lyric Opera Company
F. Scott Fitzgerald Theatre, Edmonton Drive & Baltimore Road, Rockville, Md. (301) 445-0020.
Vienna Light Opera
James Madison High School Auditorium, 2500 James Madison Drive, Vienna, Va. (703) 281-2570.

CONCERT HALLS

Alexandria Roller Rink
807 North St. Asaph Street, Alexandria, Va. (703) 836-2199.

Baird Auditorium
Smithsonian Institution, National Museum of Natural History, 10th Street & Constitution Avenue, NW. 357-1300.

Capitol Centre
Harry Truman Drive, Landover, Md. (301) 350-3900.

Carter Barron Amphitheater
4850 Colorado Avenue, NW. 426-0486.

The Concert Hall
Kennedy Center, 2700 F Street, NW. 467-4600.

Coolidge Auditorium
Library of Congress, 1st Street & Independence Avenue, SE. 707-5502.

Corcoran Gallery of Art
17th Street & New York Avenue, NW. 638-3211.

Cramton Auditorium
Howard University, 620 T Street, NW. 806-7199.

DAR Constitution Hall
18th & D Streets, NW. 638-2661.

F. Scott Fitzgerald Theatre
Old Baltimore Road, Rockville, Md. (301) 445-0020.

Folger Library
201 East Capitol Street, SE. 544-7077.

Fort Dupont
Minnesota & Randale Avenues, SE. 426-7723.

Fort Ward Amphitheater
4301 West Braddock Road, Alexandria, Va. (703) 838-4834.

Glen Echo Park
MacArthur Boulevard & Goldsboro Road, Glen Echo, Md. (301) 492-6282.

Hall of Americans
OAS, 17th Street & Constitution Avenue, NW. 458-3000.

Hall of Musical Instruments
Smithsonian Institution, National Museum of American History, 8th & G Streets, NW. 357-1300.

Hirshhorn Museum Auditorium
Smithsonian Institution, 8th Street & Independence Avenue, SW. 357-1300.

Jewish Community Center
6125 Montrose Road, Rockville, Md. (301) 881-0100.

Robert F. Kennedy Stadium
East Capitol & 22nd Streets, SE. 546-3337.

Lisner Auditorium
George Washington University, 730 21st Street, NW. 994-6800.

The Lyceum
201 South Washington Street, Alexandria, Va. (703) 838-4994.

Merriwether Post Pavilion
Columbia, Md. (301) 982-1800; (800) 543-3041.

National Academy of Sciences Auditorium
21st Street & Constitution Avenue, NW. 334-2000.

The National Gallery of Art
6th Street & Constitution Avenue, NW. 737-4215.

Pierce Mill
Rock Creek Park, Beach Drive & Tilden Street, NW. 426-6908.

The Phillips Collection
1600 21st Street, NW. 387-2151.

Renwick Grand Salon
Smithsonian Institution, Renwick Gallery, 17th Street & Pennsylvania Avenue, NW. 357-1300.

Smithsonian Institution
Constitution Avenue between 10th and 14th Streets, NW. 357-2700.

Sousa Hall
Marine Barracks, 8th & I Streets, NW. 433-5714.

Warner Theater
513 13th Street, NW. 626-1050.

T. C. Williams High School
3330 King Street, Alexandria, Va. (703) 824-6800.

Wolf Trap Farm Park
1551 Trap Road, Vienna, Va. (703) 255-1860.

Concert Information

For information on major concerts in the area, call:

Q-107: 829-7625.
Ticketron: 432-0200.
WAVA: (703) 533-1328.
WHFS: (301) 577-1001.

MOVIE THEATERS: FIRST RUN

Avalon I & II
5612 Connecticut Avenue, NW. 966-2600.

Capitol Hill Cinemas 1 & 2
507 8th Street, SE. 547-1210.

Dupont Cinema
1350 19th Street, NW. 872-9555.

Embassy
1927 Florida Avenue, NW. 387-1344.

K-B Cerberus
3040 M Street, NW. 337-1311.

K-B Cinema
5100 Wisconsin Avenue, NW. 363-1875.

K-B Fine Arts
1919 M Street, NW. 223-4438.

K-B Foundry 7
1055 Thomas Jefferson Place, NW. 337-0094.

K-B Janus 3
1660 Connecticut Avenue, NW. 232-8900.

K-B Paris
Mazza Galerie, 5300 Wisconsin Avenue, NW. 686-7700.

Key
1222 Wisconsin Avenue, NW (Georgetown). 333-5100.

MacArthur 1, 2, 3
4859 MacArthur Boulevard, NW. 337-1700.

Outer Circle Theaters 1 & 2
4849 Wisconsin Avenue, NW. 244-3116.

Senator Theatre
3950 Minnesota Avenue, NE. 398-3083.

Stanton Art Theatre
3100 18th Street, NE. 526-3312. (X-rated films.)

Tenley Circle, 1, 2, 3
4200 Wisconsin Avenue, NW. 363-4340.
Uptown
3426 Connecticut Avenue, NW. 966-5400.
West End 1, 2, 3, 4
23rd & L Streets, NW. 293-3152.
West End 5, 6, 7
23rd & M Streets, NW. 452-9020.
Wisconsin Avenue 6
4000 Wisconsin Avenue, NW. 244-0880.

MOVIE THEATERS: REVIVAL

American Film Institute
Kennedy Center, 2700 F Street, NW. 785-4600.
Biograph
2819 M Street, NW (Georgetown). 333-2696.
Carmichael Auditorium
National Museum of American History, Constitution Avenue at 14th Street, NW. 357-2700.
Jenifer Cinema I & II
5252 Wisconsin Avenue, NW. 244-5703.

FREE ENTERTAINMENT

Call Dial-a-Park, 619-7275, for up-to-the-minute information on free cultural events on that day. Also check the ANNUAL EVENTS chapter of this book for listings of many very special happenings, especially during the summer months, most of which are FREE.

CHURCH MUSIC

See the *Washingtonian* and the weekend *Washington Post* for current church musical programs.

TELEVISION SHOWS

For free tickets to TV shows call or write the appropriate station:
WDCA (Channel 20)
5202 River Road, Bethesda, Md. (301) 654-2600.
WETA (PBS, Channel 26)
P.O. Box 2626, Washington, DC 20013. (703) 998-2626.
WFTY (Channel 50)
12276 Wilkins Avenue, Rockville, Md. (301) 230-1550.
WJLA (ABC, Channel 7)
3007 Tilden Street, NW. 364-7777.
WRC (NBC, Channel 4)
4001 Nebraska Avenue, NW. 885-4000.

WTTG (Channel 5)
5151 Wisconsin Avenue, NW. 244-5151.
WUSA (CBS, Channel 9)
4001 Brandywine Street, NW. 364-3900.

RADIO STATIONS

In radio jargon: MOR = "middle of the road."

AM Stations

WABS: 780. Religious/Sacred Music
WAGE: 1200. Top 40/News
WCMD: 1560. MOR
WCPT: 730. CNN News
WCTN: 950. Religious
WDCT: 1310. Inspirational/News
WFAX: 1220. Religious
WGMS: 570. Classical
WILC: 900. Contemporary Latin
WINX: 1600. Adult Contemporary
WMAL: 630. News/Talk
WMDO: 1540. Latin Music/News
WMZQ: 1390. Country
WNTR: 1050. News/Talk
WOL: 1450. Soul
WPGC: 1580. Business News
WPWC: 1480. Country
WTOP: 1500. News/Sports/Talk
WUST: 1120. Gospel: Talk & Music
WWDC: 1260. Personality/MOR
WWRC: 980. Talk
WYCB: 1340. Inspirational

FM Stations

WAMU: 88.5. Arts/Information (NPR)
WASH: 97.1. Adult Contemporary
WAVA: 105.1. Top 40
WCXR: 105.9. Classic Rock
WDCU: 90.1. Jazz/Information
WETA: 90.9. Information (NPR)/Classical
WFRE: 99.9. Easy Listening
WGAY: 99.5. Easy Listening
WGMS: 103.5. Classical
WGTS: 91.9. Educational/Cultural
WHFS: 99.1. Progressive
WHUR: 96.3. Urban Adult
WJFK: 106.7. Classic Rock
WJZE: 100.3. Jazz/Adult Contemporary
WKYS: 93.9. Urban Contemporary
WLTT: 94.7. Adult Contemporary
WMJR: 107.7. Oldies
WMJS: 92.7. Easy Listening
WMMJ: 102.3. Adult Contemporary
WMUC: 88.1. Progressive
WMZQ: 98.7. Country
WPFW: 89.3. Jazz/Community Radio
WPGC: 95.5. Contemporary Crossover
WWDC: 101.1. Album Rock
WXTR: 104.1. Oldies Hits

NIGHTLIFE

Blues Alley

DRINKING AGE

The legal drinking age for wine, beer, and all other alcoholic beverages in Washington, DC, Maryland, and Virginia is 21. If you are blessed with a youthful appearance be prepared to show ID.

NIGHTSPOTS INDEX

The following is an index of the clubs you will find in this section. The categories that appear in parentheses are: Bluegrass/Country, Comedy, Dance Bars & Clubs, Dinner/Dancing, Eclectic, Ethnic, Jazz, Piano Bars, Rock. Complete descriptions follow index.

See also RESTAURANTS, Entertainment.

BLUEGRASS/COUNTRY

The Birchmere
3901 Mount Vernon Avenue, Alexandria, Va. (703) 549-5919. Rustic bluegrass club, also country, folk, and acoustic. Features the Seldom Scene every Thursday. "Names" have been known to drop by. Music Tuesday to Thursday at 8:30pm, Friday and Saturday from 9pm to midnight. Burgers, sandwiches till 11pm. From the bar beer, wine, and soft drinks only. Cover charge varies; no minimum. No credit cards. Tickets also available at Ticketron. *OPEN 7 nights 7pm-1am.*

COMEDY

Chelsea's
1055 Thomas Jefferson Street, NW. 298-8222. The popular political-satire group Capitol Steps

ickles the funny bone at this Georgetown club every other Saturday at 8pm. Persian music Wednesday and Sunday nights, salsa music Thursday and Friday. Cover varies; minimum for the Capitol Steps. AC, MC, V. *OPEN Wed, Thurs & Sun till 2am; Fri & Sat till 3:30am.*

Comedy Cafe
1520 K Street, NW. 638-JOKE. DC's premier all-comedy stop. A mix of top local and national acts (the likes of Jay Leno, Yakov Smirnoff, Larry "Bud" Melman). Shows Friday at 8:30 and 10:30pm; Saturday at 7, 9, and 10pm. Thursday is Open Mike Night from 8:30pm to 11pm. A la carte nibbles or full dinners. Cover (higher on the weekend); no minimum.

Garvin's Comedy Club
Cafe Maxime, 1825 I Street, NW. 726-1334. The laugh's on them Tuesday to Thursday at 8:30pm, and every Friday and Saturday at 8:30 and 10:30pm with fine professionals to tickle your funny bone. Plush surroundings in which to dine and laugh. Cover charge; two-drink minimum. Reserve Friday and Saturday. AE, CB, DC, MC, V. *OPEN Mon-Thurs 11am-2am; Fri & Sat 11am-3am.*

DANCE BARS & CLUBS

From 17th to 20th Streets, between L and M Streets, there is a high concentration of singles' bars/night spots. See also RESTAURANTS, Bars & Burgers.

The Black Rooster Pub
1919 L Street, NW. 659-4431. For draft and dart lovers, an attractive, lively "English pub." Dancing to discs Wednesday to Saturday. Overstuffed sandwiches till 10pm. No cover; no minimum. AE, CB, DC, MC, V. *OPEN Mon-Sat 11:30am-1am.*

The Bottom Line
1716 I Street, NW. 298-8488. Rugby players' hangout. Dancing to pop and rock oldies from Tuesday to Saturday starting at 9pm. Happy Hour Monday to Friday from 5 to 7:30pm. Burgers, omelettes, and salads till 10:30pm. No cover; no minimum. AE, CB, DC, MC, V. *OPEN Mon-Thurs 11am-1:30am; Fri & Sat 11am-2:30am.*

The Chapter III
900 1st Street, SE. 488-4462. Large club for disco dancing draws a predominantly black crowd. No jeans or athletic shoes. Age minimum 21. Cover charge; no minimum. AE, CB, DC, MC, V. *OPEN Thurs, Sun & Mon 9pm-3am; Fri & Sat 9pm-5am.*

Chesapeake House
746 9th Street, NW. 347-3600. Monday to Thursday from 8:30pm to 2am and Friday and Saturday from 8:30pm to 3am, it's a gay bar with go-go boys and disco. Cover charge; no minimum. MC, V. *OPEN Sun- Thurs 5pm-2am; Fri & Sat 5pm-3am.*

Chicago
1330 19th Street, NW. 463-8888. Terrific new dance club (formerly Mirage) where the d.j. plays rhythm and blues, New Wave high-energy Wednesday to Thursday from 9pm to 2am; Friday and Saturday till 3am. Chicago Bar & Grill serves an American grill menu till 1am. No jeans or athletic shoes. Cover; no minimum. AE, MC, V. *OPEN Mon-Thurs 11:30am-2am; Fri 11:30am-3am; Sat 6pm-3am. Sun brunch 11am-7pm.*

Duddington's Underground
319 Pennsylvania Avenue, SE. 544-3500. Subterranean Capitol Hill bar. Oldies discs and youngies dancing. A d.j. spins records Thursday to Saturday from 9pm; jukebox the rest of the time. Good singles' meeting bar. Happy Hour Monday to Friday from 5 to 8pm. Food till midnight Monday to Wednesday; till 10pm Thursday to Saturday. No cover; no minimum. AE, CB, DC, MC, V. *OPEN Sun-Thurs 11:30am-11pm; Fri & Sat 11:30am-midnight.*

Engine Room
Channel Inn Hotel, 650 Water Street, SW. 554-2400. Dance to soft rock and enjoy the waterfront view, Monday to Friday from 8pm to 1am. Light food till 11pm. Jacket and tie requested. No cover; no minimum. AE, DC, MC, V. *OPEN Mon-Sat 11am-1am.*

15 Minutes
1030 15th Street, NW. 408-1855. Hot high-energy spot for alternative, hip-hop, funk, reggae played by a d.j., as well as live blues, alternative rock, soul, and rockabilly bands (except Sunday). There are also poetry readings on Mondays, and acoustic jazz on Tuesdays, in the "koffee-haus." Friday and Saturday there is a free buffet from 5 to 1:30am. Cover; varies with the bands. AE only. *OPEN Sun-Thurs 5pm-2am; Fri 5pm- 3am; Sat 8pm-3am.*

Fifth Column
915 F Street, NW. 393-3632. In the old Equitable Bank Building, a new upscale dance club on three floors: two dance floors, TV monitors, laser lights, and local art on display. Draws an under-40 professional crowd. Proper attire; no jeans. Membership. Cover for nonmembers. *OPEN Wed, Thurs & Sun 9pm-2am; Fri & Sat 9pm-3am.*

The Fraternity House
2122 P Street, rear, NW. 223-4917. A young, collegiate gay bar located in a former stable. The d.j. disco starts at 9pm every night. Video bar upstairs where entertainment videos and TV are shown; also a pool table and pinball machines. No drag, please! Cover charge Wednesday through Saturday; minimum. No credit cards. *OPEN Mon-Wed 4pm-2am; Thurs 4pm-4am; Fri & Sat 4pm-5am (bar till 2:30am).*

Jenkins Hill
223 Pennsylvania Avenue, SE. 544-6600. The famed, fashionable pub on "the Hill" subdued during the week goes wild on Friday and Saturday nights when a d.j. spinning oldies and rock 'n' roll takes over beginning at 9pm till closing. Steaks, ribs, burgers till 1am. Champagne

brunch Saturday and Sunday from 10:30am to 3pm. No cover; no minimum. AE, CB, DC, MC, V. *OPEN Sun-Thurs 11:30am-midnight; Fri & Sat 11:30am-3am.*

The Lost & Found
56 L Street, SE. 488-1200. Handsome, off-the-beaten-track gay bar/restaurant/d.j. disco. Dinner till 11pm. Special: Annual Summer Sleaze Ball. Cover charge Friday and Saturday; no minimum. AE, MC, V. *OPEN Wed- Sun 7pm-2am.*

Paul Mall
3235 M Street, NW. 965-5353. Crowded and lively Georgetown bar. Live bands play disco and rock from 9pm, spontaneous dancing (tiny floor); lots of hustle and bustle. Redskins and Bullets team members have been known to wet their whistles here. Light fare served. Reserve. Cover charge Friday and Saturday; no minimum. AE, CB, DC, MC, V. *OPEN Sun-Thurs 7pm-2am; Fri & Sat 7pm-3am.*

Rumors
1900 M Street, NW. 466-7378. Extremely popular singles' bar with dining and dancing. The d.j. spins mostly Top 40 and oldies from 5pm during the week and from 9pm on weekends. Burgers, nachos, steaks, and seafood till 11pm. Minimum age, 21. Shirts with collars; no jeans, athletic shoes, or sandals. No cover; no minimum. AE, CB, DC, MC, V. *OPEN Sun-Thurs 11:30am-2am; Fri & Sat 11:30am-3am.*

Samantha's Restaurant
1823 L Street, NW. 223-1823. Tastefully decorated restaurant with stained glass, oak paneling, and a skylight. A d.j. spins big band sounds Wednesday from 5pm to 1am; pop and rock 'n' roll, Thursday to Saturday from 9pm till closing. Young professional crowd. Fireplace ablaze in winter; outdoor dining in summer. Continental menu. Food till 10pm. No athletic footwear. No cover; no minimum. No reservations. AE, CB, DC, MC, V. *OPEN Mon-Thurs 11:30am-1:30am; Fri & Sat 11:30am-2:30am.*

The Sky Dome
Holiday Inn Crowne Plaza, 300 Army Navy Drive, Arlington, Va. (703) 892-4100. This room, with its panoramic view of DC, slowly revolves, completing a full circle every hour. Dancing every Tuesday to 50s and 60s sounds, Wednesday is karaoke night, and there's a d.j. the rest of the week. Happy Hour is from 4:30 to 7pm. Sandwiches till closing. No cover; no minimum. AE, CB, DC, MC, V. *OPEN Mon-Thurs 4pm-midnight; Fri & Sat 4:30pm 2am.*

The Spy Club
805 5th Street, NW, downstairs. 289-1779. Elegant club under Notte Luna, draws a well-dressed upscale crowd for dancing to "lite disco" or conversation in one of the intimate plush spaces like the traditional library setting or the Cuban motif room. In all, a class act. On Fridays they open early for a happy hour. Jacket and tie preferred; no collarless shirts, sneakers, or jeans. Cover charge. AE, MC, V. *OPEN Thurs & Sat 8pm-3am; Fri from 5pm.*

The Third Edition
1218 Wisconsin Avenue, NW. 333-3700. A d.j spins Top 40 and just about anything else in this saloon where a college-age crowd dances. Thursday to Saturday from 9:30pm to 3am, upstairs; Sunday, 9:30pm, downstairs. Food till midnight, Sunday till 11pm. Burgers, steaks, and salads. Sunday brunch from 10:30am to 3pm. Open-air patio. No athletic shoes or T-shirts. Cover upstairs Friday and Saturday; minimum. Reserve. AE, DC, MC, V. *OPEN Mon-Thurs 11:30am-1:30am; Fri & Sat 11:30am-2:30am; Sun 10:30am-1:30am.*

Tracks
1111 1st Street, SE. 488-3320. Huge club attracts a mixed gay and straight crowd. Within its 20,000 square feet there are eight bars and an outdoor dance floor. Tuesdays are Lesbo-a-Go-Go nights; Wednesday is R&B night; Thursday for progressive modern music; Friday night is "straights" night with industrial techno music; Saturday is men's night ("all white gay men"); Sunday features house music. There's food from the cafe. Cover charge. AE, MC, V. *OPEN Tues-Thurs 8pm till the party's over; Fri-Sat from 8am; Sun 8pm-3:30am.*

Winston's
3295 M Street, NW. 333-3150. Where the 18-to-25-year-old set come to dance to "oldies but goodies" and Top 40 records spun by a d.j. nightly from 9pm. Sandwiches till 1:30am Sunday to Thursday and till 2:30am Friday and Saturday. Dress jeans only; no T-shirts. Cover charge Friday and Saturday; no minimum. No reservations. AE, MC, V. *OPEN Sun-Thurs 7pm-2am; Fri & Sat 7pm-3am.*

DINNER/DANCING

F. Scott's
1232 36th Street, NW. 342-0009. F. Scott Fitzgerald would have been comfortable in his namesake bar/restaurant. Its Art Deco decor is sophisticated and stylish. Dancing to 30s and 40s mellow records. Good people-watching late-night spot. Northern Italian menu, interesting drinks. Jackets; no jeans. Age minimum, 21. No cover charge; no minimum. Reserve for dinner. AE, CB, DC, MC, V. *OPEN Tues-Thurs 7pm-2am; Fri & Sat 7pm-3am.*

Hogate's
9th Street & Maine Avenue, SW. 484-6300. Attractive seafood restaurant on the Potomac with a comfortable lounge for listening or dancing to Top 40 tunes while enjoying the wonderful waterfront view. Above-25 crowd. Music Monday to Sunday from 8pm till closing. Raw bar seven days, 11am till closing. Sunday brunch buffet till 2:30pm; lunch buffet Monday to Friday from 11am to 2pm; Saturday lunch noon to 3pm. Dinner till 10pm Monday to Thursday, till 11pm Friday and Saturday, and till 10pm Sunday. No cover; no minimum. Reserve for six or more for

dinner. AE, CB, DC, MC, V. *OPEN Mon-Thurs 11am-12:30am; Fri & Sat 11am-2am; Sun 10:30am-10pm.*

River Club
See RESTAURANTS, American.

Spirit of Washington
Washington Boat Lines, 602 Water Street, SW. 554-8000. From late May to November, the Moonlight Dance Cruise is featured on this 125-foot ship. Cruise the Potomac from 11:30pm to 2am while you dance. Live band and Mother Nature supply the mood. Cash bar. Snacks available. Great for large groups. Reserve. Call ahead to find out when she sails.

The View Lounge
Marriott Key Bridge, 1401 Lee Highway, Rosslyn, Va. (703) 524-6400. Wonderful view of Georgetown, Great Falls, and the Potomac. Dancing to live music Tuesday to Saturday from 9pm till closing. Wednesday is Ladies' Night featuring a free buffet. Dinner in The View restaurant (*see* RESTAURANTS, Rooms with a View). Hungry Hour Monday to Friday from 4 to 8pm an all-you-can-eat buffet for a minimal charge. Jacket required; no jeans. No cover; no minimum. Reserve. AE, CB, DC, MC, V. *OPEN Mon-Fri 4pm-1am; Sat 6pm-2am.*

ECLECTIC

dc space
443 7th Street, NW. 347-4960 or -1445. Casual restaurant and alternative performance space. Soft jazz, rock, New Wave, theater, art shows, films. Call for current schedule. "California"-style food—fresh vegetables and fruit, burgers, too—Monday to Saturday till 9pm. Happy Hour Monday to Thursday from 4pm to 7pm; Friday from 4pm to 9pm. Cover charge for some shows; no minimum at night. No cover at back bar. AE, MC, V. *OPEN Mon-Thurs 11:30am-2am; Fri & Sat 11:30am-3am.*

Food for Thought
1738 Connecticut Avenue, NW. 797-1095. Very earthy and homey bar and "healthy food" restaurant, presents live folk, jazz, rock, and bluegrass from 6pm to midnight. Vegetarian food, chicken and fish, too, till 11:30pm, Friday and Saturday till 12:30am. No cover; no minimum (but the hat does get passed). No-smoking section. Reserve for ten or more. AE, MC, V. *OPEN Mon 11:30am-3pm, 6pm-midnight; Tues-Thurs 11:30am-midnight; Fri & Sat 11:30am-1am; Sun 5pm-midnight.*

Kilimanjaro
1724 California Street, NW. 328-3838 (recording). Terrific Adams-Morgan spot for African, Latin, and Caribbean dance music. Calypso, reggae, and New World beat. Cover, higher on weekends. *OPEN Tues-Thurs noon-2am; Fri & Sat 6pm-3am; Sun 6pm-2am.*

Round Table
4859 Wisconsin Avenue, NW. 362-1252. Very

friendly, small restaurant/club. Downstairs, live music, rock to jazz, every night from 9:30pm till closing. Continental menu till 10:30pm, in restaurant only. No cover; no minimum. Reserve for ten or more. AE, CB, MC, V. *OPEN Mon-Thurs 11:30am-2am; Fri 11:30am-3am; Sat noon-3am; Sun 6:30pm-1am.*

ETHNIC

The Dubliner
520 North Capitol Street, NW. 737-3773. Guinness on tap, Harp and Irish whiskey, fish 'n' chips, and lots of blarney in this spirited, wild Irish bar. Irish groups perform nightly Monday to Thursday from 9pm to 1:30am; Friday and Saturday from 9pm to 2:30am; and Sunday from 7:30pm to midnight—there's plenty of opportunity to sing along. Steaks, burgers, lamb chops, too, every night till 11pm. No cut-offs or tank tops. No cover; no minimum. AE, CB, DC, MC, V. *OPEN Sun-Thurs 11am-2am; Fri & Sat 11am-3am.*

Gallagher's Pub
3319 Connecticut Avenue, NW. 686-9189. Comfortable neighborhood Irish bar with folk singing Thursday from 8:30pm to midnight; Friday and Saturday from 9:30pm to 1:30am. Groups play Irish, folk, bluegrass, or rock. Sunday is Open Mike Night. Irish stew is the house specialty served till midnight Sunday to Thursday, till 1am Friday and Saturday. No cover; no minimum. AE, CB, DC, MC, V. *OPEN Sun-Thurs noon-2am; Fri & Sat noon-3am.*

Ireland's Four Provinces
3412 Connecticut Avenue, NW. 244-0860. One of Washington's best-loved Irish bars. Irish and Celtic folk singing Tuesday to Thursday from 9pm to 1:15am; Friday and Saturday from 9:15pm to 2:15am; Sunday from 8:30pm. Guinness and Harp on tap, served in pint glasses, and the fish 'n' chips are some of the reasons why. Steaks, chops, corned beef and cabbage till 11pm. Cover charge on Friday and Saturday; no minimum. AE, CB, DC, MC, V. *OPEN Sun-Thurs 5pm-2am; Fri 5pm-3am; Sat 4pm-3am.*

Ireland's Own
132 North Royal Street, Alexandria, Va. (703) 549-4535. Enthusiasm, Irish song, and Harp and Guinness on tap. No cover. AE, MC, V. *OPEN 7 days 10am-2am.*

Irish Times Pub
14 F Street, NW. 543-5433. Guinness on tap at this low-frills typical Irish pub frequented by a middle-aged, "young at heart" crowd. Singer in residence, Pete Papageorge, Wednesday and Thursday from 8:30pm to 12:30am; Friday and Saturday from 9pm to 1:30am. Food till 11pm. No cover; no minimum. No reservations. AE, CB, DC, MC, V. *OPEN Sun-Thurs 10:30am-2am; Fri & Sat 10:30am-3am.*

Murphy's
713 King Street, Alexandria, Va. (703) 548-1717. Amiable Old Town Irish pub (there's a clone of

this original in DC, at 2609 24th Street, NW; 462-7171) features live Irish folk music every night from 9pm and in winter a warming fire in the hearth. Burgers, steaks, and seafood till midnight. Reserve (except Friday and Saturday). AE, CB, DC, MC, V. *OPEN 7 days 11am-2am.*

JAZZ

Blues Alley
1073 Wisconsin Avenue, NW, in the rear. 337-4141. Follow the discerning crowds of jazz buffs down the alley to this popular (most often picked as DC's best), attractive, brick-walled Georgetown spot for the country's top names in contemporary, progressive, and traditional jazz. Shows Sunday to Thursday at 8 and 10pm; Friday and Saturday at midnight as well. Fine New Orleans cajun specialties for dinner. Cover; minimum. Must reserve! AE, CB, DC, MC, V. *OPEN 7 days 6pm-2am.*

Ibex
5832 Georgia Avenue, NW. 726-1800. One part cozy jazz bar, the other a New York-style dance club with live music and comedy. Cover varies for live shows; no cover for jazz lounge. *OPEN Tues-Thurs till 3am; Fri & Sat till 4am.*

Il Porto Ristorante
121 King Street, Alexandria, Va. (703) 836-8833. Old Town Italian restaurant features Johnny ("Crazy Otto") Maddox playing ragtime and boogie piano, Tuesday to Saturday from 8:30pm to midnight. Cover; no minimum. Reserve. AE, MC, V. *OPEN 7 days 11:45am-midnight.*

The Market Inn
200 E Street, SW. 554-2100. Popular with members of Congress, this 15-year-old bar provides a relaxing spot to listen to live jazz and pop, Monday to Friday from 11:30am to 1am; Saturday from 7pm; Sunday from 6pm to midnight. Extensive menu (101 items in all) features fresh lobster, available till 1am. Happy Hour Monday to Friday from 3pm to 6pm. Healthy-sized drinks. No cover; no minimum. Reserve for dinner. AE, CB, DC, MC, V. *OPEN Mon-Thur 11:30am-midnight; Fri & Sat 11:30am-1am; Sun 11:30am-midnight.*

One Step Down
2517 Pennsylvania Avenue, NW. 331-8863. Small atmospheric jazz club, smoke-filled and jammed. Music Thursday to Monday from 9 or 10pm to 1 or 2am. Eclectic light food available till 1am, Friday and Saturday till 2am. Saturday and Sunday afternoon jam sessions from 3pm to 7pm (and no cover). Special: a jukebox stocked with classic jazz records. Cover and minimum vary. No reservations. AE, CB, DC, MC, V. *OPEN Mon-Thurs 10am-2am; Fri 10am-3am; Sat noon-3am; Sun noon-2am.*

The Saloon
3239 M Street, NW. 338-4900. The Georgetowners' hangout. Live jazz every night—Sunday to Thursday from 9pm to 2am; Friday and Saturday from 9pm to 3am. Comfortable, nontouristy. Burgers, deli sandwiches, and seafood specialties till 1:30am. NY sirloin steak special, Tuesday and Wednesday from 6pm to 1am. Monday and Tuesday there is a Beer Night Special. Cover Wednesday to Saturday; one-drink minimum per set. CB, DC, MC, V. *OPEN Sun-Thurs 3pm-2am; Fri & Sat 3pm-3am.*

Takoma Station Tavern
6914 14th Street, NW. 829-1999. A black professional crowd comes to this friendly spot to hear live jazz by local talent nightly (except Sunday, which is reggae night) in the bar. Food ranges from chili to stuffed shrimp. Music starts at 6:30 pm till . . . . AE, MC, V. No cover; two-drink minimum at tables. *OPEN Sun-Thurs 4pm-2am; Fri & Sat 4pm-3am.*

Twins Lounge
5516 Colorado Avenue, NW. 882-2523. Live jazz nightly starting at 9:45pm by local and visiting talent. Best night: Sunday for their jazz jam from 9pm to 1am. MC, V. Food or drink minimum; no cover. *OPEN Sun-Thurs 4pm-2am; Fri & Sat till 3am.*

The Wharf
119 King Street, Alexandria, Va. (703) 836-2834. The Quarter Deck Lounge, a cozy, beamed-ceilinged, upstairs nightspot in Old Town, features good live local jazz every night from 9pm to 12:30am. Appetizers available upstairs. Downstairs, a seafood restaurant serves till 10pm Sunday and Monday; till 10:30pm Tuesday to Thursday; till 11pm Friday and Saturday. Sunday brunch. Cover charge after 9pm; no minimum. AE, MC, V. *OPEN Sun & Mon 10:30am-10pm; Tues-Thurs 10:30am-10:30pm; Fri & Sat 10:30am-11pm.* Upstairs *OPEN 7 days till 1:30am.*

PIANO BARS

The Bar—Capitol Hilton
1001 16th Street, NW. 393-1000. Mirrors mirrors everywhere in this piano bar and lounge. Pianist plays Tuesday through Saturday from 5pm to 8pm. No cover; no minimum. AE, MC, V. *OPEN 7 days 10am-1:30am.*

Capitol View Lounge
Hyatt Regency Washington, 400 New Jersey Avenue, NW, 11th floor. 737-1234. For cocktails and piano music and a magnificent view of the Capitol. Music Monday to Saturday, 7pm until 11pm. AE, CB, DC, MC, V. *OPEN 7 days 5:30pm-2am.*

The Fairfax Bar
Ritz Carlton Hotel, 2100 Massachusetts Avenue, NW. 293-2100. An intimate lounge with fireplaces and sofas where a pianist entertains from 5pm to 1am every night but Sunday. Everything about this spot is sophisticated. Light fare served from 11am to 11pm. English High Tea Monday to Friday from 3pm to 5pm. Jacket after 5pm. No cover; no minimum. AE, CB, DC, MC, V. *OPEN 7 days 11am-2am.*

The Garden Terrace Lounge
Four Seasons Hotel, 2800 Pennsylvania Avenue, NW. 342-0444. This elegant lobby-lounge is bi-level, plush, and plant-filled. Get comfy and listen to jazz piano music every day from 4pm to 2am. Proper attire. No reservations. AE, CB, DC, MC, V.

John Hay Room
Hay-Adams Hotel, 800 16th Street, NW. 638-6600. Elegant setting. The piano is mirror-tiled and the pianist plays here and at the (White) House across the street. Music Monday to Saturday from 6:30pm to 11:30pm, Sunday from 7pm to 11pm. Frequented by White House staffers. Proper attire. No cover; no minimum. AE, CB, DC, MC, V. *OPEN 7 days 11am-1am.*

ROCK

The Bayou
3135 K Street, NW. 333-2897. Longtime super-charged showcase for top names on the rock, folk, and blues scene. Dancing on nonconcert nights; local bands Friday and Saturday. Call for current roster. Tickets may be purchased through the Bayou box office after 8pm and through Ticketron and Hecht's TicketCenter. Cover charge; no minimum. No credit cards. *OPEN Sun-Thurs 8pm-midnight; Fri & Sat 8pm-2:30am.*

Club Soda
3433 Connecticut Avenue, NW. 244-4084. Good oldies rock 'n' roll club where the 50s and 60s live. Live bands Thursday to Saturday and alternate Wednesdays at 10pm. No credit cards. *OPEN Sun-Thurs 4pm-2am; Fri & Sat 4pm-3am.*

dc space
see Eclectic.

Deja Vu
2119 M street, NW. 452-1966. Popular lively 50s and 60s rock club with space for 2,000 dancing fools. Six different rooms, three dance floors (one of them is the largest in DC). Thursday nights and the fourth Friday of every month there are jitterbug contests for cash prizes. Happy Hour Thursday and Friday from 4:30pm to 7pm; Friday is WLIT night, featuring a d.j. from that radio station. Theme parties throughout the year. Shirts with collars; no athletic shoes or "grubby" jeans. Minimum age, 21. No cover; no minimum. AE, CB, DC, MC, V. *OPEN Sun-Thurs 8pm-2am; Fri & Sat 8pm-3am.*

The East Side
1824 Half Street, SW. 488-1205. Former warehouse (formerly the Pier) located in an industrial sector. Two levels, three bars. Upstairs Saturday, showcase of local and national rock talent. Downstairs, high-energy dancing to videos. Cover varies with groups. *OPEN Fri & Sat 11pm-5am.*

9:30 Club
930 F Street, NW. 393-0930. Excellent DC showcase club for New Wave. Live shows; punk, New Wave, and rock bands. Wednesday, Thursday, and Sunday first band strikes up at 9:30pm; Friday and Saturday at 10:30pm and midnight. Recorded music with a d.j. as well. Two bars, video, and lots of dancing. Light fare till closing. ID required. Cover charge; no minimum. No credit cards. *OPEN Tues, Wed, Thurs & Sun 8pm-2am; Fri & Sat 9pm-3am.*

Roxy Showcase Club
1214 18th Street, NW. 296-9292. National and local New Wave, R&B, high-energy reggae bands every Thursday, Saturday, and Sunday; progressive d.j. Wednesday and Friday. Good sound system, spare decor. Cover varies with the act. Call for concert schedule. Tickets at the box office, Hecht's TicketCenter, or phone charge, 432-0200. MC, V.

RESTAURANTS

Au Pied de Cochon

RESERVATIONS

Telephone ahead to make a reservation, since this will determine that the particular restaurant is still in business and that a table will be available. If reservations are not accepted, you can determine whether to expect a long wait prior to being seated.

TIPPING

The rule of thumb is approximately 15 percent of the total (exclusive of tax, which is 9 percent). Generally, Washington restaurants do not add a service charge.

KEY TO SYMBOLS

The price of dinner at these restaurants has been classified on the basis of a complete dinner for two, excluding wine, tax, and tip, as follows:

$	$25 or less
$$	$26 to $40
$$$	$41 to $60
$$$$	More than $60
$$$$ +	More than $100

The key used for meals served is:

B	Breakfast
L	Lunch
D	Dinner

The key used for credit cards is:

AE	American Express
CB	Carte Blanche
DC	Diners' Club
MC	MasterCard
V	Visa

RESTAURANT INDEX

Washington, DC, has nearly 5,000 restaurants. The following represent a good cross section of every type of food and price range. Recommended dining in nearby Virginia and Maryland is also included. In addition to the usual ethnic categories and cross-references, I have included the following special listings for your convenience and pleasure: Afternoon Tea; Bars & Burgers; Breakfast/Brunch; Entertainment; Fireplaces; Fish & Seafood; Garden/Outdoor Dining; Inexpensive Lunch; Late Night/24 Hours; No-Smoking Areas; Rooms with a View; Soul/Southern; Steak. The restaurant may be found in the category listed in parentheses. A complete description of each restaurant follows the index.

The Supreme Court Building Cafeteria
(Cafeterias)
Sushi-Ko (Japanese)
Szechuan (Chinese)
Tabard Inn (Continental)
Taberna del Alabardero (Spanish)
Tandoor (Indian)
Taverna Cretekou (Greek)
Taverna the Greek Islands (Greek)
Terrace Cafe (Inexpensive Lunch)
Terrazza (Italian)
Thai Room (Thai)
Thai Taste (Thai)
Tiberio (Italian)
Tila's (American)
Timberlake's (Bars & Burgers)
Tony & Joe's Seafood Place (Fish & Seafood)
Tony Cheng's Mongolian (Chinese)
The Top O' the Town (Rooms with a View)
Tout Va Bien (French)
Trader Vic's (Polynesian)
Trattu (Italian)
Twenty-One Federal (American)
Twig's (Breakfast/Brunch)
Two Continents in the Sky (Rooms with a View)
Vie de France (Breakfast/Brunch)
Vietnam Georgetown (Vietnamese)
Vietnam Taste-Pho 79 (Vietnamese)
The View (Rooms with a View)
Vincenzo (Italian)
West End Cafe (American)
Willard Room (American)
Yannick's (French)
Yenching Palace (Chinese)
Yosaku (Japanese)
Zed's Ethiopian Cuisine (Ethiopian)

RESTAURANTS

Afghan

Bamiyan
3320 M Street, NW, upstairs; 338-1896. And 300 King Street, Alexandria, Va; (703) 548-9006. Also 808 King Street, Alexandria (called Hakim), (703) 683-9008. Authentic Afghan cuisine (described as a blend of Middle Eastern and Indian). Universally recommended as appetizer or main dish: aushak, scallion-filled dumplings topped with yogurt and meat sauce and sprinkled with mint. Other fascinating combos add up to a distinctive dining experience. Order à la carte. Reserve. MC, V. *OPEN 7 days 5.30pm-11pm.* $
Khyber Pass
2309 Calvert Street, NW, upstairs. 234-4632. Good lamb and beef kebabs. The aushak is as good here as at Bamiyan (former partners). Freshly baked Afghan bread. Reserve. AE, MC, V. *OPEN 7 days 5:30pm-11pm.* $

Afternoon Tea

Most of the deluxe hotels serve afternoon tea. The following are standouts.

Coeur de Lion
See American.
Four Seasons Hotel
2800 Pennsylvania Avenue, NW. 342-0444. The Garden Terrace provides a tranquil setting. Floor-to-ceiling windows, comfortable armchairs, and piano music from 4pm. Tea, finger sandwiches, assorted breads, biscuits, scones, Devonshire cream, and preserves. AE, CB, DC, MC, V. *Served 7 days 3pm-4:30pm.* $
Ritz Carlton Hotel
2100 Massachusetts Avenue, NW. 293-2100. In the Fairfax Bar with fireplaces for prix-fixe tea with finger sandwiches, scones, and pastries. AE, CB, DC, MC, V. *Served 7 days 2:30pm-5pm.* $
The Sheraton Carlton Hotel
923 16th Street, NW. 638-2626. The grand Palm Court is the setting for tea with finger sandwiches, fruit tarts, pastries. Everything à la carte. AE, CB, DC, MC, V. *Served Mon-Sat 2:30pm-5:30pm.* $

American

This category includes the so-called New American cooking as well as the traditional. (See also Bars & Burgers; Cafeterias; and Steak.)
Adirondacks
Union Station, 50 Massachusetts Avenue, NE. 682-1840. In the restored historic Presidential Suite of Union Station. California cuisine as showcased at owner Michael McCarty's restaurant in Santa Monica. Here chef Gethin Thomas highlights the natural flavors of quality seasonal ingredients such as duck with sun-dried cherries and ginger and pork loin with sherry vinegar. The space is spectacular and well used for private functions. Reserve. AE, CB, DC, MC, V. *L Mon-Fri noon-2pm. D 7 days 6pm-9pm.* $$$$+
America
Union Station, 50 Massachusetts Avenue, NE. 682-9555. Dine indoors, outdoors, upstairs, downstairs, or at the bar of this dramatic yet comfortable component of the Union Station renaissance. Extensive menu runs the gamut from fluffernutters to caviar, with hefty-sized offerings of sandwiches, salads, entrees, burgers, and gluttonous desserts. Service is earnest but slow. Good people-watching spot. No-smoking area. AE, CB, DC, MC, V. *OPEN Mon-Fri 11:30am-2am; Sat & Sun 11:30am-2:30am.* $
American Cafe
*227 Massachusetts Avenue, NE; 547-8500. And National Place, 13th & F Streets, NW, 626-0770. Also 1211 Wisconsin Avenue, NW, 944-9464; 5252 Wisconsin Avenue, NW, 363-5400; and Union Station, 50 Massachusetts Avenue, NE, 682-0937. A home-grown chain of open, light, airy, conveniently located outposts featuring a menu of fresh regional American basics—soups, salads, sandwiches. The chili is quite good and desserts are worth saving room for. Note: There's nothing grilled or fried so you won't find a burger. The youthful servers are inexperienced at best. *Outdoor dining in season. Reserve for 5 or more only. AE, CB, DC, MC, V. *OPEN Sun-Thurs*

1am-3am; Fri & Sat 11am-4am. *Sun champagne brunch 11am-4pm. Hours may vary at some locations; call for specifics. Happy Hour Monday to Friday from 4 to 7pm, in some locations.* $

Cheesecake Factory
Chevy Chase Pavilion, 5345 Wisconsin Avenue, NW. 364-0500. A multi-faceted transplant from Southern California boasts a 15-page menu featuring dishes with Asian, Latin, and traditional American orientations. In addition to the popular bar, there's a bakery cafe for drinks, snacks, and desserts, including 38 varieties of cheesecake. No-smoking area. No reservations. AE, MC, V. *OPEN Mon-Thurs 11:30am-11:30pm; Fri & Sat 11:30am-12:30am; Sun 10am-11pm. Downstairs bar OPEN one hour later than restaurant.* $$

City Cafe
2213 M Street, NW. 797-4860. In the West End, a sophisticated two-story urban cafe from restauranteur Nora Poullon. Here, as at Nora, the purity of what is fed to what is served is stressed (animals are raised in a "stress-free, pesticide-free environment"). Cafe traditionals—salads, pizza, grilled foods—get an original twist and in most cases are quite successful. Reserve. MC, V. *OPEN Mon-Fri noon-10pm; Sat 5pm-11pm. CLOSED Sun.* $$

Coeur de Lion
Henley Park Hotel, 926 Massachusetts Avenue, NW. 638-5200. The fine contemporary American fare served in this lovely downtown hotel is being discovered. The brick-walled dining room with atrium is a serene spot for lunch, dinner, or brunch. Afternoon tea is served in the Wilkes Room, an English-style parlor off the lobby. Reserve. AE, DC, MC, V. *B 7 days 7:30am-10:30am. L Mon-Sat 11:30am-2:30pm. D 7 days 6pm-10pm. Sun brunch 11:30am-2:30pm. Afternoon tea 7 days 4pm-6pm.* $$$$

Duke Zeibert's
Washington Square, 1050 Connecticut Avenue, NW, upstairs. 466-3730. Duke has long been in the business of thickening the waistlines of well-known and well-placed Washingtonians. In this vast, handsome new quarters with floor-to-ceiling windows and lovely dining terrace in season, they do business over meat and potatoes, and those New York-deli style favorites: chopped liver, matzo ball soup, and chicken in the pot. His crab cakes are as celebrated as his clientele and his heated rivalry with former manager, former heir apparent Mel Krupin. Reserve. AE, CB, DC, MC, V. Valet parking in the evening. *OPEN Mon-Sat 11:30am-11:30pm; Sun 5pm-11:30pm. CLOSED Sun in July & Aug.* $$$

Foggy Bottom Cafe
River Inn, 924 25th Street, NW. 338-8707. A small, lively spot in the Kennedy Center vicinity for nicely prepared, often inventive, always fresh food. A good Sunday brunch destination. Reserve, especially for pretheater. AE, CB, DC, MC, V. *B 7 days 7am-10am. L Mon-Fri 11:30am-2pm. D Tues-Sat 5:30pm-11:30pm; Sun & Mon 5:30pm-10:30pm. Sun brunch 10am-2pm.* $$

Hard Times Cafe & Hard Times Rockville
1404 King Street, Alexandria, Va; (703) 683-5340. And 1117 Nelson Street, Rockville, Md; (301) 294-9720. Chili is the mainstay—every which way—including two-, three-, four-, and five-way (chili, spaghetti, cheese, onions, and kidney beans); Cincinnati-, Texas-, and vegetarian-style, too. Coney Islands (smoked sausage, chili, cheese, and onions on a bun), sandwiches, and salads. C&W on the jukebox. Beer and wine only. No reservations. MC, V. *OPEN Sun-Thurs 11:30am-10pm; Fri & Sat 11:30am-11pm.* $

Herb's
Holiday Inn Governor House, 1615 Rhode Island Avenue, NW. 333-4372. An inviting spot downtown, best for lunch or brunch in the garden courtyard in season. Stick with the appetizers or try the sesame chicken salad, one of the better choices. No-smoking section. Reserve. AE, CB, DC, MC, V. *OPEN 7 days 7am-midnight.* $$

Lafitte
Hampshire Hotel, 1310 New Hampshire Avenue, NW. 296-7600. Well-seasoned and tasty Creole cooking in an attractive Art Deco setting. The trendy crowd dines on braised duck with Creole mustard; batter-dipped fried crayfish tails; Cajun popcorn; barbecued shrimp sauteed with fresh rosemary, black pepper, garlic, and a bit of Dixie beer; seafood gumbo; quail stuffed with andouille sausage; and don't miss the chocolate raspberry torte. Live piano music at lunch and dinner. Good breakfast/brunch spot for wonderfully seasoned eggs Benedict and Cajun hash browns. Jacket and tie required. *B Mon-Fri 7am-10am; Sat & Sun 8am-11am. L Mon-Fri 11am-2:30pm. D 7 days 5:30pm-10:30pm.* $$$

Lucie
Embassy Row Hotel, 2015 Massachusetts Avenue, NW. 939-4250. Handsome Art Deco-inspired hotel dining room where chef Jim Papovich turns out very fine contemporary American cuisine. The multi-course prix-fixe dinner is a fine introduction. Reserve. AE, CB, DC, MC, V. *B 7 days 7am-10am. L 7 days 11:30am-2pm. D Mon-Sat 6pm-10pm; Sun 6pm-9:30pm. Sun brunch 11:30am-2:30pm.* $$$$

McPherson Grill
950 15 Street, NW. 638-0950. Close to the White House, a sophisticated yet comfortable Art Deco dining room. A favorite of power brokers and anyone else who likes deftly prepared fresh grilled meats and fish among other treats on the daily changing menu of American regional fare, all in a congenial setting. Well-priced wine list. No-smoking area. Reserve. AE, DC, MC, V. *L Mon-Fri 11:30am-2:30pm. D Mon-Sat 5:30pm-10pm. CLOSED Sun.* $$$

Mel Krupin's
Washington Court Hotel, 525 New Jersey Avenue, NW. 879-7919. The power diner's room close to the Capitol. Best for the prime ribs and prime sirloin via New York, aged on the premises. Chopped liver, matzo ball soup, and

crab-stuffed flounder. Good wine list. Jackets required. Reserve for dinner only. AE, CB, DC, MC, V. *OPEN 7 days 6:30am-11pm.* $$$$

The Monocle on Capitol Hill

107 D Street, NE. 546-4488. Popular Victorian-era styled spot on the Hill favored by legislators and lobbyists for lunch; quieter "civilian" clientele at dinnertime. Menu focuses on regional seafood specialties; good homemade pastries. Fireplace in winter. Jacket requested. Reserve. AE, CB, DC, MC, V. *OPEN Mon-Fri 11:30am-midnight; Sat 6pm-11pm (except July & Aug). CLOSED Sun.* $$$

Morrison-Clark Inn

Massachusetts Avenue & 11th Street, NW. 898-1200. Modern American regional cuisine in a lovely turn-of-the-century setting complete with fireplaces. The freshest of ingredients, imaginatively combined, to produce some of the district's loveliest meals. Reserve. AE, CB, DC, MC, V. *L Tues-Fri 11:30am-2pm. D Tues-Sun 6pm-10pm. Sun brunch 11am-2pm.* $$$

Mrs. Simpson's

2915 Connecticut Avenue, NW. 332-8300. A small romantic restaurant named for the Mrs. Simpson who-would-be-queen-but-became-a-duchess. The frequently changing New American menu emphasizes fresh ingredients in dishes like lamb chops with oregano and Pommery mustard, calf's liver with mustard chive sauce, and for dessert, sour cream chocolate cake with heavy cream, lemon meringue mousse. Wonderful Sunday brunch. Reserve. AE, CB, DC, MC, V. *D Sun-Thurs 5:30pm-10pm; Fri & Sat 5:30pm-11pm. Sun brunch 10:30am-2:30pm.* $$

New Heights

2317 Calvert Street, NW, upstairs. 234-4110. Creative and original New American fare in a spacious, sparsely accented, and serene Art Deco setting one flight up overlooking Rock Creek Park. The menu changes with the availability of ingredients, desserts are beautiful as well as tempting; good wine list. Pleasant service. Outdoor cafe in season. No-smoking area. Reserve. AE, DC, MC, V. *OPEN Sun-Thurs 6pm-10:30pm; Fri & Sat 6pm- 11:30pm. Weekend brunch 11am-2:30pm.* $$

Nicholas

The Mayflower Hotel, 1127 Connecticut Avenue, NW. 347-8900. This small distinguished hotel dining room serves innovative New American cuisine in beautifully serene surroundings. Excellent value prix-fixe dinners. Reserve. AE, CB, DC, MC, V. *L Mon-Fri noon-2:30pm. D 7 days 6pm-10:30pm.* $$$

Nora

2132 Florida Avenue, NW. 462-5143. Washingtonians have long beat a path to this one for the homemade soups, breads, noodles, and desserts; the additive-free meat; the organic produce; and mainly for the refreshing point of view, which was way ahead of its time. Skylit dining area; outdoor cafe. MC, V. *OPEN Mon-Thurs 6pm-10pm; Fri & Sat 6pm-10:30pm.* $$$

O'Brien's Pit Barbecue

1314 East Gude Drive, Rockville, Md; (301) 340-8596. And 6820 Commerce Street, Springfield Va; (703) 569-7801. Also 7305 Waverly Street Bethesda, Md, (301) 654-9004. No-frills Formica and plastic. Cafeteria-style (table service at the Waverly Street location only). Famous with those in the know for serving the best barbecued ribs and brisket this side of the Lone Star State. Great chili, too. Draft beer in frosty plastic beer mugs. No reservations. MC, V. *OPEN Sun-Thurs 11am-10pm; Fri & Sat 11am-11pm.* $

Occidental/Occidental Grill

1475 Pennsylvania Avenue, NW. 783-1475. The name and the black-and-white photographs of the famous who had sipped and supped at the original (among them Justice Oliver Wendell Holmes, "Buffalo Bill" Cody, John Philip Sousa, John D. Rockefeller, and the Duke of Windsor) are all that remain of the old Occidental lost to the wrecker's ball. It was an important gathering place for political Washington and those in the press who covered it. (Indeed, an important piece of the Cuban missile crisis drama was played out there.) The new Occidental still attracts DC powermongers with its New American fare in a welcoming, re-created, turn-of-the-century atmosphere in both the downstairs grill, with its handsome bar, comfy banquettes, and more casual (and less costly) menu, and the more formal upstairs dining room (take the elevator). Separate menus in each change weekly. Reserve. AE, CB, DC, MC, V. Dining Room *L Mon-Fri 11:45am-2:30pm. D Mon-Sat 6pm-10:30pm.* $$$$ Grill *OPEN Mon-Sat 11:30am-11:30pm.* $$

Portner's

109 South St. Asaph Street, Alexandria, Va. (703) 683-1776. Basic American food in a converted firehouse with a skylit top floor. Elegant but inexpensive dining from the Hamburger Hamlet folks. More formal upstairs. Fireplace in winter; lots of singles year-round. Good brunch choice. Reserve. AE, DC, MC, V. *OPEN Mon-Thurs 11:30am-11pm; Fri & Sat 11:30am-midnight. Sun brunch 10:30am-11pm.* $

Prime Rib

2020 K Street, NW. 466-8811. Prime power brokers meat-and-potatoes choice is a luxurious setting—with prices to match (lower at lunch). Attractive expense-account, lobbyist, lawyer crowd. Excellent prime rib and steak; fried potato skins. Piano music in the bar Monday to Friday from 12:30pm to 2:30pm, and also Monday to Saturday from 7pm to 11pm. Interested interesting people at the bar in the pm. Free dinner parking. Jacket required. Reserve! AE, CB, DC, MC, V. *L Mon-Fri 11:30am-3pm. D Mon-Thurs 5pm-11pm; Fri & Sat 5pm-11:30pm. CLOSED Sun.* $$$

Red Hot & Blue

1600 Wilson Boulevard, Arlington, Va. (703) 276-7427. Authentic Memphis barbecue and pulled-pig sandwiches those are the reasons for the line. Expect to wait and you won't be disapooointed or resort to carryout. MC, V. *OPEN Mon-Thurs 11am-10pm; Fri 11am-11pm; Sat noon-11pm; Sun noon-9pm.* $

Red Sage
605 14th Street, NW. 638-4444. Chef/owner Mark Miller, a culinary master of contemporary southwestern cuisine (via the Coyote Cafe in Santa Fe), has spared no expense (rumors put it at $7 million) to bring Washington a mytho-logical Western wonderland. Santa Fe crafts-men are responsible for the artistry of the din-ing complex with chili bar, and downstairs, a lavish multi-level dining extravaganza. The boldly flavored chili-enlivened cooking is, at presstime, running a poor second to the dining room decor that has natives agog, but expec-tations are high that Mr. Miller's kitchen will in time also shine. In the meantime, with a menu and wine list that are fairly priced, you can af-ford to sit back and enjoy the lavish view. AE, CB, DC, MC, V. Reserve. Chili Bar *OPEN Mon-Thurs 11:30am-1:30am; Fri & Sat 11:30am-2:30am; Sun 5:30pm-1:30am. Dining Room L Mon-Sat 11:30am-2:15pm. D 7 days 5:30pm-10:30pm.* $$$

River Club
3223 K Street, NW. 333-8118. Quite good con-temporary American cuisine with cross-cultural accents, in a sophisticated Art Deco supper-club setting. To add to the retro feel, between the bar and the dining rooms is a well-used (into the wee hours) dance floor, where couples sway to a live contemporary jazz band from 7 to 10pm, followed by a d.j. spinning '50s to '90s music till 2am, on Saturday till 3am. To ease the pain on the pocket, the menu offers grazing opportuni-ties with appetizers and half-portions of main courses, and fine wines are available by the glass. Stylish singles ranging from the 20s to the 50s understandably love this place—it's such a swellegant, elegant party! No-smoking dining area. Valet parking. Jacket required for gentle-men. Reserve. AE, DC, MC, V. *D Mon-Thurs 5:30pm-11:30pm; Fri & Sat 5:30pm-midnight. Dancing Mon-Thurs till 2am; Fri & Sat till 3am.* $$$$

The 1789
1226 36th Street, NW. 965-1789. Near George-town University. Traditional elegance in a won-derfully restored two-story federal town house and a fine, albeit expensive, nouvelle American menu. Game dishes in season. Good wine list. Four charming dining rooms, one with fireplace ablaze in winter. Jackets required. Reserve. AE, CB, DC, MC, V. *OPEN Sun-Thurs 6pm-10pm; Fri & Sat 6pm-11pm.* $$$$

Tila's
2 Wisconsin Circle, Chevy Chase, Md. (301) 652-8452. Southwestern fare right above the Friendship Heights Metro station. The youngish crowd that gathers after work loves this huge place for the 95-foot bar, the salsa, the potent drinks, and the desserts. Keep it simple and you might even have a good meal. No-smoking area. Reserve. AE, MC, V. *OPEN Mon-Thurs 11:30am-*

10pm; Fri 11:30am-10:30pm; Sat noon-10:30pm; Sun noon- 9pm.* $$

Twenty-One Federal
1736 L Street, NW. 331-9771. In a few short years, this smart newcomer has made it to the top of nearly everyone's best list. Chef Bob Kinkead's modern American seasonal menu draws raves. Choices may include short ribs braised in zinfindel, spit-roasted chicken with cornbread dressing and Smithfield ham gravy, and linguini with salmon and scallops in black bean sauce. Though prices have recently been scaled back, the tab will still make a dent. Noisy at lunch. Reserve. AE, MC, V. *L Mon-Fri 11:30am-2:30pm. D Mon-Fri 5:30pm- 9:30pm; Sat 5:30pm-10pm.* $$$$

West End Cafe
One Washington Circle, NW. 293-5390. An at-tractive, sophisticated (albeit noisy) spot for New American cooking. Seasonal fresh ingredi-ents, grilled shiitake mushrooms, calf's liver with mustard-watercress sauce, duck with raspberry sauce. Wine bar. Light fare, too. Piano music adds romance. Reserve. AE, CB, DC, MC, V. *B Mon-Fri 7am-10am; Sat & Sun 8am-10:30am. L Mon-Fri 11:30am-2:30pm. D Mon-Thurs 6pm-11:30pm; Fri & Sat 6pm-midnight; Sun 6pm-1am. Weekend brunch 11:30am-3pm.* $$

Willard Room
Willard Hotel, 1401 Pennsylvania Avenue, NW. 637-7440. A sumptuous dining room located in the gorgeous restored turn-of-the-century hotel. Beautifully prepared and presented American fare; great choice for Sunday brunch 11am to 2pm. No-smoking section. Jacket and tie at din-ner. Valet parking. Reserve. AE, CB, DC, MC, V. *B Mon-Fri 7am-10am. L Mon-Fri 11:30am-3pm. D 7 days 6:30pm-10pm.* $$$$

Bars & Burgers

(See also NIGHTLIFE, Dance Bars & Clubs.*)*

Brickskeller
1523 22nd Street, NW. 293-1885. Friendly pop-ular pub with a reverence for the brew—over 400 imported and close to 200 domestic brands of beer are stocked. Upstairs: dart and game room; downstairs: restaurant. Backgammon, chess, video games, too. Dance floor, d.j. plays oldies and soft rock from 7:30pm to 2am, Friday and Saturday till 3am. Burgers, steaks, sandwiches, and pizza till 1am. AE, CB, DC, MC, V. *OPEN Mon-Thurs 11:30am-2am; Fri 11:30am-3am; Sat 6pm-3am; Sun 6pm-2am.* $

Clyde's of Georgetown
3236 M Street, NW. 333-9180. (Enter from M Street or through Georgetown Park.) Long re-nowned as a popular Georgetown institution, it still draws crowds, both local and out-of-towners—albeit the food has gone downhill as the prices have edged upward. Best rooms for dining: the lush Atrium or the pretty Omelette Room. Best time: brunch. Otherwise the best bites are the burgers and the very special fries. The bar draws a young singles' crowd. Shirts

with collars required. Reserve. AE, CB, DC, MC, V. *OPEN Mon-Thurs 11:30am-2am; Fri 11:30am-3am; Sat 9am-3am; Sun 9am-2am. Weekend brunch 10am-4pm; or the Omelette Room for breakfast Mon-Fri 7:30am-11:30am.* (*See also* Rooms with a View: Clyde's of Tysons Corner.) $ in the Omelette Room; $$ in the Atrium.

Hamburger Hamlet
3125 M Street, NW; 965-6970. And 5225 Wisconsin Avenue, NW; 244-2037. Also 10400 Old Georgetown Road, Bethesda, Md, (301) 897-5350. Popular home of the haute burger, and it's terrific with fries and onion rings. Also great omelettes, malts, and hot fudge cake. Kids like the crayons on the table. Outdoor dining (except M Street) and no-smoking sections at all locations. Wisconsin Avenue locale has a fireplace in the winter. Reserve for 10 or more. AE, DC, MC, V. *OPEN Sun-Thurs 11am-midnight; Fri & Sat 11am-1am.* $

The Hawk 'n Dove
329 Pennsylvania Avenue, SE. 543-3300. Popular Capitol Hill spot attracts congressional staffers at lunchtime because of its location and relaxed atmosphere. Burgers, salads, omelettes; three working gas fireplaces. Reserve for 20 or more only. AE, CB, DC, MC, V. *B & L Mon-Fri 10am-4pm. D 7 days 4pm-midnight. Brunch: Sat 10am-3:30pm; Sun 9:30am-3:30pm.* $

Houston's
1065 Wisconsin Avenue, NW. 338-7760. Also, *12256 Rockville Pike, Rockville, Md. (301) 468-3535. Great spot for burgers grilled over hickory and oak, chili, or ribs, but you have to like crowds, too. Expect a wait. No reservations. AE, MC, V. *OPEN Sun-Wed 11:30am-11pm; Thurs 11:30am-midnight; Fri & Sat 11:30am-1am. *OPEN Mon-Thurs 11:15am-11pm; Fri & Sat 11:15am-midnight; Sun 11am-10pm.* $

Jenkins Hill
223 Pennsylvania Avenue, SE. 544-6600. Great bar burgers and the best bloody Mary in town. Favorite of those who work on the Hill—lots of "shop talk." Sandwiches till 1am. No reservations. AE, CB, DC, MC, V. *OPEN Mon-Thurs 11:30am-12:30am; Fri 11:30am-3am; Sat 11am-3am; Sun 10:30am-midnight. Weekend brunch 10:30am-3pm.* $

J. Paul's
3218 M Street, NW. 333-3450. Popular (especially weekends) albeit noisy Georgetown watering hole. Raw bar, hickory burgers, smoked ribs, and sweet potato chips. AE, CB, DC, MC, V. *OPEN Mon-Thurs 11:30am- 2am; Fri & Sat 11:30am-3am; Sun 10:30am-2am.* $

Millie & Al's
2440 18th Street, NW. 387-8131. "It's been there forever"—Adams-Morgan's beloved neighborhood bar. Draft beer and a kind of raunchiness that is fast disappearing as old makes way for trendy. Italian food till 11:30pm. Great pizza; homemade rolls. A jukebox, of course. Reserve. No credit cards. *OPEN Mon-Thurs 4pm-2am; Fri & Sat noon-3am; Sun 2pm-2am.* $

Murphy's
713 King Street, Alexandria, Va. (703) 548-1717 A dark, inviting Irish tavern in Old Town for good pub grub (fish and chips, Irish stew, burgers), camaraderie, draft beer and ale, and a blazing fire in winter. Folk singing in the pm (*see also* NIGHTLIFE, Ethnic). Hale and hearty crew on the weekends. On Sunday you can have an Irish country breakfast (among other choices), with unlimited champagne, from 10am to 3pm. Reserve except Friday and Saturday nights. AE, CB, DC, MC, V. *OPEN 7 days 11am-midnight. Bar till 2am. Sun brunch 10am-3pm.* $

Old Ebbitt Grill
See Late Night/24 Hours.

Timberlake's
1726 Connecticut Avenue, NW. 483-2266. This friendly, noisy Dupont Circle neighborhood bar serves good burgers, sandwiches, salads, and brew to the locals. Well-stocked jukebox. No reservations. AE, CB, DC, MC, V. *OPEN Mon-Thurs 11:30am-2am; Fri 11:30am-3am; Sat 10:30am-3am; Sun 10:30am-2am. Weekend brunch 10:30am-3pm.* $

Breakfast /Brunch

Au Bon Pain
The Shops at National Place, 1331 Pennsylvania Avenue, NW. 638-9560. Flaky, fresh-baked croissants, wonderful cafe au lait, and fresh o.j. make this a good, inexpensive quick stop for breakfast for early risers or while waiting for the Shops to open at 10am (or if you're staying at the J.W. Marriott or the Willard). Self-service. No credit cards. *OPEN Mon-Fri 6:30am-8pm; Sat 7am-8pm; Sun 7am-5pm.* $

Market Lunch
Eastern Market, 7th & C Streets, SE. 547-8444. There can be no more colorful nor hectic spot for an early morning breakfast—especially on Saturday—than this no-frills outpost in the bustling Eastern Market. Blueberry pancakes; egg sandwiches; French custard toast with blueberries, strawberries, or peaches; grits; and more. (They also have some of the best crab cakes in DC.) It's self-service and the queue starts forming at 7:15am. Prices are low, plates are plastic, and the seating, inside and out, limited. No reservations. No credit cards. *B Tues-Sat 7:30am-10:55am. L Tues-Sat 11am-2:30pm.* $

Twig's
Capitol Hilton, 16th & K Streets, NW. 393-1000. A roll call here at breakfast, from 6:30am to 10:30am, would turn up more than a few congressmen. Specialties: pancakes with maple butter, bacon, and spiced apples; Delicate Thins, crepes rolled up with maple butter and syrup, with bacon or sausages on top. AE, CB, DC, MC, V. *OPEN 7 days 6:30am-10pm.* $$

Vie de France
The Esplanade, 1900 K Street, NW. 659-0055. *Le petit dejeuner.* Fresh-baked croissants and café. Sandwiches and nightly specials. Fresh sea trout every night. No-smoking section. Re-

serve for dinner. AE, MC, V. *OPEN Mon-Fri 7:30am-9pm. CLOSED Sat & Sun.* $

In addition to the above, the following also offer breakfast or Saturday and/or Sunday brunch:

American Cafe (American)
Aux Beaux Champs (French)
Bice (Italian)
Big Wong (Chinese)
Bistro Français (French)
Bombay Club (Indian)
Bombay Palace (Indian)
Chaucer's (Continental)
Chez Grand-mere (French)
Cities (Continental)
Coeur de Lion (American)
The Dandy (Rooms with a View)
Florida Avenue Grill (Soul/Southern)
Foggy Bottom Cafe (American)
The Guards (Steak)
Harrington Cafeteria (Cafeterias)
The Hawk 'n Dove (Bars & Burgers)
Herb's (American)
Hogate's (Fish & Seafood)
Jenkins Hill (Bars & Burgers)
Jockey Club (Continental)
Kalorama Cafe (Vegetarian)
Kramer Books & Afterwords, A Cafe (Late Night/24 Hours)
La Brasserie (French)
La Colline (French)
Lafitte (American)
Library of Congress Cafeteria (Cafeterias)
Lucie (American)
Morrison-Clark Inn (Americn)
Mrs. Simpson's (American)
Murphy's (Bars & Burgers)
National Museum of American History Cafeteria (Cafeterias)
New Heights (American)
Old Ebbitt Grill (Late Night/24 Hours)
Patent Pending (Cafeterias)
Patisserie Cafe Didier (Inexpensive Lunch)
Powerscourt (Continental)
Roof Terrace (Rooms with a View)
The Senate Cafeteria (Cafeterias)
Sequoia (Rooms with a View)
Sholl's Cafeteria (Cafeterias)
The Supreme Court Building Cafeteria (Cafeterias)
Szechuan (Chinese)
Tabard Inn (Continental)
Tandoor (Indian)
Taverna Cretekou (Greek)
Timberlake's (Bars & Burgers)
The View (Rooms with a View)
West End Cafe (American)
Willard Room (American)

Cafeterias

Washington is rich in that most democratic of dining institutions, the cafeteria. No preferential

treatment here. You take your tray and wait your turn.

Buffet/Cascades Cafe
National Gallery of Art, 6th Street & Constitution Avenue, NW, lower level. 347-9401. Boffo contemporary self-service cafeteria, the Buffet for hot and cold lunches, salad bar, and desserts; waitress-service Cascades for a changing menu of hot entrees, sandwiches, salads, beer, and wine. Sunny atrium area, cascading waterfall view. Buffet: No-smoking section; no reservations; no credit cards. Cascades: No reservations; AE, MC, V. *OPEN 7 days noon-5pm.* $

Harrington Cafeteria
Harrington Hotel, 428 11th Street, NW. 628-8140. This cafeteria serves over 2,000 people a day! Menu features the usual in cafeteria fare—open-face sandwiches, burgers, stews, roasts, desserts. Very inexpensive. *B & L 7 days 7:30am-2:30pm. D 7 days 5:30pm-8:30pm.* $

Library of Congress Cafeteria
Library of Congress, 1st Street & Independence Avenue, SE, 6th floor. 707-5000. Plain surroundings and fare at rock-bottom prices. Snack bar in basement Monday to Saturday from 7am to 4pm. No-smoking section. No credit cards. *OPEN (to the public) B Mon-Fri 9am-10:30am. L Mon-Fri 12:30pm-3pm. CLOSED Sat & Sun.* $

National Museum of American History Cafeteria
Constitution Avenue between 12th & 14th Streets, NW, lower level. 357-1300. Marriott Corporation-run self- service cafeteria. Sandwiches, burgers, and hot entrees—plus a view of the Washington Monument. No alcohol. No reservations. No credit cards. *B 7 days 10am-11am. L & D 7 days 11am-5pm.* $

Patent Pending
National Portrait Gallery/National Museum of Art, 9th & G Streets, NW. 357-1300. Small, charming restaurant for consistently good soups, salads, sandwiches, nitrate-free hot dogs, homemade pastries. Nice idea: half sandwich with salad or soup. In fine weather, outdoor dining in garden with sculpture and fountains. No-smoking section (the employees insisted on it). Beer and wine only. No reservations. No credit cards. *B Mon-Fri 10am-10:30am. L 7 days 11am-3pm.* $

The Senate Cafeteria
Dirksen Senate Office Building, Constitution Avenue & 1st Street, NE. 224-3121. It's fun to take the Senate subway from the Capitol Building and to have some Senate bean soup (menu mainstay since 1904) or Maryland crab cakes. Tables outdoors in the courtyard in summer. *OPEN 7 days to the public only before noon & after 1:30pm.* $

Sholl's Cafeteria
1990 K Street, NW. 296-3065. There are almost as many tourists here as on the Mall. But Washingtonians of every persuasion come, too (and have for over 50 years), for the high-quality food—fresh produce, lean meats, home-baked pastries and breads—at low prices. Good breakfast choice. No alcohol. No reservations. Yes,

usually a line—but it moves fast. No credit cards. B Mon-Sat 7am-10:30am. L Mon-Sat 11am-2:30pm. D Mon-Sat 4pm-8pm. CLOSED Sun. $

The Supreme Court Building Cafeteria
East Capitol & 1st Streets, NE. 479-3246. Small and modern, it serves the best Capitol Hill cafeteria food. Sandwiches, salads, hot entrees. No-smoking section. No alcohol. No reservations. No credit cards. B Mon-Fri 7:30am-10:30am. L Mon-Fri 11:30am-2pm. CLOSED Sat & Sun. $

Caribbean

Cafe Atlantico
1819 Columbia Road, NW. 575-2233. Tightly packed funky Adams-Morgan hot spot for well-seasoned Caribbean cooking. Cod fritters, shrimp and potato croquettes, yucca fritters, octopus fricasseed with red wine. Caribbean dancing starts one hour after the kitchen closes from Wednesday to Saturday. Reserve. AE, MC, V. OPEN Sun-Wed 5:30pm-11pm; Thurs-Sat 5:30pm-midnight. $$

Fish, Wings & Tings
2418 18th Street, NW. 234-0322. A small, bright, funky Adams-Morgan cafe for such Caribbean delights as jerk chicken, curried shrimp, grilled fish, goat, and ital stew—a fresh vegetable amalgam. Hectic, as those in the know wait for a free table (there's no coffee to linger over) and others wait for take-out. No alcoholic beverages. No reservations. AE only. OPEN Mon-Thurs noon-10pm; Fri & Sat noon-11pm. CLOSED Sun. $

Chinese

Big Wong
610 H Street, NW. 638-0116. This bustling basement Chinatown restaurant is a good bet for low-priced Cantonese cooking, especially in the wee hours. There's dim sum for lunch (11am to 3:30pm) and bargain specials. Good steamed and noodle dishes; Hong Kong specialties. Sunday is popular with families. Beer only. Takeout, too. Reserve. MC, V. OPEN 7 days 11am-3am.$

China Inn
631 H Street, NW. 842-0909. Order as the Chinese patrons do and you will have Cantonese food as it should be prepared. Recommended: "smoked" crabs, steamed chicken with Chinese sausage, spareribs with black bean sauce, whole poached sea bass, duck with watercress. Ask about "Banjo Duck" one day ahead. Reserve. AE, MC, V. OPEN Mon-Thurs 11am-1am; Fri & Sat 11am-2am; Sun 11am-1:30am. $$

Fortune
5900 Leesburg Pike, Falls Church, Va. (703) 998-8888. Fortunate indeed is the diner who comes here for the enticing dim sum served daily between 11am and 3pm. Steamed shrimp balls, stuffed duck's feet, shark-fin dumplings among so much more. Reserve. AE, DC, MC, V. OPEN Sun-Thurs 11am-11pm; Fri & Sat 11am- 2am. $

Hunan Chinatown
624 H Street. 783-5858. More formal and modern than most of its Chinatown neighbors, this competently run spot serves consistently fine dishes from a limited menu. Tea-smoked duck, stir-fried spinach with garlic, pan-fried dumplings, and still-in-the-shell shrimp coated with spicy salt. Reserve for large parties. AE, CB, DC, MC, V. OPEN Sun-Thurs 11am-11pm; Fri & Sat 11am-1am. $

Hunan Garden
2104 Viers Mill Road, Rockville, Md. (301) 340-6880. Excellent cuisine of Hunan province. Specialties are savory and hot. Wonderful tea lunch (tien hsin) on Saturday and Sunday. Reserve for 4 or more. AE, MC, V. OPEN 7 days 11am-10pm. $

Mr. Yung's
740 6th Street, NW. 628-1098. A range of seasonal, ofttimes exotic, authentic Cantonese dishes, in addition to the usuals, as well as dim sum (11am to 3pm), makes this an interesting and rewarding choice for Chinese fare in Chinatown. Standouts include whole fried shrimp steamed in a lotus leaf, soup with shredded roast duck, noodles and snow cabbage. Reserve. AE, MC, V. OPEN 7 days 11am-midnight. $

Szechuan
615 I Street, NW, upstairs. 393-0130. This Chinatown restaurant is still considered by many to serve the best Szechuan around. A very wide choice of beautifully seasoned Szechuan and Hunan dishes. Good choices are hot and sour soup, shredded duck Szechuan style, shredded chicken, shredded crispy beef, Szechuan shrimp balls, or the crisp whole fish (favored by the Chinese clientele). Weekend northern Chinese tea lunch (tien hsin), more interesting than usual dim sum. Free parking. Reserve for 4 or more only. AE, MC, V. OPEN Mon-Thurs 11am-11pm; Fri & Sat 11am-midnight; Sun 11am-10pm. Dim sum Sat & Sun 11am-2:30 pm. $$

Tony Cheng's Mongolian
619 H Street, NW. 842-8669. In this Chinatown eatery, choices are kept to a minimum. Choice #1: a charcoal-fired hot pot in which you cook your own meat, seafood, and vegetables (and here the staff is very helpful). Choice #2: a Mongolian barbecue—after you pick and season your raw vegetables and meat, hand them to the grill chef for cooking on the cast-iron grill. Both are all-you-can-eat choices that are too popular on weekends. Reserve. AE, MC, V. OPEN Sun-Thurs 11am-11pm; Fri & Sat 11 am-midnight. $

Yenching Palace
3524 Connecticut Avenue, NW. 362-8200. Long-established, large, and popular restaurant known for its very fine house specialties reflecting the cuisine of China's northern provinces. Their very special whole Peking duck requires no advance notice and is served with thin pancakes and an onion and bean sauce. Well known as the site of the secret meeting between U.S. and Soviet negotiators that successfully resolved the 1962 Cuban missile crisis. Free park-

ng. Reserve. AE, CB, DC, MC, V. *OPEN Sun-Thurs 11:30am-11pm; Fri & Sat 11:30am-11:30pm.* $$

Continental

Chaucer's
Canterbury Hotel, 1733 N Street, NW. 296-0665. Clubby wood-paneled and skylit hotel dining room on pretty residential Dupont Circle-area street. The creative menu is small but satisfying. Coarse rabbit pâté, oysters in beurre blanc with salmon caviar, roast duckling with blueberry compote. Desserts, made on premises, include a delicious crème brulee. A warming fireside in winter. Reserve. AE, CB, DC, MC, V. *B Mon-Fri 7am-10am; Sat & Sun 7:30am-10am. L Mon-Fri 11:30am-2pm. D 7 days 5:30pm-10pm. Sun brunch 11:30am-2:30pm.* $$

Cities
2424 18th Street, NW. 328-7194. Every few months this trendy Adams-Morgan bar/restaurant changes its decor, menu, and attitude to honor a different world city. It's a fascinating scene, especially late in the pm, and in the upstairs disco, from 10pm on into the wee hours. Great open-to-the street cafe and brunch with soft classical music accompaniment. Reserve. AE, CB, DC, MC, V *D Mon-Thurs 5pm-11pm; Fri & Sat 5pm- 11:30pm; Sun 5pm-10pm. Sun brunch 11am-3pm.* $$$

Jockey Club
Ritz Carlton Hotel, 2100 Massachusetts Avenue, NW. 659-8000. The Ritz Carlton Hotel's beautifully elegant restaurant and bar continues to attract the town's political heavyweights and visiting celebs (it was the Kennedys' favorite during the Camelot era). Good veal and seafood dishes, great cheesecake; impeccable service. Fireplace in the cocktail lounge. (*See also* NIGHTLIFE, Piano Bars: The Fairfax Bar.) Jacket and tie required. *B Mon-Fri 6:30am-11am; Sat & Sun 6:30am-11:30am. L Mon-Fri noon-2:30pm. D 7 days 6pm-11:30pm. Weekend brunch noon-2:30pm.* $$$$

Old Angler's Inn
10801 MacArthur Boulevard, Potomac, Md. (301) 365-2425. Idyllic and oh-so-romantic setting. Century-old country inn with a fireplace in the lounge in winter. Outdoor dining on a large flagstone terrace in summer. But neither the food nor the service match what nature and history have provided. Best for a drink and romance. Free parking. Jacket requested. Reserve. AE, CB, DC, MC, V. *L 7 days noon-2:30pm. D 7 days 6pm-10pm.* $$$$

Powerscourt
Phoenix Park Hotel, 520 North Capitol Street, 2nd floor. 737-3776. By virtue of location, good food, and inviting old-world setting, this hotel dining room is fast becoming a Capitol Hill meeting place. The continental cooking has an Irish lilt—steak is flamed in Irish whiskey, and there is potato soup on the menu (updated with lobster); for dessert, mousse flavored with Bailey's Irish

Cream. Valet parking in the evening. Reserve. AE, DC, MC, V. *B Mon-Sat 7am-10am. L Mon-Sat 11:30am-2:30pm. D Mon-Fri 5:30pm-10pm; Sat 5pm-10pm. CLOSED Sun.* $$

Tabard Inn
1739 N Street, NW. 833-2668. There's a small eccentric Dupont Circle hotel with a most welcoming fireplace lounge (great for drinks before or after dinner) and an interesting continental menu for casual dining in the informal skylit, low-ceilinged dining room, or in summer in the walled patio garden. Popular with local journalists and lovers who like to linger over lunch. Reserve for dinner only. MC, V. *B Mon-Fri 7am-10am; Sat & Sun 8am-10am. L Mon-Fri 11:30am-2:45pm. D Mon-Thurs 6pm-10:30pm; Fri & Sat 6pm-11pm; Sun 6pm-10pm. Weekend brunch 11am-2:45pm.* $$

Delicatessen

Carnegie Deli
Embassy Suites Hotel, 8517 Leesburg Pike, Vienna, Va. (703) 790-5001. A genuine New York deli in a hotel lobby in the suburbs—I guess Washingtonians didn't wish hard enough. Oversized sandwiches of deli meat are the signature. No-smoking section. No reservations. AE, CB, DC, MC, V. *OPEN Sun-Thurs 11am-10pm; Fri & Sat 11am-midnight.* $

Hofbergs
5240 Randolph Road, Rockville, Md; (301) 770-0777. And 3 Research Court, Rockville, Md, (301) 670-0024. Also 7913 Tuckerman Lane, Potomac, Md; (301) 299-1740. If you can't go to New York for a good deli sandwich, come here. Huge combos, good Reuben. Beer and wine only. No reservations. MC, V. *OPEN Mon-Thurs 8am-9pm; Fri & Sat 8am-10pm; Sun 8am-7pm.* $

Entertainment

The following feature live entertainment. (See also NIGHTLIFE *section of this book.)*

Anna Maria's (Italian)
Cafe Lautrec (French)
Charley's Crab (Fish & Seafood)
Duangrat's (Thai)
El Bodegon (Spanish)
El Caribe (Latin American)
Food for Thought (Vegetarian)
Four Seasons Hotel (Rooms with a View)
Hogate's (Fish & Seafood)
Joe & Mo's (Steak)
Kalorama Cafe (Vegetarian)
Katmandu (Indian)
Kramer Books & Afterwords, A Cafe
  (Late Night/24 Hours)
Lafitte (American)
Las Pampas (Latin American)
Market Inn (Fish & Seafood)
Murphy's (Bars & Burgers)
Old Europe Restaurant & Rathskeller

(German/Austrian)
Perry's (Late Night/24 Hours)
Prime Rib (American)
Red Sea (Ethiopian)
River Club (American)
Roof Terrace (Rooms with a View)
Taverna the Greek Islands (Greek)
Twenty-One Federal (American)
The View (Rooms with a View)
West End Cafe (American)

Ethiopian

Meskerem
2434 18th Street, NW. 462-4100. Not the usual dark den where people gather to eat with their hands. This is a skylit, sunny-yellow dining room and dining loft with the traditional messobs—coiled straw baskets that serve as tables. The so-called national dish of Ethiopia, kitfo, raw beef spiced with fresh green chilis; and the shrimp wat, a stew generously seasoned with their fiery berbere sauce, are great authentic choices. Sans silverware, the spongy crepelike bread, injera, is used to scoop up the food. Colorful dining experience. Reserve. AE, DC, MC, V. *OPEN Mon-Thurs 5pm-midnight; Fri-Sun noon-midnight.* $
Red Sea
2463 18th Street, NW. 483-5000. Lively casual eatery in Adams-Morgan for those ubiquitous Ethiopian stews—the mild alechas and the spicier wats. All authentically seasoned and all eaten with the fingers wrapped around the thin crepe-like bread. Friday and Saturday there's live native music. Reserve but expect a wait. AE, CB, DC, MC, V. *OPEN 7 days 11:30am-2am.* $
Zed's Ethiopian Cuisine
3318 M Street, NW. 333-4710. The traditional wats and injera stand out at this Ethiopian restaurant in Georgetown. Also good here the broiled short ribs, beef with collard greens, and chicken sauteed in butter and onions. Reserve for 4 or more only. AE, MC, V. *OPEN Sun-Thurs 11am-11pm; Fri & Sat 11am-2am.* $

Fireplaces

The following have working fireplaces when winter chills:

A. V. Ristorante (Italian)
Chaucer's (Continental)
Dominique's (French)
Geranio (Italian)
El Bodegon (Spanish)
Geranio (Italian)
The Guards (Steak)
Hamburger Hamlet (Bars & Burgers)
The Hawk 'n Dove (Bars & Burgers)
Iron Gate Inn (Middle Eastern)
L'Auberge Chez Francois (French)
La Chaumière (French)
The Monocle on Capitol Hill (American)
Morrison-Clark Inn (American)

Murphy's (Bars & Burgers)
Old Angler's Inn (Continental)
Petitto's (Italian)
Portner's (American)
Ritz Carlton Hotel (Afternoon Tea)
The 1789 (American)
Tabard Inn (Continental)
Tout Va Bien (French)

Fish & Seafood

Aux Fruits de Mer
1329 Wisconsin Avenue, NW. 333-2333. Busy Georgetown cafe for fresh Maine lobster (inexpensive). There's also much for those who don't like fish. Daily specials. All served with French fries and great ratatouille (evidence of its relationship to Au Pied de Cochon). No reservations. AE, CB, DC, MC, V. *OPEN Sun-Thurs 11:30am-2am; Fri & Sat 24 hours.* $
Charley's Crab
Connecticut Connection, 1101 Connecticut Avenue, NW, atrium level. 785-4505. Attractive stop (literally, it's at the Farragut North Metro station) for the nightly bouillabaisse. Great for people watching. Piano Monday to Friday from 5pm to 10pm. No-smoking section. Reserve. AE, CB, DC, MC, V. *L Mon-Fri 11:30am-3pm. D Mon-Fri 5pm-10pm; Sat 5pm-9:30pm. CLOSED Sun.* $$$
Crisfield
8012 Georgia Avenue, Silver Spring, Md; (301) 589-1306. And *Lee Plaza, 8606 Colesville Road, Silver Spring, Md; (301) 588-1572. This anachronism, with decor described as "early shower tile," is without doubt the area's best for consistently fresh, simply-prepared seafood. The French fries and cole slaw are worthy accompaniments. Line-ups are usual. Beer and wine only. Free dinner parking. No reservations. No credit cards. *OPEN Tues-Thurs 11am-10pm; Fri & Sat 11am-11:30pm; Sun noon-9:30pm. CLOSED Mon.* *Newer location, more attractive and inviting. AE, DC, MC, V. *OPEN Mon-Thurs 11am-10pm; Fri & Sat 11am- 11:30pm. CLOSED Sun.* $$
Dancing Crab
4611 Wisconsin Avenue, NW. 244-1882. Informal, no-frills setting for all-you-can-eat specials (Tuesday to Thursday from 7 to 10pm) of seafood: hard-shell crabs, steamed or raw clams, shrimp or raw oysters. Outdoor dining in season. Reservations accepted. AE, DC, MC, V. *OPEN Mon-Fri 11am-10:30pm; Sat noon-10:30pm; Sun 3pm-10:30pm.* $
Harvey's
1001 18th Street, NW. 833-1858. Lincoln is said to have eaten in this oldest of Washington restaurants (1858). Noted for the freshness of its fish, the strength of its drinks, and its fine wine list. Great crab cakes and gumbo. Free dinner parking. Jackets required; no jeans or athletic shoes. Reserve! AE, CB, DC, MC, V. *L Mon-Fri 11am-3pm. D 7 days 5:30pm-10pm. CLOSED Sun in summer.* $$$

Hogate's
800 Water Street, SW. (9th Street & Maine Avenue.) 484-6300. Cavernous seafood restaurant touted mainly because it overlooks the Potomac. The Mariner's Platter is a popular choice, so, too, the Sunday brunch. Pleasant spot for cocktails with a jazz accompaniment. Outdoors in season. AE, CB, DC, MC, V. OPEN Mon- Thurs 11am-11pm; Fri 11am-midnight; Sat noon-midnight; Sun 10:30am-1pm. Sun brunch 10:30am-2:30pm. $

Market Inn
200 E Street, SW. 554-2100. A dimly lit remnant of former bustling market area. Great New England clam chowder; crab Norfolk; live lobster tank. Stick with the straightforward. Reportedly favored by Supreme Court justices at lunch. Sidewalk cafe in summer. Piano and bass daily from noon to closing. Free parking. Reserve. AE, CB, DC, MC, V. OPEN Mon-Thurs 11am-11pm; Fri & Sat 10:30am-midnight; Sun 10:30am-11pm. $$

Sea Catch
Canal Square, 1054 31 Street, NW. 337-8855. Seafood cooking raised a notch above the traditional by chef Frederick Lange. In addition to the frequently changing menu, many consider this to be among the very best crab cakes in the area. Nice weather affords the opportunity to dine on the awning-covered deck overlooking the canal. No-smoking available. Reserve. AE, CB, DC, MC, V. L Mon-Fri noon-2:30pm. D Mon-Sat 6pm-10pm. CLOSED Sun. $$$

Tony & Joe's Seafood Place
Washington Harbor, 3000 K Street, NW. 944-4545. Located in Georgetown, on the Potomac, it's a popular spot mainly for it seasonal umbrella-shaded patio affording river-filled views while dining on seafood. The well- priced buffet brunch is your best bite, Sunday from 11am to 2pm. Reserve. AE, MC, V. OPEN Sun-Thurs 11am-11pm; Fri & Sat 11am-midnight. $$

Vincenzo
See Italian.

French

Aux Beaux Champs
Four Seasons Hotel, 2800 Pennylvania Avenue, NW. 342-0810. Luxurious serene setting and ambitious French cuisine in the deluxe Georgetown hostelry. The food is deftly prepared and presented, desserts are lavish, and the prices are expense-account. Excellent brunch venue. Free valet parking. Reserve. AE, CB, DC, MC, V. B Mon-Fri 7am-10am. L Mon-Fri noon-2:30pm. D Mon-Sat 6:30pm-10:30pm; Sun 6:30pm-10pm. Weekend brunch 11am-2:30pm. $$$$ +

Bistro Français
See Late Night/24 Hours.

Cafe Lautrec
2431 18th Street, NW. 265-6436. Casual (both the ambience and the service) French bistro in the lively Adams-Morgan area. Good daily specials. Highly recommended North African cous-

cous served Friday and Saturday. Good wine list. Sidewalk cafe in season. Live music nightly from 9:30pm. Reserve for 6 or more. D Sun-Thurs 5pm-2am; Fri & Sat 5pm-3am. $

Chez Grand-mere
3057 M Street, NW. 337-2436. Simple, French country-style cooking in a like ambience. Nice selection of meat, veal, and fish entrees; daily specials. Reasonable wine list. Reserve. AE, CB, DC, MC, V. L Mon-Fri 11:30am-3pm. D Sun-Thurs 5:30pm-11pm; Fri & Sat 5:30pm-midnight. Sun brunch 11:30am-5pm. $$

Dominique's
1900 Pennyvania Avenue, NW. 452-1126. Popular for elegant French food, attentive service, and a generally festive aura. Choices are always fresh, often unusual (rattlesnake), always beautifully prepared. Good lunch value and bargain pre- and posttheater prix-fixe meals. Fireplace in winter. Bastille Day race (see ANNUAL EVENTS, July: Bastille Day Waiters Race). Valet dinner parking. Jacket and tie requested. Reserve. AE, CB, DC, MC, V. OPEN 7 days 5:30pm-11:30pm. $$

Jean Louis
Watergate Hotel, 2650 Virginia Avenue, NW. 298-4488. Nouvelle, or as the famed chef Jean-Louis Palladin aptly calls it, "imaginative," cuisine. Interesting combinations, beautifully prepared and graciously served; alas, stratospherically priced. There is a great-value four-course prix-fixe dinner Monday to Saturday from 5:30pm to 6:30pm, but don't expect to linger over it. An exceptional wine list. Free parking. Reserve. AE, CB, DC, MC, V. OPEN Mon-Sat 5:30pm-10pm. CLOSED Sun. $$$$ +

L'Auberge Chez Francois
332 Springvale Road, Great Falls, Va. (703) 759-3800. Worth a drive to one of the best in the area and the most romantic. Deservedly popular for wonderful Alsatian specialties in a charming country inn setting. Fire ablaze in winter, outdoor tables on the lawn under the trees during the summer. Jacket and tie required. Reserve at least two weeks in advance (no reservations for garden). AE, DC, MC, V. OPEN Tues-Sat 5:30pm-9:30pm (last seating); Sun 2:30pm-7:45pm (last seating). CLOSED Mon. $$$

La Bergerie
218 North Lee Street, upstairs, Alexandria, Va. (703) 683-1007. Elegant Alexandria restaurant distinctive for its robust Basque specialties, as well as French classics: garbure Béarnaise, pipérade Basquaise, confit de canard, and the traditional seafood platter with garlic tomato sauce. Save room for dessert. Reserve. AE, CB, DC, MC, V. L Mon-Sat 11:30am-2:30pm. D Mon-Sat 6pm-9:30pm. $$$

La Brasserie
239 Massachusetts Avenue, NE. 546-9154. A favorite of Capitol Hill legislators and residents, for informal yet gracious dining at the indoor cafe or the umbrella-shaded outdoor sidewalk terrace. Authentic brasserie specialties include la bourride (fish soup), bouches (puff pastries with sea-

food or chicken), foie gras terrine, and a must: hot crème brulee for dessert. Reserve, especially on weekends. AE, DC, MC, V. *OPEN 7 days 11:30am-10pm. Sun brunch 11:30am-4pm.* $$$$

La Chaumière
2813 M Street, NW. 338-1784. Popular with Georgetowners. Old-fashioned rustic country inn ambience: beamed ceiling, massive central fireplace. In the cozy upstairs dining room, always satisfying French country food with a seafood emphasis. Algerian couscous on Wednesday; cassoulet on Thursday; homemade sausages; game in season. Gracious service. Reserve. AE, CB, DC, MC, V. *L Mon-Fri 11:30am-2:30pm. D Mon-Sat 5:30pm-11pm. CLOSED Sun.* $$$

La Colline
400 North Capitol Street, NW. 737-0400. This large, spare, contemporary French bistro is without doubt the best place to dine on Capitol Hill. The consistently fine yet most affordable menu boasts a selection of classic yet inventive French cooking. The menu changes daily with seasonal offerings and includes a few Cajun dishes. Wild mushroom terrine, gratin of fresh crayfish, lamb chops with green peppercorn butter, saute of lamb with garlic, shrimp Creole. Every Friday there's bouillabaisse and cassoulet. Quite good desserts and quality wines by the glass. Excellent value prix-fixe dinner. Breakfast here is popular with the congressional contingent. Reserve. AE, CB, DC, MC, V. *B Mon-Fri 7am-10am. L Mon-Fri 11:30am-3pm. D Mon-Sat 6pm-10pm. CLOSED Sun.* $$

La Fourchette
2429 18th Street, NW. 332-3077. Good country French cooking at reasonable prices distinguishes this charming rustic little bistro in Adams-Morgan. Meat and fish specials nightly. Must finale: Crêpes Belle Escale. Limited but good wine list. Sidewalk cafe for interesting multi-cultural people watching. Reserve. AE, CB, DC, MC, V. *L Mon-Fri 11:30am-2:30pm. D Mon-Fri 4pm-10:30pm; Sat 4pm-11pm; Sun 4pm-10pm.* $

La Maree
1919 I Street, NW. 659-4447. Cozy dining room on two levels of a town house distinguish this charmer—perfect for a quiet lunch or a romantic pretheater repast. The focus is on seafood; best are the daily specials and the bouillabaisse (available daily). Also seasonal game dishes; excellent pastries. Good buy prix-fixe dinner. Jacket requested. Free parking at 1919 Pennsylvania Avenue, NW. Reserve. AE, DC, MC, V. *L Mon-Fri 11:30am-2pm. D Mon-Thur 5:30pm-9:30pm, Fri & Sat 5:30pm-10pm.* $$$

Lavandou
3321 Connecticut Avenue. 966-3003. The menu of this cozy storefront in Cleveland Park is an exciting culinary celebration of the Provençal region of France. The menu features hearty soups and an emphasis on fresh fish and grilled meats, all robustly seasoned. Reserve. AE, MC, V.

OPEN Sun & Mon 5pm-10pm; Tues- Thu 11:30am-10pm; Fri 11:30am-11pm; Sat 5pm 11pm. $

Le Caprice
2348 Wisconsin Avenue, NW. 337-3394. Those in the know—and those who are known—easil fill the 40 seats of this intimate modest two-stor town house French bistro—one of the best i town. The former chef of the French embass wears the toque here and the seasonal menu i always a treat. Updated French classics beaut fully presented: oyster-stuffed ravioli with lobste sauce, roast quail nesting in fried potatoes braised veal shank niçoise, duck breast gar nished with fresh fruit, chicken and wild mush rooms baked in pastry. There are always tw daily specials and an excellent value three course prix-fixe lunch and dinner. Don't skip dessert. Reserve. AE, CB, DC, MC, V. *L Tues-F 11:45am-2pm. D Tues-Sun 6pm-9:30pm CLOSED Mon.* $$$

Le Gaulois
1106 King Street, Alexandria, Va. (703) 739 9494. The original site was lost to the wrecker' ball, but Alexandria has gained one of the bes for *cuisine bourgeoise.* In a two-story rustic set ting, Bernard Baudrand continues the tradition of outstanding dining at unbeatable prices Bargain-priced Mini Cafe at lunch. Reserve AE, DC, MC, V. *OPEN Mon-Thurs 11:30am 10:30pm; Fri & Sat 11:30am-11pm. CLOSED Sun.* $$

Le Lion d'Or
1150 Connecticut Avenue, NW. 296-7972. Outstanding is the word most often used. For cuisine classical and nouvelle, it's Washington's consistently best by far. Great well-priced wine list. Wonderful soufflés. Free parking. Reserve AE, CB, DC, MC, V. *L Mon-Fri noon-2pm. D Mon-Sat 6pm-10pm. CLOSED Sun.* $$$$

Maison Blanche
1725 F Street, NW. 842-0070 or -2263. Wonderful elegant French dining within walking distance of that other White House. Heir apparent to now-defunct San Souci. (Check with Art Buchwald on that point.) Moderately priced pre- and posttheater menu Monday to Saturday from 6pm to 7pm and 10pm to 11pm. Lunchtime attracts heavyweights including Executive Branch staffers and journalists. Free valet parking at dinner. Reserve! AE, CB, DC, MC, V. *L Mon-Fri 11:45am-2:30pm. D Mon-Sat 6pm-11pm. CLOSED Sun.* $$$$

Patisserie Cafe Didier
See Inexpensive Lunch.

Tout Va Bien
1063 31st Street, NW. 965-1212. Comfortable intimate Georgetown bistro for good onion soup, pâté, and other simple French fare. Charming setting with fireplace in winter; greenhouselike garden room year-round. Good value. Wine and beer only. Reserve. AE, MC, V. *L Mon-Sat 11:30am-2:30pm. D Mon-Thurs 5:30pm-10pm; Fri & Sat 5:30pm-11:30pm; Sun 5:30pm-11pm.* $$

Yannick's
Radisson Plaza Hotel, 5000 Seminary Road, Alexandria, Va. (703) 824-0297. Famed chef Yannick Cam, who presided over Le Pavillon until its demise, now performs his culinary magic across the Potomac. Many of his imaginative signature dishes are available on the à la carte menu; there is also a choice of a four-course or a six-course tasting menu at dinner. Less pricey than his former venue, but still up there. Reserve. AE, CB, MC, V. *L Mon-Fri 11:30am-2pm. D Mon-Thurs 6pm-10pm; Fri & Sat 5:30pm-10:30pm.* $$$$

Garden/Outdoor Dining

The following have outdoor dining facilities in season:

Adams-Morgan Spaghetti Garden (Italian)
America (American)
American Cafe (American)
Armand's Chicago Pizzeria (Italian)
A. V. Ristorante (Italian)
Bangkok Gourmet (Thai)
Booeymonger (Late Night/24 Hours)
Cafe Lautrec (French)
Cafe Splendide (German/Austrian)
Calvert Cafe (Middle Eastern)
C. F. Folks (Inexpensive Lunch)
Dancing Crab (Fish & Seafood)
Duke Zeibert's (American)
Four Seasons Hotel (Rooms with a View)
Gary's (Steak)
Hamburger Hamlet (Bars & Burgers)
Herb's (American)
Hogate's (Fish & Seafood)
Iron Gate Inn (Middle Eastern)
Kalorama Cafe (Vegetarian)
Kramer Books & Afterwords, A Cafe
  (Late Night/24 Hours)
L'Auberge Chez Francois (French)
La Brasserie (French)
La Fonda (Mexican)
La Fourchette (French)
Lauriol Plaza (Spanish)
Market Inn (Fish & Seafood)
Market Lunch (Breakfast/Brunch)
New Heights (American)
Nora (American)
Notte Luna (Italian)
Old Angler's Inn (Continental)
Patent Pending (Cafeterias)
Petitto's (Italian)
Sea Catch (Fish & Seafood)
The Senate Cafeteria (Cafeterias)
Sequoia (Rooms with a View)
Sfuzzi (Italian)
Sky Terrace Lounge (Rooms with a View)
Star of Siam (Thai)
Tabard Inn (Continental)
Taverna Cretekou (Greek)
Thai Taste (Thai)
The Top O' the Town (Rooms with a View)
Vietnam Georgetown (Vietnamese)
Yosaku (Japanese)

German/Austrian

Cafe Splendide
1521 Connecticut Avenue, NW. 328-1503. In a European tearoom ambience, good value, satisfying Austrian fare. Recommended: the salad splendide, homemade soups, and the crusty Austrian burger, seasoned with green pepper; wonderful omelettes and glorious homemade pastries, of course. Outdoor cafe in season. Reserve. No credit cards. *OPEN Tues-Sun 11am-11:30pm. CLOSED Mon.* $

Old Europe Restaurant & Rathskeller
2434 Wisconsin Avenue, NW. 333-7600. The city's oldest (1948) and best for authentic, well-prepared, hearty German food: schnitzel, sauerbraten, liver dumplings. Game in season. German beer, good selection of Rhine wines. Entertainment nightly. Seasonal festivals galore. Free parking. Reserve. AE, CB, DC, MC, V. *L Mon-Sat 11:30am-3pm. D Mon-Thurs 5pm-10pm; Fri & Sat 5pm-11pm; Sun 4pm-10pm.* $$

Greek

Taverna Cretekou
818 King Street, Alexandria, Va. (703) 548-8688. Whitewashed, Greek Island-pretty with a brick-walled, flower-ringed, awning-shaded patio garden in summer. Nicely prepared and served traditionals; terrific leisurely brunch spot. Reserve. AE, CB, DC, MC, V. *L Tues-Sat 11:30am-2:30pm. D Tues-Sun 5pm-10:30pm. Sun brunch 11am-3pm. CLOSED Mon.* $$

Taverna the Greek Islands
307 Pennsylvania Avenue, SE. 547-8360. Quite good Greek food at this Capitol Hill restaurant. Specialty: exohiko (lamb, olives, and cheese wrapped in filo pastry). Greek wines by the glass. Live bouzouki music on occasion. No-smoking area. Reserve for dinner only. AE, DC, MC, V. *OPEN Mon-Sat 11am-midnight; Sun 4pm-midnight.* $$

Indian

Aditi
3299 M Street, NW. 625-6825. Small, modern, highly-thought-of Indian restaurant where olive oil is utilized in the cooking instead of the usual clarified butter. Consistent standouts include stir-fried lamb, vegetarian "meatballs," wonderful pilafs. Try the budget-priced multi-course feast. Reserve. AE, DC, MC, V. *L Tues-Sun 11:30am-2:30pm. D Sun-Thurs 5:30pm-10pm; Fri & Sat 5:30pm-10:30pm.* $

Bombay Club
815 Connecticut Avenue, NW. 659-3727. British Raj atmosphere, just a short walk from the White House. The elegant setting and the light well-seasoned cuisine has scores of fans. Recommended: the broiled scallops; the Bombay Thali, a vegetarian assortment; marinated salmon fillet roasted in the tandoor oven; and the yogurt-marinated baby lamb chops. Champagne

brunch is served on Sunday. Reserve. AE, MC, V. *L Mon-Fri 11:30am-2:30pm. D Mon-Thurs 6pm-10:30pm; Fri & Sat 6pm-11pm. Sun brunch 11:30am-2:30pm.* $$$

Bombay Palace
1835 K Street, NW. 331-0111. Attractive link in a national chain of upscale Indian dining rooms. Those who like it hot love this spot. Recommended: the lamb or chicken pilaf, the tandoor prawns, lamb vindaloo, and the vegetable curries. Prix-fixe menu; bargain weekend brunch. Reserve. AE, CB, DC, MC, V. *L Mon-Fri noon-3pm. D 7 days 5:30pm-10pm. Weekend brunch noon-3pm.* $$$

Katmandu
1800 Connecticut Avenue, NW. 483-6470. An interesting albeit tightly packed choice for the cuisines of Nepal and Kashmir. The emphasis is on charcoal-grilled meats and shish kebabs. Very good Indian curries, too. Live Indian music occasionally. No-smoking section. Reserve. AE, CB, DC, MC, V. *L 7 days 11:30am-2:30pm. D Sun-Thurs 5:30pm-11pm; Fri & Sat 5:30pm-11:30pm.* $$

Madurai
3318 M Street, NW, upstairs. 333-0997. In Georgetown, the vegetarian cuisine of southern India. An interesting blending of spices by the kitchen's sure hand produces a fine array of dishes each with its own unique taste. Recommended are the made-to-order breads (paratha and poori), the fragrant navatan with nine vegetables, and the mushroom curry with tomatoes and onions. On Sunday there's a great value prix-fixe all-you-can-eat buffet. Skip the desserts. No-smoking area. Reserve. AE, CB, DC, MC, V. *L Mon-Sat noon-2:30pm; Sun noon-4pm. D 7 days 5pm-10pm.* $

Tandoor
3316 M Street, NW; 333-3376. And 2623 Connecticut Avenue, NW; 483-1115. Also 719 King Street, Alexandria, Va, (703) 548-1739. On the first floor of this fine two-story Indian restaurant is the in-view clay tandoor oven, out of which come the sizzling tandoori specialties of the house. The murgh tandoori is a standout; so are the breads. If you like your food highly seasoned, speak up—curries are custom-spiced here. Reserve. AE, CB, DC, MC, V. *L 7 days 11:30am-2:30pm. D 7 days 5:30pm-10:30pm.* $$

Inexpensive Lunch

Most of the museums offer opportunities to have a snack without spending a great deal of money. (See also Bars & Burgers and Cafeterias.)

C. F. Folks
1225 19th Street, NW. 293-0162. A casual no-frills diner for lunch only—but what a lunch it is. Hearty sandwiches and a small selection of modestly priced specials, featuring a different cuisine daily, are listed on a blackboard. Monday there is Cajun jambalaya and fried catfish; Tuesday, Mexican dishes are featured; Wednesday is the day for Indian and Italian; Thursday

and Friday you dine on seafood. Crowds are the norm. Outdoor tables in season. No alcohol. No reservations. No credit cards. *OPEN Mon-Fri 11:45am-3pm. CLOSED Sat & Sun.* $

Dutch Treat
1710 L Street, NW; 296-3219. And *1901 L Street, NW; 223-9420. For lunching alfresco—a treat from Holland—broodje haus. Half or whole sandwiches on broodje rolls, smoked salmon, chicken salad, ham, roast beef, and carrot salad. All to go and so inexpensive you won't have to go Dutch treat. *Steam table for hot entrees and sandwiches to go. Catering, too. No credit cards. *OPEN Mon-Fri 7:30am-4pm; Sat (Oct-May) 10am-3pm. CLOSED Sun.* $

Kramer Books & Afterwords, A Cafe
See Late Night/24 Hours.

Patisserie Cafe Didier
3206 Grace Street, NW. 342-9083. Tucked away on a short street behind Georgetown Park is this tiny 10- table jewel of a French tearoom/bakery. Stop in for a continental breakfast of flaky croissant (the best this side of Paris) or a light lunch sandwich, soup, salad, or quiche, or just go anytime for nothing short of the best pastries in town. P.S.: The hot chocolate is made with *real* chocolate. No reservations. No credit cards. *OPEN Tues-Sat 8am-7pm; Sun 8am-6pm. CLOSED Mon.* $

Terrace Cafe
National Gallery of Art, 6th Street & Constitution Avenue, NW, 4th level. 842-6025. More subdued than its lower-level cafeteria counterpart. For complete meals or dessert and coffee. Overlooks the Mall. Beer and wine only. No reservations. AE, MC, V. *OPEN Mon-Sat 11:30am-4pm; Sun noon-4pm.* $

Italian

Adams-Morgan Spaghetti Garden
2317 18th Street, NW. 265-6665. Home-style Italian cooking of the value-for-volume variety. It's hearty, filling, and inexpensive. Good family spot; children's portions. Small but very special menu. All pasta portions are cooked to order al dente. Wonderful roof garden in season. No reservations. AE, MC, V. *OPEN 7 days noon-midnight.* $

Anna Maria's
1737 Connecticut Avenue, NW. 667-1444. Attractive, cheerful downtown Italian restaurant. Best are the homemade pastas. Live entertainment, mostly jazz, Monday to Friday from 8pm to 1am; Saturday from 10pm to 3am; and Sunday from 8pm to 1am. Reserve. AE, CB, DC, MC, V. *OPEN Mon-Thurs 11am-1am; Fri 11am- 3pm; Sat 5pm-3am; Sun 5pm-1am.* $$

Armand's Chicago Pizzeria
4231 Wisconsin Avenue, NW; 686-9450. Express delivery, 363-5500. And *111 King Street, Alexandria, Va; (703) 683-0313. The first in DC with Chicago-style deep-dish pizza. Collegiate crowds. Outdoors, too. No reservations. AE, CB, DC, MC, V. *OPEN Mon-Thurs 11:30am-*

midnight; Fri & Sat 11:30am-2am; Sun noon-midnight. *Sun-Thurs 11am-11pm; Fri & Sat 11am-1am. $

A. V. Ristorante
607 New York Avenue, NW. 737-0550. Popular, eccentric, and longtime (over 30 years, and little has changed) restaurant with few frills for wonderfully hearty Italian fare. Good thin-crust pizza, bargain Italian wines. Fireplace in winter, large (seats 60) garden in summer. Reserve for 10 or more. AE, CB, DC, MC, V. OPEN Mon-Fri 11:30am-11pm; Sat 5pm-midnight. CLOSED Sun. $$

Bice
601 Pennsylvania Avenue, NW. 638-2423. Everyone's favorite new restaurant is this upscale trattoria via Milano (the original was founded in Tuscany in 1926). Wonderful pastas, risottos, grilled dishes and game in season. It's a wonderful dolce vita addition to the neighborhood. Reserve. AE, DC, MC, V. L Mon-Fri 11:30am-2:30pm. D Mon-Sat 5:30pm-midnight; Sun 5:30pm-10:30pm. Sun brunch 11:30am-2pm. $$$$

De Carlo
4822 Yuma Street, NW. 363-4220. Huge family-oriented neighborhood Italian restaurant. Everything made on premises, from pasta to pastries. Reserve. AE, MC, V. L Mon-Fri 11:30am-2:30pm. D Mon-Sun 5:30pm-10pm. $

Filomena
1063 Wisconsin Avenue, NW. 338-8800. This dark and bustling, tightly packed, moderately priced Italian trattoria, known for its enticing pasta dishes, is a popular Georgetown lunch and dinner spot. Don't stray from the pasta; fill up on salad, dessert, and the anisette or amaretto liqueurs proffered free to each table after dinner. Jacket requested. Reserve. AE, MC, V. OPEN Mon & Tues 5pm-11pm; Wed-Sun 11:30am-11pm. $$

Fio's
3636 16th Street, NW. 667-3040. A throwback—from the decor to the prices to the records in the jukebox. The unpretentious home-style Southern Italian food is very good and equally cheap. Daily specials of roast duck, rabbit, and veal supplement the regular pizza, pasta, and vegetable menu. The waitresses are friendly if not fast. Note: Some food is cooked without salt for sodium watchers. Reserve for 5 or more only. AE, CB, DC, MC, V. OPEN Tues-Sun 5pm-11pm. CLOSED Mon. $

Galileo
1110 21st Street, NW. 293-7191. This longtime foodies "in" spot, in an expansive new home, is highly recommended for the authentic and varied Northern Italian dishes created by chef Roberto Donna. The unusual menu changes twice daily, as does the list of wines available. Choices might include risotto with porcini mushrooms, or a pumpkin puree, homemade noodles with crab meat, leg of lamb roasted with rosemary, grilled shrimp still in the shells; game in season. Wonderful olive and herb bread. Reserve! AE, CB,

DC, MC, V. L Mon-Fri noon-2:30pm. D Mon-Thurs 5:30pm-10pm; Fri & Sat 5pm-10:30pm; Sun 5pm-10pm. $$$

Geppetto
2917 M Street, NW; 333-2602. And *10257 Old Georgetown Road, Bethesda, Md; (301) 493-9230. There are daily specials and sandwiches in this cacophonous cafe, but almost everyone comes for the white pizza, considered by many the best in town. For dessert, the creamy ricotta cheese pie. A nice place to take the kids. No reservations. AE, CB, DC, MC, V. OPEN Mon-Thurs noon-11pm; Fri & Sat noon-1am; Sun 4pm-11pm. *OPEN Mon-Thurs 11:30am-9:30pm; Fri & Sat 11:30am-11pm; Sun noon-9pm. $

Geranio
724 King Street, Alexandria, Va. (703) 548-0088. Lovely welcoming Italian restaurant of note. Simple preparations: the salads, especially the tomato and mozzarella with olive oil and basil (seasonal); the soups and the pastas (half portions available) are all freshly made. Daily specials, always a treat. Fireplace in winter. Reserve. AE, MC, V. L Mon-Fri 11:30am-2:30pm. D Mon-Sun 6pm-10:30pm. $$

I Matti
2436 18th Street, NW. 462-8844. Roberto Donna's (of Galileo fame) inviting and lively Adams-Morgan trattoria. The frequently changing menu features rustic Italian specialties including delicious thin-crust pizzas, wonderful antipasti, grilled fish, and more. Impressive wine list. Reserve! AE, DC, MC, V. OPEN Mon-Thurs noon-11pm; Fri & Sat noon-11:30pm; Sun 11:30am-10pm. $$

I Ricchi
1220 19th Street, NW. 835-0459. Opened in 1989, this handsome, high-ceilinged hot spot has become the most recommended Italian restaurant in the district—giving Galileo a run for your money. Tuscan specialties predominate, with meat and poultry, including game, grilled over a wood fire. Free valet parking after 6pm. Reserve! AE, DC, MC, V. L Mon-Fri 11:30am-2:30pm. D Mon-Thurs 5:30pm-10:15pm; Fri & Sat 5:30pm- 10:30pm. CLOSED Sun. $$$$

Notte Luna
809 15th Street, NW. 408-9500. A lively stylish Italian cafe for satisfying pizzas, pastas, and other boutique Italian fare. Great desserts, noisy bar; sidewalk dining in season. No-smoking area. Reserve. AE, MC, V. OPEN Mon-Fri 11am-11pm; Sat & Sun 5pm-midnight. $$

Obelisk
2029 O Street, NW. 872-1180. In spare but elegant surroundings, the refined Italian cooking of chef Peter Pustan is garnering bravos. The limited but interesting menu changes nightly. Feast on wonderful antipasti, carpaccio, pastas, and grilled main courses, all utilizing the freshest seasonal ingredients. For dessert, don't pass up the poached fruit with zabaglione. Reserve! MC, V. OPEN Mon-Sat 6pm-10pm. CLOSED Sun. $$$$

Odeon Cafe

1714 Connecticut Avenue, NW. 328-6228. Trendy, Art Deco-detailed two-story dining room and balcony that overlooks the noisy scene in the pm (it's a popular neighborhood lunch spot). Italian boutique foods such as calamari or carpaccio to start, or a half portion of pasta. Good main course choices: the great tricolor pasta with bolognese or the spicy fettuccine campagna. Best of the pizzas: the bianca—with sausage, garlic, and fontina—and the Margherita—with tomato, mozzarella, and basil. Also available, grilled chicken and shrimp. Reserve. AE, MC, V. *OPEN Mon-Thurs 11:30am-10:30pm; Fri 11:30am-11:30pm; Sat & Sun 5pm-11:30pm.* $$

Paolo's

1303 Wisconsin Avenue, NW. 333-7353. A bright bustling informal Georgetown cafe for zesty inexpensive Italian fare—including pizzas from a wood-burning oven, with a choice of trendy or traditional toppings. Generous portions of pasta and salads, too. During the week the kitchen closes at midnight, but pizza is available till 1am; Friday & Saturday the full menu till 12:30am and pizza until 2am. No reservations, so expect a wait to get in on the party. AE, CB, MC, V. *OPEN Mon-Thurs 11:30am-2am; Fri & Sat 11am-3am; Sun 11am-2am.* $$

Paper Moon

See Late Night/24 Hours.

Petitto's

2653 Connecticut Avenue, NW. 667-5350. The specialty is pasta, well prepared in a variety of often distinctive dishes (half portions available). Wonderful antipasto. Four fireplaces ablaze in winter; outdoor cafe for summer. Good choice. Private dining room for parties of 10 to 14. Reserve! AE, CB, DC, MC, V. *L Mon-Fri 11:30am-2:30pm. D Mon-Sat 6pm-10:30pm. CLOSED Sun except in summer.* $$

Pines of Rome

4709 Hampden Lane, Bethesda, Md. (301) 657-8775. Extremely popular, highly informal neighborhood trattoria. Hearty Italian home cooking from all regions; bargain-priced family-style dinners; good white pizza and great cannoli for dessert. Beer and wine only. No reservations. AE, CB, DC, MC, V. *OPEN Sun & Mon 11:30am-10pm; Tues-Thurs 11:30am-11pm; Fri & Sat 11:30am-11:30pm.* $$

Pizzeria Uno

3211 M Street, NW; 965-6333. And at Union Station. A slice of Chicago comes to DC. From the windy city comes the famed, filling, deep-dish pizza. Also sandwiches and salads. No reservations. Takeout, too. AE, MC, V. *OPEN Sun-Thurs 11am-1am; Fri & Sat 11am-2am.* $

Primi Piatti

2013 I Street, NW. 223-3600. Also at Tysons Corner. Enormous post-modern Italian trattoria featuring the simple yet newly chic modern Italian fare that is now all the rage: homemade breads, risottos, polenta, carpaccio, pizza from a wood-burning oven, Tuscan-style grilled and roasted dishes and, of course, tiramisu for dessert. It's

hectic, noisy, and satisfying (if you don't mind the latter). No reservations. AE, CB, DC, MC, V. *L Mon-Fri 11:30am-2:30pm. D Mon-Sat 5:30pm-10:30pm.* $$$

Sfuzzi

Union Station, 50 Massachusetts Avenue, NE. 842-4141. The theatrical setting is unparalleled not so the food, in this postmodern Italian cafe (albeit a part of a Dallas-based chain). The pizza, pasta, and grilled dishes are secondary to the noisy "scene," and when the bill comes you might be tempted to make one. Choice of downstairs cafe or upstairs dining room. Outdoors in season. No-smoking area. Reserve. *L Mon & Tues 11:30am-2:30pm; Wed-Sat 11:30am-5:30pm. D Sun-Thurs 5:30pm-10pm; Fri & Sat 5:30pm-midnight. Sun brunch 11am-3pm.* $$$$

Terrazza

710 King Street, Alexandria, Va. (703) 683-6900. Deservedly revered formal Old Town restaurant for wonderful but pricey Northern Italian dining. (Same owner as Tiberio.) Glorious pastas, spinach ravioli, linguini with clam sauce, squid salad. Well-selected, moderately priced wine list. Jacket required. Reserve. AE, CB, DC, MC, V. Valet parking (dinner only). *L Mon-Fri 11:30am-2:30pm. D 7 days 6pm-10pm.* $$

Tiberio

1915 K Street, NW. 452-1915. Contemporary artwork lines the walls of this tastefully elegant Northern Italian restaurant. Standouts: the fresh, rich pasta dishes—cannelloni pulcinella, agnolotti freschi alla crema. A sophisticated dining experience—for which you will pay handsomely. Free dinner valet parking. Jacket required. Reserve. AE, CB, DC, MC, V. *L Mon-Fri 11:45am-2:30pm. D Mon-Sat 6pm-10pm. CLOSED Sun.* $$$$

Trattu

1823 Jefferson Place, NW. 466-4570. Small, friendly, charming, brick-walled Italian trattoria in Dupont Circle, serves distinctive and satisfying dishes from a limited menu. Recommended starter: the spinach-stuffed agnolotti in cream sauce. Be forewarned: It's noisy. Reserve for dinner only. AE, MC, V. *L Mon-Fri 11:30am-2:30pm. D 7 days 5:30pm-11pm.* $$

Vincenzo

1606 20th Street, NW. 667-0047. Charming, very well regarded Dupont Circle area spot for authentic Italian cooking featuring fresh seafood and now also poultry and meat specials. The grilled whole fish is wonderful, as are the pastas, perfectly al dente but available only with a full dinner (here you do as the Romans do). Seating capacity has been doubled by enclosing the courtyard. Reserve. AE, MC, V. *L Mon-Fri noon-2pm. D Mon-Sat 6pm-10pm. CLOSED Sun.* $$$$

Japanese

Hisago

Washington Harbor, 3050 K Street, NW. 944-4181. An elegant branch of a Tokyo chain serves exquisite sushi at prices to match. The authentic kaiseki cuisine—artful multi-course meals based on seasonal ingredients—varies daily. Dine in the modern dining room or in traditional tatami rooms (surcharge). Also good, the shabu-shabu and sukiyaki. Reserve. AE, DC, MC, V. *L Mon-Fri noon-2:30pm. D Sun-Thurs 6pm-10:30pm; Fri & Sat 6pm-11pm.* $$$$ +

Japan Inn
1715 Wisconsin Avenue, NW. 337-3400. Handsome handcrafted Japanese restaurant, popular for very good grilled beef, chicken, or shrimp, prepared at communal table/grill by chefs cum entertainers. Tempura bar as well as traditional tatami rooms (second floor) for shoeless dining on sukiyaki and shabu-shabu. Reserve. AE, CB, DC, MC, V. *L Mon-Fri noon-2pm. D Mon-Thurs 6pm-10pm; Fri & Sat 6pm-10:30pm; Sun 5:30pm-9:30pm.* $$

Mikado
4707 Wisconsin Avenue, NW. 244-1740. Serene and small old-time Japanese restaurant in upper northwest for top-rated sushi and sashimi; exceptional yellowtail. Warm sake soothes. Reserve. AE, CB, DC, MC, V. *L Tues-Fri 11:30am-2pm; Sat noon-2:30pm. D Tues-Sun 5:30pm-10pm. CLOSED Mon.* $$

Perry's
See Late Night/24 Hours.

Sakura Palace
7926 Georgia Avenue, Silver Spring, Md. (301) 587-7070. Rated by many as the area's best Japanese restaurant. Sushi and sashimi bar as well as a wide variety of Japanese-style dishes: tempura, teriyaki, sukiyaki; also daily specials. Videotaped Japanese TV programs at the sushi bar and authentic tatami rooms. In sum, most enjoyable, albeit service is Eastern-slow. No-smoking section. Jacket requested. Reserve. AE, MC, V. *L Tues-Fri 11:30am-2:30pm. D Tues-Fri 5:30pm-10pm; Sat & Sun 5pm-10:30pm. CLOSED Mon.* $$

Sushi-Ko
2309 Wisconsin Avenue, NW. 333-4187. A low-key Japanese oasis in Georgetown for an extensive selection of what devotees call the freshest-possible sushi and sashimi in town. Sushi bar (it was DC's first), booths or tables; always full to capacity. Tempura, teriyaki, and *udon suki.* Sake, Japanese beer. Free parking. Reserve. AE, MC, V. *L Tues-Fri noon-2:30pm. D Mon-Fri 6pm-10:30pm; Sat 5pm-10:30pm; Sun 5pm-10pm.* $$

Yosaku
4712 Wisconsin Avenue, NW. 363-4453. Modest, informal neighborhood restaurant for tasty sushi. The dining room has a reasonably priced Japanese menu. Good value. Seasonal outdoor dining. Upstairs Japanese lounge. No reservations. AE, DC, MC, V. *L Mon-Fri 11:30am-2:30pm; Sat & Sun noon-3pm. D Sun-Thurs 5:30pm-11pm; Fri & Sat 5:30pm-midnight.* $$

Late Night/24 Hours
(*See also* Bars & Burgers *as well as the* NIGHTLIFE *chapter.*)

Au Pied de Cochon
1335 Wisconsin Avenue, NW. 333-5440. Even those ashamed of their French recommend the "pig's foot" (it's served here, cold). A casual, authentic French brasserie and bar with down-to-earth bistro food and prices. Great onion soup, cheese omelette, and cold Maine lobster; good daily specials. Nice mix of natives and tourists. Enclosed sidewalk cafe for Georgetown watching. Extremely popular, expect a wait in the pm. No reservations. AE, CB, DC, MC, V. *OPEN 7 days, 24 hours.* $$

Bistro Français
3128 M Street, NW. 338-3830. A bustling very French bistro and more subdued dining room combined make up this longtime popular, late-night Georgetown spot. Terrific onion soup, confit of duck, Moroccan couscous, fish soup, and roast loin of pork. Good place for a late-night supper, snack, or drink. Reserve. AE, CB, DC, MC, V. *OPEN Sun-Thurs 11am-3am; Fri & Sat 11am-4am. Weekend brunch 11am-4pm.* $

Booeymonger
3265 Prospect Street, NW; 333-4810. And 5252 Wisconsin Avenue, NW; 686-5805. Outrageous, overstuffed, innovative sandwiches. Beer and wine only. No reservations. No credit cards. *OPEN 7 days 8am- midnight.* $

Hard Rock Cafe
999 E Street, NW. 737-ROCK. Another link in the worldwide chain of rock 'n' roll memorabilia-bedecked eateries featuring good burgers, fries, BBQ, hot fudge brownies, LOUD taped music, the ubiquitous sweatshirt (most don't go home without one), and a wait to get in. Close to the FBI headquarters, it attracts the young and the tourist. AE, MC, V. *OPEN 7 days 11am-2am.* $

Kramer Books & Afterwords, A Cafe
1517 Connecticut Avenue, NW. 387-1462. Two favorite pastimes—eating and reading—combined in this popular bookstore/cafe, where even if you're solo it's welcoming. Full-service cafe for dinner or just light fare: soups, salads, sandwiches; great for a delicious dessert and frothy cappuccino (decaf, too) or perhaps breakfast (till 11:30am) with the *New York Times* (available in the front). Great sidewalk cafe. P.S.: No one minds if you read at the table as long as you've purchased the book. Live music Friday and Saturday from 9pm to midnight. No reservations. AE, MC, V. *OPEN Sun-Thurs 7:30am-12:30am; Fri & Sat 24 hours. Sun brunch 10:30am-2:30pm.* $

Old Ebbitt Grill
675 15th Street, NW. 347-4800. The setting is sensuous turn-of-the-century (albeit re-created); this is really the new Old Ebbitt, the original having been demolished. There is flickering gaslight, mahogany walls, potted palms, brass and marble fittings, and muraled ceilings; and don't miss the bathrooms. There are two bars, dining rooms seating 200, and an oyster bar. The range of food is wide with examples of New American offerings; play it safe, stay simple. Best, still, is the generous burger. There is a new lunch and

dinner menu daily and a Cruvinet allows for a fine wine selection by the glass. Good spot for after theater (Ford's, the Warner, and the National are close by). Reserve. Garage or valet parking. AE, CB, DC, MC, V. *OPEN Mon-Fri 7:30am-1am; Sat 8am-1am; Sun 9:30am-1am. Sun brunch 10am-3pm.* $$

Paper Moon
1073 31st Street, NW. 965-6666. This Georgetown once-hot-now-not spot draws mainly an undemanding undergrad crowd who like the pizza main courses—including one with the ubiquitous sun-dried tomatoes, another with four cheeses. Large bowls of upscale pastas, too. Active bar scene. Service is akin to a Keystone Kops routine but without the laughs. Reserve. AE, MC, V. *OPEN Sun-Thurs 5pm-midnight; Fri & Sat 5pm-1am.* $$

Perry's
1811 Columbia Road, NW. 234-6218. Vast Adams-Morgan hot spot where the young and arty go for sushi and the hip urban attitude. Late-night dining till midnight weekdays, till 1am on the weekend. Japanese-style sing-along (karaoke) Monday, Friday & Saturday from 10:30pm. In season, the wonderful roof deck is the perfect place for a cocktail. Reserve. AE, CB, DC, MC, V. *OPEN Sun-Thurs 6pm-2am; Fri & Sat 6pm-3am.* $

The following serve food till at least 11pm:

Adams-Morgan Spaghetti Garden (Italian)
America (American)
American Cafe (American)
Anna Maria's (Italian)
Armand's Chicago Pizzeria (Italian)
Austin Grill (Mexican)
Aux Fruits de Mer (Fish & Seafood)
A. V. Ristorante (Italian)
Bamiyan (Afghan)
Bice (Italian)
Big Wong (Chinese)
The Brickskeller (Bars & Burgers)
Cafe Atlantico (Caribbean)
Cafe Lautrec (French)
Cafe Splendide (German/Austrian)
Calvert Cafe (Middle Eastern)
Cheesecake Factory (American)
Chez Grand-mere (French)
China Inn (Chinese)
Cities (Continental)
Clyde's of Georgetown (Bars & Burgers)
Clyde's of Tysons Corner (Rooms with a View)
Dominique's (French)
Duke Zeibert's (American)
El Caribe (Latin American)
Filomena (Italian)
Fio's (Italian)
Foggy Bottom Cafe (American)
Food for Thought (Vegetarian)
Fortune (Chinese)
Four Seasons Hotel (Rooms with a View)
Geppetto (Italian)
The Guards (Steak)

Hamburger Hamlet (Bars & Burgers)
The Hawk 'n Dove (Bars & Burgers)
Herb's (American)
Hogate's (Fish & Seafood)
Houston's (Bars & Burgers)
Hunan Chinatown (Chinese)
I Matti (Italian)
Jenkins Hill (Bars & Burgers)
Jockey Club (Continental)
J. Paul's (Bars & Burgers)
Katmandu (Indian)
Khyber Pass (Afghan)
La Fonda (Mexican)
La Plaza (Spanish)
Las Pampas (Latin American)
Lauriol Plaza (Spanish)
Le Steak (Steak)
Maison Blanche (French)
Market Inn (Fish & Seafood)
Mel Krupin's (American)
Meskerem (Ethiopian)
Millie & Al's (Bars & Burgers)
The Monocle on Capitol Hill (American)
Morton's of Chicago (Steak)
Mrs. Simpson's (American)
Mr. Yung's (Chinese)
Murphy's (Bars & Burgers)
Notte Luna (Italian)
Occidental Grill (American)
Pan-Asian Noodles & Grill (Thai)
Paolo's (Italian)
Pines of Rome (Italian)
Pizzeria Uno (Italian)
Portner's (American)
Prime Rib (American)
Red Sage (American)
Red Sea (Ethiopian)
River Club (American)
Roof Terrace (Rooms with a View)
Sam & Harry's (Steak)
Sky Terrace Lounge (Rooms with a View)
Star of Siam (Thai)
Szechuan (Chinese)
Taverna the Greek Islands (Greek)
Timberlake's (Bars & Burgers)
Tony Cheng's Mongolian Restaurant (Chinese)
Tony & Joe's Seafood Place (Fish & Seafood)
The Top O' the Town (Rooms with a View)
Trader Vic's (Polynesian)
Trattu (Italian)
Two Continents in the Sky (Rooms with a View)
Vietnam Georgetown (Vietnamese)
West End Cafe (American)
Yenching Palace (Chinese)
Yosaku (Japanese)

Latin American

El Caribe
1828 Columbia Road, NW; 234-6969. And 3288 M Street, NW; 338-3121. Also 8130 Wisconsin Avenue, Bethesda, Md, (301) 656-0888. The original is located on Adams-Morgan's so-called Latin Row, but they all feature well-prepared

specialties of Spain, Peru, Bolivia, and Argentina. Hearty entrees are accompanied by rice and black beans. Strolling guitarist Monday to Saturday from 9pm to 11pm, and Sunday from 7pm to 9pm. Georgetown location a bit roomier with slightly higher prices. Reserve. AE, CB, DC, MC, V. *OPEN 7 days 11am-11pm.* $$

Las Pampas
3291 M Street, NW. 333-5151. A carnivore's delight. Bi-level Argentine restaurant for grilled, marinated beef. Start with the empanadas. The parillada—a mixed grill for two—is a good-bet main course accompanied by Argentinean wine. Strolling guitarists from 8pm. Reserve. AE, CB, DC, MC, V. *OPEN Sun-Thurs 11am-11pm; Fri 11am-1am; Sat 5pm-1am.* $$

Mexican

Austin Grill
2404 Wisconsin Avenue, NW. 337-8080. Bright, bustling Tex-Mex on Upper Wisconsin for margaritas that pass the test, great chili, beef and bean burritos, grilled pork chop, and carnitas. Yes! President Bush ate here, too. Reserve, but a long wait is to be expected. AE, MC, V. *OPEN Mon 5:30pm-11pm; Tues-Fri 11:30am- 11pm; Fri & Sat 11:30am-midnight; Sun 11:30am-10:30pm.* $

Enriqueta's
2811 M Street, NW; 338-7772. And *1832 Columbia Road, NW; 328-0937. There's nothing fast about this food—it's authentic Mexican food—flavorful, fresh, and interesting. Great chicken mole and regional seafood dishes, all in lively partylike settings. Reserve for 4 or more only. AE, CB, DC, MC, V. *L Mon-Fri 11:30am-2:30pm. D Sun-Thurs 5pm-10pm; Fri & Sat 5pm-11pm. *OPEN Sun-Thurs 5pm-10:30pm; Fri & Sat 5pm-11:30pm.* $$

La Fonda
1639 R Street, NW. 232-6965. Bright-tiled and stucco setting to enjoy unimaginative but nonetheless satisfying Mexican specialties. Wonderful sidewalk cafe in season. Reserve for 6 or more. AE, CB, DC, MC, V. *OPEN Mon-Thurs 11:30am-11pm; Fri 11:30am-midnight; Sat & Sun 11:30am-10pm.* $

Lauriol Plaza
See Spanish.

Mixtec
1792 Columbia Road, NW. 332-1011. In Adams-Morgan, Pepe Montesinos's (of Enriquita's) casual atmospheric storefront outpost of authentic Mexican cooking. Soft homemade tortillas with charcoal-broiled strips of pork or beef topped by a spicy salsa cruda. On Saturday and Sunday devotees of tripe stew are in for a treat. Reserve. No credit cards. *OPEN Mon-Thurs 11am-10:30pm; Fri & Sat 11am-11:30pm; Sun 11am-10pm.* $

Rio Grande Cafe
4919 Fairmont Avenue, Bethesda, Md. (301) 656-2981. This pseudo-warehouselike outpost of Tex-Mex cooking is deservedly popular for pork

tamales sauced with chili, tacos al carbon, grilled spareribs, fajitas. No reservations, a wait will be certain. AE, CB, DC, MC, V. *OPEN Sun-Thurs 11:30am-10:30pm; Fri & Sat 11:30am-11:30pm.* $

Middle Eastern

Bacchus
1827 Jefferson Place, NW; 785-0734. And *7945 Norfolk Avenue, Bethesda, Md; (301) 657-1722. Small, attractive, albeit tight, quarters (Bethesda is more spacious) for feasting on Lebanese appetizers (maza) or choose kebab (don't stray from the aforementioned). Suffer the service. Reserve. AE, MC, V. *L Mon-Fri noon-2:30pm. D Mon-Thurs 6pm-10pm; Fri & Sat 6pm-10:30pm. CLOSED Sun. *OPEN Sun 6pm-10pm.* $$

Calvert Cafe
1967 Calvert Street, NW. 232-5431. Locals, diplomats, journalists come for the consistently fine Middle Eastern food, the low prices, and the omnipresence of Mama Ayesha, who runs this unassuming, fun (the waiters have been known to belly dance) spot. Outdoor cafe in summer. Reserve on weekends. No credit cards. *OPEN 7 days 11:30am-midnight.* $

Iron Gate Inn
1734 N Street, NW. 737-1370. The Middle Eastern specialties run second to the setting, which is one of the most charming in any season. In summer dine under a real grape arbor in one of DC's loveliest outdoor settings; in winter, indoors, in the former carriage house, dine in a stall warmed by a fire or upstairs in the hayloft (The Hunt Room)—so dark—it's a great rendezvous for lovers and spies. Reserve for dinner only. AE, CB, DC, MC, V. *OPEN Mon-Fri 11:30am-10pm; Sat 5:30pm-10pm. CLOSED Sun.* $

Nizam's
23 Maple Avenue West, Vienna, Va. (703) 938-8948. Quite good authentic Turkish food in a suburban setting. Good baked lamb topped with kasseri cheese, braised lamb shank with tomato sauce and yogurt, and a delicious baked moussaka. On Tuesday and Friday through Sunday the döner kebab (thin-sliced marinated meats roasted on a spit) are available. Baklava for dessert. Well worth the trip. Reserve. AE, CB, DC, MC, V. *L Tues-Fri 11am-3pm. D Tues-Thurs 5pm-10pm; Fri & Sat 5pm-11pm; Sun 4pm-10pm. CLOSED Mon.* $

No-Smoking Areas

The following have no-smoking areas:

America (American)
Buffet/Cascades Cafe (Cafeterias)
Carnegie Deli (Delicatessen)
Charley's Crab (Fish & Seafood)
Cheesecake Factory (American)
Food for Thought (Vegetarian)
Hamburger Hamlet (Bars & Burgers)

Herb's (American)
Katmandu (Indian)
Library of Congress Cafeteria (Cafeterias)
Madurai (Indian)
McPherson Grill (American)
New Heights (American)
Notte Luna (Italian)
Pan-Asian Noodles & Grill (Thai)
Patent Pending (Cafeterias)
River Club (American)
Sakura Palace (Japanese)
Sea Catch (Fish & Seafood)
Sfuzzi (Italian)
The Supreme Court Building Cafeteria
  (Cafeterias)
Taverna the Greek Islands (Greek)
Tila's (American)
Vie de France (Breakfast/Brunch)

Pizza

See Italian.

Polynesian

Trader Vic's
The Capitol Hilton Hotel, 16th & K Streets, NW. 347-7100. Of another time and place. Drink enough mai tais and you won't remember if you're in the Trader Vic's in DC, London, Chicago, or San Francisco. Feast on the appetizers, they're delicious and filling—and don't go near the entrees. Reserve. AE, CB, DC, MC, V. *L Mon-Fri 11:30am-2:30pm. D Mon-Fri 5pm-11:30pm; Sat 5pm-11pm. CLOSED Sun.* $$$

Rooms with a View

Clyde's of Tysons Corner
8332 Leesburg Pike, Vienna, Va. (703) 734-1900. Formal continental dining in the Grill Room; The Cafe, Oyster Bar, Main Bar, and Palm Terrace share a menu featuring pastas, burgers, salads, and sandwiches as well as dinner entrees. Extravagantly and elaborately decorated. Go to eat and gape, the room *is* the view. Jackets after 5pm in the Main Bar and Grill Room. Valet parking for dinner. Reservations accepted for all rooms. AE, CB, DC, MC, V. *OPEN Mon-Sat 11am-2am; Sun 10am-2am. Sun brunch 10am-4:30pm.* $$$

The Dandy
Zero Prince Street, Alexandria, Va. (703) 683-6076 or -6090. This 97-foot riverboat takes you from Old Town to Georgetown and back for a 3-hour or so (18 miles) candlelight dinner cruise. Also Sunday brunch at 12:30pm for a 2½-hour cruise. Jacket required; no jeans. Reserve! AE, CB, DC, MC, V. *Departs Tues-Sun at 7:30pm.* $$

Four Seasons Hotel
2800 Pennsylvania Avenue, NW. 342-0444. Windows full of views of Rock Creek Park are the special attraction. The Garden Terrace is a comfortable, lovely spot for a light lunch, late snack,

or afternoon tea (served daily from 3pm to 4:30pm). Pianist daily from 4pm to closing. During the summer the outdoor Plaza Cafe is open daily from 11:30am to 8pm. Salads and sandwiches available till closing. No reservations. AE, CB, DC, MC, V. *OPEN Sun-Thurs 11am-12:30am; Fri & Sat 11am-1:30am.* $$

Capitol View Club
Hyatt Regency Washington, 400 New Jersey Avenue, NW, 11th floor. 737-1234. Ascend in glass-enclosed elevators to this newly renovated dining room overlooking the Capitol. Steak, seafood pastas. Private club at lunchtime. Jacket required; no jeans. (*See also* NIGHTLIFE, Piano Bars: Capitol View Lounge.) Reserve. AE, CB, DC, MC, V. *D Mon-Sat 6pm-10pm.* $$$

Roof Terrace
Kennedy Center, 2700 F Street, NW. 416-8555. The basics here are quite good (stick with them) and the view of the city superb. Harpist Thursday to Saturday from 6pm to 11pm. Cocktail lounge serves appetizers and hors d'oeuvres. Suffer the service. Jacket and tie requested. Reserve! AE, CB, DC, MC, V. *L 7 days 11:30am-3pm. D 7 days 5:30pm-9pm; after-theater menu, 9:30pm till ½ hour after curtain goes down. Sun brunch 11:30am-3pm.* $$

Sequoia
Washington Harbor, K & Thomas Jefferson Streets, NW. 944-4200. The area's most elaborate and extravagant dining venue. The two-story, glass-walled dining room faces the river—the upstairs bar is the best vantage point. Outside, across the water, is the Kennedy Center. In season, dining or just having a sunset cocktail at the bar on the terraced patio leading down to the river's edge is a plus. Reserve. AE, CB, DC, MC, V. *OPEN Sun-Thurs 11:30am-midnight; Fri & Sat 11:30am-1am. Weekend brunch 11:30am-4pm.* $$

Sky Terrace Lounge
Hotel Washington, 15th Street & Pennsylvania Avenue, NW. 638-5900. The spectacular view of L'Enfant's Washington from the outdoor terrace makes this a popular and comfortable stop for a drink. Light menu nightly till 1am. A wait can be expected. No reservations. AE, CB, DC, MC, V. *OPEN May-Oct. 7 days 11am-1am.* $

The Top O' the Town
Prospect House, 14th & North Oak Streets, Arlington, Va. (703) 525-9200. Via the glass-enclosed elevator to the most spectacular view of the city. Covered outdoor terrace from which you can hear the Marine Band performing at the Iwo Jima Memorial on Tuesday evenings in summer. No jeans, T-shirts, or athletic shoes. Reserve! AE, MC, V. Terrace *OPEN Apr-Oct, Sun-Thurs 5pm-midnight; Fri & Sat 5pm-2am.* Restaurant *L Mon-Fri noon-3pm. D Sun-Thurs 6pm-10pm; Fri & Sat 6pm-11pm.* $$

Two Continents in the Sky
Hotel Washington, 15th Street & Pennsylvania Avenue, NW. 638-5900. In summer, elegant rooftop continental dining room with a wonderful view of the Mall. The terrace (*see* Rooftop Ter-

ace) is one of the town's most popular spots for a cocktail with hors d'oeuvres while watching the sun set. Unforgettable! Reserve. AE, CB, DC, MC, V. *OPEN May-Oct, 7 days 11am-1am.* **$$**

The View
Marriott Key Bridge, 1401 Lee Highway, 14th floor, Rosslyn, Va. (703) 524-6400. Prix-fixe nouvelle cuisine, lovely luxurious mirrored setting but most of all an extraordinary view of the Lincoln, Washington, and Jefferson memorials and the Kennedy Center. From the lounge, the view is of Great Falls, Georgetown, and the Potomac, with dancing to live entertainment. Jacket required; no jeans. Reserve. AE, CB, DC, MC, V. *OPEN Mon-Thurs 5pm-10pm; Fri 5pm-11pm; Sat 6pm-11pm; Sun 5:30pm-9:30pm. Sun champagne brunch 10am-2:30pm.* **$$$**

Soul/Southern

Blues Alley
See NIGHTLIFE, Jazz.

Florida Avenue Grill
1100 Florida Avenue, NW. 265-1586. This throwback of a diner (with counter and booths) serves wonderful hearty Southern-style food from morning till night. Salmon cakes, ham hocks, Southern-fried chicken, grits, homemade biscuits and corn bread, and for dessert, bread pudding. Popular with cab drivers, especially for their down-home country breakfast. No alcohol. No reservations. No credit cards. *OPEN Mon-Sat 6am-9pm. CLOSED Sun.* **$**

Lafitte
See American.

Red Hot & Blue
See American.

Spanish

El Bodegon
1637 R Street, NW. 667-1710. A pleasantly appointed, fun place for hearty Spanish fare. In the bar, tapas for upscale grazing, but the fun is in the dining rooms, where you can feast on *paella à la Valenciana* and *arroz con pollo y chorizo* while being entertained by strolling guitarists and Flamenco dancing nightly. Fireplace in winter. Free parking. Reserve. AE, CB, DC, MC, V. *L Mon-Fri noon-2:30pm. D Mon-Sat 5:30pm-10:30pm. CLOSED Sun.* **$$**

La Plaza
1847 Columbia Road, NW. 667-1900. An inviting stylish outpost in Adams-Morgan for some of the best—and best-priced—Spanish fare in town. Charbroiled steak, fine roast duck, seafood stew, roast pork, paella, and great drinks. Valet parking. Reserve. AE, CB, DC, MC, V. *OPEN 7 days noon-11:30pm.* **$$**

Lauriol Plaza
1801 18th Street, NW. 387-0035. The party spills out like a piñata onto the street of this Adams-Morgan favorite. The traditional Spanish/Mexican dishes are secondary to the atmosphere. Inviting umbrella-shaded sidewalk

tables; lethal margaritas. Reserve. AE, CB, DC, MC, V. *OPEN 7 days 11am-11:30pm.* **$**

Taberna del Alabardero
1776 I Street, NW. 429-2200. A luxurious choice for refined contemporary Spanish fare prepared as nowhere else. The tapas bar, serving weekdays from noon to 10:30pm, weekends from 6pm to 10pm, is a standout. In the dining room, seasonal offerings may include a casserole of quail with white beans, a mixed seafood grill with romescu sauce, or cabbage stuffed with salt cod. Great desserts. Reserve. AE, CB, DC, MC, V. *L Mon-Fri noon-3pm. D Mon-Thurs 6pm-10pm; Fri & Sat 6pm-10:30pm.* **$$$$**

Steak

Gary's
1800 M Street, NW. 463-6470. Go for the delicious, thick, well-aged steaks and the stiff drinks; everyone else does. Nonbeef choices, too, and great chocolate mousse pie. Outdoor cafe in summer. Reserve! AE, CB, DC, MC, V. *OPEN Mon-Fri 11:30am-10:30pm. CLOSED Sat & Sun.* **$$$**

The Guards
2915 M Street, NW. 965-2350. This longtime Georgetown steak and chop house is inviting in every season. In winter the dark wood-paneled interior with its three fireplaces ablaze couldn't be more comforting, and in summer the secluded gardenlike atrium is great for romance. Wonderful steak, prime rib, and rack of lamb to boot, as well as a fine wine selection. Reserve. AE, MC, V. *OPEN Sun-Thurs 11:30am-11pm; Fri & Sat 11:30am-midnight. Weekend brunch 11:30am-5pm.* **$$$**

Joe & Mo's
1211 Connecticut Avenue, NW; 659-1211. And 7345 Wisconsin Avenue, Bethesda, Md; (301) 656-8501. Another capital movers and shakers spot and a macho beef lover's dream come true; great prime ribs, excellent aged steaks, lobster, and fresh seafood. Other pluses: the bread, onion rings, and potato pancakes. Entertainment Friday and Saturday nights. Free parking till 6:30pm. Reserve. AE, CB, DC, MC, V. *OPEN Mon-Thurs 11:30am-10pm; Fri & Sat 11:30am-10:30pm. CLOSED Sun.* **$$$**

Le Steak
3060 M Street, NW. 965-1627. Choices are kept to a minimum here. The herb and mustard sauce sets this steak apart (noncarnivores may have swordfish). Preceded by onion soup or *salad verte* with a wonderful vinaigrette and accompanied by perfect *pommes frits*. Your only choices are the wine and dessert. It's a delightfully simple, satisfying meal in an intimate French bistro setting. Jacket requested. Reserve. AE, CB, DC, MC, V. *OPEN 7 days 5:30pm-11pm.* **$$**

Mel Krupin's
See American.

Morton's of Chicago
Georgetown Court, 3251 Prospect Street, NW. 342-6258. Via Chicago, Morton's is a noisy re-

minder of the quintessential steak joint. It boasts a masculine clubby atmosphere for the town's best well-aged steaks, cooked as requested. Portions are enormous—there are legendary two- and three-pound porterhouse steaks, as well as huge lobsters and superior prime rib. Chocolate souffle for the hogs among us. Pricey and noisy. Jacket and tie suggested. Reservations are now taken even after 7pm. Free parking. AE, CB, DC, MC, V. *OPEN Mon-Sat 5:30pm-11pm; Sun 5pm-10pm.* $$$$

The Palm
1225 19th Street, NW. 293-9091. A la the original in New York, political and sports cartoons and caricatures cover the walls. It draws the power mongers of DC for the reliability of the steaks, the addictive cottage fries, the size of the lobsters, and the NY cheesecake. Best if someone else is picking up the tab, which can be very heavy indeed. Everything à la carte. Free dinner valet parking. Reserve. AE, CB, DC, MC, V. *OPEN Mon-Fri 11:45am-10:30pm; Sat 6pm-10:30pm. CLOSED Sun.* $$$$

Prime Rib
See American.

Sam & Harry's
1200 19th Street, NW. 296-4333. Handsome new clubby powerhouse whose porterhouse and prime rib rivals that of Morton's (they're from Chicago, too). Also fine, the stuffed baby chicken, the pork chops, and the humongous lobsters. Reserve. AE, CB, DC, MC, V. *L Mon-Fri 11:30am-2:30pm; at the bar, 2:30pm-5:30pm. D Mon-Sat 5:30pm-11pm. CLOSED Sun.* $$$$

Swiss

Les Trois Visages de la Suisse
1990 M Street, NW. 293-1990. In an elegant setting, the cuisine and wines of Switzerland's three regional "faces"—French, Italian, and German. Choice of formal dining room or the more casual subterranean grotto with bar and church-bench seating, where the specialty is a choice of meat or fish, cooked by a waiter at the table, on a square of sizzling granite. Interesting albeit expensive adventure. Reserve. AE, CB, DC, MC, V. *L Mon-Fri 11:30am-2:30pm. D Mon-Sat 6pm-10:30pm. CLOSED Sun.* $$$$

Thai

Bangkok Gourmet
523 South 23rd Street, Arlington, Va. (703) 521-1305. Spicy Thai offerings that do not compromise. Good lemon grass soup, shrimp with chili, and garlic beef with basil. Fine specials include curried grouper, oysters with garlic, grilled salmon stuffed with leeks, and baby eggplant with black bean sauce. Outstanding Thai choice. Patio dining in summer. Reserve. AE, CB, DC, MC, V. *L 7 days 11am-3pm. D 7 days 5:30pm-10pm.* $

Duangrat's
5878 Leesburg Pike, Bailey's Crossroads, Va. (703) 820-5775. Touted by many as the area's

finest Thai restaurant. Feast on noodles with curried duck topping, deep-fried flounder with chili sauce, beef with green curry. Pleasant surroundings and service. Classic Thai dancing upstairs every Friday and Saturday evening. Reserve. AE, CB, DC, MC, V. *L 7 days 11:30am-2:30pm. D Sun-Thurs 5pm-10pm; Fri & Sat 5pm-11pm.* $$

Pan-Asian Noodles & Grill
2020 P Street, NW; 872-8889. And 1018 Vermont Avenue, NW; 783-8899. Bright, casual, good-value Dupont Circle spot for homey filling Asian fare. Wonderful appetizers, noodles, meal-sized bowls of broth with noodles, and grills. Try the drunken or cozy noodles. Good, too, the grilled chicken and the satays. Great place to go with a group and share. Service is friendly and efficient. Wine & beer only. No smoking upstairs. Carryout available. Reserve for 4 or more. *L Mon-Sat 11:30am-2:30pm. D Sun-Thurs 5pm-10pm; Fri & Sat 5pm-11pm.* $

Ploy
2218 Wisconsin Avenue, NW. 337-2324. Aficionados call this the best Thai cooking in the District. In a contemporary cafe setting, choose stuffed duckling, marinated roast quail, prawns in a spicy minced-pork sauce. Reserve. AE, MC, V. *L 7 days 11:30am-3pm. D Sun-Thurs 5pm-10pm; Fri & Sat 5pm-11pm.* $

Star of Siam
1136 19th Street, NW. 785-2838. Thai curries are the specialty of this well-regarded District Thai restaurant. Outside dining in season. Reserve. AE, DC, MC, V. *OPEN Mon-Sat 11:30am-11pm; Sun 4pm-10pm.* $

Thai Room
5037 Connecticut Avenue, NW. 244-5933. DC's longest running Thai restaurant, best for those who like it hot. There are no compromises here and it's an adventure for all but the timid (there are some milder choices). Reserve. AE, DC, MC, V. *OPEN 7 days 11:30am-10pm.* $

Thai Taste
2606 Connecticut Avenue, NW; 387-8876. And *8553 Rockville Pike, Rockville, Md; (301) 340-8897. This Thai restaurant with Art Deco and neon-enhanced decor is a popular spot for those who like it hot. Pork and string beans with chili paste, soft-shell crabs with chili, fried beef with chili paste and coconut milk, garlic soup with red curry, fried salted beef. This is a combo of Chinese and Thai and there are dishes for the less adventurous palate, including grilled whole sea bass and duck with mixed vegetables. Attentive, helpful staff. Sidewalk cafe. Reserve. AE, CB, DC, MC, V. *OPEN Mon-Sat 11:30am-10:15pm; Sun 5pm-10:15pm. *OPEN Mon-Thurs 11:30am-9:30pm; Fri & Sat 11:30am-10:30pm; Sun 5pm-9:30pm.* $

Vegetarian

Food for Thought
1738 Connecticut Avenue, NW. 797-1095. The main focus is vegetarian, but there's chicken and

ish, too. Good soups and great salads. Also burgers and nitrate-free hot dogs. Nondescript setting at best. Live music from noon to 3pm and from 6pm to midnight (*see also* NIGHTLIFE, Eclectic). No-smoking section. Reserve for 10 or more. AE, MC, V. *OPEN Mon 11:30am-3pm & 6pm-midnight; Tues-Thurs 11:30am-midnight; Fri 11:30am-1am; Sat 5pm-1am; Sun 5pm-midnight.* $

Kalorama Cafe
2228 18th Street, NW. 667-1022. Small, friendly neighborhood restaurant serves a nice shrimp tempura; daily vegetarian specials. Live classical and jazz guitar Tuesday to Thursday from 6pm to 10pm, and Friday and Saturday from 6pm to 11pm. Outdoor flower-filled patio in summer. Beer and wine only. No reservations. No credit cards. *L Tues-Sat 11:30am-3pm. D Tues-Sat 6pm-10pm. Sun brunch 11am-3pm. CLOSED Mon.* $

Madurai
See Indian.

Paru's Indian Vegetarian
2010 S Street, NW. 483-5133. Small, no-frills storefront for a limited but interesting number of inexpensive, strictly vegetarian dishes. The best masala dosai (crispy, thin pancake filled with potato curry) around. No alcohol. Reserve. No credit cards. *OPEN Mon-Sat 11:30am-8:45pm. CLOSED Sun.* $

Vietnamese

East Wind
809 King Street, Alexandria, Va. (703) 836-1515. In Old Town, consistently wonderful Vietnamese food in a relaxed setting. Pricey in relation to the competition. Reserve. AE, DC, MC, V. *L Mon-Fri 11:30am-2:30pm. D Mon-Thurs 6pm-10pm; Fri & Sat 6pm-10:30pm; Sun 5:30pm-9:30pm.* $$

Germaine's
2400 Wisconsin Avenue, NW, upstairs. 965-1185. A wonderful outpost in upper Georgetown, for Vietnamese—really pan-Asian—specialties. Vietnamese spring rolls; Indonesian sates (prepared in view); Korean kim chi; Japanese teriyaki; Szechuan cold noodles. The decor is skylit and soothing, the food outstanding, the service gracious. Favored by media and political types. Asian beers. Reserve. AE, CB, DC, MC, V. *L Mon-Fri 11:30am-2:30pm. D Sun-Thurs 5:30pm-10pm; Fri & Sat 5:30pm-11pm.* $$$

Queen Bee
3181 Wilson Boulevard, Arlington, Va. (703) 527-3444. One of the area's best for well-prepared Vietnamese cuisine. Wonderful soups to be shared, roast pork with sweet soy sauce, deep-fried whole fish, and roast quail. Reserve. MC, V. *OPEN 7 days 11am-10pm.* $$

Vietnam Georgetown
2934 M Street, NW. 337-4536. One of DC's most popular ethnic restaurants. Nearly everyone starts with *cha gio* (crispy rice-paper-wrapped egg rolls). Also good are the soups, albeit blander than one would expect, and the shrimp and noodles. The rear outdoor patio is a plus; the slow service, a minus. No reservations. MC, V. *OPEN Sun-Thurs 11am-11pm; Fri & Sat 11am-midnight.* $

Vietnam Taste-Pho 79
2007 Viers Mill Road, Rockville, Md. (301) 279-8870. Choose from the regular menu of Vietnamese dishes or have *pho* (a meal-size bowl of beef and noodle soup). Other good choices are the spring rolls, lemon grass chicken, fried whole flounder, and char-grilled meatballs to wrap in a rice crêpe. Reserve. AE, MC, V. *OPEN Mon-Thurs 11:30am-10pm; Fri & Sat 11am-10:30pm; Sun 10:30am-9:30pm.* $

SHOPPING

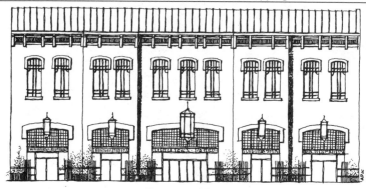

Georgetown Park

There are three main shopping sectors: the Old Downtown area, where the older large department stores are located and where several new shopping complexes have added new excitement; lower Connecticut Avenue between K and R Streets for very fine specialty shopping; and Georgetown, which, on M between 28th and 34th streets and on Wisconsin from M to Q Streets, is akin to a giant agora, where boutiques of every sort vie for your attention.

DEPARTMENT STORES

Hecht's
Metro Center, 12th & G Streets, NW; 628-6661. And in suburbs. A new, $40 million, five-level flagship store for this local retailing stalwart, in the heart of the downtown renaissance. More moderately priced trendy fashions for the whole family and anything you need for the home. AE, MC, V, Hecht's charge. *OPEN Mon-Sat 10am-8pm; Sun 11:30am-6:30pm.*

Lord & Taylor
5225 Western Avenue, NW; 362-9600. And in suburbs. Small version of New York store. Stable, strong on American designers. Clothes for women, men, children. Furnishings, gifts. AE, Lord & Taylor charge. *OPEN Mon-Fri 10am-9:30pm; Sat 10am-7pm; Sun noon-6pm.*

Neiman-Marcus
Mazza Gallerie, 5300 Wisconsin Avenue, NW; 966-9700. And Tysons II. The status store—from Dallas. Great half-yearly sales. AE, Neiman-Marcus charge. *OPEN Mon-Fri 10am-8pm; Sat 10am-6pm; Sun noon-5pm.*

Saks Fifth Avenue
5555 Wisconsin Avenue, Chevy Chase, Md. (301) 657-9000. Just over the "border" from DC, high-quality fashions for men and women. AE, DC, MC, V, Saks charge. *OPEN Mon & Thurs 10am-9pm; Tues, Wed, Fri & Sat 10am-6pm; Sun noon-5pm.*

Woodward & Lothrop
11th & F Streets, NW; 347-5300. And in suburbs. Since 1880, Washington's full-service department store for the whole family, affectionately and universally dubbed "Woodies." AE, MC, V, Woodies charge. *OPEN Mon-Sat 10am-8pm; Sun noon-5pm.*

DC SHOPPING MALLS

Georgetown Park
M Street & Wisconsin Avenue, NW. 298-5577. Billed as a "shopping park." Charming Victorian-era motif enhances this multi-million dollar Georgetown mall, DC's largest. Over 100 shops, including branches of many of the best known. A must Georgetown stop! Mall *OPEN Mon-Fri 10am-9pm; Sat 10am-7pm; Sun noon-6pm. Restaurant hours may vary.*

Les Champs
Watergate, 600 New Hampshire Avenue, NW. A collection of 30 famous upscale boutiques including Pierre Cardin, Gucci, Yves Saint Laurent, Mario Valentino. *OPEN Mon-Sat 10am-6pm.*

Mazza Gallerie
5300 Wisconsin Avenue, NW (at the District/Maryland line). 966-6114. A skylit four-level atrium boasting 51 of the most luxurious shops in town, including Neiman-Marcus. Concierge service, call 686-9515. *OPEN Mon-Fri 10am-8pm; Sat 10am-6pm; Sun noon 5pm.*

The Pavilion at the Old Post Office
1100 Pennsylvania Avenue, NW. 289-4224. New shopping in a very old DC landmark. The Old Post Office Building provides the unique setting for a three-level retail/restaurant complex clustered around a soaring skylit court. Novelty items abound; it's a good spot to find inexpensive momentos of DC. Extra treat: free noontime concerts daily. Added in 1992: The East Atrium containing additional shops, a food court, and a

Size Comparison Chart for Clothes

Ladies' dresses, coats & skirts

American -	3	5	7	9	11	12	13	14	15	16	18
Continental -	36	38	38	40	40	42	42	44	44	46	48
British -	8	10	11	12	13	14	15	16	17	18	20

Ladies' blouses & sweaters

American -	10	12	14	16	18	20
Continental -	38	40	42	44	46	48
British -	32	34	36	38	40	42

Ladies' stockings

American -	8	8½	9	9½	10	10½
Continental -	1	2	3	4	5	6
British -	8	8½	9	9½	10	10½

Ladies' shoes

American -	5	6	7	8	3	10
Continental -	36	37	38	39	40	41
British -	3½	4½	5½	6½	7½	8½

Children's clothing

American -	3	4	5	6	6X
Continental -	98	104	110	116	122
British -	18	20	22	24	26

Children's shoes

American -	8	9	10	11	12	13	1	2	3
Continental -	24	25	27	28	29	30	32	33	34
British -	7	8	9	10	11	12	13	1	2

Men's suits

American -	34	36	38	40	42	44	46	48
Continental -	44	46	48	50	52	54	56	58
British -	34	36	38	40	42	44	46	48

Men's shirts

American -	14	15	15½	16	16½	17	17½	18
Continental -	37	38	39	41	42	43	44	45
British -	14	15	15½	16	16½	17	17½	18

Men's shoes

American -	7	8	9	10	11	12	13
Continental -	39½	41	42	43	44½	46	47
British -	6	7	8	9	10	11	12

Men's hats

American -	6⅞	7⅛	7¼	7⅜	7½	7⅝
Continental -	55	56	58	59	60	61
British -	6¾	6⅞	7⅛	7¼	7⅜	7½

theater showing a 50-minute film showcasing the history and character of DC. *OPEN 7 days.* (For more on the building *see also* SIGHTSEEING, Viewpoints: Old Post Office Clock Tower, *and* HISTORIC & NEW WASHINGTON, Historic Buildings and Areas: Old Post Office Building.)

The Shops at National Place
Enter: F street between 13th & 14th streets, NW, or from the J.W. Marriott, 1331 Pennsylvania Avenue, NW. 783-9090. Another Rouse company production (Harborplace in Baltimore, South Street Seaport in New York, Faneuil Hall in Boston, etc.). A lively four-tiered retail mall with over 85 shops and eateries will entice you to this revitalized strip of Pennsylvania Avenue. All the regulars are here including Benetton, The Limited, and Banana Republic; the Food Hall on level four for feasting on fast food. It's all extremely pleasant. *OPEN Mon- Wed & Fri-Sat 10am-7pm; Thurs 10am-8pm; Sun noon-5pm.*

Union Station
50 Massachusetts Avenue, NE. 371-9441. The street and upper levels of the fabulously restored historic station have been transformed into a shopper's paradise boasting more than 120 specialty retail stores. The East Hall is a wonderfully grand setting for a special collection of 15 museum-quality shops for much that is handcrafted. You can buy anything from a chic new head-to-toe outfit to political campaign memorabilia or a model train set. Dining opportunities abound. Don't miss! *OPEN Mon-Sat 10am-9pm; Sun noon-6pm.*

SUBURBAN MALLS

The Fashion Center at Pentagon City
1100 South Hayes Street at Army-Navy Drive & I-395, Arlington, Va. (703) 415-2400. Opened in

1989, it's the area's largest mall. Anchored by Macy's and Nordstrom, it includes 120 stores including Laura Ashley, Villeroy & Boch, and Britches. Restaurants, a food court, six movie theaters. *OPEN Mon-Sat 10am-9:30pm; Sun 11am-6pm.*

Mongomery Mall
I-270 & Democracy Boulevard, Md. (301) 469-6000. Newly gussied up and expanded with the addition of a Nordstrom and 70 new specialty shops including Abercrombie & Fitch and J. Crew. Of course, still here are Hecht's and Woodies. *OPEN Mon-Sat 10am-9:30pm; Sun noon-6pm.*

Potomac Mills
Exit 52, off I-95, Dale City, Va. (703) 826-4557. If you have to go to one discount mega-mall, make it this one. Enticements include the Nordstrom Rack, the clearance center of the store known for service (even here!), as well as bargains from the likes of Eddie Bauer, Britches, Benetton, Laura Ashley, Fiyz & Floyd, Fenn, Wright & Mason, and the wonderful Georgetown Leather Design Outlet. *OPEN Mon-Sat 10am-9:30pm; Sun 11am-6pm.*

Tysons Corner Center
9160 Chain Bridge Road (Leesburg Pike), McLean, Va. (703) 556-4600. Contains several retailing giants including Bloomingdale's, Lord & Taylor, Hecht's, Woodies, Nordstrom, and nearly 250 specialty stores including Brooks Brothers, Raleigh's Britches, and F.A.O. Schwarz. Restaurants and movie theaters as well. *OPEN Mon-Sat 10am-9:30pm; Sun noon-5pm.*

White Flint Mall
11301 Rockville Pike, Kensington, Md. (301) 468-5777. Star stores include Bloomingdale's, I. Magnin, Lord & Taylor, as well as 120 specialty shops including high-fashion contenders like Saint Laurent Rive Gauche. *OPEN Mon-Sat 10am-9:30pm; Sun noon-6pm.*

WOMEN'S CLOTHES

Boutiques

This list covers every taste, age, and price level.

Ann Taylor
Georgetown Park, 3222 M Street, NW; 338-5290. And Union Station, 50 Massachusettes Avenue, NE; 371- 8010. Also 1720 K Street, NW, 466-3544; Tysons Corner; and White Flint. Well-organized, well-stocked shops for contemporary clothing, accessories, and shoes for work and play. Moderate to expensive. AE, MC, V. Ann Taylor charge. *OPEN 7 days.*

Banana Republic
Wisconsin & M Streets, NW; 333-2554. And *The Shops at National Place, 14th & F Streets, NW; 783-1400. Also *King & South Washington Streets, Alexandria, Va, (703) 739-0888; and **Tysons Corner, 893-0540. These safari and "travel" clothes were available for years through

their amusing catalog only, now they are on almost every corner in America bringing bush jackets and vests, bandanas, khaki and faded denim back into high style (but at higher prices than in pre-chic days). Casual fun clothing and environment; modest to high prices. AE, DC, MC, V. *OPEN Mon-Sat 10am-10pm; Sun 11am-8pm.* *OPEN Mon-Sat 10am-9pm; Sun noon-7pm.* **OPEN Mon-Sat 10am-8pm; Sun noon-6pm.*

Benetton
The Shops at National Place, 1331 Pennsylvania Avenue, NW. 737-5544. Worldwide mass merchandiser of stylish, color-coordinated Italian sportswear separates; strong on sweater dressing. Colorful, youthful, casual, and affordable. AE, MC, V. *OPEN 7 days.*

Casual Corner
*1017 Connecticut Avenue, NW; 659-8344. And The Shops at National Place, 1331 Pennsylvania Avenue, NW; 737-7280. Also 408 L'Enfant Plaza East, SW, 554-5240; Georgetown Park, 3222 M Street, NW, 342-1926; and in suburbs. Popular shops where the young working woman comes for very moderately priced sportswear, dresses, coats, accessories. AE, MC, V. *OPEN 7 days.* *CLOSED Sun.*

Chanel Boutique
1455 Pennsylvania Avenue, NW. 638-5055. Can't get to Paris soon enough? Don't fret, the complete line of Chanel ready-to-wear, accessories, jewelry, fragrances, and cosmetics is right here. AE, DC, MC, V. *OPEN Mon-Sat.*

Commander Salamander
1420 Wisconsin Avenue, NW. 337-2265. DC's first funky-punky-New Wave clothes emporium. Lots of energy, loud music, fabulous accessories. Very youth-oriented. Doc Martin shoes; Stagelight cosmetics; Betsey Johnson's sexy creations. AE, MC, V. *OPEN Mon-Thurs 10am-10pm; Fri & Sat 10am-midnight; Sun noon-8pm.*

Frankie Welch
305 Cameron Street, Alexandria, Va. (703) 549-0107. An area institution. Three stories of classic high- quality designs. Her scarf designs are renowned. AE, MC, V. *OPEN 7 days.*

Georgetown Leather Design
3265 M Street, NW; 333-9333. And 1150 Connecticut Avenue, NW; 223-1855. Also Mazza Galleria, 5300 Wisconsin Avenue, NW, 363-9710. Beautiful leather and suede clothes—vests, jackets, blazers—much of it custom-designed and made on the premises. Briefcases and shoes, too. For men and women. AE, MC, V. *OPEN 7 days.*

Gianfranco Ferre
5301 Wisconsin Avenue, NW. 244-6633. The Italian designer's first freestanding boutique is a welcome showcase for his ready-to-wear for women and men. AE, MC, V. *OPEN Mon-Sat.*

Gucci
Les Champs, Watergate, 600 New Hampshire Avenue, NW; 965-1700. And Chevy Chase, Md. Also Fairfax, Va. The well-known status clothing, accessories, shoes, and leather goods—with or

without his initials. AE, CB, DC, MC, V. *OPEN Mon-Sat.*

Laura Ashley
3213 M Street, NW. 338-5481. English-country floral fashions in all-natural fabrics for the young and young at heart. Home furnishings including fabric, wallpaper, and lamps. AE, MC, V. *OPEN 7 days.*

Liberty of London
Georgetown Park, 3222 M Street, NW. 338-3711. Clothing and accessories made from the beautiful traditional English print fabrics. Fabrics by the yard, too. AE, MC, V. *OPEN 7 days.*

Limited
*1024 Connecticut Avenue, NW; 955-5710. And Georgetown Park, 3222 M Street, NW; 342-5150. Also The Shops at National Place, 1331 Pennsylvania Avenue, NW, 628-8331; and 5335 Wisconsin Avenue, NW, 686- 7513. Trendy, fashionable looks for the upwardly mobile who do not have the bank account to match; designed for 16-to-40-year-olds. They consistently replenish the stock and have markdowns that make this a place to visit often. Their own line is the number one seller in America. Au courrant accessories, too. *OPEN 7 days. *CLOSED Sun.*

Polo/Ralph Lauren Shop
1220 Connecticut Avenue, NW. 463-7460. Large selection of the well-regarded designer's clothes. On the second floor, classics for women; downstairs, classics for men. AE, DC, MC, V. *OPEN Mon-Sat.*

Saint Laurent Rive Gauche
Les Champs, Watergate, 600 New Hampshire Avenue, NW; 965-3555. And 5516 Wisconsin Avenue, Chevy Chase, Md; (301) 656-8868. Ready-to-wear from the master of fanciful dressing. AE, DC, MC, V. *OPEN Mon-Sat.*

Saks-Jandel
Les Champs, Watergate, 2522 Virginia Avenue, NW; 337-4200. And 5510 Wisconsin Avenue, Chevy Chase, Md; (301) 652-2250. A super store for designer clothes when money's no object. Gucci, Oscar de la Renta, Anne Klein, Perry Ellis. Very special furs at the Chevy Chase store. AE, DC, MC, V. *OPEN Mon-Sat.*

Style vs Freedom
Georgetown Park, 3222 M Street, NW. 333-6023. Poor choice of name for a shop that purveys a small but excellent selection of European-designed au courant clothing for men and women. Individual style; pricey. AE, MC, V. *OPEN 7 days.*

Toast & Strawberries
1617 Connecticut Avenue, NW. 234-2424. Packed with lovely clothing (many local designers are represented), gifts, and accessories. Good selection of maternity and working women's clothes. Sizes 6 to 20. Custom, too, with your fabric or theirs culled from around the world. Fun shop to poke around. Great for alterations. AE, CB, DC, MC, V. *OPEN 7 days.*

Up Against the Wall
3219 M Street, NW; 337-9316. And 1006 F Street, NW; 393-0224. Shop late every night (Friday till midnight!) at this youth-filled spot for youthful, inexpensive sportswear and separates: Gribaud, Guess, Levi's, and more, mostly jeans. Amusing accessories. AE, MC, V. *OPEN 7 days.*

Valentino Boutique
Les Champs, Watergate, 600 New Hampshire Avenue, NW. 333-8700. Valentino, St. Laurent, and Guy Laroche for women. Some accessories. AE, DC, MC, V. *OPEN Mon-Sat.*

The White House
Union Station, 50 Massachusetts Avenue, NE; 289-1639. And 3222 M Street, NW; 965-4419. All-white environment for charming all-white fashions and accessories year-round. AE, MC, V. *OPEN 7 days.*

Consignment

Clothes Encounters of a Second Kind
202 7th Street, SE. 546-4004. Ladies' resale shop for very low priced dresses, separates, bags, shoes, belts, and costume jewelry. AE, MC, V. *OPEN Mon-Sat.*

Encore of Washington
3715 Macomb Street, NW. 966-8122. Very good resale shop for high-quality American and European labels. Accessories, too. MC, V. *OPEN Mon-Sat.*

I Do, I Do
(301) 942-0322. In this Rockville shop, choose from over 200 wedding dresses including designer (all presumably worn only once), sizes 2-20, as well as the headpiece and veil, lingerie (new), and shoes. Also in stock, dresses for the mother of the bride, bridesmaids, and flower girl. No credit cards. *By appointment only.*

The Junior League Shop of Washington
3066 M Street, NW. 337-6120. Where many of DC's leading ladies donate their clothes. Good-cause consignment shop for gently worn women's and kids' conservative and some designer classics. MC, V. *OPEN 7 days.*

Not New
116 South Royal Street, Alexandria, Va. (703) 549-0649. Good consignment shop for contemporary clothing. No credit cards. *OPEN Mon-Sat.*

Once Is Not Enough
4830 MacArthur Boulevard, NW. 337-3072. Where prominent Washington ladies deposit their "I've been seen in it" gowns and day clothes. Designer labels abound, so do clothes with the original tickets still on! Jewelry, furs, men's formal wear. Always a sale rack. New kids' clothes and shoes, too. MC, V. *OPEN Mon, Wed, Fri & Sat 10am-4:30pm; Thurs 10am-8pm.*

The Pinnacle
4932 Wisconsin Avenue, NW, second floor. 244-6300. Though a bit more pricey than the others, you will find "names" Beene, Valentino, Nippon, Ungaro. MC, V. *OPEN Mon-Sat.*

Second Chance
7710 Woodmont Avenue, Bethesda, Md. (301) 652-6606. Women's previously owned, mainly designer, clothes; furs, shoes, and accessories, too. AE, MC, V. *OPEN Mon-Sat.*

Secondhand Rose
1516 Wisconsin Avenue, NW, upstairs. 337-3378. Resale boutique with a large stock of women's designer clothes; furs and accessories, too. Fashions are current and generally in great shape. MC, V. *OPEN Mon-Sat. CLOSED Mon in summer.*

Discount Clothing

Loehmann's
7241 Arlington Boulevard, Falls Church, Va; (703) 573-1510. And 5230 Randolph Road, Rockville, Md; (301) 770-0030. In some areas of the country knowing about Loehmann's is a woman's birthright; in any case it's worth a trip to their back room just for the evening clothes. Today's high fashions at low prices; no labels (or just hints); communal dressing rooms; no returns. A true bargain hunter's dream. MC, V. *OPEN 7 days.*

T. H. Mandy
1118 19th Street, NW; 659-0024. And in suburbs. Ladies, this is *the* downtown DC discount shop for better sportswear. Large selection of the season's newest looks from the likes of Argenti, Maggy London, John Meyer, and more, at prices 20 to 50 percent off retail. Service more personal than in other shops of its kind. (Isn't it nice to know you can get a bargain even if you don't own a car.) AE, MC, V. *OPEN 7 days.*

Ethnic

Nomad
2407 18th Street, NW, upstairs. 332-2998. Owned by an anthropologist, this Adams-Morgan store's motto is "Clothes for the Urban Explorer," and a Baedeker of countries is represented—Morocco, Africa, Japan, South America, Asia, China, India. Some New York and European designs, too. Also their own stylish line, designed by them and made in Morocco. Tribal pieces, accessories, bracelets and necklaces, colorful scarves. AE, MC, V. *OPEN 7 days.*

Nuevo Mundo
313 Cameron Street, Alexandria, Va. (703) 549-0040. A must in Old Town for unique and colorful clothing, jewelry (antique and new), accessories, and objects culled from travels to Europe, India, Afghanistan, China, and Africa. Some ethnic and tribal textiles, pre-Columbian pottery. AE, MC, V. *OPEN Mon-Sat.*

The Phoenix
1514 Wisconsin Avenue, NW. 338-4404. Colorful and fine imports from Mexico. Hand-loomed cotton dresses and lovely lacy Mexican wedding dresses; jewelry, pottery; decorative objects. AE, MC, V. *OPEN 7 days.*

Putumayo
Union Station, 50 Massachusetts Avenue, NE. 289-2255. An attractive selection of moderately priced clothing and accessories imported from Bolivia, Chile, Iceland, Tibet, and Afghanistan. AE, MC, V. *OPEN 7 days.*

Furs

The Fur Vault
7220 Wisconsin Avenue, Bethesda, Md. (301) 654-0555. The largest mink buyer on the East Coast. Full- service furrier (suede and leather, too) with its own storage facility. AE, CB, DC, MC, V, own revolving credit plan. *OPEN Mon & Thurs 10am-9pm; Tues, Wed & Fri 10am-7pm; Sat 10am-6pm; Sun noon-5pm.*

Miller's Furs
1335 F Street, NW. 628-5628. Fine furs since 1921—good-value prices. Some designer furs. AE, CB, DC, MC, V. *OPEN Mon-Sat.*

Mouratidis Furs, Ltd.
4400 Jenifer Street, NW. 338-2500. Fine custom-designed furs for men and women. AE, MC, V. *OPEN Mon-Sat.*

Rosendorf/Evans
1750 K Street, NW; 833-9100. And Montgomery Mall and Tysons Corner. For 85 years their furs have kept District ladies fashionably warm. Clothing, too. AE, MC, V, Rosendorf charge. *OPEN Mon-Sat.*

Saks-Jandel
See Boutiques.

Handbags

All of the department stores have stylish handbag selections.

Camalier & Buckley
1141 Connecticut Avenue, NW; 783-1431. And Mazza Gallerie and Chevy Chase. Also several suburban locations. Quality workmanship: handbags, wallets, briefcases, luggage. Gift accessories. AE, MC, V. *OPEN Mon-Sat.*

Gucci
See Boutiques.

Louis Vuitton
1028 Connecticut Avenue, NW. 296-6838. Handcrafted status luggage and handbags since 1854. For the truly secure, a line of goods without the LVs. AE, MC, V. *OPEN Mon-Sat.*

Hats

All of the major department stores have a selection of hats, especially during spring and fall.

Hats in the Belfry
1237 Wisconsin Avenue, NW. 342-2006. From caps and boaters to top hats and deerstalkers. Hats off to this shop that specializes in head gear for all seasons, all reasons, and in all sizes. AE, MC, V. *OPEN Mon-Thurs 10am-10pm; Fri & Sat 10am-midnight; Sun noon-10pm.*

Lingerie

G's
1197 20th Street, NW. 785-4488. From the routine to the risqué. Danskin, too. AE, MC, V. *OPEN Mon-Sat. CLOSED Sat in summer.*

Klein's 4 Seasons
1050 17th Street, NW; 223-4633. And 1706 G Street, NW; 789-2228. Also 410 L'Enfant Plaza,

SW; 554-3426. Good selection of ladies' lingerie; strong focus on exercise wear including Baryshnikov, Marika, and Danskin. AE, CB, DC, MC, V. *OPEN Mon-Fri.*

Slightly Laced
Crilley Warehouse, 218 North Lee Street, Alexandria, Va. (703) 836-2666. Lovely, lacy lingerie and loungewear. AE, MC, V. *OPEN Mon-Sat.*

Victoria's Secret
The Shops at National Place, 1331 Pennsylvania Avenue, NW; 347-3535. And Georgetown Park, 3222 M Street, NW; 965-5457. Also Union Station, 50 Massachusetts Avenue, NE, 682-0686; and Washington Square, 1050 Connecticut Avenue, NW, 293-7530. For her: a large selection of feminine and sexy intimate apparel and sleepwear in a charmingly intimate-though-in-a-mall setting. For him: a small selection of silk boxer shorts (not all branches). AE, MC, V. *OPEN 7 days.*

Rental

Til Midnight
1200 19th Street, NW. 331-2180. Why didn't Cinderella think of renting? Formal gowns or shorter cocktail dresses for special events, rented for a standard three days; price range $75 to $250. In addition they have excellent sales twice a year, the third week in January and in May. AE, MC, V. *OPEN Mon-Fri 10am-6:30pm; Sat noon-5pm.*

Shoes & Boots

Georgetown overflows with shoe stores.
Bally of Switzerland
Washington Square, 1020 Connecticut Avenue, NW. 429-0604. The finely crafted imported footwear, personal leather goods, leather apparel, and accessories. For men and women. AE, DC, MC, V. *OPEN Mon-Sat.*

The Bootlegger
1142 Connecticut Avenue, NW; 785-2863. And *1420 Wisconsin Avenue, NW; 333-0373. For men and women, moderately priced shoes and boots; bags, too. Great end-of-season sales. Heavy on service and loud music. AE, MC, V. *OPEN Mon-Sat. *OPEN 7 days.*

Hess for Her
2000 Pennsylvania Avenue, NW; 887-9172. And *Georgetown Park, 3222 M Street, NW; 333-7043. Also White Flint. Since 1872, fine women's shoes for dress and sport. Bass, Jourdan, Ferragamo, and Magli among many. AE, CB, DC, MC, V. *OPEN Mon-Sat. *OPEN 7 days.*

Unusual Sizes

August Max
The Shops at National Place, 1331 Pennsylvania Avenue, NW. 347-0108. Very moderately priced now fashions and accessories for the larger woman, size 14 to 24. The savvy staff can help you pull it together. AE, DC, MC, V. *OPEN 7 days.*

The Forgotten Woman
Mazza Gallerie, 5300 Wisconsin Avenue, NW. 363-0828. The woman size 14 to 24 is no longer forgotten. Indeed, here she is catered to. Designer fashions in large sizes only. AE, MC, V. *OPEN 7 days.*

Stylish Stout Shop
925 F Street, NW. 638-7219 or -1184. Large women's apparel, sizes 16 to 52. Sportswear, lingerie, foundation garments. AE, MC, V. *OPEN Mon-Sat.*

Vintage

Amarylis Vintage Company
4922 Wisconsin Avenue, NW. 244-2211. A mood-piece of a shop for clothing, furnishings, textiles, and linens, 1840 to 1940. A small selection of collectible jewelry as well. Highly browsable. AE, MC, V. *OPEN Thurs-Mon, hours vary, call first.*

Antiques Anonymous
See Specialty Shops, Jewelry.

Bird-in-the-Cage Antiques
110 King Street Alexandria, Va, upstairs. (703) 549-5114. In a clutter-filled shop there are racks of vintage clothing circa 1860 to 1960, all packed like sardines. If you have the patience you may be rewarded with an interesting and wearable frock. Also jewelry, accessories, and more, in 20,000 square feet of highly browsable "stuff." AE, MC, V. *OPEN 7 days (evenings in warmer weather).*

Classic Clothing
3146 M Street, NW. 965-2120. Vintage clothes aficionados consider this the best (actually they have virtually knocked off all of their competitors) for the breadth of the stock (especially upstairs). Decades of day and evening dresses, coats, suits, shoes, petticoats, tuxes, letter sweaters, beaded sweaters, used Levis, and much more. New, too. For men and women, and all very accessibly priced, and Russell is extremely helpful. AE, MC, V. *OPEN 7 days.*

Le Melange
1020 King Street, Alexandria, Va. (703) 548-4448. A consignment shop for antique and contemporary women's clothing. Also jewelry and accessories. AE, MC, V. *OPEN Tues, Wed, Fri & Sat 10am-5pm; Thurs till 9pm.*

MEN'S CLOTHES

Boutiques

Beau Monde
International Square, 1814 K Street, NW. 466-7070. Avant-garde fashions for men. AE, MC, V. *OPEN Mon-Sat.*

Britches of Georgetown
1247 Wisconsin Avenue, NW; 338-3330. And *1219 Connecticut Avenue, NW; 347-8994. Also Montgomery, Fair Oaks, Tysons Corner, and

Springfield malls. The young well-to-do trendy's store for the well-turned-out look in clothes and accessories, including jewelry. AE, DC, MC, V. *OPEN 7 days. *OPEN Mon- Sat.*

Britches Great Outdoors
1225 Wisconsin Avenue, NW; 333-3666. And 1200 18th Street, NW; 775-8983. Also Montgomery, Springfield, Tysons Corner, Fair Oaks, and Columbia malls, and Annapolis, Md. Very preppy shop for Shetland sweaters, khakis and cords, sportswear. Some western wear, including Stetson hats. Down wear, too. AE, MC, V. *OPEN 7 days.*

James Clothiers
1800 M Street, NW; 296-2131. And White Flint and Tysons II. A complete men's haberdashery. Armani, Zegna, Valentino, Canali, Hugo Boss, Brioni, and more. AE, CB, DC, MC, V. *OPEN Mon-Sat.*

The Polo Shop/Ralph Lauren
1220 Connecticut Avenue, NW. 463-7460. The quintessential American classics by Ralph Lauren for men, women, and children. AE, DC, MC, V. *OPEN Mon-Sat.*

Raleigh's
1133 Connecticut Avenue, NW; 833-0120. And Mazza Gallerie, 5300 Wisconsin Avenue, NW; 244-6400. Also in suburbs. Popular, large department store heavily devoted to men. Clothes by Cardin, YSL, and Hart Schaffner & Marx; accessories, toiletries, shoes. Women's clothes, too. AE, MC, V. *OPEN Mon-Sat.*

Silhouette/Hugo Boss
1517 Wisconsin Avenue, NW; 338-0120. And 1201 Connecticut Avenue, NW; 887-5081. A top shop for men's high fashion. European and new American designs are featured. AE, DC, MC, V. *OPEN 7 days.*

Consignment

A Man for All Seasons
321 7th Street, SE. 544-4432. Fine selection of consignment clothes for men—well-priced stylish suits, dress shirts, casual wear, ties, and shoes. MC, V. *OPEN Tues-Sat 11am-6pm.*

Discount

Jos. A. Bank
1118 19th Street, NW; 466-2282. And Pentagon City, Rockville, Md, and Falls Church, Va. Direct from this manufacturer, excellent first-quality this-season's clothing at 30 percent off. Traditional suits, jackets, coats, and rugged wear for both men and women. Accessories, too. AE, MC, V. *OPEN Mon-Sat.*

Shoes

Erik Harris
1429 G Street, NW. 783-1933. Stylish shoes for men and women, and the best ties in town. Interesting jewelry and gifts, too. AE, MC, V. *OPEN 7 days.*

Hess
Georgetown Park, 3222 M Street, NW; 333-7043. And White Flint and Tysons Corner. Since 1872 fine leather men's shoes for sport and dress. Jourdan and Magli among many. AE, CB, DC, MC, V. *OPEN 7 days.*

Rich's
1321 F Street, NW. 393-2100. Since 1869 their motto has been: "The world's finest men's shoes." Bruno Magli, Salvatore Ferragamo, Charles Jourdan (and the not-so-chic Bass, too). Women's and children's shoes as well. AE, CB, DC, MC, V. *OPEN Mon-Sat.*

Sports Clothes & Shoes

Abercrombie & Fitch
Georgetown Park, 3222 M Street, NW. 965-6500. The original founded in 1872. Classic men's apparel, accessories, and gifts. AE, MC, V. *OPEN 7 days.*

Eddie Bauer
1800 M Street, NW. 331-8009. Well known for clothing that keeps the chill out. AE, CB, DC, MC, V. *OPEN 7 days.*

The Gap
1217 Connecticut Avenue, NW; 638-4603. And 1267 Wisconsin Avenue, NW; 333-2657. Also 2000 Pennsylvania Avenue, NW, 429-6862; and in suburbs. Youth-oriented affordable sporty fashions. AE, MC, V. *OPEN 7 days.*

Herman's World of Sporting Goods
4350 Jenifer Street, NW; 537-1388. And in suburbs. Huge selection of athletic clothes, shoes, and equipment. AE, CB, DC, MC, V. *OPEN 7 days.*

Hudson Trail Outfitters, Ltd.
Tenley Circle, 4437 Wisconsin Avenue, NW; 363-9810. And in suburbs. "Outdoor clothing specialists"—for every season, every reason. Strong on cross-country, mountain climbing, hiking. MC, V. *OPEN 7 days.*

Traditional

Brooks Brothers
1840 L Street, NW, upstairs; 659-4650. And Chevy Chase, Md. One of America's traditions for quality conservative classics; women's department, too. AE, DC, MC, V, Brooks charge. *OPEN Mon-Sat.*

Burberry's
1155 Connecticut Avenue, NW. 463-3000. The English country-weekend look: waterproofs for men and women. The traditionally styled top coats, blazers, suits, and ties for men; suits, blazers, sweaters, skirts, and shirts for ladies; and of course, the famed trenchcoat and matching checked scarves, umbrellas, and luggage. AE, DC, MC, V. *Thurs till 7pm.*

Unusual Sizes

George & Company
427 7th Street, NW; 638-0884. And Rockville, Md, and McLean, Va. Since 1883 outfitters of big

sizes 44 to 66) and tall (sizes 38 to 56) men. Personal service. AE, MC, V. *OPEN Mon-Sat.*

BEAUTY

Beauty Specialists

(*See also* Hair.)

Daniel's
1831 M Street, NW; 296-4856. And in the Mayflower Hotel. For men and women. Deep-cleansing facials, nail sculpture, waxing. Hair styling, too. MC, V. *OPEN 7 days.*

Elizabeth Arden
5225 Wisconsin Avenue, NW. 362-9890. Elegance behind the red door. Clothes, accessories, cosmetics, perfume. Hair, body, and face specialists facials, body massage, makeup lessons; cuts, blow dry, perms, and more pampering for a price. Women only. AE, DC, MC, V, Elizabeth Arden charge. *OPEN Mon-Sat.*

Lucien et Eivind's
2233 Wisconsin Avenue, NW. 965-2100. For men and women. Skin cleansing, facials, eyebrow shaping, nail sculpture, body waxing. Massage (women only). Hair styling. MC, V. *OPEN Tues-Sat by appointment.*

MRV, Inc.
1010 Wisconsin Avenue, NW. 337-6324. Skin-care salon and boutique for men and women. Orlane products. Waxing, facials, massage. Hair styling, too. Manicures and pedicures. MC, V. *OPEN Tues-Sat, appointment advisable.*

Somebodies Body & Skin
1070 Thomas Jefferson Street, NW. 338-3822. European skin-care system for men and women; concerned with the overall look of the body. Clarins natural herbal-ingredient products. Studio for exercise classes that work with the skin-care treatment. Face treatments take 1½ hours. AE, MC, V. *OPEN Mon-Sat by appointment.*

Suissa Hair & Skin Salon
3068 M Street, NW. 333-1066. Georgetown hair and skin care salon for men and women. Cuts, perms, and coloring. Facials, waxing, manicure, and pedicure. MC, V. *OPEN Mon-Sat by appointment.*

Fragrance

Caswell-Massey
Georgetown Park, 3222 M Street, NW; 965-3224. And 1100 Pennsylvania Avenue, NW; 898-1833. This company, in business since 1752, blended cologne for George and Martha Washington! These pretty and fragrant outposts purvey a large attractive selection of soaps, creams, bath oils, and herbal treatments for face, hair, and body. AE, MC, V. *OPEN 7 days.*

Crabtree & Evelyn
Georgetown Park, 3222 M Street, NW; 342-1934. And Union Station, 50 Massachusetts Avenue, NE; 289-0670. Also in Pentagon City, Tysons Corner, Fair Oaks, and White Flint malls. England's famed all-natural toiletries and comestibles beautifully presented and packed. AE, MC, V. *OPEN 7 days.*

L'Herbier de Provence
Union Station, 50 Massachusetts Avenue, NE. 289-3843. An enticingly pretty and fragrant shop purveying French soaps, bath oils, potpourri, and dried floral topiaries. AE, MC, V. *OPEN 7 days.*

Galerie des Parfums, Inc.
3251 Prospect Street, NW. 965-5090. An extremely wide selection of perfumes and Dior cosmetics. Advice on makeup application. AE, CB, DC, MC, V. *OPEN 7 days.*

Hair

(*See also* Beauty Specialists.)

Bruno Dessange
1523 Wisconsin Avenue, NW. 337-1731. To Georgetown, via Paris and New York. Masterful haircutting. MC. V. *OPEN Mon-Sat by appointment.*

Heads Unlimited
1143 New Hampshire Avenue, NW, in the Sheraton City Centre Hotel. 785-0677. Haircut and blow dry without an appointment (for any other service, an appointment is advisable). Tinting, perms, sets. Manicures, too. MC, V. *OPEN Mon-Sat.*

Robin Weir & Company
2134 P Street, NW. 861-0444. Well-regarded stylist and salon. Cuts, color, styling. Also skin care, facials, makeup, manicures, and waxing. Ask about the "Works." For visitors: They come to your hotel. AE, MC, V. *OPEN Mon-Fri 8am-6pm; Sat 8am-4pm.*

Visage Express
3034 M Street, NW; 965-4420. And 1201 Connecticut Avenue, NW; 775-8250. Top-rated salon in Georgetown for styling, cuts, and color. You can design your own full "day of beauty." MC, V. *OPEN 7 days by appointment.*

Watergate Salon
2532 Virginia Avenue, NW. 333-3488. Full-service salon; shampoo, set; facials, makeup, eyebrow arch; manicure, pedicure. Body massage, electrolysis, and gossip galore. MC, V. *OPEN Mon-Sat.*

Makeup

"I" Natural Cosmetics
Georgetown Park, 3222 M Street, NW. 965-7546. Cosmetics, treatment preparations, and skin care made of only natural things. Makeup styling, consultation, and lessons. *OPEN 7 days.*

Pretty Is
The Shops at National Place, 1331 Pennsylvania Avenue, NW; 737-0742. And International Square, 1825 I Street, NW; 429-9595. All-natural cosmetics. Three lines of skin care: dry, oily, normal. Makeup application with purchase. Also

manicures, pedicures, and waxing. Accessories, too. AE, MC, V. *OPEN 7 days.*

FOOD & WINE

Baked Goods

Au Croissant Chaud
3222 N Street, NW. 333-7700. Exotic selection of croissants: ham, cheese, blueberry, almond, or chocolate. Almond cream pastries, fruit tarts, eclairs, Napoleons, and the breads. *Mon Dieu!* No credit cards. *OPEN 7 days.*

Bread and Chocolate
2301 M Street, NW; 833-8360. And 3251 Prospect Street, NW; 338-5722. Also 666 Pennsylvania Avenue, SE, 547-2875; and 611 King Street, Alexandria, Va, (701) 548-0992. Highly rated European-style bakery for very good European-style breads. Italian, graham, baslor, roggen, baureu, and six-grain. Lovely pastries, too, especially the chocolate truffle cake. Tearoom for eating in. All fresh-baked daily. MC, V. *OPEN 7 days.*

Marvelous Market
5035 Connecticut Avenue, NW; 686-4040. And *Union Station, 50 Massachusetts Avenue, NE; 371-9524. A word-of-mouth success story. Washingtonians rave about their home-baked sour-dough-based breads—rosemary, currant, rye, and olive—especially the olive. There's challah and brioche, too. No credit cards. *OPEN Mon-Fri 8am-8pm; Sat 8am-6pm; Sun 8am-1pm. *OPEN Mon-Sat 11am-9pm; Sun noon-6pm.*

Mayflower Wines and Spirits
2115 M Street, NW. 463-7950. What's a wine store doing under Baked Goods you ask? As lovers of European-style bread will tell you, this is the only place in DC—and Thursday is the only day—that the round panelles, French baguettes, and braided rolls baked in a brick oven in Hoboken, NJ, arrive. MC, V. *OPEN Mon-Sat 10am-9pm.*

New Crustie's Bakery
2824-A Dorr Avenue, Fairfax, Va. (703) 207-9525. Supplier of baked goods to the Mayflower Hotel and other major hotels and restaurants in DC. Now to you, too. Sinful cakes and pies, tasty breads, crusty French loaves, flaky croissants. What more could you want. No credit cards. *OPEN Mon-Sat 7am-6pm.*

Vie de France
Esplanade, 1990 K Street, NW; 659-0055. And 600 Maryland Avenue, SW; 554-7870. Fresh-baked croissants and coffee for *le petit dejeuner.* AE, CB, DC, MC, V. *OPEN Mon-Fri.*

Watergate Pastry Shop
2534 Virginia Avenue, NW. 342-1777. Official and unofficial polls (and pols) rate these the very best baked goodies in town. Specially designed cakes. Apple, cherry, and blueberry pies. French pastries and miniatures. Great cheese-cake and white chocolate mousse cake. Cake

ends for those unafraid of being an old maid (and fat). *OPEN 7 days.*

Candy

Chocolate Chocolate
Washington Square, 1050 Connecticut Avenue NW. 466-2190. So nice they named it twice. Sumptuous in taste and price. *OPEN Mon-Fri 10am-6pm; Sat noon-3pm.*

Godiva Chocolatier, Inc.
Georgetown Park, 3222 M Street, NW; 342-2232. And Union Station, 50 Massachusetts Avenue, NE; 289- 3662. Also Washington Hilton Hotel, 1919 Connecticut Avenue, NW, 332-4427. The famed elaborately boxed sweets. Sybaritic. *OPEN 7 days.*

Krön Chocolatier
Mazza Gallerie, 5300 Wisconsin Avenue, NW. 966-4946. The ultimate in taste treats—whimsical, too (though not the prices). Fantastic truffles and fresh fruit hand-dipped in chocolate. Custom orders including an inscribed solid chocolate heart. Corporate gifts. AE, MC, V. *OPEN 7 days.*

Palais du Chocolat
1200 19th Street, NW. 659-4244. The king of this palace is an award-winning chocolatier, Dominique Leborgne. Trained in France, he creates 30 types of chocolates, using crème fraiche for his filling. Note that his chocolate is 70 percent cocoa (as opposed to the usual 40 percent). AE, MC, V. *OPEN Mon-Fri 8:30am- 6:30pm; Sat 8:30am-5:30pm.*

Gourmet & Catering

Ambrosia
Mazza Gallerie, 5300 Wisconsin Avenue, NW. 362-0677. Gourmet shop filled with imported temptations: mustards, pastas, cheeses, pickles, coffees, teas, spices; wines and beer. AE, MC, V. *OPEN 7 days.*

Ann Gallagher & Company
333-4023. Elegant catering. Wedding receptions to cocktail parties. Will accommodate most menu choices. Full staff of chefs, bartenders, waitresses. No credit cards. *Call 7 days 9am-6pm.*

The French Market
1628-32 Wisconsin Avenue, NW. 338-4828. For more than 30 years this market has known what Washingtonians want on their tables even before they did—fresh game in season, European cuts of meat, charcuterie, baguettes and croissants, over 50 imported cheeses, imported condiments, fine canned goods, wine, champagne, French roast coffee. Now that's what I call one-stop shopping. Free parking in the rear. MC, V. *OPEN Mon-Sat 8:30am-6pm; Wed 8:30am-1:30pm only.*

Georgetown Coffee, Tea & Spice
1330 Wisconsin Avenue, NW. 338-3801. This tea and coffee emporium is a sensational treat. Over 50 varieties of coffee; 85 of tea, including decaf

and their own blends. French spices, Godiva chocolates, breads and cheeses, too. Also a good selection of cookware. AE, MC, V. *OPEN 7 days.*

Sutton Place Gourmet
3201 New Mexico Avenue, NW. 363-5800. Fresh meats, 600 kinds of cheese, seven different foie gras, every vegetable in and out of season; 300 brands of beer; fresh herbs. Their own chocolates made on premises (the bread and cookies are made at their Bethesda location). Fresh and packaged foodstuffs from around the world. Gourmet dishes to go from their own kitchen. Wonderful but pricey. MC, V. *OPEN 7 days.*

Health Food

The Natural Food Store
1825 Columbia Road, NW. 462-5150. Small store for strict vegetarians. Fresh organic and inorganic produce; fresh juice, soup, and sandwiches made; cheeses, too. Vitamins, books on health, natural cosmetics, and beauty aids. AE, MC, V. *OPEN Mon-Sat.*

Yes! Natural Gourmet
3425 Connecticut Avenue, NW. 363-1559. Go natural. Only pure organic foods. Fresh produce; 300 types of herb tea; 150 different nuts, grains, fruits; natural cosmetics and soaps. The first and largest natural food store in DC. AE, MC, V. *OPEN 7 days.*

Wine & Spirits

AB Liquor Company
1803 Columbia Road, NW. 234-5500. Knowledgeable owners and good prices make this a favorite spot of Adams-Morgan oenophiles. *OPEN Mon-Sat.*

Ace Beverage
3301 New Mexico Avenue, NW. 966-4444. Emphasis on personal service. Delivers. *OPEN Mon-Sat.*

Calvert Woodley
4339 Connecticut Avenue, NW. 966-4400. Top spot for wine buyers. Large stock, impressive variety. Unique feature: Bordeaux futures. Add your name to their mailing list for reminders of good sales. MC, V. *OPEN Mon-Sat 10am-8:30pm.*

Central Liquor
726 9th Street, NW. 737-2800. Volume operation offers good weekly buys on imported wines and liquors. *OPEN Mon-Sat.*

Eagle Wine & Cheese
3345 M Street, NW. 333-6655. Discount prices on wine, beer, liquor, cheese. Well respected for their good selection of wine and their knowledgeable staff. Tasting room, daily samples of cheese. Fresh-baked bread; catering; picnics; luncheons for 15 to 1,500 people. Office parties are their specialty. MC, V. *OPEN Mon-Sat.*

MacArthur Liquor
4877 MacArthur Boulevard, NW. 338-1433. A favorite of wine buyers for the knowledgeable and

helpful staff. MC, V. *OPEN Mon-Sat 10am-8:30pm.*

Mayflower Wines & Spirits
2115 M Street, NW. 463-7950. A favorite of local oenophiles and bread lovers (*see* Baked Goods). Features wine tastings from time to time. MC, V. *OPEN Mon-Sat 10am-9pm.*

Plain Old Pearson's
2436 Wisconsin Avenue, NW. 333-6666. Over 2,000 wines stocked, many at bargain prices. *OPEN Mon-Sat.*

HOME

China & Housewares

China Closet
4418 Connecticut Avenue, NW; 362-8440. And 7235 Arlington Boulevard, Falls Church, Va; (703) 698-9236. Also White Flint. Discount contemporary and imported cookware; flatware and ceramics. Just about anything you might need. AE, MC, V. *OPEN 7 days.*

Dolly Kay Designs Ltd.
5232 44th Street, NW. 966-0925. Mazza Gallerie vicinity. Elegant pottery and china; Porthault linens; collectibles, art glass, gift items. AE, MC, V. *OPEN Mon-Sat.*

Kitchen Bazaar
4401 Connecticut Avenue, NW. 244-1550. Au courant for the kitchen. Le Creuset merchandise, imported copper items from France, gadgets. Over 9,000 items for the serious cook. They will ship (for a stiff fee). MC, V. *OPEN 7 days.*

La Cuisine
323 Cameron Street, Alexandria, Va. (703) 836-4435. For very high quality cooking gear. Lovely terrines, copperware. Also a good selection of cookbooks. Call (800) 521-1176 for special orders from their catalog cum source book. MC, V. *OPEN Mon-Sat.*

Little Caledonia
1419 Wisconsin Avenue, NW. 333-4700. A nest of inviting shops packed with traditional cookware, china, furnishings; tile (nearly 100 designs); fabric; stationery, cards; kids' stuff, too. Great spot for gift browsing and buying when you haven't a clue. AE, MC, V. *OPEN Mon-Sat.*

Martin's of Georgetown
1304 Wisconsin Avenue, NW. 338-6144. The longtime (50 plus years) Washington source for fine china and crystal including Baccarat, Herend, Ginori, and Lalique; silver by Buccellati, Tiffany, and Christofle; Kaiser and Boehm porcelain. Antique and contemporary. Also a wonderful selection of fanciful baskets. AE, MC, V. *OPEN Mon-Sat.*

Williams-Sonoma
Mazza Gallerie, 5300 Wisconsin Avenue, NW. 244-4800. Well-known and well-stocked cookware specialty shop from California. AE, MC, V. *OPEN Mon-Fri 10am-8pm; Sat 10am-6pm; Sun noon-5pm.*

Furniture

(*See also* Specialty Shops, Antiques & Collectibles.)

The Bombay Company
Georgetown Park, 3222 M Street, NW. 333-0852. Their specialty is reproduction English-style accent furnishings, lamps, mirrors, brass accessories, and framed prints, all affordably priced. The look—but not too close—is heirloom. AE, MC, V. *OPEN 7 days.*

Conran's Habitat
Georgetown Park, 3227 Grace Street, NW. 298-8300. Via London and New York, a top name in contemporary furnishings. The renovated 18th-century warehouse building crossing the canal is stocked with attractive, colorful housewares, fabrics, and life-style (simple, carry out) furniture. Now more sophisticated than it was at the start. AE, MC, V. *OPEN 7 days.*

Door Store
3140 M Street, NW; 333-7737. And in suburbs. Emphasis is on the contemporary oak and maple furniture hand- and factory-made. Plastic, teak, marble, and glass items. Household accessories; imports from Italy, Hungary, Czechoslovakia, Romania. AE, MC, V. *OPEN 7 days.*

This End Up
The Shops at National Place, 1331 Pennsylvania Avenue, NW; 783-1187. And 117 King Street, Alexandria, Va; (703) 549-2974. Also in suburbs. Rugged handcrafted yellow pine furniture, fashioned after packing crates contemporary and highly affordable. Choice of 50 fabrics. Lamps, accessories, and wall hangings as well. AE, MC, V. *OPEN 7 days.*

The Wicker Shoppe
Old Town Market, 210 North Lee Street, Alexandria, Va. (703) 548-7773. Everything you ever wanted in wicker, rattan, and willow. MC, V. *OPEN 7 days.*

Rugs

Bloomingdale's at White Flint and Tysons Corner has a good oriental rug gallery. See also Specialty Shops, Antiques & Collectibles.

Adabi Oriental Rug Gallery
3323 Connecticut Avenue, NW. 362-1116. Old and new handmade oriental, Persian, Chinese, Indian, Romanian, and Pakistani rugs. Services: washing, repairs, appraisals, and will ship anywhere. MC, V. *OPEN 7 days.*

David's Antique Rugs
4918 Wisconsin Avenue, NW. 338-4141. Antique, new, and used decorative kilims and nomadic rugs; tapestries, pillows. Restoration, appraisals, and cleaning are their specialty. MC, V. *OPEN Mon-Sat.*

Nazarian
4801 Massachusetts Avenue, NW, Suite 200. 364-6400. Since 1920, oriental rugs and carpets: new, antique, semi-antique. Repairs, cleaning, appraisals, and storage. Expert advice. Free parking. No credit cards. *OPEN Mon-Sat.*

Pasargad Carpets, Inc.
Dupont Circle, 1351 Connecticut Avenue, NW. 659-3888. Since 1904 direct importers of fine Persian and oriental rugs. One of the largest selections in the country. Low prices. Repairs and cleaning, too. AE, MC, V. *OPEN 7 days.*

SPECIALTY SHOPS

Antiques & Collectibles

Alcoforado Arts and Antiques
1673 Wisconsin Avenue, NW. 338-6717 or -0486. A rare and refined selection of medieval to late 18th- century antiques. No credit cards. *OPEN 7 days 11am-5pm.*

Antiques Anonymous
2627 Connecticut Avenue, NW. 332-5555. Not far from the National Zoo, a worthwhile stop for collectors of estate jewelry, with a good selection of Art Deco as well as Bakelite, Mexican silver, and 40s costume. In addition, vintage clothes Victorian to 50s. It's packed with stuff (even New York dealers buy here). AE, MC, V. *OPEN Mon-Sat 11am-6pm.*

Antiques-on-the-Hill
701 North Carolina Avenue, SE. 543-1819. A longtime spot, across from Eastern Market, now under new management. Antiques, bric-a-brac, quilts. Much clutter but don't let that fool you, they know what they've got and it's priced accordingly. Clothing; oak and Victorian furniture. AE, MC, V. *OPEN Tues-Sun.*

A Bit of Britain
607 South Washington Street, Alexandria, Va. (703) 836-3420. All things British—old and new. English pine country furniture, Lloyd Loom wicker, porcelain, china, antique accessories. Upstairs, Victorian linen and lace. MC, V. *OPEN Tues-Sun.*

Cherishables Antiques
1608 20th Street, NW. 785-4087. Lovely inviting shop purveys 18th- and 19th-century American furniture, folk art, and quilts; decorative accessories. Both country and formal. Contemporary sofas and decorative items also. Modern fabrics follow through the antique themes. AE, MC, V. *OPEN Mon-Sat.*

Christ Child Opportunity Shop
1427 Wisconsin Avenue, NW. 333-6635. Benefiting community programs for children. Go directly upstairs (the shop is a hodgepodge downstairs) for what may be the largest selection of antiques and collectibles in Georgetown. You will find on consignment higher-ticket items, including silver, china, paintings, rugs, quilts, embroidered shawls and kimonos. Many a dealer makes a morning stop here—they (and now you) know that new merchandise is put out every day. Friendly, highly browsable albeit not exactly cheap. No credit cards. *OPEN Mon-Sat 10am-3:45pm only. CLOSED August.*

The Georgetown Antiques Center
2918 M Street, NW. 338-3811. Two shops (Michael Getz Antiques and Cherub Antiques Gallery) under one roof provide a pleasant browsing opportunity. You will be tempted by the very fine collection of art, antiques, Georgian to Art Deco. British watercolors and drawings, silver, furnishings. They will ship anywhere. AE, MC, V. *OPEN 7 days.*

Joy's Blair House Antiques
1663 Wisconsin Avenue, NW. 338-5349. An *extremely* cluttered shop in which the collector with a good eye may spot a find, the aptly named owner could not be more accommodating. No credit cards. *OPEN Mon-Sat 11am-5pm.*

Lenore and Daughters
130 South Royal Street, Alexandria, Va. (703) 836-3356. Several inviting rooms full of 19th-century silver, china, oil paintings, antique prints, and jewelry. Nice spot, nice owner. AE, MC, V. *OPEN Mon-Sat.*

Lloyd's Row
119 South Henry Street, Alexandria, Va. (703) 549-7517. Fine 18th-century American and English furnishings. Paintings, prints; silver and brass accessories. No credit cards. *OPEN Tues-Sat.*

Marston Luce
1314 21st Street, NW. 775-9460. American and European, some early 18th, and 19th century, American folk art, painted furniture, quilts, and porcelain. Specializes in garden items and architectural pieces such as columns, windows, classical detailing. AE, MC, V. *OPEN Mon-Sat 11am-6pm.*

Miller & Arney
1737 Wisconsin Avenue, NW. 338-2369. Quality American and European furniture, mainly from the 18th and 19th centuries. Rugs, paintings, silver, glass, china. AE, MC, V. *OPEN Mon-Sat.*

Reflections Antiques
310 North Fairfax Street, Alexandria, Va. (703) 683-6808. Mainly antique brass lighting from 1850 to 1930, including chandeliers with original gas lighting, early electric, or a combination of gas and electric; wall lights and sconces; table and floor lamps. Also antique furniture of the same period—armoires (a specialty), desks, marble-top dressers and night tables. It's a handsome shop. AE, MC, V. *OPEN 7 days.*

Rocky Road to Kansas
Carriage House Shops, 215 South Union Street, upstairs, Alexandria, Va. (703) 683-0116. A charming, well- stocked find for lovers of antique quilts—19th century to the 1930s—as well as new ones from Kansas and Pennsylvania. Crib quilts, wall hangings, table covers, basic quilting supplies, and books; also made-from-old-quilts pillows and stuffed animals, door stops, and draft dodgers (with long tails). Other charming prairie folk art including "dingy dolls" made from old fabric and notions. MC, V. *OPEN 7 days.*

Rooms & Gardens
1631 Wisconsin Avenue, NW. 965-3820. A unique and inviting antique shop in Georgetown with a very personal point of view. The inside/outside European gardenlike atmosphere, created by mainly French furnishings and accessories, including the wonderful turn-of-the-century *pique-assiette*, is one you will want to transport to your room and garden. Interior and garden design services available. AE, MC, V. *OPEN Tues-Sat 10am-6pm; Sun 1-5pm.*

Susquehanna Antiques
3216 O Street, NW. 333-1511. Quality 18th- and early 19th-century American and European antiques (mainly furniture). MC, V. *OPEN Mon-Sat.*

Trojan Antiques & Teacher's Pet
Old Town Market, 210 North Lee Street, Alexandria, Va. 549-9766. The area's largest selection of well-priced vintage costume jewelry. In addition, an eclectic mix of antiques and collectibles, including miniatures, old Christmas ornaments, kitchen items, advertising memorabilia. Contemporary country crafts, too. AE, MC, V. *OPEN 7 days.*

Warehouse Antiques
Crilley Warehouse, 218 North Lee Street, Alexandria, Va. (703) 548-2150. Specializes in turn-of-the-century English pine. MC, V. *OPEN 7 days.*

Antiques & Flea Markets

Wonderful alternatives to mall shopping; best for treasure hunters and those in the mood for serendipity.

Flea Market at Eastern Market
7th Street & North Carolina Avenue, SE. (703) 534-7612. Though the usually bustling market itself is closed on Sunday, on that day there is a good outdoors collection of approximately 70 to 100 vendors purveying antiques, collectibles, and handmade crafts. It's the perfect place to Christmas shop no matter what time of year. Good spots to eat nearby. *OPEN March-Nov, 10am-5pm.*

Georgetown Flea Market
The Parking Yard of Family Rosario Adult Education Center, Wisconsin Avenue between S & T Streets, NW. (703) 296-4989. Across from the "social" Safeway is this longtime well-run flea market where approximately 60 to 100 vendors purvey everything from old tools, to antique coins, watches, silver, and furniture, to vintage and just plain used clothing. You're sure to find something; a lot of this town's antique dealers can be found here buying. Snack stand. *OPEN first Sun in March-last Sun in Dec, 9am-5pm.*

Farmer's Flea Market
7155 Wisconsin Avenue, NW, Bethesda, Md. This is on Wednesday and Saturday the Bethesda Farmwoman's market, but on Sunday it becomes quite a good flea market with approximately 75 vendors selling old and new merchandise *OPEN March-Nov, 9am-5pm.*

A Thieves Market
8101 Richmond Highway, Alexandria, Va. ' 360-4200. Eighteen shops for antiques

lectibles: jewelry, china, furniture, rugs, paintings, silver. Of varying quality. *OPEN 7 days.*

The Washington Antiques Center Limited
209 Madison Street at Fairfax, Alexandria, Va. (703) 739-2484. Fifty permanent dealers selling 18th-, 19th-, and 20th-century American, European, and Oriental furniture, paintings, porcelain, bronzes, jewelry, silver, and books. Free parking on weekends. *OPEN Wed-Mon 11am-6pm.*

Auctions

Adam A. Weschler & Son
905 E Street, NW. 628-1281. Since 1890. A little bit of everything appears at the weekly auctions, every Tuesday at 9:30am. American, English, and European furniture and decorative pieces, fine arts, jewelry, and 20th-century art including Art Deco and Art Nouveau; oriental art and furniture. Inspection one week prior to auction.

Laws Auction House
7209 Centreville Road (Route 28), Manassas, Va. (703) 361-3148. Inspection all day Monday and Friday. Weekly auctions on Monday and Friday nights. Six catalog auctions a year.

G. Sloan & Company, Inc.
4920 Wyaconda Road, Rockville Pike, Rockville, Md. (301) 468-4911. Eight catalog auctions yearly for fine antiques. Auctions held throughout the year, usually on Saturday, mainly for household items, in Rockville, Md. Call for further information. Appraisals.

Books: General

Bartleby's
7710 Woodmont Avenue, Bethesda, Md. (301) 654-4373. Considered one of the area's best. Fiction, nonfiction, literary criticism, philosophy, science, poetry, unusual press books. New and antiquarian. AE, MC, V. *OPEN Mon-Sat 10am-8pm; Sun noon-6pm.*

B. Dalton
1776 K Street; 872-0863. And The Shops at National Place, 1331 Pennsylvania Avenue, NW; 393-1468. Also Mazza Gallerie, 5300 Wisconsin Avenue, NW, 393-1468. Over 25,000 titles; quite good, well-stocked national chain bookstore. Helpful service. Good DC book section. AE, DC, MC, V. *OPEN 7 days.*

Books Unlimited
2729 Wilson Boulevard, Arlington, Va. (703) 525-0550. Crowded treasure trove of fiction—new and backlist. Also Judaica, feminist, and children's books. Children's play area. MC, V. *OPEN Mon, Wed & Fri 10am-9pm; Tues, Thurs & Sat 10am-6pm.*

Borders Book Shop
11500 Rockville Pike, Md. (301) 816 1067. With more than 300,000 books in stock (125,000 titles arranged within 30 sections), this newcomer is without a doubt the area's heavyweight among booksellers. Setting it apart also is the classical music (live on Friday evenings), author readings

and appearances, clean rest rooms, and the large adjacent shop for children's books (*see also* KIDS' WASHINGTON, Children's Shopping: Borders Book Shop for Kids). AE, MC, V. *OPEN Mon-Sat 9am-11pm; Sun 11am-8pm.*

Bridge Street Books
2814 Pennsylvania Avenue, NW. 965-5200. Good selection of current fiction, literary criticism, politics, psychology, philosophy, film, women's studies, Judaica. MC, V. *OPEN Mon-Thurs 10am-7pm; Fri & Sat 10am-11pm; Sun 1-6pm.*

Calliope Bookshop
3424 Connecticut Avenue, NW. 364-0111. The bookstore that book lovers love. Good selections, including hard-to-find titles. The specialty is literature, including low-priced remainders. Also history, psychology, art, music, travel, photography, and women's studies. AE, MC, V. *OPEN Mon-Sat 10am-10pm; Sun noon-9pm.*

Chapters Literary Bookstore
1512 K Street, NW. 347-5495. Well stocked with new and backlist fiction; strong in literature, poetry, criticism. A sweet touch: cookies and sherry are served every Friday afternoon. Special orders, gift wrapping, and mailing. AE, MC, V. *OPEN Mon-Fri 10am-6:30pm; Sat 11am-5pm.*

Francis Scott Key Bookstore
1400 28th Street, NW. 337-4144. It's the quintessential bookstore and has been a Georgetown institution since 1939. They invite you to browse and even serve you tea. Piled high with current books, mostly hardcover. Art, biography, travel; good children's book selection. They special order, will do an out-of-print search, have a delivery service, take phone orders, gift wrap, and mail. MC, V. *OPEN Mon-Sat 9:30am-5pm.*

Kramer Books & Afterwords
1517 Connecticut Avenue, NW. 387-1400. A unique bookstore/cafe (*see* RESTAURANTS, Late Night/24 Hours). Good selection in all fields: best-sellers, classics, history, politics, literary criticism. Newspapers and periodicals, too. AE, MC, V. *OPEN Sun-Thurs 8am-1am; Fri & Sat 24 hours.*

Olsson's Books & Records
1307 19th Street, NW; 785-1133. And 1239 Wisconsin Avenue, NW; 338-9454. Also 106 South Union Street, Alexandria, Va, (703) 684-0077. Extremely popular complete bookstore. Hardcover and paperback, fiction and nonfiction. Small press, history, politics. *Washington Post* hardcover best-sellers 25 percent off retail. They will order almost any book in print if not in stock. Also a separate music section with a good selection of new LPs and CDs. AE, MC, V. (*See also* Records.) *OPEN 7 days.*

Politics & Prose Bookstore
5015 Connecticut Avenue, NW. 364-1919. Very personal full-service bookstore. Fiction, nonfiction, Penguin classics, Washington politics, art, psychology, cooking. Special orders, shipping, gift wrapping. Frequent author readings. Monthly calendar of events. MC, V. *OPEN Mon-Sat 10am-10pm; Sun 11am-6pm.*

Trover Shop
1031 Connecticut Avenue, NW; 659-8138. And
*800 15th Street, NW; 347-2177. Also **227
Pennsylvania Avenue, SE, 543-8006. Wide selection of paperbacks; all the current fiction and
nonfiction. Penguin classics; good magazine selection. Gift items. Cards, too. MC, V. *OPEN Mon-
Sat. *OPEN Sun-Fri. **OPEN 7 days.*

Waldenbooks
1700 Pennsylvania Avenue, NW; 393-1490. And
*Georgetown Park, 3222 M Street; 333-8033.
Best-sellers, general books. Foreign language,
travel, politics, current events, self-help, and
computer books. AE, MC, V. *OPEN Mon-Sat.
Lloyd's*OPEN 7 days.*

Books: Discount

Crown Books
2020 K Street, NW; 659-2030. And 1710 G
Street, NW; 789-2277. Also 3131 M Street, NW,
333-4493; and many other locations including
suburbs. Well known for its great selection of
hardcover and paperback books and magazines, all at substantial discounts. Bestsellers
(hardcover) 40 percent off and paperbacks 25
percent off. Remainders at greater savings. MC,
V. *OPEN 7 days 9am-8pm.*

Books: Antiquarian, Old & Used

Booked Up
1209 31st Street, NW. 965-3244. Antiquarian
bookstore in Georgetown. Rare first editions,
good-condition used and out-of-print books. In a
charming setting. Great for collectors. No credit
cards. *OPEN Mon-Sat.*

Capitol Hill Books
657 C Street, SE. 544-1621. When you have finished browsing at Eastern Market pop into this
secondhand shop strong on out-of-print history
and modern first editions. No credit cards. *OPEN
Mon-Fri 11am-7pm; Sat 9am-6pm; Sun noon-
5pm.*

Estate Book Sales
2914 M Street, NW. 965-4274. On three floors in
Georgetown: scholarly, used, and out-of-print
books. AE, MC, V. *OPEN 7 days 11am-7pm.*

Idle Time Books
2410 18th Street, NW. 232-4774. Browsable
Adams-Morgan bookshop. Two and a half floors
of used and out-of-print books. Review copies of
new books at discount. MC, V. *OPEN 7 days
11am-10pm (at least).*

Secondhand Prose
5010 Connecticut Avenue, NW. 364-8280. A
good selection of all categories of used books
with a special emphasis on psychology, politics,
and history. Sometimes first editions and collector's items. They buy as well. MC, V. *OPEN Tues-
Sat noon-8pm; Sun noon-6pm.*

Second Story Books
Dupont Circle, 2000 P Street, NW; 659-8884.
And 602 King Street, Alexandria, Va; (703) 548-
2742. Also 4836 Bethesda Avenue, Bethesda,
Md, (301) 656-0170. Very good source: used,

rare, and out-of-print books. Free (albeit a $1
tax) search service. Old *Life* magazines, too.
Highly amenable to browsing. Secondhand LPs,
CDs, and videos stocked as well. AE, MC, V.
OPEN 7 days 10am-10pm.

Books: Special Interest

American History Museum Shop
National Museum of American History, Constitution Avenue between 12th & 14th Streets, NW.
357-1784. This bookstore specializes in American history and culture. A 10 percent discount
for Smithsonian members. AE, MC, V. *OPEN 7
days.*

American Institute of Architects Bookstore
1735 New York Avenue, NW. 626-7475. Specializes in architecture books and gifts. AE, MC, V.
OPEN Mon-Fri.

Backstage
2101 P Street, NW. 775-1488. A whole room dedicated to scripts and theater-oriented books,
over 3,000 titles. Books on dance, opera, film,
theater, and TV. Special search service. Merchandise also includes greasepaint, masks,
dancewear, and much more. AE, MC, V. *OPEN
Mon-Sat (and the occasional Sun).*

Franz Bader Gallery & Bookstore
1911 I Street, SE. 337-5440. Art books, art history, graphics techniques. Books on photography, architecture, design. *OPEN Mon-Sat 10am-
6pm.*

Cheshire Cat Children's Book Store
See KIDS' WASHINGTON, Children's Shopping.

International Language Center
1753 Connecticut Avenue, NW (inside the News
Room). 332-2894. Books, magazines, audiovi-
sual tapes in 120 languages. Great hours! AE,
MC, V ($25 minimum). *OPEN Mon-Fri 7am-
10pm; Sat 7am-11pm; Sun 7am- 9pm.*

Victor Kamkin Bookstore
4956 Boiling Brook Parkway, Rockville, Md.
(301) 881-5973. This is the largest Russian-
language bookstore outside of Moscow. Inventory of over 150,000 titles, includes everything
from political treatises to cookbooks. Upstairs for
dissident and emigre authors. V, MC. *OPEN
Mon-Sat 9am-5pm.*

Sidney Kramer Books
1825 I Street, NW. 293-2685. In business for
nearly 50 years. Expert on economics, foreign
affairs, political science, and management. One
of the few stores that specializes in books of this
kind. Special orders. AE, MC, V. *OPEN Mon-Fri
9am-6:30pm; Sat 10am-5pm.*

Lambda Rising
1625 Connecticut Avenue, NW. 462-6969. Gay-
and lesbian-oriented books, magazines, and
newspapers; records, cards, and gifts. AE, MC,
V. *OPEN 7 days 10am-midnight.*

The Map Store
1636 I Street, NW. 628-2608. One of the area's
best for maps and guides, foreign and domestic
nautical charts, topographic maps; globes. *
OPEN Mon-Sat.

Preservation Shop
1600 H Street, NW. 842-1856. Books about historic preservation. Run by the National Trust for Historic Preservation; their own publications make nice gifts. Free literature on preservation efforts. For mail order, call 673-4200. MC, V. *OPEN Mon-Sat.*

Schoenhof's Foreign Books
3160 O Street, NW. 338-8963. French, German, Italian, Russian, and Spanish (some other languages, too) literature and children's books. Dictionaries and cassettes in 50 languages. Records of spoken arts—poetry, recitals. Special orders. MC, V. *OPEN Mon-Sat.*

Travel Books & Language Center, Inc.
4931 Cordell Avenue, Bethesda, Md. (301) 951-8533; (800) 220-2665. Terrific shop for peripatetic and armchair travelers. Guides, maps, atlases, dictionaries, language books, cassettes. Histories as well as books on tape for listening to while you drive. AE, MC, V. *OPEN Mon-Sat 10am-9pm; Sun noon-5pm.*

Travel Merchandise Mart
1425 K Street, NW. 371-6656. Good selection of travel guides and maps, lanquage books, and tapes. Small selection of travel items. MC, V. *OPEN Mon-Fri 9am-5pm.*

Yes! Bookshop
1035 31st Street, NW. 338-7874. Extensive stock of books: holistic medicine, nutrition; philosophy, mysticism, medicine, and other East-West disciplines for mind and body. CDs and tapes: classical, Eastern, and medieval music. AE, MC, V. *OPEN 7 days.*

Crafts

Appalachian Spring
1415 Wisconsin Avenue, NW; 337-5780. And Union Station, 50 Massachusetts Avenue, NE; 682-0505. A charming selection of American handmade contemporary country items: quilts, pottery, dolls, toys, rag rugs, pewter, woodenware, ironwork, jewelry, and kaleidoscopes. AE, MC, V. *OPEN 7 days.*

Elder Crafters Shop
405 Prince Street, Alexandria, Va. (703) 683-4338. A nonprofit consignment shop featuring unique handcrafted items made by men and women over 55 years of age. Quilts, dolls and their houses, furniture, jewelry, scarves and sweaters, infant clothing and artwork, handmade ornaments, wooden toys, boxes, and game sets. MC, V. *OPEN Tues-Sat 10am-4pm.*

Torpedo Factory Art Center
105 North Union Street at King Street, Alexandria, Va. (703) 838-4565. A massive WW I torpedo factory recycled as an arts and crafts studio and retail complex. All media. Fun to browse, observe, or purchase. *OPEN 7 days 10am-5pm.*

Drugstores

Morgan Pharmacy
3001 P Street, NW. 337-4100. A charming, old-fashioned Georgetown pharmacy where the em-

phasis is on personal service. Prescriptions, sundries, and a helpful, courteous staff—not only to regulars but to travelers in need. MC, V. *OPEN Mon-Sat 8:30am-6pm.*

People's
14th Street & Thomas Circle, NW, off Vermont Avenue; 628-0720. And 7 Dupont Circle, NW; 785-1466. They are all over town, and they carry everything you might need in the way of medications, cosmetics, and more. Prescriptions filled around the clock at these two. *OPEN 7 days, 24 hours.*

Ethnic

(*See also* Women's Clothes: Ethnic.)

Bamboozled!
1499 22nd Street, NW. 659-5050. Spacious, Dupont Circle-area shop is well stocked with unique imports from all over the world. Women's clothes including lovely kimonos for evening, accessories, jewelry, serious and not so. Small affordable children's items and much that is handcrafted. Good gift buying; friendly, helpful staff. AE, MC, V. *OPEN Mon-Sat.*

Discoveries
207 Ramsay Alley, Alexandria, Va. (703) 548-9448. A gift shop/gallery of carpets, papyrus paintings, jewelry, sculpture, and art, mainly African. Brass and copper, rugs, textiles, and leather from Egypt, North and West Africa. All handmade, hand-picked, hand-packed, and lovingly purveyed. AE, MC, V. *OPEN 7 days.*

Ginza, Inc.
1721 Connecticut Avenue, NW. 331-7991. Futons—Japanese bedding; comforters, too. China, sake sets, baskets, fans, pillows, jewelry, kimonos, and tabis. Books on Japanese culture. MC, V. *OPEN Mon-Sat.*

Indian Craft Shop
Department of the Interior, 1800 C Street, NW. 737-4381. A wonderful stock of authentic handcrafted American Indian-made crafts. Silver and turquoise jewelry; dolls, pottery, rugs, baskets. Also ivory and soapstone carvings from Alaska. MC, V. *OPEN Mon-Fri 8:30am-4:30pm.*

Fabric

Cherishable Antiques
See Antiques & Collectibles.

G Street Fabrics
Mid-Pike Plaza, 11854 Rockville Pike, Rockville, Md. (301) 231-0990. Imported silks, woolens, cottons; remnants, including some couture fabrics; notions, upholstery fabrics, too. Just about everything for sewing plus how-to classes (call 231-8982 for newsletter and schedule) and videos to rent on sewing and fashion. For mail order, call (301) 231-8960. AE, MC, V. *OPEN Mon-Fri 10am-9pm; Sat 10am-6pm; Sun noon-5pm.*

Jo-Ann Fabrics
1223 Connecticut Avenue, NW. 628-9855. At this and 20 other locations throughout the metropolitan area you'll fill all your sewing needs. Slip-

cover, upholstery, and drapery fabrics; patterns, needles, and notions; craft and quilting supplies. AE, MC, V. *OPEN Mon-Sat.*

Liberty of London
Georgetown Park, 3222 M Street, NW. 338-3711. England's traditional print fabrics by the yard. Wide range for dress, drapery, and upholstery. Also clothing and accessories in Liberty prints. AE, MC, V. *OPEN 7 days.*

Framing

Grafix
2904 M Street, NW. 342-0610. (Formerly, Revival Processes Custom Framing.) Conservation framing using acid-free materials. Over 800 frames from which to choose. Antique prints and vintage posters are more reasons for going here. MC, V. *OPEN Mon-Sat.*

Mickelson Gallery
707 G Street, NW. 628-1734. Washington's oldest and largest custom-framing facility. Dedicated to framing of fine art to museum specifications. AE, MC, V. *OPEN Mon-Sat.*

The Old Print Gallery
1220 31st Street, NW. 965-1818. This lovely gallery shop for 18th- and 19th-century prints and maps is a perfect place to have custom framing done. (*See also* MUSEUMS & GALLERIES, Galleries.) MC, V. *OPEN Mon-Sat.*

Venable-Neslage Gallery
1803 Connecticut Avenue, NW. 462-1800. Largely restoration and conservation framing but will do custom-design framing for anything— tapestries, fans, collars, medals. (*See also* MUSEUMS & GALLERIES, Galleries.) AE, DC, MC, V. *OPEN Tues-Sat.*

Gifts

Candlewyck of Alexandria
320 King Street, Alexandria, Va. (703) 548-2279. Charming shop for candles of every shape, for every occasion, in a variety of fragrances. Holders, sticks, gifts. AE, MC, V. *OPEN Mon-Sat.*

Carnation Station
109 North Pitt Street, Alexandria, Va. (703) 836-1604. Not your ordinary flower shop. Fresh, silk, and dried flowers. Choose from an unusual selection of European flowers. Gift items such as rocking horses, hand-painted and blown glass vases, gourmet candies and foods for gift baskets. Extensive line of fanciful ribbons. MC, V. *OPEN Mon-Sat.*

Contrast
Union Station, 50 Massachusetts Avenue, NE, West Hall, 371-0566. A well-chosen selection of unusual contemporary gifts from all over the world. AE, MC, V. *OPEN 7 days.*

Dallas Alice
The Shops at National Place, 1331 Pennsylvania Avenue, NW. 628-8686. Specializes in silk-screened tees and sweatshirts; colorful, witty, and amusing. Good DC souvenirs and gifts. More expensive than the usual, but then they are not the usual. Mail order. AE, MC, V. *OPEN 7 days.*

Fit to a Tee
Georgetown Park, 3222 M Street, NW; 965-3650. And The Small Mall, 118 King Street, Alexandria. Va; (703) 836-0938. Quality tees and sweatshirts for the whole family, including infants. Hand-painted and hand- screened, featuring Washington themes as well as Gary Larson's "Far Side." Here, too, Gorby tees, the true future collectible. AE, MC, V. *OPEN 7 days.*

Soon S. Hong
At the Pavilion at the Old Post Office. Mr. Hong beautifully executes, in watercolor, artistic name writing combined with oriental symbolism. The result is a beautiful and meaningful rendering of a person's name, a perfect gift. Symbols he may use include happiness (sitting birds), flowers (beauty), sun (fame), or bamboo (honesty). The cost is amazingly low considering the skill. He is at this location *Mon-Sat 10am-8pm.* He also accepts mail order; call for details, (703) 847-0410.

Music Box Center
918 F Street, NW (inside the National Union Building). 783-9399. Choose from over 500 melodies and 1500 boxes, then create a personalized box as a gift using your photo of a loved one, or a special occasion invitation. Orders take three weeks to fill. Among the boxes in stock are antique, multiple tune, and Russian lacquer boxes. No credit cards. *OPEN Mon-Fri 10am-6pm; Sat 10am-3pm.*

The Nature Company
Union Station, 50 Massachusetts Avenue, NW; 842-3700. And 1323 Wisconsin Avenue, NW; 333-4100. For the save-the-earth-minded, a shop that owes its vision to the likes of Charles Darwin, Rachael Carson, and Jacques Cousteau. Fun, educational, and ecologically responsible toys, books, gifts such as bird feeders and wind chimes. AE, MC, V. *OPEN 7 days.*

Jewelry

See also Antiques & Collectibles *for shops stocked with antique and estate jewelry.*

Boutique Cartier
Mayflower Hotel, 1127 Connecticut Avenue, NW; 887-5888. And 5454 Wisconsin Avenue, Chevy Chase, Md; (301) 654-5888. Les must de Cartier: They are all here. Jewelry, watches, leather goods, pens, lighters. Repairs and free appraisals of Cartier merchandise. AE, DC, MC, V. *OPEN Mon-Sat.*

Charles Schwartz & Son
Mazza Gallorie, 5300 Wisconsin Avenue, NW; 363-5432. And in Willard Hotel, 1401 Pennsylvania Avenue, NW; 363-5432. Fine jewelry, china, crystal; Wedgwood and Waterford commemorative objects. Gift items. AE, CB, DC, MC, V. *OPEN Mon-Sat.*

Duehring Jewelers
6935 Wisconsin Avenue, Chevy Chase, Md. (301) 652-0252. Since 1926, jewelry manufacturers and expert watch repair. Omega specialist. MC, V. *OPEN Mon-Sat.*

Galt & Brothers
607 15th Street, NW. 347-1034. In business since 1802, they are America's oldest jewelers. Renowned diamond specialists; rare stones, too. Gold, sterling, flatware. Repair service. AE, MC, V, their own charge. *OPEN Mon-Sat.*

Imposters
Georgetown Park, 3222 M Street, NW; 625-2363. And Union Station, 50 Massachusetts Avenue, NE; 842- 4462. Also the Shops at National Place, 783-1508. Keep 'em guessing, with their popular three-strand "Barbara Bush pearls," and other fabulous faux (though pricey) gems including copies of Bulgari, Cartier, and Rolex classics, not to mention Princess Di's engagement ring. AE, MC, V. *OPEN 7 days.*

The Mineral Kingdom
338-5505. In Georgetown, imported and one-of-a-kind custom-designed jewelry in 14-, 18-, or 22-karat gold only (silver by special request). Repairs and in-depth appraisals. AE, DC, MC, V. *OPEN by appointment only.*

Rubini
632 North Washington Street, Alexandria, Va. (703) 548-5509. Gold, platinum, sterling, and gemstone handcrafted jewelry; also some textiles. Jewelry repair. AE, MC, V. *OPEN Mon-Sat.*

Tiny Jewel Box
1143 Connecticut Avenue, NW. 393-2747. Open since 1930, this lovely little shop has Washington's best collection of antique and estate jewelry. Appraisals, too. AE, CB, DC, MC, V. *OPEN Mon-Sat.*

VIP Antiques
1665 Wisconsin Avenue, NW. 965-0700. Quite a good selection of vintage costume jewelry including Bakelite and signed pieces from the likes of Hattie Carnegie, Eisenberg, and Haskell. MC, V. *OPEN Mon-Sat (sometimes Sun) noon-6pm.*

Ylang Ylang
Mazza Gallerie, 5300 Wisconsin Avenue, NW. 966-1199. Ritzy glitz to wear on the ears, neck, and wrists straight from Rodeo Drive. The jewels may not be rare but the prices are. AE, MC, V. *OPEN 7 days.*

Newspapers: Foreign & Out-of-Town

Central Periodicals
3109 M Street, NW. 338-2955. Out-of-town and foreign magazines and newspapers. Specialty computer books. *OPEN Mon-Sat 10am-10pm; Sun 10am-9pm.*

The News Room
1753 Connecticut Avenue, NW. 332-1489. The town's most comprehensive news store. Out-of-town and foreign newspapers and magazines. *OPEN Mon-Thurs 7am-10pm; Fri & Sat 7am-11pm; Sun 7am-9pm.*

Pens

Fahrney's Pens Inc.
1430 G Street, NW. 628-9525. Fine writing instruments—Sheaffer, Parker, Cross, Ester-

brook, Montblanc, and many more. Wide price range. Desk accessories and calligraphy sets, too. In business for over 60 years; repairers of presidential pens since Hoover. AE, MC, V. *OPEN Mon-Sat.*

Washington Inkwell
See Stationery.

The Washington Pen Company
Union Station, 50 Massachusetts Avenue, NE, East Hall. 289-2054. A unique and very fine selection of writing instruments and accessories including inkwells. AE, MC, V. *OPEN 7 days.*

Records

Olsson's Books & Records
1239 Wisconsin Avenue, NW (Georgetown); 338-9544 (books), 338-6712 (records). And 1307 19th Street, NW (Dupont Circle); 785-1133 (books), 785-2662 (records). Also 1200 F Street, NW (Metro Center), 347- 3686 (books) and 393-1853 (records); 106 South Union Street, Old Town, Alexandria, Va, (703) 684-0077 (books) and (703) 684-0030 (records). Wide and wonderful selection of books, records, and tapes. Good prices and good choice of imports. They ship worldwide. (*See also* Books: General.) AE, MC, V. *OPEN 7 days.*

Orpheus Records
3249 M Street, NW. 337-7970. Used and out-of-print records; some new. Collector's items at good prices. Rock, jazz, and R&B are the main focus, with a limited selection of classical. If you can't find it elsewhere, this store usually has it. MC, V. *OPEN 7 days.*

Record Mart
217 King Street, Alexandria, Va. (703) 683-4583. Rare and hard-to-find 45s and LPs: rock, jazz, opera, Big Band, classical, movie and Broadway soundtracks, easy listening, soul, comedy. MC, V. *OPEN 7 days.*

Second Story Books
See Books: Antiquarian, Old & Used.

Tower Records
2000 Pennsylvania Avenue, NW. 331-2400. Large—18,000 square feet—emporium well stocked with CDs and cassettes. Rock, jazz, classical in a fun, flashing, funky setting. AE, MC, V. *OPEN year-round, 9am-midnight.*

Sports Equipment

Athlete's Foot
Georgetown Park, 3222 M Street, NW. 965-7262. Athletic footwear and accessories. Almost every top brand—Nike, Adidas, Reebok, etc. AE, MC, V. *OPEN 7 days.*

The Bike Shop
District Hardware, 2003 P Street, NW. 659-8686. In the Dupont Circle area, a fine selection of quality 10-speed bikes. Accessories and supplies for all your biking needs. Wheelchair repair, too. AE, MC, V. *OPEN Mon-Sat.*

Herman's World of Sporting Goods
350 Jenifer Street, NW; 537-1388. And in suburbs. Chain store for discount sporting goods from running shoes to boxing equipment. Good selection of sports apparel for men and women. Complete line of sporting equipment. AE, DC, MC, V. OPEN 7 days.

Racquet & Jog
3225 M Street, NW; 333-8113. And 4959 Elm Street, Bethesda, Md; (301) 986-0558. Clothes, shoes, and equipment: jogging, tennis, racquetball, squash, platform tennis, and badminton. AE, MC, V. OPEN Mon-Sat.

Stationery

Dempsey & Carroll
Georgetown Park, 3300 M Street, NW. 965-3830. This firm, founded in 1878 (in New York), purveys fine hand-engraved stationery. Choose from over 200 monogram styles. AE, MC, V. OPEN 7 days.

Perfect Papers, Inc.
3238 P Street, NW. 342-7301. This wonderful Georgetown shop is a find for anyone interested in things to write with and on. Ink wells, desk and writing accessories, hand-painted paper, decorative gift boxes, pens, inks, wraps, ribbons, portfolios, journals, photo albums, and scrapbooks. MC, V. OPEN 7 days.

Washington Inkwell
The Pavilion at the Old Post Office, 1100 Pennsylvania Avenue, NW. 289-4160. Chock-full of calligraphy books and implements; framed calligraphed quotes; fine pens; cards and notepads; rubber stamps; Washington posters and postcards. AE, MC, V. OPEN 7 days.

Tobacconists

A. Garfinkel
1585 I Street, NW. 638-1175. International tobacconist for more than a century. Importers and distributors of cigars from all over the world. To-

bacco; cigarettes, too. There's a blending bar (former President Richard Nixon smoked one of their blends). Expert pipe repair as well. They will mail anywhere. AE, CB, DC, MC, V. OPEN Mon-Fri.

Earthworks Tobacconists
1724 20th Street, NW. 332-4323. In stock: 60 different private label and European pipe tobaccos. Pipes by Dunhill, Savinelli, Ben Wade, Peterson, Talamona, James Upshall, Sasieni. A 19th-century apothecary case displays antique pipes and accessories. More than 250 imported brands of cigarettes; one of the largest snuff bars anywhere. AE, MC, V. OPEN Mon-Sat.

Georgetown Tobacco & Pipe Shop
3144 M Street, NW. 338-5100. And in suburbs. Good selection of pipes and smoker's accessories. Exclusive distributor of "Georgetown" products. Dunhill and Dupont lighters. Worldwide mail-order service. AE, MC, V. OPEN 7 days.

J.R. Tobacco
1667 K Street (enter 17th between K & L Streets). 296-3872. An entire store devoted to cigars—very brand you can name at substantial discount. The shop, owned by the former owner and manager of Paul Young's restaurant, is actually a giant humidor. Catalog available; they ship anywhere in the world. MC, V. OPEN Mon-Fri 8am-5:30pm; Sat 10am-3pm.

The Scottish Merchant & John Crouch, Tobacconist
128 King Street, Alexandria, Va; (703) 548-2900. And Metropolitan Cigars, 921 19th Street, NW; 223-9648. Quality pipes including Dunhill; quality cigars including Palomino, Montecruz, Macanudo, Portagas, among others. Scientifically designed walk-in humidor (Metropolitan). Blending bar. Also clan tartan ties and other Scottish merchandise. AE, MC, V. OPEN 7 days.

W. Curtis Draper
640 14th Street, NW. 785-2226. Since 1887, fine cigars, tobacco, pipes, and accessories. Blending bar. Mail and phone orders. AE, MC, V. OPEN Mon-Sat.

TRAVEL
&
VACATION
INFORMATION

British Embassy

PASSPORTS

During peak travel times, apply at least three weeks in advance of scheduled departure. Definitely call before going, since certain information and documentation are necessary. Some renewals can be done through the mail.

State Department—Passport Office
1425 K Street, NW. 783-8200. *OPEN Mon-Fri 8am-4:15pm. CLOSED Sat, Sun & holidays.*

Express Visa Service
2150 Wisconsin Avenue, NW, Suite 20. 337-2442. They will handle the necessary paperwork involved in getting a passport, visa, or other foreign travel documents. You fill out the application, they'll get it processed and present you with the finished product. Great service for busy travelers and worth the fee. *Call Mon-Fri 9am-6pm.*

Passport Photographs

Two identical photos are needed. These can be done by any photographer as long as they fit the required specifications. For details, call 783-8200.

American International Passport Photos
1425 K Street, NW. 393-0276. In the same lobby as the State Department Passport Office. Color or black-and-white photos while you wait. *OPEN Mon-Fri 8am-5pm. CLOSED Sat & Sun.*

INOCULATIONS & VACCINATIONS

To ascertain what vaccinations are required for the countries you intend to visit, and where you can get them, contact your local health department office. For information, call 673-6715, Monday to Friday, 9am to 4:30pm.

Traveler's Medical Service
2141 K Street, NW, Suite 408. 466-8109. They give vaccinations and general, helpful information for those who travel abroad. Pre- and post-

travel health problems are dealt with; there is a charge for services rendered. Yellow fever vaccinations: Monday, Wednesday, and Thursday from 1:30 to 4:30pm. *OPEN Mon-Fri 9:30am-12:30pm & 1:30-4:30pm.*

OTHER IMPORTANT NUMBERS

Immigration & Naturalization Service
307-1501
U.S. Customs Service
General Information: 566-8195

CURRENCY EXCHANGE

Most DC banks do not as a policy exchange foreign currency, so it is best to arrive with some American dollars. At Dulles International Airport, lower level, there is a Foreign Currency Service. OPEN 7 days 9am-8:15pm.

If you are going abroad, it's best to buy some foreign currency before you leave. You can purchase currency at the following exchange offices:

First American Bank N.A.
740 15th Street, NW; 637-7755. And 1800 K Street, NW; 637-2666. All branches exchange currency; the two listed here also sell. The others can sell with 24-hour notice. *OPEN Mon-Fri 8:30am-3:30pm.*

Riggs National Bank
835-6000. Eight branches located throughout DC. *OPEN Mon-Thurs 9am-3pm; Fri hours vary, call individual office.*

Ruesch International Monetary Services
825 14h Street, NW. 408-1200. *OPEN Mon-Fri 9am-5:30pm.*

Thomas Cook Currency Services
1800 K Street, NW. 872-1233; (800) 368-5683. *OPEN Mon-Fri 9am-5pm.*
Georgetown Park, 3222 M Street, NW, 3rd level.

38-3325. *OPEN Mon-Fri 10am-9pm; Sat 10am-7pm; Sun noon-6pm.*
Union Station, 50 Massachusetts Avenue, NE. 371-9219. *OPEN Mon-Sat 10am-9pm; Sun noon-5pm.*

TRAVELER'S CHECKS

Banks and almost all shops accept them. (The banks usually require photo identification, such as passport or driver's license.)
American Express Travel Service
1150 Connecticut Avenue, NW. 457-1300.
1001 G Street, NW. 393-0095.
Mazza Gallerie, 5300 Wisconsin Avenue, NW. 362-4000.
Tysons Corner Shopping Center, McLean, Va. (703) 893-3550.
Seven Corners, Va. (703) 534-0828.
Springfield Mall, Springfield, Va. (703) 971-5600.
White Flint Shopping Center, Kensington, Md. (301) 468-2023.
   For refunds for lost or stolen American Express Traveler's Cheques, call (800) 221-7282.

LOST PROPERTY

Buses
DC Metro buses: 600 5th Street, NW, 5th floor, room 5C. 962-1195.
Greyhound: 12th Street & New York Avenue, NW. 289-5145.

Railroads
Union Station 289-8355; Amtrak 906-3104.

Subways (Metro)
600 5th Street, NW, 5th floor, room 5C. 962-1195.

Airports
Baltimore-Washington International Airport
Call the State Police Station at the airport, (301) 859-7040.
Dulles International Airport
Call the Airport Police, (703) 471-4114.
Washington National Airport
Call the Airport Police, (703) 685-8034.

Taxicabs
Contact the police at 767-7586.

TRAVELER'S AID

(See also BASIC INFORMATION, Information Centers.)

Telephone Language Bank
A service for non-English-speaking people from the community as well as foreign visitors. Over 50 languages available. Staffed by volunteers. Call 783-6540 till 11pm for assistance; there is also a 24-hour answering service for emergency calls.
Traveler's Aid Society
512 C Street, NE. 546-3120. Nationwide non-profit organization that helps robbery victims, lost persons, wayward children, and travelers with problems. Works with the police. *OPEN Mon-Fri 9am-5pm.* Also located on the lower concourse of Dulles International Airport and at Washington National Airport. *OPEN 7 days 10am-9pm.*

Lost Anywhere
Contact the nearest police station. *See* HELP!, Emergency, Police Stations.

Lost Child
The police: 911.

Lost Dog
Washington Humane Society, SPCA
7319 Georgia Avenue, NW. 333-4010. For any animal emergency, call 576-6664, 24 hours a day, 7 days a week. Also put up notices in shops in the area of loss with a description of your pet and your phone number only. Ads in local neighborhood publications are also helpful. *OPEN 7 days 8am-4:30pm.*

CAR HIRE

Drive Yourself
Avis
Domestic Reservations and Information: (800) 331-1212. International: (800) 331-1084. Out of Town: (800) 228-9650.
1722 M Street, NW. 785-5840.
Union Station. 789-0742.
8333 Fenton Street, Silver Spring, Md. (301) 587-9090.
Also located at Dulles International, Washington National, and Baltimore-Washington Airports. Call (800) 331-1212.
Budget Rent-A-Car
4727 Wisconsin Avenue, NW. 244-7437.
From DC and Virginia phones, (800) 527-0700.
Hertz
24-hour information and reservations domestic and worldwide: (800) 654-3131.
901 11th Street, NW. 628-6174.
Locations at Washington National and Dulles International Airports, call (800) 654-3131.

Chauffeur-Driven

Admiral Limousine Service
1243 First Street, SE. 554-1000. Washington's largest limo service. Chauffeur-driven Cadillacs, limousines, sedans. By the hour, week, or month. *24-hour service.*

Carey Limousine
4530 Wisconsin Avenue, NW; 362-7400. And 768 South 23rd Street, Arlington, Va; (703) 892-2000. Limousines. Uniformed, multilingual chauffeurs. Short and long distance. *24-hour service.*

International Limousine Service
2300 T Street, NE. 388-6800. Cadillacs, limousines. Multilingual chauffeurs. *24-hour service.*

BUS STATIONS

Greyhound-Trailways
1005 1st Street, NE. For fare and schedule information, call (301) 565-2662.

TRAIN STATIONS

Alexandria Station
110 Callahan Drive, Alexandria, Va. For reservations, call 484-7540.

Capitol Beltway Station
Lanham, Md. For reservations, call 484-7540.

Union Station
50 Massachusetts Avenue, NW. 371-9441; Amtrak 484-7540.

AIRPORTS

Baltimore-Washington Airport
Baltimore, Md. (301) 261-1001. Thirty-one miles northeast of downtown DC.

Washington-Dulles International Airport
Arlington, Va. Call individual airline for information. Twenty-eight miles west of downtown DC.

Washington National Airport
Alexandria, Va. Call individual airline for information. This airport is served by the Metro, making it only 15 minutes from downtown.

AIRLINES

Aerolineas Argentinas
1825 K Street, NW. 296-8078; (800) 333-0276.

Air Canada
1000 16th Street, NW. 638-3348; (800) 776-3000.

Air France
Contact your local travel agent or call (800) 237-2747.

Air-India
1612 K Street, NW. 785-8989; (800) 223-7776

Air Jamaica
Contact your local travel agent or call (800) 523-5585 or (301) 859-1760.

Air New Zealand
Contact your local travel agent or call (800) 262-1234.

Alaska Airlines
Contact your local travel agent or call (800) 426-0333.

Alitalia Airlines
1001 Connecticut Avenue, NW. 331-1841; (800) 223-5730.

ALM Antillean Airlines
Contact your local travel agent or call (800) 327-7230.

American Airlines
1721 K Street, NW. (800) 433-7300. Locations also at the Capitol Hilton Hotel, Crystal Gateway Marriott, and 122 South Washington Street, Alexandria, Va.

Avianca Airlines
1115 Massachusetts Avenue, NW. 347-3626; (800) 284-2622.

Braniff International
Contact your local travel agent or call (800) 272-6433.

British Airways
(800) 247-9297.

British West Indian Airways
Contact your local travel agent or call (800) 327-7401.

Canadian Airlines
Contact your local travel agent or call (800) 426-7000.

Cathay Pacific Airways
1000 Connecticut Avenue, NW. 833-9393; (800) 233-2742.

China Airlines
1648 K Street, NW. 833-1760.

Commuter Airways
Contact your local travel agent or call (800) 321-3342.

Continental Airlines
(800) 231-0856.

Ecuatoriana Airlines
1650 L Street, NW. 296-3129; (800) 328-2367.

El Al Airlines
1730 Rhode Island Avenue, NW. 296-5440; (800) 223-6700.

Finnair
1901 Pennsylvania Avenue, NW. 659-8233; (800) 950-5000.

Hawaiian Airlines
Contact your local travel agent or call (800) 367-5320.

Iberia Airlines
1725 K Street, NW. 293-1453; (800) 772-4642.

Icelandair
Contact your local travel agent or call (800) 223-5500.

Japan Air Lines
1130 Connecticut Avenue, NW. 223-3310; (800) 525-3663.

KLM Royal Dutch Airlines
1730 K Street, NW. 331-1328; (800) 777-5553.
Korean Air Lines
1154 15th Street, NW. 785-3644; (800) 223-1155.
Kuwait Airways
1150 Connecticut Avenue, NW. 296-4644.
Lan-Chile Airlines
1717 K Street, NW, Suite 412. 628-2868; (800) 735-5526.
Lufthansa Airlines
1101 16th Street, NW. 296-5608; (800) 645-3880.
Mexicana Airlines
(800) 531-7921.
Northwest Airlines
Capital Hilton Hotel, 16th & K Streets, NW. 737-7333.
Olympic Airways
1000 Connecticut Avenue, NW. 659-2511; (800) 223-1226.
Pakistan International Airlines
1511 K Street, NW. 737-0037.
Philippine Airlines
(800) 435-9725.
Qantas Airways
1825 K Street, NW. (800) 227-4500.
Republic Airlines
Contact your local travel agent or call 347-0448.
Royal Air Maroc
1511 K Street, NW. 393-2243.
Royal Jordanian Airline
(800) 223-0470.
Sabena World Airlines
1725 K Street, NW. 833-9600; (800) 955-2000.
Scandinavian Airlines
1725 K Street, NW. 833-2424; (800) 221-2350.
Singapore Airlines
1050 17th Street, NW. 466-3748; (800) 742-3333.
Swissair
1717 K Street, NW. 296-5380; (800) 221-4750.
Taca International Airlines
1010 16th Street, NW. 234-7006.
TAP Air Portugal
Contact your local travel agent or call (800) 221-7370.
Thai Airways International, Ltd.
Contact your local travel agent or call (800) 426-5204.
Trans World Airways (TWA)
Domestic: (800) 221-2000. International: (800) 892-4141.
Trump Shuttle
(800) 247-8786.
United Airlines
(703) 742-4600; (800) 241-6522.
USAir
1601 K Street, NW. 783-4500.
1830 K Street, NW.
1001 G Street, NW.
2345 Crystal Drive, Arlington, Va.
Varig Brazilian Airlines
1725 K Street, NW. 331-8913; (800) 468-2744.

Viasa Venezuelan International Airways
Contact your local travel agent or call (800) 221-2150.

EMBASSIES & LEGATIONS

Afghanistan Embassy
2341 Wyoming Avenue, NW. 234-3770.
Embassy of Algeria
2133 Wyoming Avenue, NW. 265-2800.
Embassy of Argentina
1600 New Hampshire Avenue, NW. 939-6400.
Embassy of Australia
1601 Massachusetts Avenue, NW. 797-3000.
Austrian Embassy
2343 Massachusetts Avenue, NW. 483-4474.
Embassy of the Bahamas
2220 Massachusetts Avenue, NW. 319-2660.
Embassy of the State of Bahrain
3502 International Drive, NW. 342-0741.
Embassy of Bangladesh
2201 Wisconsin Avenue, NW. 342-8372.
Embassy of Barbados
2144 Wyoming Avenue, NW. 939-9200.
Belgian Embassy
3330 Garfield Street, NW. 333-6900.
Embassy of Bolivia
3014 Massachusetts Avenue, NW. 483-4410.
Botswana Embassy
3400 International Drive, NW. 244-4990.
Brazilian Embassy
3006 Massachusetts Avenue, NW. 745-2700.
British Embassy
3100 Massachusetts Avenue, NW. 462-1340.
Bulgarian Embassy
1621 22nd Street, NW. 387-7969.
Burundi Embassy
2233 Wisconsin Avenue, NW. 342-2574.
Embassy of the Republic of Cameroon
2349 Massachusetts Avenue, NW. 265-8790.
Embassy of Canada
501 Pennsylvania Avenue, NW. 682-1740.
Embassy of the Republic of Cape Verde
3415 Massachusetts Avenue, NW. 965-6820.
Embassy of the Central African Republic
1618 22nd Street, NW. 483-7800.
Embassy of Chad
2002 R Street, NW. 462-4009.
Embassy of Chile
1732 Massachusetts Avenue, NW. 785-1746.
Embassy of People's Republic of China
2300 Connecticut Avenue, NW. 328-2500.
Colombian Embassy
2118 Leroy Place, NW. 387-8338.
Embassy of Costa Rica
1825 Connecticut Avenue, NW. 234-2945.
Embassy of Cyprus
2211 R Street, NW. 462-5772.
Embassy of Czechoslovakia
3900 Linnean Avenue, NW. 363-6315.
Embassy of Denmark
3200 Whitehaven, NW. 234-4300.
Dominican Republic Embassy
1715 22nd Street, NW. 332-6280.

Embassy of Ecuador
2535 15th Street, NW. 234-7200.
Embassy of Egypt
2300 Decatur Place, NW. 234-3903.
Embassy of El Salvador
1010 16th Street, NW. 331-4032.
Ethiopian Embassy
2134 Kalorama Road, NW. 234-2281.
Embassy of Finland
3216 New Mexico Avenue, NW. 363-2430.
Embassy of France
4101 Reservoir Road, NW. 944-6000.
Embassy of the Republic of Gabon
2034 20th Street, NW. 797-1000.
Embassy of Germany
4645 Reservoir Road, NW. 298-4000.
Embassy of Ghana
3512 International Drive, NW. 686-4520.
Embassy of Greece
2211 Massachusetts Avenue, NW. 667-3168.
Embassy of Grenada
1701 New Hampshire Avenue, NW. 265-2561.
Embassy of Guatemala
2220 R Street, NW. 745-4952.
Embassy of Guinea
2112 Leroy Place, NW. 483-9420.
Embassy of Guyana
2490 Tracy Place, NW. 265-6900.
Embassy of Haiti
2311 Massachusetts Avenue, NW. 332-4090.
Embassy of Honduras
3007 Tilden Street, NW. 966-7702.
Embassy of Hungary
3910 Shoemaker Street. 362-6730.
Embassy of Iceland
2022 Connecticut Avenue, NW. 265-6653.
Embassy of India
2107 Massachusetts Avenue, NW. 939-7000.
Indonesian Embassy
2020 Massachusetts Avenue, NW. 775-5200.
Embassy of Iraq
1801 P Street, NW. 328-7314.
Embassy of Ireland
2234 Massachusetts Avenue, NW. 462-3939.
Embassy of Israel
3514 International Drive, NW. 364-5500.
Embassy of Italy
1601 Fuller Street, NW. 328-5500.
Ivory Coast Embassy
2424 Massachusetts Avenue, NW. 483-2400.
Embassy of Jamaica
1651 Pennsylvania Avenue, NW. 628-2679.
Embassy of Japan
2520 Massachusetts Avenue, NW. 939-6700.
Embassy of Jordan
3504 International Drive, NW. 966-2664.
Embassy of Kenya
2249 R Street, NW. 387-6101.
Korean Embassy
2370 Massachusetts Avenue, NW. 939-5600.
Embassy of the State of Kuwait
3500 International Drive, NW. 365-2200.
**Embassy of the Lao People's Democratic
Republic**
2222 S Street, NW. 332-6416.

Embassy of Latvia
4325 17th Street, NW. 726-8213.
Embassy of Lebanon
2560 28th Street, NW. 939-6300.
Embassy of Lesotho
2511 Massachusetts Avenue, NW. 797-5533.
Embassy of Liberia
5303 Colorado Avenue, NW. 723-0437.
Lithuanian Embassy
2622 16th Street, NW. 234-5860.
Luxembourg Embassy
2200 Massachusetts Avenue, NW. 265-4171.
Embassy of Madagascar
2374 Massachusetts Avenue, NW. 265-5525.
Malawi Embassy
2408 Massachusetts Avenue, NW. 797-1007.
Embassy of Malaysia
2401 Massachusetts Avenue, NW. 328-2700.
Embassy of Mali
2130 R Street, NW. 667-6857.
Embassy of Malta
2017 Connecticut Avenue, NW. 462-3611.
Mauritius Embassy
4301 Connecticut Avenue, NW. 244-1491.
Embassy of Mexico
1019 19th Street, NW. 293-1710.
Embassy of Morocco
1601 21st Street, NW. 462-7979.
Embassy of Mozambique
1990 M Street, NW. 293-7146.
Embassy of Myanmar
2300 S Street, NW. 332-9044.
Royal Nepalese Embassy
2131 Leroy Place, NW. 667-4550.
Netherlands Embassy
4200 Linnean Avenue, NW. 244-5300.
New Zealand Embassy
37 Observatory Circle, NW. 328-4800.
Embassy of Nicaragua
1627 New Hampshire Avenue, NW. 939-6531.
Embassy of Niger
2204 R Street, NW. 483-4224.
Embassy of Nigeria
2201 M Street, NW. 882-1500.
Embassy of Norway
2720 34th Street, NW. 333-6000.
Embassy of Oman
1717 Massachusetts Avenue, NW. 387-2014.
Embassy of Pakistan
2315 Massachusetts Avenue, NW 930-6200.
Embassy of Panama
2862 McGill Terrace, NW. 483-1407.
Embassy of Papua New Guinea
1615 New Hampshire Avenue, NW. 745-3680.
Embassy of Paraguay
2400 Massachusetts Avenue, NW. 483-6960.
Embassy of Peru
1700 Massachusetts Avenue, NW. 833-9860.
Philippine Embassy
1617 Massachusetts Avenue, NW. 483-1414.
Polish Embassy
2224 Wyoming Avenue, NW; 232-4517. And
2640 16th Street, NW; 234-3800.
Embassy of Portugal
2125 Kalorama Road, NW. 328-8610.

Embassy of Qatar
600 New Hampshire Avenue, NW. 338-0111.
Embassy of Romania
1607 23rd Street, NW. 232-4747.
Russian Embassy
1125 16th Street, NW. 628-7551; 939-8916.
Embassy of Rwanda
1714 New Hampshire Avenue, NW. 232-2882.
Embassy of Saudi Arabia
601 New Hampshire Avenue, NW. 342-3800.
Embassy of Senegal
2112 Wyoming Avenue, NW. 234-0540.
Embassy of Sierra Leone
1701 19th Street, NW. 939-9261.
Embassy of the Republic of Singapore
1824 R Street, NW. 667-7555.
Embassy of Somali Democratic Republic
600 New Hampshire Avenue, NW. 342-1575.
South African Embassy
3051 Massachusetts Avenue, NW. 232-4400.
Embassy of Spain
2700 15th Street, NW. 265-0190.
Embassy of Sri Lanka
2148 Wyoming Avenue, NW. 483-4025.
Embassy of the Sudan
2210 Massachusetts Avenue, NW. 338-8565.
Embassy of Republic of Surinam
4301 Connecticut Avenue, NW. 338-8565.
Embassy of the Kingdom of Swaziland
3400 International Drive, NW. 362-6683.
Swedish Embassy
600 New Hampshire Avenue, NW. 944-5600.

Embassy of Switzerland
2900 Cathedral Avenue, NW. 745-7900.
Embassy of Syria
2215 Wyoming Avenue, NW. 232-6313.
Embassy of Tanzania
2139 R Street, NW. 939-6125.
Royal Thai Embassy
2300 Kalorama Road, NW. 483-7200.
Embassy of Togo
2208 Massachusetts Avenue, NW. 234-4212.
Embassy of Trinidad and Tobago
1708 Massachusetts Avenue, NW. 467-6490.
Embassy of Tunisia
1515 Massachusetts Avenue, NW. 862-1850.
Embassy of Turkey
2523 Massachusetts Avenue, NW. 483-5366.
Embassy of Uganda
5909 16th Street, NW. 726-7100.
Embassy of the United Arab Emirates
600 New Hampshire Avenue, NW. 338-6500.
Embassy of Uruguay
1918 F Street, NW. 331-1313.
Embassy of Venezuela
1099 30th Street, NW. 342-2214.
Embassy of Yugoslavia
2410 California Street, NW. 462-6566.
Embassy of the Republic of Zaire
1800 New Hampshire Avenue, NW. 234-7690.
Embassy of the Republic of Zambia
2419 Massachusetts Avenue, NW. 265-9717.
Embassy of the Republic of Zimbabwe
1608 New Hampshire Avenue, NW. 332-7100.

HELP!

Children's Hospital

EMERGENCY

Emergency services 24 hours a day, 7 days a week.

Abused Child
727-0995

Deaf Emergency
727-9334

Drugstores
People's
14th Street and Thomas Circle, NW, off Vermont Avenue; 628-0720. And 7 Dupont Circle, NW; 785-1466.

Fire
911

Poison
625-3333

Police
911

Public Assistance/Emergency Assistance Unit
727-4326

Rape Hotline/Crisis Center
333-RAPE (7273)

AIDS Hotline
332-AIDS

VD Hotline
832-7000

Police Stations
1st District
415 4th Street, SE. 727-4655. Substation: 500 E Street, SE. 727-4660.
2nd District
3320 Idaho Avenue, NW. 282-0070.
3rd District
1620 V Street, NW. 673-6930.
4th District
6001 Georgia Avenue, NW. 576-6745.
5th District
1805 Bladensburg Road, NE. 727-4510.
6th District
100 42nd Street, NE. 727-4958.
7th District
1324 Mississippi Avenue, SE. 767-8020.
Harbor Branch
550 Water Street, SW. 727-4582.

Police Services

For location of your nearest district police headquarters and for general information, call 727-4326.

Ambulance

Huntemann Ambulance Service, Inc.
5732 Georgia Avenue, NW. 726-5700 or -0190. Covers DC, Maryland, and Virginia. *24 hours, 7 days a week.*
Bethesda-Chevy Chase Rescue Squad, Inc.
5020 Battery Lane, Bethesda, Md. (301) 652-1000. Covers upper and NW DC, Bethesda, Potomac, Chevy Chase, and other areas. *24 hours, 7 days a week.*

Hospital Emergency Rooms

Alexandria Hospital
4320 Seminary Road, Alexandria, Va. (703) 379-3065. Cardiac intensive care unit. Drug and alcohol detoxification unit. Emergency psychiatric help.
Arlington Hospital
1701 North George Mason Drive, Arlington, Va. (703) 558-5000. Cardiac intensive care unit. Poison control index.
Children's National Medical Center
111 Michigan Avenue, NW. 745-5000. Screening clinic. All pediatric specialties. Burn and pe-

diatric shock trauma units. (Parent permitted to accompany child into treatment.)

D.C. General Hospital
19th Street & Massachusetts Avenue, SE. 675-5400. Cardiac intensive care unit.

Fairfax Hospital
3300 Gallows Road, Falls Church, Va. (703) 698-3111. Cardiac and neonatal intensive care units. Psychiatric emergencies. Level 1 Trauma Center.

Fair Oaks Hospital
3600 Joseph Siewick Drive, Fairfax, Va. (703) 391-3644. Cardiac intensive care unit. Drug and alcohol emergencies.

Georgetown University Medical Center
3800 Reservoir Road, NW. 784-2118. Cardiac and neonatal intensive care units. Trauma center. Pediatric and psychiatric emergency care. Poison control center.

George Washington University Hospital
901 23rd Street, NW. 994-3211. Cardiac and neonatal intensive care units. "Sudden death" management for heart attacks. Trauma center. Neurosurgery and psychiatric emergency care.

Greater Laurel-Beltsville Hospital
7100 Contee Road, Laurel, Md. (301) 497-7954. Cardiac intensive care unit. Psychiatric emergency care.

Greater Southeast Community Hospital
1310 Southern Avenue, SE. 574-6541. Cardiac and neonatal intensive care units. Psychiatric emergency care.

Hadley Memorial Hospital
4601 Martin Luther King Jr. Avenue, SW. 574-5750. Coronary care unit. Family Health Clinic.

Holy Cross Hospital of Silver Spring
1500 Forest Glen Road, Silver Spring, Md. (301) 905-0100. General emergency care. Drug and alcohol emergency care.

Howard University Hospital
2041 Georgia Avenue, NW. 865-1131 or -1116. Cardiac and neonatal intensive care units. Trauma center.

Jefferson Memorial Hospital
4600 King Street, Alexandria, Va. (703) 931-9700. Cardiac intensive care unit.

Eugene Leland Memorial Hospital
4400 Queensbury Road, Riverdale, Md. (301) 699-2000. Cardiac intensive care unit.

Montgomery General Hospital
18101 Prince Philip Drive, Olney, Md. (301) 774-7800. Burn and cardiac intensive care units. Psychiatric, drug, and alcohol emergency care available.

Mount Vernon Hospital
2501 Parkers Lane, Mount Vernon, Va. (703) 664-7111. Cardiac intensive care unit. Psychiatric, drug, and alcohol emergency care.

National Hospital for Orthopedics & Rehabilitation
2455 Army Navy Drive, Arlington, Va. (703) 553-2417; (703) 920-6700. Cardiac intensive care unit. Advanced life-support-trained emergency unit. Psychiatric, drug, and alcohol emergency care.

Northern Virginia Doctors' Hospital
601 South Carlin Springs Road, Arlington, Va. (703) 671-1200. Cardiac and surgical intensive care units. Alcoholic and psychiatric services.

Prince George's General Hospital
Cheverly, Md. (301) 618-2000. Cardiac and neonatal intensive care unit. Psychiatric, drug, and alcohol emergency care. Protective services for abused children.

Providence Hospital
1150 Varnum Street, NE. 269-7000. Cardiac intensive care unit. Dialysis unit. Psychiatric and alcohol emergency care.

Shady Grove Adventist Hospital
9901 Medical Center Drive, Rockville, Md. (301) 279-6000. Cardiac and neonatal intensive care units. Psychiatric emergency care. Alcohol and drug acute care.

Sibley Memorial Hospital
5255 Loughboro Road, NW. 537-4000. Cardiac intensive care unit.

Southern Maryland Hospital
7503 Surratts Road, Clinton, Md. (301) 868-8000. Cardiac intensive care unit.

Suburban Hospital
8600 Old Georgetown Road, Bethesda, Md. (301) 530-3100. Cardiac intensive care unit. Shock trauma center. Psychiatric emergency care. Alcohol and drug emergency care.

V.A. Medical Center
50 Irving Street, NW. 745-8000. Cardiac and surgical intensive care units. Psychiatric emergency care.

Washington Adventist Hospital
7600 Carroll Avenue, Takoma Park, Md. (301) 891-7600. Cardiac intensive care unit. Alcohol detoxification unit. Psychiatric emergency care.

Washington Hospital Center
110 Irving Street, NW. 877-7000. Cardiac and neonatal intensive care units. Burn unit. Shock trauma unit. Eye emergencies; dialysis; alcohol detoxification.

ASSISTANCE

These organizations help and advise anyone in need—the ill, the lonely, the victimized, the desperate, and those people who simply need solutions to problems. Remember that 24 hours a day, 7 days a week, there is police assistance.

General

District of Columbia Department of Human Services
Information Center: 724-5466. This city agency provides public assistance in many areas. Call for referral to appropriate divisions. Social services include adoption, day care, foster care, protective services, paternity and child care enforcement, Medicaid, food stamps, youth services, vocational rehabilitation.

American Red Cross National Capital Chapter
2025 E Street, NW. 728-6400. Courses on CPR, caring for the elderly and sick, first aid, home nursing, prenatal education and child care, and staying healthy over 50 program. *OPEN Mon-Fri 9am-5pm.*

Board of Education
415 12th Street, NW. 724-4044. General information and special information for preschool-age children, high school and adult education. Handicapped resources information as well. *OPEN Mon-Fri 8am-4:30pm.*

Catholic Charities Social Services
1438 Rhode Island Avenue, NE. 526-4100. Counseling for both the family and individual members of the family. *OPEN Mon-Fri 9am-4:45pm.*

Salvation Army
503 E Street, NW. 783-4050. Other locations as well. General counseling on family problems. Help with transitional shelter. Food and clothing assistance. *OPEN Mon-Fri 8:30am-4:30pm.*

Mayor's Command Center
2000 U Street, NW. 727-6161. Handles any kind of emergency ranging from toxic waste to mugging. They give advice, assistance, and act as a referral service, too. *OPEN 24 hours, 7 days a week.*

Consumer Education & Information
614 H Street, NW. 727-7000.

DC Help
832-4357. Handles complaints and questions about city services.

Crime Victims

See Assistance, General: Mayor's Command Center.

Disaster Relief

(*See also* Assistance, General: Mayor's Command Center.)

American Red Cross
2025 E Street, NW. 728-6401. Financial assistance, food, shelter, and clothing given to meet family needs caused by disaster. Help is available *24 hours, 7 days a week.*

Drug Abuse

The following is a list of the programs sponsored by the DC government. They offer drug abuse and detoxification programs as well as counseling. You must go to the Central Intake Division first, and they will refer you to a clinic from there. All clinics are OPEN weekends and holidays 8-11:30am.

Central Intake Division
1400 Q Street, NW. 727-0660. *OPEN Mon-Fri 8:15am-4:45pm.*

CEASED
433 9th Street, NE. 727-0620. *OPEN Mon-Fri 7:30-10:30am & 1-2pm; weekends & holidays 6-9am.*

Detox-Abstinence
1905 E Street, SE. 727-5163. *OPEN Mon-Fri 7:30am-3pm.*

SHACK
123 K Street, SE. 727-0483. *OPEN Mon-Fri 9am-5:30pm; Sat & Sun 7:45am-10:30am.*

TRAIN I
59 M Street, NE. 727-0580. *OPEN Mon-Fri 7:30am-3pm.*

TRAIN II
DC General Hospital, 19th Street & Massachusetts Avenue, SE. 727-3920. *OPEN Mon-Fri 10:30am-6pm.*

Women's Services
DC General Hospital, 19th Street & Massachusetts Avenue, SE. 727-5166. *OPEN Mon-Fri 8:30am-4pm.*

Youth Abstinence
2146 24th Place, NE. 576-7314. Programs for minors. *OPEN Mon-Fri 8am-5:30pm.*

Rape

Rape Crisis Center
P.O. Box 21005, Washington, DC 20009. 333-RAPE (7273). This nonprofit women's organization gives very helpful information and general services to rape victims. Referral, individual and group counseling, and aid. Call them 24 hours a day, 7 days a week, and they'll tell you where to come right away. They will even escort you to the hospital, police, or court if need be. Self-defense classes, too.

INDEX

Other I LOVE city guides by Marilyn J. Appleberg

America's most acclaimed urban travel books—
in new, updated editions

I Love Boston
I Love Chicago
I Love Los Angeles
I Love New York
I Love San Francisco

NOTES

NOTES

NOTES

NOTES

Hotel p. 14

1. Bureau of Engraving & Printing p. 25
2. The Capitol p. 25
3. The FBI p. 26
4. The National Archives p. 26
5. U.S. Naval Observatory p. 27
6. Vietnam Veterans Memorial p. 27
7. National Air & Space Museum p. 81
8. Tech2000 p. 84
9. Tourmobile - Mount Vernon Tour p. 23
10. NASA Space Flight Ctr. p. 102